# THE AZTECS

THE

# AZTECS

## THE HISTORY OF THE INDIES OF NEW SPAIN

*by Fray Diego Durán*

TRANSLATED, WITH NOTES, BY

DORIS HEYDEN AND

FERNANDO HORCASITAS

*Introduction by Ignacio Bernal*

**ORION PRESS**

*New York*

THIRD PRINTING

© 1964 by The Orion Press, Inc.

All rights reserved

Library of Congress Catalog Card Number: 63-19949

Designed by Wladislaw Finne

Manufactured in the United States of America

The quotation on page 355 is from The Aztecs of Mexico by George Vaillant,
copyright © 1941, 1962
by Doubleday & Company, Inc.
Reprinted by permission of the publisher.

The material quoted in notes 61 and 62 is reprinted from
Florentine Codex, Vol. 2, translated by Anderson and Dibble,
by permission of the School of American Research,
Santa Fe, New Mexico.

# CONTENTS

## *The History of the Indies of New Spain*

# ILLUSTRATIONS

COLOR

MAPS

# INTRODUCTION

"A book, written by a Dominican friar, a kinsman of mine, which was the most exact account based on ancient records that I have ever seen," writes the scholar Juan de Tovar in his famous letter to Father José de Acosta in reference to Fray Diego Durán's *Historia*. This letter is undated but must have been written between 1586 and 1588. It is, therefore, the first reference, though indirect, to Durán's work and his first praise. "This is the finest in its field that I have ever seen" is the opinion of Agustín Dávila Padilla, who would one day be Archbishop of Santo Domingo. It is probable that these were the only two men within a period of three hundred years to see the *Historia de las Indias de Nueva España e Islas de Tierra Firme*. Tovar was related to Durán and undoubtedly was the Jesuit most versed in "things about the Indians." Dávila Padilla was, like Durán, a Dominican. Therefore, one being a relative and the other a member of the same religious order, it might be suspected that they had personal reasons to exaggerate the value of the unpublished chronicle. Today it is believed and it is my own opinion that both these scholars realized the extraordinary importance of Durán's work, since they were the only ones among those who saw it, capable of evaluating it.

During the following two and one half centuries other authors—León Pinelo, Alonso Franco, Eguiara, Clavijero, Beristáin, etc., mentioned the *Historia* without being familiar with it. Frequently they went so far as to alter the name of the author: Eguiara calls him "Pedro" and Clavijero refers to him as "Fernando." Durán is a remarkable case of the incomprehension or ill luck that sometimes falls upon the historian. His work, finished in 1581, was seen by only a few contemporaries; afterwards no one seems to have known the manuscript, which was preserved in Spain until the nineteenth century.

We do not know with precision the date on which the learned José Fernando Ramírez discovered the existence of Durán's manuscript in the National Library of Madrid, but we know that in 1854 an exact copy, made under Ramírez' orders, was finished. This does not mean, however, that it was published immediately. Ramírez, like many other Mexicans then and now, combined historical research with administrative and political occupations. He was eventually to become Mexican Minister of Foreign Affairs. These activities consumed valuable time and his adventure-filled life prevented the termination and publication of many manuscripts and studies. The historical archives of the National Museum of Anthropology in Mexico City preserve numerous volumes containing the unpublished manuscripts of this scholar. For this reason the first volume of Durán's chronicle which contains the *Historia* up to Chapter LXVIII did not appear until 1867. According to an unpublished letter to García Icazbalceta of April 13 of that year, Ramírez had left Mexico on January 20 en route to Europe, during the last throes of the Empire of Maximilian. Never to return, he died in Bonn on March 4, 1871. In the letter we have just mentioned, he speaks of the publication of the first volume of Durán and one receives the impression that he saw the printed edition before he left Mexico. Therefore the printing of it must have taken place at the end of 1866 or during the first days of the new year. In any case, Ramírez, now ruined and far away from his native land, was unable to continue his great work. The remainder of the manuscript together with the plates (which had already been reproduced, but not distributed) were considered lost at the end of Maximilian's rule, with which Ramírez collaborated. Years later Alfredo Chavero removed these papers from a mouldy storehouse in the College of Mines, where they were rotting along with many other treasures which had been "put away" in order to avoid their loss in the confusion of the times. The director of the museum, Alcaraz, had taken no pains to rescue these precious documents. Therefore, it was not until 1880 that Chavero released the second volume in which the *Historia* is completed, and in which are included the other two books: *The Rites* and *The Calendar*. Chavero's edition, however, did not contain Ramírez' study, announced in the first volume, which had been lost. It was also at this time that forty-nine plates of the Atlas, bearing water stains from the storehouse, were also released.

The Ramírez-Chavero edition modifies the spelling and very bad punctuation of the original manuscript to some extent, but it does not correct these sufficiently to make easy reading. Durán's paragraphs are interminable—at times they cover an entire chapter—and his antiquated form of writing makes reading difficult. Furthermore, this cannot be considered a critical edition as numerous notes and indexes—essential in these cases—are lacking. In spite of all these defects this edition not only definitely saved from oblivion one of the most important documents on ancient Mexico that exists, but also made it available to scholars. In 1952 a re-edition appeared, but it contributed nothing new; a genuinely critical edition of this book, basic for the study of Aztec history, is indispensable. Because of this we are happy that Durán's *Historia*, though incomplete, is appearing in its first translation into another language. The fact that it is not the whole original text may lessen its scholarly value, but for the first time in history the lay reader will easily become acquainted with this magnificent text which justly may be called one of the principal keys to the roots of Mexican culture.

We do not know the title Durán gave his work. On the reverse of the first plate of the Atlas can be read an inscription written by a copyist: "Historia de las Indias de N. i islas y tierra firme." These words seem to be taken from the title of the first chapter to which the copyist added "Historia" and completed the "N" to mean *Nueva España* (New Spain). Even so, this title is inexact, as Durán not only dealt with history but with many other things. He did not discuss the islands (we assume that this means the Antilles) nor "Tierra Firme" (the mainland which later would be the Audiencia of Panama). Ill luck, which has pursued Durán, does not stop there, since because of an inexplicable confusion, in Ramírez' edition the work is called "Historia de la Nueva España i Islas de Tierra Firme," or "History of New Spain and of the Islands of the Mainland." It is difficult to imagine "islands" on the mainland; therefore I suppose that this must have been simply an error.

This translation covers the entire *Historia de las Indias* but does not include the books dedicated to rites and the calendar. Properly speaking, this is more an adaptation of the original text, eliminating tedious repetitions, modernizing the punctuation and simplifying the spelling, in order to make the story accessible to the general reader. It has no pretensions of being a translation for specialists, who will prefer to consult the original Spanish text.

We know little about the life of Fray Diego Durán. Through a written accusation which he presented before the Inquisition in 1587 we discover that he was born in Seville fifty years before, which means that the date of his birth must have been around 1537. As a small child (in 1542?) he came to New Spain. This is clear, since (among the few facts that he records about his own life) when speaking of the city of Texcoco, he states that "my teeth were not born there but my second teeth came out there." After having spent his childhood in that city which had been "the Athens of America," he entered the Dominican Order on May 8, 1556, in the monastery of Saint Dominic in Mexico City. In September of 1559 he was ordained a deacon in this establishment and in 1561 was sent to the province of Oaxaca, an area of great importance to the men of his Order. The length of his stay in that region is unknown; he is never mentioned among Dominicans who labored in Oaxaca at that time. Durán himself never speaks of his stay in that province. I believe that he must have remained there a short time, and it is probable that ill health prevented him from gaining fame there. What little information he gives on his work as a missionary mentions the area surrounding Mexico City. There is no doubt that his knowledge of the Nahuatl language (which he had learned as a child in Texcoco) would serve him better in this region. His book was begun at least by 1574, although one must admit that Durán's entire life since 1542 was a subconscious preparation for it. The *Historia* was finished in 1581 and our chronicler died in 1588.

Two important facts may be deduced from these scant biographical data: Fray Diego Durán was exposed in an intense manner to Indian culture in Texcoco, one of its principal centers, and his thirty-two years of life as a Dominican were spent in intimate contact with these people. We also know that he had a relative especially important in the field of ancient history, who lived in Texcoco and who later became a Jesuit, Father Juan de Tovar, whom we have already mentioned. Durán was also able to work at the Indian school at Santiago Tlatelolco, near the heart of Mexico City, perhaps collaborating with the Franciscan Bernardino de Sahagún, the foremost authority in his time on pre-conquest Aztec culture.

It is as part of this world of Spanish friars devoted to research on the ancient civilizations of Central Mexico that we must place Durán, in one of the most important periods of Mexican historiography. Only thus can we understand the intricate relationships that exist between the writings of Durán and those of his contemporaries.

Durán's entire work, though it forms a single corpus, actually is divided in three treatises; "the first contains seventy-eight chapters on the history of Mexico from its origins to the Conquest and complete subjection of the country by the Spaniards, ending with Cortés' expedition to Honduras. . . ." At the end of this book can be read: "The present work was finished in the year 1581." The second treatise contains twenty-three chapters on Mexican deities, rites, feasts and temples. The third, divided into two sections, consists of nineteen chapters on the Mexican calendar. This third part is in reality, according to Durán himself, a continuation of the second treatise. It was finished in 1579. Therefore, even though it appears at the end of Ramírez' and Chavero's edition, it is really the first. Actually, the entire order of the edition is incorrect. As Garibay has pointed out, this is a serious defect in the Ramírez-Chavero edition. Beauvois has reorganized the text in a more logical fashion, in the manner planned by Durán. Actually Durán had planned to write a fourth book (or third, if Two and Three are to be considered one work). This was to contain *huehuetlatolli*, ancient Aztec speeches and sermons, plus other matters which had been omitted in his previous books. Unfortunately our chronicler died before this work could be written.

Fray Diego Durán lived in a golden age of chronicles written on ancient Mexico —the second half of the sixteenth century. The fury of warfare had passed and it was possible to approach the Conquest as an historical episode. However, the pre-Hispanic epoch was still sufficiently close and there not only existed individuals born before the arrival of Cortés and bearers of the ancient civilization, but also many groups who for all practical purposes were living a pre-Spanish life. The Franciscans, Dominicans, the descendants of the Indian rulers, and even aged conquerors filled reams of paper which described the ancient Indian ways as reported by the "elders" of Tula, Texcoco, Mexico-Tenochtitlan, and numerous other cities. Many chronicles were produced—some of them superb. This corpus is unique in the Americas. All of this marvelous production of material on the native cultures, however, is not only due to the activities of the friars of the latter half of the sixteenth century, but also to the fact that great libraries of painted books had already existed before the Conquest. These books today are called "codices" and even though they are sadly diminished in number they constitute a highly valuable mass of original material. The codices were commonly used by the missionary and Indian chroniclers for their writings as they themselves often attest. All these historians utilized two basic sources: the pre-Hispanic manuscripts in picture writing and living informants. Bernardino de Sahagún seems to have used live informants more extensively than historians such as Durán and Ixtlilxochitl of Texcoco, who base their chronicles on written sources. Often, of course, these manuscripts had to be explained by informants. Ixtlilxochitl tells us that in ancient times "there were writers for each branch of knowledge. Some composed the historical annals, setting in order the events that took place every year, stating the day, month and hour. Others recorded the genealogies and descendants of the kings, lords and personages of high lineage; they would make note of those who were born and cancel the dead. Others painted the limits, boundaries and border stones of the cities, provinces and villages, and of the fields and plantations, indicating their owners. Yet others made records of the laws, and the rites and ceremonies performed in pagan times. The priests made records regarding the temples of the idols, of their idolatrous doctrines and the feasts of their false gods and their calendars. And finally, there were philosophers and wise men among them who recorded in picture writing the sciences they were versed in. They also taught the chants which dealt with these sciences and with their historical traditions." A number of these documents have been preserved. They are few compared to those which perished but they suffice to prove to us that such books did exist and that there were different schools of scribes just as Ixtlilxochitl affirms.

But how did these pictographic documents, so difficult to interpret for the European mind, become well-organized history books, such as that of Durán? One must remember the manner in which the ancient books were conceived. Because of the nature of native hieroglyphic writing, these codices could only serve as a sort of *aide-mémoire*. Essentially they were only lists of events which certain well-trained individuals in special schools learned how to "read" out loud, elaborating on the action of events, which could not be described adequately by picture writing; they added adjectives and reproduced conversations or any other pertinent commentaries that had been memorized. So it was that the pictures were only a guide which allowed the commentator to narrate a story which was to be told to a group of listeners. Poems, speeches by historical personages and many other things —in prose or poetry—were memorized and the skillful "reader" would include them as he went along in his narration. Tovar, in his letter to Acosta, explains the procedure followed by missionaries, probably since the time of Father Olmos: "It is to be noted that even though the Indians had different figures and characters with which they wrote, these were not so perfect as our own letters. However, they did not omit a word when they quoted what was written. Each reader kept an accurate account of this oral tradition in his mind and had memorized the words and the general order of these speeches. The latter were composed by the orators and recorded in picture writing. That the texts might be preserved with the exact words that their orators and poets had used, they would be taught to the young nobles who were to succeed the speakers. With this continuous repetition the oral versions were memorized word for word. The natives preserved the most famous orations which were composed in each generation by teaching these to the young men who were to become eloquent speakers. In this manner many discourses were passed on exactly from generation to generation, until the coming of the Spaniards. The latter wrote down many of these speeches or chants in our alphabet, and I personally saw these. In this way the ancient traditions have been preserved."

So it was that European writing was used after the Conquest in order to record earlier history and form a permanent and fixed corpus of documents. To this praiseworthy task the friars and the indigenous historians dedicated their lives. Among them the role of Durán is outstanding. "Its main value," writes Garibay of Durán's *Historia*, "is that it is the first and only chronicle of the sixteenth century that gives us a harmonious view of Tenochtitlan."

Since the seventeenth century there has been much discussion regarding the relationship between Durán's *Historia* and those of the other chroniclers.

The most superficial observation shows us that there are a number of chronicles, all of them written in the second half of the sixteenth century, which are very similar—sometimes almost identical. Besides the *Historia* there exist Tezozomoc's *Crónica Mexicana*, the *Códice Ramírez*, the *Historia de la venida de los indios* by Juan de Tovar, and Chapter VII of the *Historia Natural y Moral de las Indias* by José de Acosta. There is no doubt that there is a direct relationship among these documents, which, incidentally, are nearly all of first-rate importance. In this introduction we shall not discuss all the details of the problem, as they would be of interest only to specialists in this field. However, in order to grasp the *Historia* of Durán more fully, it is necessary to understand the general outline of this confusing situation, which began during the early part of the seventeenth century when Dávila Padilla stated that Acosta based his Chapter VII on the work of Durán. Over the centuries affirmations—some correct and some false—were made regarding this problem. But, in general, all of them are of little importance before the manuscript of the *Historia* was published. When, in the middle of the nineteenth century, the first edition appeared, the problem began to be understood. Recent scholarly studies such as those of Barlow and Sandoval have been based on profound knowledge of all the documents mentioned above together with others that shed light on the situation. These studies have revealed much to us, although there are still many enigmatic points.

It is evident that Acosta—he himself says so—used the manuscript of Tovar as a basis for his Chapter VII. This is not a problem. It is also evident that the *Códice Ramírez* and the *Història de la venida de los indios* by Tovar (only part of which has been published) are the same document, recorded, however, in two copies with slight variations. Both of them are, therefore, the *Historia* by Juan de Tovar. Tovar himself states, in his famous correspondence with Father Acosta, that he based a large part of his writings on Durán's *Historia*. It could be thought then that we have only two basic sources whose origin and relationship should be studied—Durán and Tezozomoc.

Nevertheless, the problem is more complex, as Tovar states that the *Historia* to which we have referred is the *second* that he wrote and we will call it *Tovar II*. *Tovar I*, therefore, is missing. We must keep this in mind. Further investigation reveals that Tezozomoc and Durán are derived from a common source, even though they are far from being identical, as they both used new material apart from their original source. It had been thought that their similarity was due to their both having used *Tovar I*, which is not extant. It is a fact that Durán mentions with complete honesty a "Chronicle" that he followed. Tezozomoc also used it, even though he does not say so clearly. With this information the problem again might appear to have been solved: Tovar wrote a first chronicle (*Tovar I*) which has been lost, and it served as a basis for Durán on the one hand, and for Tezozomoc on the other, even though both utilized additional oral and written material. The *Códice Ramírez (Tovar II)* served as a basis for Acosta but not for Durán or for Tezozomoc. Tovar himself says that as he had sent his first book to Spain, he did not have it available to consult and therefore wrote his second version from memory, making use of information furnished him by his kinsman Durán (who, in turn, it has been said, had taken them from *Tovar I*). In a scholarly article, Barlow indicates a certain doubt that events took this course, mainly because of some inconsistency in dates in the Indian calendar that appear in the *Códice Ramírez*. Barlow suspects the existence of an earlier chronicle which would not be *Tovar I* and which he names the *Crónica X*, and from which he thinks the other histories—in their different forms—are derived.

The Indian date of the *Códice Ramírez* as studied by Caso could only have fallen between 1536 and 1539 in the Christian calendar. Tovar could not possibly have written his work at this time as he was born in 1543. Therefore, it is evident that we are dealing with an earlier chronicle, called by Barlow the *Crónica X*, that cannot be the same as *Tovar I*. So it is that we are dealing with two lost chronicles. However, we must remember that there are different schools of thought as to the interpretation of the native calendar and that Durán did not have an understanding of it. It is probable that Tovar did not have a grasp of this either. It is also possible that the date given by the *Códice Ramírez* is an error. In spite of the fact that the date may be erroneous, there are other aspects of the matter that lead us to think that the *Crónica X* did exist, independent of *Tovar I*.

Tovar, in his letter to Acosta, after mentioning that he had been unable to recover his first *Historia*, writes, ". . . as I then looked deeply into these matters and spent much time on them, a great deal remained in my memory. Aside from that I consulted a book, done by a Dominican friar, a kinsman of mine, which was the most exact account based on ancient records, that I have ever seen. This refreshed my memory in order to write my chronicle (*Tovar II*), which now Your Reverence has read." Is it not unlikely that Tovar would fail to mention that the book of his "kinsman" Durán is based upon Tovar's own first work?

It could be expected that when Tovar wrote to Acosta, sending him *Tovar II*, indicating that he had written it from memory, and based on Durán, he would have revealed that Durán's chronicle had been based on *Tovar I*. This revelation would not necessarily have been made because he wished to belittle Durán or even less to boast that Durán had written his chronicle based on *Tovar I*. Rather, he might have done so because he wished Acosta to be advised that Tovar's second work was trustworthy and not only composed from memory. For, had it been based on Durán (and if the latter had been practically the same as *Tovar I*), this meant that *II* was fundamentally *Tovar I*. Let us remember that what Acosta sought was to be sure that his sources were accurate. It seems to me that all of this leads to a belief in the existence of a *Crónica X*, which is not *Tovar* but the original source used for *Tovar I*, Durán and Tezozomoc.

However, there is another problem involved, and that is the fact that Tovar, in his letter, explains clearly to Acosta the manner in which he wrote his first chronicle. He did not take it from another similar document but from several painted manuscripts and written accounts which he tried to organize into a history of the events in their consecutive order. To achieve the latter, he found it necessary to use a number of indigenous informants. Therefore, it is probable that Tovar's work is not based on the *Crónica X*, or at best Tovar used the latter as only one of his sources.

I feel that the painted manuscripts and written accounts mentioned by Tovar as the basis of his first *Historia* could be part of the material gathered by Olmos. This Franciscan missionary arrived in Mexico in 1528 and we know that he was concerned with Indian history at least since 1533, as he had been commissioned to study it by Sebastián Ramírez de Fuenleal and Fray Martín de Valencia, high civil and religious authorities, as is narrated by the early ecclesiastical writer Mendieta. Olmos gathered numerous documents. Perhaps these are the "ancient records," some of which have been preserved, even though his own history has been lost.

Be it as it may, Garibay, the eminent Nahuatl scholar and critic of ancient Aztec literature, has demonstrated the immense importance of Olmos' work, which, unfortunately, for the most part has been lost, but whose pioneer research methods set the standards for all the important scholars of the sixteenth century—not excluding Sahagún. This gathering of material included "interviews" with informants, in the manner of the modern ethnologist. Besides these, the scholar then gathered and examined all available written material. Is it possible that these documents, compiled by Olmos, were in part those used by Tovar and Durán? To prove this would require an enormous comparative study which would be out of place here. I have only tried to indicate briefly the antecedents of the great *Historia de las Indias* of Durán.

It may be wise to point out to the reader that when Durán refers to the ancient "crónica" the translators have used the term *Chronicle*. This *Chronicle* signifies to them the unrecorded or lost documents which I have just identified as perhaps being those collected by Olmos.

It is important to discuss the source material used by the ancient historians in order to evaluate their statements, to see whether we may draw trustworthy conclusions from the information contained in them. However, it is not necessary to fall into what the historian Edmundo O'Gorman has rightly called "the excessive quest for originality in information." Much less are we concerned with the problem of plagiarism which has been so thoroughly discussed in past times. It matters little that one historian reproduced the words of another, as long as the source that he used was a good one. From a moral point of view it would be absurd to try to apply our modern ethical standards to an age when no such standards existed and the restating of what a previous writer had recorded was no sin.

The profound knowledge of the mind of ancient Mexico shown by Durán is not to be found even in Sahagún. A good example of this is given to us by Garibay when this scholar refers to certain difficulties in the understanding of the esoteric meaning of the ancient Aztec poems. While Sahagún "sees visions and demons . . . another writer, Durán—with more profound knowledge, with more human sympathy—had listened to ancient traditions told by the natives, since childhood." These natives were still permeated with the ancient culture at Texcoco. Durán writes that "all these chants are filled with metaphors so obscure that very few persons can understand them unless their significance is studied and discussed. I have listened with great attention to what they sing and after hearing the words and metaphors, which at first seem nonsense, I find them to be meaningful thoughts, after I have examined them and meditated upon them. . . ." Durán's authority is definitive.

It is this sensitive perception of the Indian soul which makes Durán unique among the Dominicans. The Order of Preachers, more intellectual than the Franciscans, believed—as Garibay has clearly expressed—in the total renovation of the Indian world, in "erasing the past in order to instill the new faith of Christ." Though Durán did not forget the principles of his Order, he had an enormous sympathy toward the indigenous culture, toward the native ways of life and even toward the landscape of the Valley of Mexico, the scenery of Texcoco of his infancy.

The truth is that Durán, though a Spaniard by blood, was in reality a mestizo or hybrid. His childhood gave him a fluent knowledge not only of Nahuatl but also of the indigenous culture. It is evident that though he writes in Spanish, he seems to be thinking in Nahuatl. Rather—he mixes both cultures in such a way that they are difficult to separate. Fundamentally this is what places Durán at the very roots of Mexican culture and explains the historiographical climate in which he achieved his work.

We would like to be able to answer this question: Why did Durán write the *Historia*? What was his aim? Durán was not a professional historian, as Antonio de Herrera was to be later. He was a Dominican missionary whose task was the conversion of the Indians. His interest in history and ethnography was merged with the aims of his profession. The sixteenth century linguists who left us excellent dictionaries and grammars of many Indian languages did not learn them as an intellectual pastime. Their aim was to make themselves understood by the natives to whom they preached, so their writings were to facilitate the task of later friars in learning the languages. In like manner historian-ethnographers *needed* to understand the indigenous culture, grasp its present and past in order to reach the soul of their flock, thus converting it to Christianity. When Durán produced his works, fifty years had passed since the Conquest. The conversion of the Indians, at least in Central Mexico, should have been accomplished by then, and the basic obstacles eliminated, if it is true—as has been said—that the conquered Indians came in hordes, anxious to receive the new faith. Is it not possible that Durán, like many other alert men, realized that the conversion had been superficial, that in reality under the slight veneer of Christianity the ancient religion was still thriving? Ramón Iglesia is of this opinion. He believes that because of this situation Durán throws himself into "the study of the ancient religion, not in a cold impartial or simply descriptive way, but using this study as an indispensable weapon in order to uproot the old faith. That is why his book condemns not only the deeds of the non-clerical conquerors who wished to impose the Gospel at sword's point but also the complacent attitude of many friars who had allowed themselves to be deceived by the apparent success of their missionary labor."

Durán himself clearly explains the principal aim of his work: to destroy "ancient idolatry and false religion." But this will not be possible, he adds, "no matter how hard we work, if we do not understand the old religion profoundly." Therefore, he looks upon his chronicle as a basically pragmatic work which will be an aid in the labor of proselytism.

Durán, like almost all the historians of his century, is of the opinion that the purpose of history is to analyze the eternal struggle between God and the Devil, between good and evil, and that the role of man is to take part in this struggle in order to achieve the triumph of God on earth. However, in this there is a contradiction which Durán does not express clearly but that is nonetheless present. We do not know how he solved this. Since the conversion of the natives is the work of God, and God is the direct mover of history, the evangelization should have been successful, judging by the large groups of Indians that came running to receive baptism. Durán understood the Indian soul only too well. During his childhood he had lived too close to the native not to realize that baptism in many cases was an empty ceremony which changed the mentality of the neophyte little or not at all and that the Indian continually returned to his ancient practices. The solution to this problem evidently consisted in intensifying the preaching, but well-instructed preaching, an evangelization that does not rely exclusively on the zeal of the missionary. The latter must fully understand not only the ancient tongue but also the religion and culture in order to fight them with more effective weapons.

All of this may explain another interesting aspect of Durán: his open sympathy for the Indians which cannot be reconciled with his bitter criticism of them at times. The truth is that while he loves them in many ways he detests them as recalcitrant idolators. He cannot understand in reality how there may exist virtues in those who are without or only apparently within the flock of Christ. Let us not forget that he is a Dominican and that the Order of Preachers was precisely the organization that wielded the weapon of the Inquisition, attacking the heretic and, above all, the relapsed convert. But Durán was not the Inquisitor as shown in melodramas, nor was he a fanatic, blind to things of the world. As Garibay expresses with clarity, "he was an enthusiast of the Indian way of life even though he did not abandon the moderation of his own intellectual manner." In Durán, as in many other men, there exists a duality which forces him to be strict and almost inexorable in matters of the Faith, but which permits him to feel and understand a culture which he does not wish to destroy but to evangelize.

In this he is a typical product of his age. Durán, who lived in the second half of the sixteenth century, could not have had a completely medieval mentality. He belongs to the Renaissance and no matter how he may react against some new ideas, he realizes that the heathens, though lost spiritually, possess valuable things. Pagan Greek and Roman culture was fashionable in that time. Man had discovered what those peoples learned, how they progressed, and had realized the greatness of their art and of their deeds. In the same way the ancient Mexicans had obviously been mistaken in their religion but this did not mean that they had lacked admirable traits worthy of being studied and preserved. Durán believed that the study of ancient history—history is a teacher—could uproot the diabolical arts and show at the same time the positive aspects and the innate goodness of the ancient peoples.

*Ignacio Bernal*

# THE HISTORY OF
# THE INDIES OF
# NEW SPAIN

WHICH TREATS OF THE POSSIBLE PLACE OF ORIGIN OF THE INDIANS
OF THE INDIES AND MAINLAND OF THIS NEW WORLD

In order to discuss the real and truthful account of the origin and beginnings of
these Indian nations, so mysterious and remote to us, and to discover the real truth
about them, some divine revelation or spirit of God would be needed. However,
lacking this, it will be necessary to make conjectures and reach conclusions through
the many proofs that these people give us with their strange ways and manner of
conduct and their lowly conversation, so like that of the Hebrews. Because of their
nature we could almost affirm that they are Jews and Hebrew people, and I believe
that I would not be committing a great error if I were to state this fact, considering
their way of life, their ceremonies, their rites and superstitions, their omens, and
false dealings, so related to and characteristic of those of the Jews. The Holy Scrip-
ture is witness of this and we shall use it as our testimony.[1]

As proof of this opinion, we know that these newly arrived nations and Indian
people, coming from strange and remote regions, made a long and tedious journey
until they came to take possession of this country, and they passed many years in
reaching this place. One gathers this from the traditions and paintings and from
talking to the old people.

There are many people who tell fables. Some say that the Indians were born of
springs of water; others say that they were born of caves, or that their race is that
of the gods, all of which is clearly legend and shows that they themselves are
ignorant of their origin and beginnings. They always profess to have come from
strange lands and I have found this depicted in their ancient painted manuscripts,
where they portray the great periods of hunger, thirst, and nakedness, with innumerable afflictions, that they suffered until they reached this country and
settled in it.[2]

Because of all these things my suspicions are confirmed that these natives are
part of the ten tribes of Israel which Shalmaneser, King of the Assyrians, captured
and took to Assyria in the time of Hosea, King of Israel, and in the time of Ezekias,
King of Jerusalem, as can be read in the fourth *Book of Kings*, Chapter XVIII,
where one finds that Israel was carried out of its own land to Assyria. It also says
that this remote and distant country had never been inhabited before. There was
a long and tedious journey of a year and a half to the region where today are found
these people of the Islands and the Mainland toward the west beyond the seas.

Other evidence found in Holy Writ that can be cited to prove this idea is that
God, through Hosea, had promised to multiply these people like the sands of the

sea, and the fact that they have taken possession of the world shows clearly and manifestly how great was this multiplication. But leaving the Biblical text and coming to what all of us saw in this country, a thing that amazed us was the number of people found here. This was observed by the Spaniards who came early to this country, before the great plague when so many people died that not even a third of the Indians who had existed here survived, and this does not include the innumerable men, women, and children who had been killed by the Spaniards during the Conquest a few years earlier.

The Indians have traditions regarding a great man who, after suffering many afflictions and persecutions on the part of his countrymen, gathered the multitude of his followers and persuaded them to flee from that persecution to a land where they could live in peace. Having made himself leader of those people, he went to the seashore and moved the water with a rod that he carried in his hand. Then the sea opened and he and his followers went through. And the enemies, seeing this opening made, went behind him, but the waters returned to their place and the pursuers were never heard of again.[3]

What clearer proof need we that these people were Jews than the story of the flight from Egypt, wherein Moses moved the waters with his rod, the sea opened, a path appeared, and, after Pharaoh followed with his army, God returned the sea to its place, all the enemy being then drowned in the deep? If the previous account were not convincing enough, I should like to tell about another event that the Indians claim happened on their long migration.

While they were camped by some hills, a frightful earthquake occurred. The earth opened and swallowed certain evil men, an occurrence which filled the other people with dread. Having seen the painting of this event, I was reminded of the *Book of Numbers*, where it is told how the earth opened her mouth and swallowed up Korah and Dathan and Abiron.

In the same Indian painting was shown how sand or very fine hail rained on them, and when I inquired what this meant, the people told me that sand from the sky rained on their forefathers continually during the journey that they made to reach this land. If I am not deceived, this must be the manna with which God sustained the Jews in the desert, as Chapter XVI of *Exodus* relates.

The first words in *Genesis* are: "In the beginning God created the heavens and the earth." In this way an aged man from Cholula, about a hundred years old, began to describe their origins to me. This man, who from sheer age walked bent over toward the earth, was quite learned in ancient traditions. When I begged him to enlighten me about some details to put into this history, he asked me what I wanted him to narrate. I realized I had found an old and learned person, so I answered, "The beginning of the world!" He responded, "Take pen and paper, because you will not be able to remember all that I shall tell you.

"In the beginning," said this ancient man, "before light or sun had been created, this world lay in darkness and shadows and was void of every created thing. It was all flat, without a hill or ravine, surrounded on every side by water, without even a tree. And then, when the light and sun were born in the east, men of monstrous stature appeared and took possession of this country. These giants, desirous of seeing the birth of the sun and its setting, decided to go seek dawn and dusk and they separated into two groups. One band walked toward the west and the other toward the east. The latter walked until the sea cut off their route; from here they decided to return to the place from which they had set out, called *Iztaczollin ineminian.*

"Not having found a way to reach the sun but enamored of its light and beauty, they decided to build a tower so high that its summit would reach unto Heaven. And gathering materials for this building, the giants found clay for bricks and an excellent mortar with which they began to build the tower with great swiftness.

"When they had raised it as high as they could (it seemed to reach to Heaven), the Lord of the Heights became angry and said to the inhabitants of the Heavens, 'Have you seen that the men of the earth have built a lofty and proud tower in order to come up here, enamored as they are of the light of the sun and of its beauty? Come, let us confound them, it is not just that the earthlings, made of flesh, mingle with us.' Then swift as lightning those who dwell in the Heavens came out from the four regions of the world and tore down the tower that had been constructed. And the giants, bewildered and filled with terror, fled in all directions."[4]

We have now seen how an Indian relates the creation of the world, and I believe it is not necessary to suggest that the reader compare this with Chapters I and II of *Genesis.* The sixth and eleventh chapters of this Book deal with giants and the tower of Babel and how man, ambitious to reach Heaven, moved only by his desire to praise his own name, built the tower and because of this was confounded by God. Therefore I am convinced, and wish to convince others, that those who tell this account heard it from their ancestors; and these natives belong, in my opinion, to the lineage of the chosen people of God for whom He worked great marvels. And so the knowledge and the paintings of the things of the Bible and its mysteries have passed from father to son. The people attribute them to this land and say that they took place here, for they are ignorant of their own beginnings.

It cannot be denied that there have been giants in this country. I can affirm this as an eyewitness, for I have met men of monstrous stature here. I believe that

5

there are many in Mexico who will remember, as I do, a giant Indian who appeared in a procession of the feast of Corpus Christi. He appeared dressed in yellow silk with a halberd at his shoulder and a helmet on his head. And he was all of three feet taller than the others.

During such a long and tedious journey as that which the Indians pursued to come to this land they experienced great hardships. They tell of famines, plagues, thirst, tempests, wars, locusts, and hailstorms that destroyed their fields which they had sown along the way, and a thousand other obstacles and troubles that I find described in their chronicles. They undoubtedly brought chieftains and priests to guide them and instruct them in their ceremonies, but I doubt that these things be taken from the Biblical account. Seeing that their stories are so like those found in the Holy Scriptures I cannot help but believe that these Indians are the children of Israel.

They made sacrifices in the mountains, and under shaded trees, in the caves and caverns of the dark and gloomy earth. They burned incense, killed their sons and daughters and sacrificed them and offered them as victims to their gods; they sacrificed children, ate human flesh, killed prisoners and captives of war. All of these were also Hebrew ceremonies practiced by those ten tribes of Israel, and all were carried out with the greatest ritual and superstitions that it is possible to conceive. And what makes me firmly believe that these Indians are of Hebrew lineage is their strange obstinacy in not casting out these idolatries and superstitions, for they pay them much heed just as their ancestors did.

> *". . . and they worshipped their idols*
> *Which became a snare to them.*
> *And sacrificed their sons and daughters to devils.*
> *And they poured out innocent blood:*
> *The blood of their own sons and daughters,*
> *Whom they sacrificed to the idols of Canaan."*
>
> (Psalm 105.)

The only knowledge of their origins that I have obtained from my Indian informants tells of the seven caves where their ancestors dwelt for so long and which they abandoned in order to seek this land, some coming first and others later until these caves were totally deserted. The caves are in Teocolhuacan, which is also called Aztlan, "Land of Herons," which we are told is found toward the north and near the region of La Florida.[5]

Therefore, I shall now give the true account of these nations and their migration

6

emostracion de las queuas, donde aultauan
los mexicanos antes, de conquistar esta
tierra —

deuenden allos suçe
ineços, ques vna
generaçion balerosa
de que sepreçian como noso
tros dlos godos, ylos Rome
nos dlos troyanos.

*Chicomóztoc, the Seven Caves, land of origin of the*
*Aztecs. Below: Early nomadic life among the Chichimecs.*
*From the* Atlas, *the picture book accompanying*
*Durán's text. Photo Reg Van Cuylenburg.*

from the place of the caverns, although my own opinion of their origin seems more logical. But in everything I subject myself to the correction of the Holy Catholic Church.

Thus seven tribes of people went out from Chicomoztoc, the Seven Caves. As they do not know their real origin, they claim that their ancestors were born of these caves, as they have no information relating to previous times.

CHAPTER II WHICH TREATS OF HOW THESE INDIANS CAME OUT FROM THEIR
SEVEN CAVES IN ORDER TO COME TO THIS LAND

The Indian nations emerged from those seven caves, where they had lived a long time, in the year of Our Lord 820.[6] It took them more than eighty years to reach this country because of the many delays that took place. Along the way they built towns and settled in places which they saw were peaceful and pleasant, but as they explored the country they found other sites that were better and more favorable so they abandoned the first ones and went on. The old people, the sick and those who became exhausted were left behind.

The Indians erected great and curious buildings along the way, so that today remains of these edifices are found in many places. For this reason they tarried greatly in coming here, although the distance is so short that it can be covered in a month. The cause of this was their stopping to sow and to gather, and their lingering to rest and build towns, all this being consistent with their natural temperament which is deliberate and slow. In that way they reached this part of New Spain in the year 902.[7]

The people who first left the caves were the following six tribes: the Xochimilca, the Chalca, the Tecpanec, the Colhua, the Tlalhuica, and Tlaxcalans. It should be noted, however, that not all these bands left together nor in the same year. In this way they abandoned the region of the caves, one tribe doing what it saw another do. These people are fond of imitating others, like monkeys or sheep: if one jumps they all jump after him.

All of them left except the Aztecs, who remained behind due to a divine command which will be spoken of later. These people affirm that God had promised them this land, for they are the people He held near and best beloved, like the tribe of Judah among the Jews. The Aztecs, faithful to the divine order, did not abandon the place of the caves for three hundred and two years, so the other tribes came first and took possession of this land. The Aztecs came to live here three hundred and one years after the arrival of the others.

The Xochimilca were the first to arrive and they made a circuit of the great lake. They saw that the place they occupy today was good earth, so they settled there. They took possession of the mountain ridge that today belongs to the Xochimilca nation and which stretched as far as a town called Tuchimilco or Ocopetlayuca, by another name. Other towns that form part of this nation and are called by the same name include Ocuituco, Tetelaneyapan, Tlamimilulpan, Xumiltepec, Tlacotepec, Zacualpa and Temoac, Tlayacapa and Totlapa and Tepoztlan, Chimalhuacan, Ehecatzinco and Tepetlixpan, with all the other towns subject to Chimalhuacan. All of these are part of the Xochimilca nation, including Cuitlahuac, Mizquic, and Colhuacan.

Soon afterwards the second band arrived. These were the Chalca lineage, who on their arrival joined the Xochimilca and adjusted their common boundaries pacifically. They took as capitol the town of Tlalmanalco. Chieftains of that generation went out from here to live in those places that were in this province: Amecameca, Tenango, and all of those of Quaxuclipas, Ayotzinco, Chalco Atenco, and San Martin.

The Tecpanecs came after the Chalca and settled in their principal center which was Tacuba, although the court and principal people resided in Azcapotzalco. After some time had passed, the lords spread out and occupied the towns of Tacubaya, Coyoacan, Azcapotzalco, Tlalnepantla, Tenayuca, and the entire ridge that runs to the border of the country of the Otomi tribe.

The fourth to arrive was the Texcocan band, a group as numerous as that of Xochimilco. They were accompanied by many illustrious men. This fact is proved by the order and fine planning with which their city was built and the beauty with which they adorned and maintained it. They took as their capital that place which is now the city of Texcoco, and from here they dispersed in order to build towns such as the other tribes had done. Some went to Huexotla and others to Coatlichan where the court of that nation resided long before they moved to Texcoco. Still others built in Tepetlaoztoc, Acolman, Chiautlatecas, Tlantepechpa, Otumba, and many other villages which I shall not mention so as not to waste time and paper.

All that stretch of lake shore around Texcoco is inhabited by people who in every way are educated and courteous, clever, of fine speech, elegant, and polished. Their refined style in speaking is so outstanding that it reminds one of the Castilian of Toledo in Spain. In comparison with these people, the others seem coarse and rough.[8] Some will think that I am partial in speaking so well of Texcoco;

10

although I did not acquire my milk teeth in that city, I got my second ones there. Since the remarkable things of Texcoco have been extolled by others, everything I say is already well known.

When the lake was completely encircled by these four tribes who occupied its shores and shared the land among themselves, the Tlalhuica came, a very rough people in every way and of coarse speech. As the newcomers found everything occupied they settled in the place that they inhabit today: Cuernavaca in the hot country, now the Marquesado, called thus because it belonged to the Marquis, Don Hernando Cortés. This is certainly one of the most beautiful lands in the world, and if it were not for the great heat it would be another Garden of Eden. There are delightful springs, wide rivers full of fish, the freshest of woods, and orchards of many kinds of fruits, many of them native to Mexico and others to Spain, which supply all the neighboring cities with fruit. It is full of a thousand different fragrant flowers. This place is very rich in cotton and the commerce in this product is carried on here by people from all over the country.

After these five tribes had settled, the people of Tlaxcala, originally Texcala, arrived and, seeing that there was now no place where they could establish themselves on this side of the mountain, went behind the snow-capped ridges to live. They chose Tlaxcala as capital of their dominion, but as they were very numerous the lords dispersed toward Huexotzinco, Calpan, and Cholula. If I were to mention all the lands the Tlaxcalans took possession of, it would tire the reader without purpose as the innumerable towns, dwelling places and villages are well known. The King our lord has seen fit to exempt them from all tribute, as they were loyal and faithful subjects in the conquest of this country.

When these six tribes had settled, they recorded in their painted books the type of land and kind of people they found here. These books show two types of people, one from the west of the snow-covered mountain toward Mexico, and the other on the east, where Puebla and Cholula are found. Those from the first region were Chichimecs and the people from Puebla and Cholula were "The Giants," the *Quiname*, which means "men of great stature."

The few Chichimecs on the side of Mexico were brutal, savage men, and they were called *Chichimecs* because they were hunters.[9] They lived among the peaks and in the harshest places of the mountain where they led a bestial existence. They had no human organization but hunted food like the beasts of the same mountain, and went stark naked without any covering on their private parts. They hunted all day for rabbits, deer, hares, weasels, moles, wildcats, birds, snakes, lizards, mice, and they also collected locusts, worms, herbs, and roots. Their whole life was reduced to a quest for food. In order to kill a snake they spent an entire day crouching behind a bush, watching the snake at its lair as a cat will wait for a mouse. These people slept in the hills inside caves, or under bushes, without any heed for sowing, cultivating, or gathering. They did not worry about the morrow but ate what they had hunted each day.

Thus men and women went to the hills together, reminding one of a dog in a rubbish heap seeking something on which to gnaw. As the women accompanied their husbands, they left their children well glutted with milk, hanging in little rush baskets from branches of trees, until they returned from the hunt. These few Chichimecs were so spread out that they had little contact with each other. They adored no gods, and had no kind of ritual, nor did they recognize any ruler. They lived a carefree life according to natural law.

When the new nations came, these savage people showed no resistance or anger, but rather awe. They fled toward the hills, hiding themselves there. They hid in the way that they flee from us today, because it is true that we have not shown ourselves to be so kind and loving as to induce them to do otherwise. The newly arrived people seeing, then, that the land was left unoccupied, chose at will the best places to live in.

The other people who were found in Tlaxcala and Cholula and Huexotzinco are said to have been "Giants."[10] These were enraged at the coming of the invaders and tried to defend their land. I do not have a very true account of this, and therefore will not attempt to tell the story that the natives told me even though it was long and worth hearing, of the battles that the Cholultecs fought with the Giants until they killed them or drove them from the country.

These Giants lived no less bestially than the Chichimecs, as they had abominable customs and ate raw meat from the hunt. In certain places of that region enormous bones of the Giants have been found, which I myself have seen dug up at the foot of cliffs many times. These Giants flung themselves from precipices while fleeing from the Cholultecs and were killed. The Cholultecs had been extremely cruel to the Giants, harassing them, pursuing them from hill to hill, from valley to valley, until they were destroyed.

Even if we detain the reader a little, I should like to tell the manner in which the people of Cholula and Tlaxcala annihilated that evil nation. This was done by treason and deceit. They pretended to want peace with the Giants, and after having assured them of their good will they invited them to a great banquet. An ambush was then prepared. Some men slyly robbed the guests of their shields, clubs, and swords. The Cholultecs then appeared and attacked. The Giants tried to defend themselves, and, as they could not find their weapons, it is said that they tore branches from the trees with the same ease as one cuts a turnip, and in this way they defended themselves valiantly. But finally all were killed.

Once the Giants were annihilated the Cholultecs and Tlaxcalans built their cities without any opposition. They settled the boundaries among themselves, they intermarried, they lived in peace, cultivating their lands and building their homes. They had no ceremonies and had no idols, adoring only the sun which they worshipped as God, the creator and cause of all things. They sacrificed to him the following way: when any game was killed they removed the bloodstained arrow and offered it to the sun, recognizing him as a god.

From this time on the Chichimec barbarians acquired a little culture and lived like rational people and wore clothing, as things which had seemed natural to them before now were regarded as shameful. They also made huts in which to live. They began to have relations with the other people, and to trade and bargain with them, losing the fear they had, becoming related to them by marriage, beginning to have lords, recognizing the authority of some men over others. They congregated and opened their eyes to distinguish good from evil, and abandoned their savage life. But these Chichimecs always stayed in the hills and retired to the mountains, separated from the others.

Three hundred and two years after the six bands of people had left the caves where they had lived, in the region of Aztlan and Teocolhuacan, the seventh tribe, the Aztecs, came to this land. They believed that the earth had been promised to them by their gods. All of the Aztecs were idolatrous and felt favored by these gods, aside from which they were bellicose, courageous, and undertook great feats and exploits fearlessly. They were a people with a certain amount of culture. As they tarried much on their journey, and as it is my intention to relate their history, it is necessary to write a special chapter regarding the events that took place during their migration. They suffered great trials in the hope that the country that was promised them by their prophets and chieftains would be really the promised land and that it would be fertile and full of plenty. Anyone whose eyes are free of prejudice knows that the above description is true of this country, for, among all the lands in the world, this one can compare with the finest.

The Aztecs brought with them an idol called Huitzilopochtli,[11] who had four custodians to serve him. He prophesied to them in secret all the happenings that would take place on their journey. The people held this idol in such reverence and awe that no one but his keepers dared approach or touch him. He came concealed in a coffer of rushes, so that not one of the natives had ever seen the form of their idol. The priests made the people adore the idol as a god, preaching to them the law they were to follow, and the ceremonies and rites to be observed in honor of their divinity. This they did in all the places where they set up camp, like the children of Israel when they wandered in the wilderness.

13

The feats of the Aztecs are always so full of adventure that those who are not acquainted with these people will be pleased to hear of them and of their origin. I am aware of the great difficulties in relating these ancient histories, especially since they begin so far back. The early friars burned the Aztec books and writings and thus we lost important documents. The old people who could write this history are no longer alive to tell of the settling of this country. It was they whom I would have consulted for my chronicle.

It also seems to me that it will be impossible to tell everything that has occurred in this New World, as it is such a large country. There are so many kingdoms, cities, and villages here, so many large towns where innumerable people lived, divided into many nations, ways of life, and languages, as well as dress and customs. The good and bad fortunes that befell a single one of these nations would be enough for one painstaking historian. He would still have too much to do in writing the exploits of a single people, even though he abbreviated the history, which is what I have attempted here. I shall refer to the most obvious facts, for there are some remains of the past that lead us to an understanding of former events. Even if we had no more record than the carvings of the ancient kings at Chapultepec and other antique sculptures, these alone would suffice to tell of the origin and great deeds of these people. Although these figures do not tell the whole story, at least they are an indication of the greatest achievements of these nations.

In the year 1193 after the birth of our Redeemer, Jesus Christ, the Aztec nation reached this land. These people, like the others who populated the country, departed from seven caves in a land called Aztlan. This name could mean "Whiteness" or "Place of the Herons." Because of this the people were called Aztec which means "People of Whiteness." They were also called Mecitin or Mexicans, in honor of the priest and lord who guided them, whose name was Meci. The entire tribe took this name, just as the Romans took theirs from Romulus, the founder of Rome. The Aztecs now have another name, which they acquired after they took possession of this land: Tenochca, because of the *tenochtli*, or prickly pear cactus, that sprang from the rock in the place where they built their city. In this sense Tenochca means "The owners of the prickly pear cactus."[12]

The Aztecs left the seven caves in order to seek the Promised Land. According to traditions left by their priests and certain painted manuscripts, there were long delays in the migration and on these stops they inhabited many lands, fertile places abounding in water and forests.

14

In some places they stayed as long as twenty years, in others fifteen, and in others ten. In a painting that I was shown in Santiago Tlatelolco, I saw depicted many towns founded during this migration, some of them still inhabited and others now abandoned. Because the people in the latter places died off, only vestiges of the buildings and temples have remained. The first thing the people did in each place where they stopped was to construct a temple.

When the temple was ready to receive the coffer in which their god was carried, they planted maize, chilli—which is like pepper—and other crops. If their god decreed a good harvest, then they reaped; if he determined otherwise, they abandoned the fields. Everything was left except the ripened maize. Frequently the harvesting was left to old men and women and the sick who were not strong enough to go on. In this way places were settled and were left with sustenance. This was the purpose of the Aztecs, to populate those places with their people and become rulers of the land.

We have mentioned how this nation brought with it a principal god without whom they dared not move. They also carried seven other gods which represented the seven caves out of which the seven tribes had emerged. These seven deities had their titles to indicate godly superiority, as today titles denote noblemen:

The god of the first band was called Yopican Tecuhtli, Lord of Yopican, Place of the Tecpanecs; the second, Tlacochcalcatl Tecuhtli, Lord of the House of the Dart; the third, Huitznahuacatl Tecuhtli, Lord of the South; the fourth, Cuatecpan Tecuhtli, Lord of the Eagle Place; the fifth, Chalmecatl, Lord of the Jade Lineage; the sixth, Tlacatecpanecatl, Lord of the Men's Palace; the seventh, Izquitecatl, Lord of the Place of Toasted Corn.

The Aztec people went through the land of the Chichimecs. They saw all of this new country and the plains of Cibola, but nothing in that land pleased them, and they came to rest in the province that is now called Michoacan, "Land of Fish," in a place called Patzcuaro.

It should be noted that the Aztecs and those who are now called the Tarascans of Michoacan, and those of the province of Malinalco, were of the same band and all had come out of the seventh cave, all speaking the same language. When they reached Patzcuaro and saw that it was so peaceful and pleasant, the priests consulted their god. They begged that though this was not the land that had been promised them, he allow them to leave part of their group here.[13]

The god Huitzilopochtli answered the priests in dreams, telling them that he was happy to do what they asked of him. He ordered that when certain men and women went to bathe in the great lake, those who remained on the shore should steal their clothes. So, in a furtive manner, some of the Aztecs went to the camp and stole the garments, leaving the others naked. While those in the lake were still enjoying the water the others broke camp and left the place, following the route indicated by their god.

After the people in the lake had bathed contentedly, they came out and looked for their clothes but could not find them. Realizing that this was a trick of the others, they came to the camp and found it abandoned, no one being there to tell them what route the Aztecs had taken. Naked and forsaken and not knowing where to go, they decided to stay there and settle the land. Those who tell this story say that they remained dressed only in their own skins, men as well as women, and as they were there a long time they came to lose shame and leave their private parts uncovered. These people did not previously use loincloths nor mantles, but rather long tunics that reached the floor, like the robes of the Jews. I saw some of these robes some time ago, and I understand that they are still used among the countrymen of that province.

The god of the Aztecs had a sister who was called Malinalxochitl, Wild Grass Flower, who came with the tribe. She was very beautiful and was possessed of such intelligence that she became skillful in the magic arts. Her cunning was so great that she caused much harm in the tribe and made herself feared in order to be adored later as a goddess. The people had endured her because she was the sister of Huitzilopochtli, but finally they asked the latter to try to get rid of her for the sake of the tribe. The god advised the priests through dreams, as was his custom, to abandon her in the place that he would indicate, together with her attendants and certain elders.

In order to please the people, the priest told everyone of this revelation. He said:

"Your god, who beholds your sufferings,
Says that his sister, with her cunning and evil dealings, is dangerous to you.
He is very offended by this and filled with wrath toward her
Because he sees the power she has acquired by illicit means
Over fierce and harmful creatures.
She slays those who anger her with magic spells,
By sending snakes and scorpions, centipedes or deadly spiders, to bite them.
Therefore, in order to free you from this affliction,
And because of the love he has for all of you,
It is his will that this night, when she is in the first slumber
Together with her followers, we depart and abandon her.
Not one of us will remain to show her the way.
Your god says that he did not come here to bewitch the people
Or control by these means.

16

He yearns to save them through the strength of their own hearts
And the might of their arms. He wishes to extol his own name
On raising the Aztec nation to the heavens.
He will make them lords of gold and silver,
Lords of splendid feathers of many colors and of precious stones.
Your people, the Aztecs, will build houses and temples
Of jade and rubies in his name,
As he is the lord of precious stones in this earth.
And he will be lord of cacao and of richly worked mantles.
For these reasons has been his blessed coming; he has deigned
To guide us through this wilderness, to give us repose
And to bestow upon us a reward for the trials that we have
Undergone and those that we are still to endure.
Therefore he commands that his kinswoman be abandoned
In this place with her evil sorcery."

After the priest had spoken, all those who were not followers of Malinalxochitl went away. They abandoned her and her attendants who were asleep. The Aztecs then followed the road toward Tula,[14] their deity leading them, and finally reached the summit of the hill Coatepec.

When the morning came Malinalxochitl found herself alone with her followers. She wept sorrowfully and bemoaned the departure of her brother who had thus mocked her. As she did not know the way she asked advice of her aides, who then led her to a place now called Malinalco, where she and her partisans settled. It is the custom of these people to name a town for its founder, which is also a Hebrew practice. The people of Malinalco to this day have the reputation of being sorcerers and it is said that they inherited this gift from the woman who founded the city.

The Aztec nation was now divided into three parts. One had stayed in Michoacan where they invented a special language so as not to be taken for Aztecs, as they were offended at the humiliation they had suffered. Another part of the nation remained in Malinalco. Very few people reached Coatepec, although they who did were strong and courageous. Along the way, in two places called Ocopita and Acahualtzinco where they replenished their provisions, they left certain aged or sick persons, and this diminished their numbers.

As the Aztecs went into the land of Tula, the Chichimecs and mountaineers of those regions became uneasy and showed their displeasure. The Otomi people[15] were especially annoyed, complaining, "What people are these? What effrontery to dare occupy our lands without permission! They must be a vile people!"

The Aztecs, not heeding these complaints, soon built the temple of their divinity with the sacrifice stone which they used as an altar, around which were placed the other gods whom I have described. When they had settled down in their shelters around the temple, in the order which their god and their priest decreed, some to the east and others to the west, some to the south and others to the north, then in a vision the god commanded the priests to dam up the water of a river that passed close by. The water was to flow through the plain and form a lake around the hill where they had settled because the god wished to make a model of the promised land of the future.

When the dam was made, the river flowed over and covered the entire plain, forming a great lagoon. The Aztecs planted willows, cypresses, and poplars. They filled the banks with rushes and reeds, the lake began to swell with all kinds of fish. Water fowl appeared, ducks, wild geese, herons covered the lagoon, and many other kinds of birds that are found and breed today by the lake of Mexico.

The place became filled with water flowers and cattails which attracted thrushes and magpies, some red, others yellow. Their singing and chattering created great harmony and gladdened the entire place. The Aztecs were here so contented (although it was no more than a model of the promised land) that they did not want to leave it in order to search for the real promised land.

For this reason, they sang and danced with songs inspired by the beauty and luxuriant verdure of the place, exclaiming to their god, Huitzilopochtli:

"O Huitzilopochtli, here is your abode!
This is the place to which you were sent.
It is here where your name should be extolled,
On the mountain of Coatepec! It is now yours to rejoice
In the gold and silver, the precious stones and shining feathers
Of many colors, rich and precious mantles and cacao
And other splendid things.
From here you will conquer the four regions of the world
With the strength of your chest, of your head, and your arm.
Here your name will receive glory and honor.
This is the capital of your kingdom.
Command your custodians to call the people together!
Let the pilgrimage end here so the Aztecs may now repose
And rest from their hardships!"

18

The deity, Huitzilopochtli, was greatly angered, saying: "Who are they who dis-

*The training of children in Aztec society. From the*
**Codex Mendoza,** *painted in early Colonial times by
Aztec scribes. Courtesy American Museum
of Natural History, New York.*

regard my will? Are they by chance mightier than I? Tell them I will take vengeance against them before tomorrow, so they will not dare to give opinions in those things that I have determined and for which I am here. They must learn that they are to obey me alone!"

They say that the face of the idol at that point became so ugly and frightening, with its diabolical scowl, that the Aztecs were filled with terror.

At midnight, when everything was quiet, the people heard a great noise in a place called Teotlachtli, the Divine Ball Court, and in the Tzompanco, Skull Rack, dedicated to the divinity. When morning came they found the principal instigators of the rebellion dead there, together with the woman called Coyolxauhqui. All the breasts had been opened and the hearts removed. From this came the accursed belief that Huitzilopochtli ate only hearts, and thus was established the practice of sacrificing men and opening their breasts to remove their hearts in order to offer them to the devil, their god, Huitzilopochtli.

When the Aztecs saw the severe punishment that their god had inflicted upon the guilty, they were greatly frightened. But the wrath of Huitzilopochtli did not end here.

In order to demonstrate further his fury he ordered his priests to open the dam they had made and let the waters run their former course. The priests did not dare disobey. They removed the defenses and broke the dam, letting the waters run. They did this against their will because these waters had surrounded them and sustained them and had given them tranquillity.

When the lagoon was destroyed the reeds and the rushes began to dry up, the trees withered also, and the freshness disappeared. The fish and frogs and all of the insects that breed in the water perished, all that the people used for their food. The water fowl flew away and the region became as dreary and desert-like as it had been before. When the Aztecs saw the barrenness of the place which they had thought would be Mexico, they decided to consult their god as to what he wished them to do. They believed he would now be appeased by the shedding of blood and the destruction. Time dissolves anger and softens hearts.[16]

When the people consulted him, he commanded them to leave that site and go on to Tula. This they did presently. The Aztecs reached Tula in the year 1168 where they stayed a very short time. From Tula they continued on to Atitlalaquian and from there to Tequixquiac. They stayed at Tequixquiac on borrowed land for a few years, sowing the fields for their sustenance.

From this place they went on to another called Tzompanco. They wished to repose here but they met opposition from the local inhabitants and had some encounters with them. Then they continued to the town of Xaltocan. Here, as they

21

found the natives more friendly, they sowed their fields of corn and chilli and other seeds that they had brought with them. They made earth walls for their safety and, after they had harvested their crops, they gathered their provisions and came to Ehecatepec, and from here to Tolpetlac. Finally they entered the territory of the Tecpanecs. The Tecpanecs were the people of Azcapotzalco and Tacuba and Coyo-acan, an illustrious nation who at that time ruled over the other tribes.

The Aztecs finally came to rest at Chapultepec, "Hill of the Grasshopper," where with much dread they constructed a camp of huts and fortified the place as best they could. When they consulted their god about their course of action, they were told to await the change of events, since the deity would know what measures to take and would advise them at the right time. But he added that they should be prepared for what was to come, since that was not the place he had chosen for their home. This chosen land was near, but first they would meet great opposition from two nations, so the Aztecs should make their hearts strong.[17]

Awed by this answer, the people chose a captain from among their most noble men to command and guide them. The chieftain they designated was Huitzilihuitl, "Hummingbird Feather." He was a skillful man of courageous heart.

After he had been elected, Huitzilihuitl ordered the hill terraced with encircling walls, about two yards apart. At the top the walls leveled off to form a spacious courtyard. Here the people gathered and fortified the heights. They stood guard day and night diligently, they placed the women and children in the middle surrounded by the soldiers, and they repaired their arrows, wooden swords, and spears. They also carved stone points and made stones for their slings and for their defense.

CHAPTER IV WHICH TREATS OF WHAT BEFELL THE AZTECS AFTER THEIR ARRIVAL AT CHAPULTEPEC

After the Aztecs had come to the hill Chapultepec and had camped there, they were advised by their god Huitzilopochtli that this was not the promised land and that they should make preparations for war.

Although the Aztecs were fearful, they gathered their strength and courage and were on guard. They built their defense works and prepared their arms as best they could, seeing that they were in the midst of many other peoples who showed them no friendliness.

But in order to relate this story in the correct order, we must remember what was narrated in the last chapter where we described a sister of Huitzilopochtli, named Malinalxochitl. As she was harmful to the people and possessed evil arts, Huitzilopochtli had ordered his tribe to abandon her, leaving her with her followers. So it was that they abandoned this woman, who was totally ignorant of the road to be followed by her brother. She remained behind for some time and then went on to found the province of Malinalco.

This Malinalxochitl, a wicked sorceress, later gave birth to a son and taught him all her tricks and witchcraft. When he was old enough she told him of the offense done her by her brother Huitzilopochtli when he abandoned her, separating her from the rest of the tribe. The son's heart was filled with wrath and, moved by his mother's tears, he promised to seek out his uncle Huitzilopochtli and with his arts and cunning, destroy the god and his Aztec followers.

When the mother saw her son's determination she helped him prepare to look for his uncle, inciting all the nations to destroy Huitzilopochtli with their most fiendish skills and cunning. And in this way, roaming from one place to another, Copil—as he was called—set out for Chapultepec.

Copil wandered from town to town, kindling the fire of wrath against the Aztecs, inflaming the tribes to destruction, claiming that the Aztecs were pernicious men of perverse customs. The tribes were alarmed and determined to massacre the Aztecs. A conspiracy was formed among the cities of Azcapotzalco, Tacuba, Coyoacan, Xochimilco, Colhuacan, and Chalco, in order to surround the Aztecs and annihilate them. When the evil Copil saw that his plan was about to be carried out, he went up to the top of a small hill called Tetepetzinco, "Little Stone Hill," at the shore of the lake, to watch the destruction of the Aztec tribe. Copil was determined to rule over all their lands as soon as the annihilation he desired had taken place.

But the outcome of the struggle was different from what Copil desired. The god Huitzilopochtli discovered his nephew's perversity and warned the Aztecs through the priests. He instructed them to go to that hill before they were surrounded, catch Copil unaware, slay him and bring the god his heart. In order to carry this out the Aztec warriors were to take an image of the divine Huitzilopochtli with them. One of the priests, Cuauhtloquetzqui, took the idol on his shoulders and led the Aztecs to the hill. There they caught Copil unprepared and murdered him. They cut out his heart and presented it to his uncle, the deity. Huitzilopochtli commanded his priest to place himself in the marsh, in the midst of the reeds, and to cast the heart into the middle of the lake with all his strength. This he did, and the heart fell in a place now called Tlalcocomolco. The Aztecs say that out of this heart sprouted the prickly pear cactus where later the city of Mexico was built.[18] They also say that in the place where Copil was killed hot springs began to gush. These springs are called Acopilco, which means "Water of Copil."

Although Copil was now dead, the enmity against the Aztecs continued unabated. Burning with ire, their enemies surrounded Chapultepec Hill where the Aztecs were peacefully gathered. When the siege began the Aztecs realized that they were in great peril but they were so moved by the weeping of their women and children that they took heart, showing much courage.

The men of Chalco began to attack on all sides as they wished to massacre all the men and women, but Huitzilihuitl, Humming Bird Feather, Lord of the Aztecs, urged his people to face the Chalca fearlessly. The chieftain of these Chalca was Cacamatecuhtli, Lord of the Tender Maize. Although their leader was captured in the first skirmish, the Aztecs were not totally routed. Gathering the women, children, and old people in their midst and crying out to their god for help, they hacked their way through the enemy ranks until they reached a town called Tacubaya which they found deserted and where they entrenched themselves.

When the Chalca saw the harm that had been done to them they did not attempt to follow the Aztecs but contented themselves with carrying away the captured king to Colhuacan where they killed him, and through him the Chalca took revenge for all the damage they had received.

The Aztecs renewed their strength and repaired their arms. At this time they invented a weapon, a type of propelled spear that we call *fisga*.[19] When they were all armed with this type of weapon the Aztecs went on to Mazatlan, Place of the Deer, and from here they approached Colhuacan. When they had reached this town, Huitzilopochtli spoke to the priests, saying:

"Oh, my fathers, oh, my priests, I have beheld your toil and affliction! But be of strong heart! Prepare to meet your enemies with your chests and with your heads. Send your messengers to Achitometl, monarch of Colhuacan, and boldly ask him to show you a place where you may stay. Do not hesitate to approach him fearlessly since I will soften his heart. Accept the site he shows you, be it good or bad, and settle there until the term required for your comfort and rest is completed."

The Aztecs, convinced by these arguments, sent their messengers to Colhuacan. The envoys then spoke to the king of that city:

"The Aztecs beg you to show them a place where they may stay with their wives and children, entrusting themselves to you as the most benign ruler, confident that in your mercy you will give them land, not only for building but also for sowing and reaping."

The king of Colhuacan, favorably disposed to their demands, ordered lodging

24

to be given them and everything necessary for their comfort. This was the custom among the Indians: they accommodated messengers or travelers and always gave them good lodging.

While the Aztecs reposed, Achitometl, Lord of Colhuacan, called together his chieftains and elders, exclaiming, "The humble Aztecs have sent their emissaries to request me to indicate a place in our country where they may settle. Look about you and choose the land you think I should give them!"

A thousand contradictions, questions, and answers flew from his council, but the king, always favorable to the Aztecs, decided to give them a place called Tizapan. This is the other side of Colhuacan Hill, where now two roads separate in the directions of Cuitlahuac and Chalco. Tizapan was a wilderness, occupied only by vipers and poisonous snakes. This site was given the Aztecs with malice on the part of the advisers of the king. But the Aztecs accepted the favor and occupied Tizapan, which they still possess today, for all that land around there as far as Santa Marta and Los Reyes is subject to the city of Mexico.

When they reached this place, the people began to make huts and shelters. On seeing the great number of reptiles that were there they were horrified at first, but later they captured these horrible beasts in order to eat them. The Aztecs ate no other meat except those vipers and lizards. They became so fond of them as food that they almost totally consumed the snakes in that place.

The people of Colhuacan were confident that little by little the reptiles would destroy the enemy. King Achitometl said to his followers, "Go and see what has happened to the Aztecs and take my greetings to them. Ask them how they have fared in the place that was granted them."

When the king's messengers went to Tizapan they found all the Aztecs untroubled and contented. Their fields were cultivated and in order, a temple had been built to their god, and the people were living in their houses. The spits and pots were replete with snakes, some roasted and others boiled.

The Colhuacan envoys went to the huts of the chieftains where they greeted them and paid their respects and relayed the message from King Achitometl. The Aztecs, who held this monarch in great honor, answered the messengers and told them how contented they were and how grateful they were for the favors granted them. But they begged two things of the king: to be allowed to trade in his city and to intermarry with the people of Colhuacan.

The emissaries, amazed by the vigor and hardiness of the Aztecs, went with this news to their ruler. They described everything they had seen and told him the requests of these people. The king and all his lords were astounded at this incredible thing, again feeling a tremendous fear of the Aztecs. Thus the king announced,

25

"Give them everything they request. I have told you that they are people favored by their god, but they are evil people. Do not anger them, for while you do them no harm they will be appeased."

From that time on the Aztecs began to go to Colhuacan and deal with the natives, trading freely and becoming related to them by marriage. Huitzilopochtli, god of the Aztecs, was an enemy of this quiet and peace and sought unrest and strife. Seeing the few benefits that he received from this peace he said to his priests:

"It is necessary that we search for a woman who should be called 'The Woman of Discord.' She will be known as 'My Grandmother' or 'My Mother' in the place where we will dwell. This is not the land where we are to make our permanent home, this is not yet the site that I have promised you. The occasion for leaving these people where we are now staying must not be peaceful but must be warlike, many dying in the exploit. Let us begin to take up our arms, our bows and arrows, our shields and swords! Let us show the world the valor of our persons! Prepare yourselves, provide yourselves with those things necessary for our defense and for an attack on our enemies. Seek a way to leave this place. Go to the king of Colhuacan, Achitometl, and ask for his daughter to serve me. He will give her to you and she will be 'The Woman of Discord.' "

The Aztecs, always heedful of the commands of their god, went to the ruler of Colhuacan and asked for his daughter to be mistress of the Aztecs and bride of their god. Achitometl loved the maiden with great affection, but he was enthralled by the idea that she should reign and be a living goddess, so he surrendered her to those who had made the request. She was taken away with great honors, and everyone—Aztecs and Colhuacans—rejoiced greatly over this transaction. When the Aztecs had carried her to their camp and placed her upon the altar, Huitzilopochtli spoke to his priests.

"I have already proclaimed that this maiden is to be 'The Woman of Discord' and the cause of enmity between you and those of Colhuacan. Now you must kill her and sacrifice her in my name. From this day on she is to be called 'My Mother.' After she is dead, flay her and with her skin dress one of the principal youths, dress him, skin and all, with womanly garments and then invite King Achitometl to come adore the goddess, his daughter, and to offer her sacrifice."

When the priests heard the command of their god and told the entire gathering, they took the young princess of Colhuacan, heiress of that kingdom, and sacrificed her. Then they skinned her and dressed one of the youths in her skin, as their deity had willed.

Then they went to the sovereign of Colhuacan and asked him to come adore his own daughter and sacrifice to her as a goddess, since Huitzilopochtli had pro-

26

claimed her his bride. It is she whom the Aztecs worshipped from that time on as the mother of the gods, calling her "Toci," "Mother," or "Grandmother."[20]

King Achitometl accepted the invitation, calling together the dignitaries of his kingdom, recommending to them that they take many offerings for the celebration of the festival in which his daughter was to become the goddess of the Aztecs and bride of Huitzilopochtli.

The Colhuacans realized that the commands of their monarch were just. They adorned themselves regally with mantles and loincloths and carried offerings of paper, incense, fine feathers, and many kinds of food for the new goddess. They took different types of birds, such as quail and water fowl, to honor the high divinity of the Aztecs and his bride. With pomp the king and his followers then left Colhuacan and went to Tizapan.

The Aztecs came out to receive them. After all had rested and eaten, the Aztecs put the priest who was dressed in the skin of the king's daughter in the chamber next to the idol, exclaiming to Achitometl, "Lord, if it please you, you may enter and see our god and the goddess who is your daughter, and make reverences to them and give them your offerings."

The king, with great confidence, arose and went to the temple. He entered the chamber of the idol and began to perform many ceremonies. He cut off the heads of the quail and the other birds and offered sacrifice by scattering the birds' blood and placing the food before the idols. Then he offered incense and flowers which he had brought for that purpose. As the room was dark he distinguished no one. Taking with his hand a brazier with fire, he threw incense into it fervently. This began to burn and the room lighted up with the fire. Thus the king suddenly perceived the priest who was seated next to the idol, dressed in his daughter's skin. This was such a frightful sight that the king was filled with a wild terror. He dropped the brazier and rushed out of the temple shouting:

"Come here, come, O my vassals of Colhuacan! Come avenge the foul deed committed by the Aztecs! They have killed my daughter and dressed a youth in her skin and have made me worship him. Death and destruction to men so evil and with such vile customs! Let not a trace of their memory remain! Let us put an end to them!"

When the Aztecs saw the tumult and heard the cries of Achitometl, and the clamor made by his subjects, they took up their weapons. They retreated with their wives and children toward the water, using the lake itself for protection at their backs. But the Colhuacans sounded the alarm in their own city and the people came out in arms. By attacking they made the Aztecs retreat farther into the water in confusion.

Finding themselves so pressed and hearing the incessant weeping of the women and children, the Aztecs regained their courage and began to throw their spears with such force that the Colhuacan forces broke apart while the Aztecs managed to reach the land and flee to Iztapalapa. The Aztecs continued to fight their pursuers until they reached a place called Acatzintitlan. Here they threw themselves into the water. They made rafts with their lances and shields, and with grass, and on these placed the children and the women, as the water was deep. When they had reached the other side they hid themselves in the reeds and rushes where they passed the night in anguish and suffering. The women and children wept and begged to be allowed to die there, as they could suffer no more.

Huitzilopochtli, the god, saw the despair of his people and realized that they could not bear more torment, so that night he spoke to his attendants: "Console the people and animate them. All these afflictions they must endure so that later they will find peace. Let them now rest here in Acatzintitlan—'Place Next to the Little Reeds.' "

The priests consoled the people who then dedicated that entire day to drying their clothes and cleaning their weapons and their bodies. A *temazcalli*, steam bath, was built where everyone bathed.

This place was later called Mexicatzinco. The name was given because of a certain lewd happening which I shall refrain from telling in order not to offend the ears of the readers, but because of this the Aztecs were driven from the site.[21]

As the Aztecs fled through the marshes one of the main elders, a priest of Huitzilopochtli, drowned. The people cremated him and honored him by giving him a very solemn burial.

By traveling through the reeds the Aztecs came to a place that is now called Iztacalco, Place of the Salt House. They celebrated their "Festival of the Hills" there, which was a very solemn ceremony. The people made many hills of dough and gave them eyes and mouths. They celebrated their festival as best they could, according to what little security they had.

From there the Aztecs continued on to what is now San Antonio and from San Antonio to a place which we call San Pablo. Here a daughter of one of the principal men of the group gave birth to a child, therefore until this day it is also called Mixiuhcan, which means "Place of Childbirth."

Thus they continued to seek for a place that would be suitable as a permanent home. Wandering among the reeds and the rushes, they came upon a beautiful spring and saw wondrous things in the waters. These things had been predicted to the Aztecs by the priests, through the command of Huitzilopochtli, their god.

The first thing they beheld was a juniper tree, all white and very beautiful, and the spring came forth from the foot of this tree.

The second thing they saw was a group of willows around the spring, all white, without a single green leaf. The reeds there were white, also, and so were the rushes surrounding the water.

White frogs and fish came out of the water. There were water snakes, too, shiny and white.

The spring flowed out from between two large rocks, the water so clear and limpid that it was pleasing to behold. The priests and the elders, remembering what their god had told them, wept with joy and became exuberant, crying out:

"We have now found the promised land
And have seen the bliss of the weary Aztec people.
There is nothing new to covet. Be consoled, sons and brothers!
Our god told us that we would see marvelous things among the reeds and
    rushes; behold them here!
However, my brothers, let us await the command of our god,
Who will tell us what we must do!"

They came to a town now called Temazcaltitlan, where they built a steam bath for women who give birth, for they have the custom of bathing these women in a hot bath five or six days after delivery.

The next night Huitzilopochtli appeared in dreams to Cuauhtloquetzqui, one of his custodians, saying:

"Now you will be satisfied that I have told you the truth. In this place where I have brought you, you have seen the things that I predicted. But wait, there is still more to come. You will remember how I commanded you to slay my nephew, Copil, ordering you to remove his heart and fling it among the reeds and rushes. This you have done. Know now that his heart fell on a stone and from this sprang a prickly pear cactus. This cactus is so wondrously tall that it bears the nest of an eagle. Each day the eagle in his nest eats the finest and most beautiful birds of the region. In his lair on the cactus he stretches out his large and comely wings to receive the heat of the sun and the freshness of the morning. You will find the eagle at all times on this tree that sprouted from the heart of my nephew Copil, and all around it you will see innumerable green, blue, red, yellow, and white plumes from the splendid birds on which the eagle feeds. The place of the cactus and the eagle I now name Tenochtitlan, 'Place near the Hard Prickly Pear Cactus.' "[22]

29

The next day in the morning, the priest Cuauhtloquetzqui, anxious to impart the revelation from his god and to inform the people of what he had seen in dreams, ordered everyone to gather, men and women, old and young. When all had gathered he began to extol the great favors that they received each day from their god. He talked especially about the happy tidings that had just been revealed. The Aztecs had already seen that day in the spring white water snakes, frogs, fish, willows and junipers, all white.

Cuauhtloquetzqui declared that another no less wonderful thing had been disclosed to prove that this was the place chosen by their god for their shelter, where they could multiply and where the Aztec nation would excel, its greatness becoming renowned. He cried out:

"Know, my children, that last night Huitzilopochtli appeared to me. Remember, on our arrival in this valley, that we went to Chapultepec Hill where the god's nephew Copil was. Copil, having resolved on war against us, used his cunning and deceit to bring our enemies around us and to kill our captain, Huitzilihuitl. Our enemies drove us from that region, but Huitzilopochtli commanded us to kill Copil and this we did, taking out his heart. And standing in the place where he commanded, I threw the heart into the reeds; it fell upon a rock. According to the revelation of our god a prickly pear cactus has grown from this heart and become a tree so tall and luxuriant that a fine eagle rests there. Huitzilopochtli commands us to look for this place. When we discover it we shall be fortunate, for there we shall find our rest, our comfort and our grandeur. There our name will be praised and our Aztec nation made great. The might of our arms will be known and the courage of our brave hearts. With these we will conquer nations, near and distant, we will subdue towns and cities from sea to sea. We will become lords of gold and silver, of jewels and precious stones, of splendid feathers and of the insignia that distinguish lords and chieftains. We will rule over these peoples, their lands, their sons and daughters. They will serve us and be our subjects and tributaries.

"Our god orders us to call this place Tenochtitlan. There will be built the city that is to be queen of all others in the country. There we will receive other kings and nobles, who will recognize Tenochtitlan as the supreme capital. And so, my

30

children, let us go among these marshes of reeds and rushes as our god has indicated. Everything he has promised us has come true!"

When the Aztecs heard what Cuauhtloquetzqui said to them, they humbled themselves before their deity. They gave thanks to the Lord of All Created Things, of the Day and the Night, Wind and Fire. Then, dividing into different groups, they went into the swamp, searching among the reeds.

Thus they returned to the clear, transparent spring they had seen the day before. Now the water rushed out in two streams, one red like blood, the other so blue and thick that it filled the people with awe. Having seen these mysterious things the Aztecs continued to seek the omen of the eagle. Wandering from one place to another, they soon discovered the prickly pear cactus. On it stood the eagle with his wings stretched out toward the rays of the sun, basking in their warmth and the freshness of the morning. In his talons he held a bird with very fine feathers, precious and shining. When the people saw the eagle they humbled themselves, making reverences almost as if the bird were a divine thing. The eagle, seeing them, bowed his head in their direction.

As the Aztecs observed this they realized that they had come to the end of their journey and they began to weep with contentment. In thanksgiving they said, "By what right do we deserve such good fortune? Who made us worthy of such grace? We have at last fulfilled our desires; we have found what we sought, our capital. Let thanks be given to the Lord of All Created Things, our god Huitzilopochtli!" They then marked the site and went to rest.

The next day the priest Cuauhtloquetzqui told the members of the company, "My children, it is only just that we be grateful to our god and that we thank him for all that he does for us. Let us go and make a small temple where our divinity can rest in the place of the prickly pear cactus. It cannot yet be of stone so let it be constructed of earth. For the present we can do no more."

The Aztecs went eagerly to the site of the prickly pear tree. By cutting out thick blocks of earth from the marsh next to the cactus they made a square platform which was to serve as foundation for the shrine, the resting place of their god. On top of this, they built a hut roofed with grass from the same water. At that time they could do no better.[23]

The Aztecs built these things on land that was not theirs. The land did not belong to them because it belonged to the people of Azcapotzalco and of Texcoco. The boundaries of their towns met here, and halfway were the limits of Colhuacan. Knowing this, the Aztecs were so pressed and fearful that even the little house of mud for their god was made with dread and trembling.

In the meantime all of them gathered together in council. Some wanted to go to the people of Azcapotzalco and to the Tecpanecs, who are the inhabitants of Coyo-acan and Tacuba, and offer their friendship, in this way subjecting themselves to these towns in order to request of them stone and wood to build their city.

But most of the Aztecs were opposed to this plan. They claimed it would be risk-ing their lives, and that instead of receiving them well the people of Azcapotzalco and Coyoacan and Tacuba would mistreat them. They suggested that on market days in these three towns, they and their wives should go sell fish and frogs and other creatures found in the lake. They would go without humility or submission, they would go, not as subjects of any town, but as lords of that place which their god had given them. In this way they would buy stone and wood and make their houses. Everyone considered this good advice and all went into the lake and along the reed-covered shores and began to hunt ducks and other water fowl. They fished and collected frogs and shrimp and all kinds of edible things. They col-lected even the worms that thrive in the water and mosquitoes from the surface of the lake. All these they took to the market place and bartered for beams and boards, small wood, lime and stone.

Although the wood and stone were not sufficient, the Aztecs began to build their temple. Little by little they filled in and consolidated the site for the city. They built foundations in the water by driving in stakes and throwing dirt and stone between the stakes. Thus they planned their city and founded it. They cov-ered the outside of the little mud shrine with a coating of small cut stones, then plastered it with a lime finish. So, although it was small and humble, the home of their god acquired a pleasing appearance.

The night after the Aztecs had finished their god's temple, when an extensive part of the lake had been filled in and the foundations for their houses made, Huitzilopochtli spoke to his priests. "Tell the Aztec people that the principal men, each with his relatives and friends and allies, should divide the city into four main wards. The center of the city will be the house you have constructed for my resting place."

These wards are the ones that still exist in the city of Mexico. They are San Pablo, San Juan, Santa María la Redonda, and San Sebastián. After the Aztecs had separated themselves into these four districts, Huitzilopochtli commanded them to distribute the gods among them and that each ward choose a special place where these divinities might be revered. Thus each neighborhood was divided into many small sections according to the number of idols it possessed. These gods were called Calpulteotl, or District Gods. I will not mention here the names of these deities as they are not relevant to this story, but we know that these wards were similar to parishes that bear the names of saints.[24]

tenochtitlan

colhuacan. pueblo.

tenayucan. pueblo

*The founding of Mexico-Tenochtitlan, the fourfold division indicating the present-day parishes of San Juan, Santa María la Redonda, San Sebastián, and San Pablo. In the center stands the eagle upon a prickly pear cactus, symbol of Mexico City, the Aztec people and, in modern times, of the Mexican nation. First page of the* Codex Mendoza, *painted in early Colonial times by Aztec scribes. Courtesy New York Public Library. Photo Reg Van Cuylenburg.*

When this division had been made and the wards placed in order, some of the elders felt that they deserved more property than they had received as they considered themselves to be in a more honored position than the others. Therefore they decided to seek a different place. By going through the reeds they found a small dry piece of land. They informed their friends and allies and all founded a new city here. This was Xaltelolco, which we call Tlatelolco and which is now the ward of Santiago in Mexico City.[25]

The elders and principal men who went there were four. One was called Atlacuahuitl, the second Huicton, the third Opochtli, and the fourth Atlacol. From what I have heard these four chieftains were restless and seditious men. From the day they left Tenochtitlan they did not get on well with their brothers, the Aztecs. This lack of understanding has been passed on to this day, for between Mexico-Tenochtitlan and Mexico-Tlatelolco is continuous dissension and rancor.

After this third division among the Aztecs—the first at Michoacan, the second at Malinalco and the third at Tlatelolco—those who had remained in the principal site of the prickly pear cactus held a meeting. They talked about the building of their city and the safety of their people. They did not feel secure from the others who had left them, especially as the latter were multiplying rapidly and expanding their territory.

Addressing the congregation, one of the elders said, "My sons and brothers, you see how our kinsmen have abandoned us and have gone to Tlatelolco to live. They have left the place, designated by our god as our home, like rebels and ungrateful men who do not recognize their good fortune. I am afraid that with their cunning they will one day wish to surpass us and subdue us. They will wish to raise themselves to a higher position and elect a king and make their own capital. Before our problems become greater I believe we should follow our own judgment and choose a king who will rule over us and over Tlatelolco as well. If you feel that he should not be of our tribe, let us bring him from outside. Azcapotzalco is near and we are on the land of that people. Or if you disagree, let him be from Colhuacan or from the province of Texcoco. Speak, O Aztecs, express your feelings!"[26]

When Meci, the elder who had proposed this, had finished speaking, everyone was in agreement. They resolved that the Aztecs would not go to Azcapotzalco nor to the province of Texcoco for a king, but as they had lived on the lands of Colhuacan and certain Aztecs had intermarried there, begetting children of both lords and peasants, they decided to choose a son of their own people. He would come from the class of nobles and would reign in Mexico.

They remembered a great lord who had come with them on their long pilgrimage but who had stayed in Colhuacan when they fled that city. He was named

Opochtzin. He had married a woman of a great family of Colhuacan and had left a son called Acamapichtli, "Handful of Reeds." The Aztecs wished Acamapichtli to come and rule over Mexico and to be lord of this city.

The people decided to go to Colhuacan and ask this favor of King Nauhyotl. For this mission they proposed to take an important gift, the best they could find within their limited resources. They chose two esteemed elders who were skillful in the art of speech and who could deliver the message to the king of Colhuacan.

These men went and offered the present, declaring, "O great lord: We, the Aztecs, your servants and vassals, are enclosed in a marshy land and surrounded by a lake filled with reeds. We are alone and forsaken by all the nations. We were guided only by our god to the place where we are now, which is within your jurisdiction and that of Azcapotzalco and of Texcoco. Now that you have permitted us to remain here, we must have a ruler to guide us and show us how we are to live, who will free us and protect us from our enemies. Because of this we appeal to you knowing that among your people there are sons of our race related by marriage to yours, who have come out of our wombs and out of yours, of your blood and of ours. We have observed that there is a son of Opochtzin here, Acamapichtli. He is the son of a daughter of yours, Atotoztli. We beg of you to give him to us for our king, that we may show him all the reverence and respect he deserves, for he is of Aztec lineage and also descendant of the sovereigns of Colhuacan."

The monarch of Colhuacan, realizing that he would not lose anything in sending his grandson to rule in Mexico, answered thus:

"O honored Aztecs, I have heard your just petition and I find satisfaction in being able to please you. Furthermore, this is an honor for me. What good does my grandson do me here? Take him with my blessings, lead him away, for it is well that he serve your god and be in the place of Huitzilopochtli and govern the creatures of the Giver of Life, Lord of the Night and of the Day and of the Wind. Let Acamapichtli rule over the waters and the lands of the Aztec people. But I warn you that if my son were a woman I would not give her to you.[27] Take him with my consent and treat him as he deserves, like your son and like my grandson."

The Aztecs thanked the king for his liberality and begged that he give them a woman of his lineage to marry to their own ruler. And so it happened that Acamapichtli was married to a noblewoman whose name was Ilancueitl. All the Aztecs, men and women, young and old, came out to receive their king and his bride and carried them with great honors to the royal apartments which, though poor at that time, had been prepared in a regal way. They seated the royal couple on two seats and solemnly declared them to be rulers of Mexico, promising them obedience and loyalty.

And one of the old men arose, saying:

34

"My son, lord and king,
Welcome to your house and city,
Here among the rushes, here among the reeds,
Where your wretched ancestors,
Where your poor grandparents and relatives,
The Aztecs, suffered and still suffer
What only the Lord of All Created Things knows.
Behold, O lord, you have come to be the help,
The shade and the refuge of this Aztec nation.
You now are in command,
You have come to be the likeness of our god Huitzilopochtli!
You must understand that we are not in our own country but in a foreign land,
And we are not certain of what will befall us tomorrow.
Behold that you have not come here to take pleasure
But to endure a new and heavy work.
You will labor, you will be a slave to all this multitude.
You must keep our neighbors contented,
Since we live within their boundaries.
Therefore, O lord, be welcome,
Both you and our lady, Queen Ilancueitl."

These words having been said, upon their heads were placed diadems similar to a bishop's mitre, which were commonly used for the coronation of kings. And thus Acamapichtli received the kingdom in his hands and promised to take charge of its defense. From this time, he made decisions regarding matters of the state.

Since I wish to deal especially with the election of this first king of Mexico, his greatness and his way of governing, (as I consider it an important part of my history) it seems best to write a special chapter on this subject. But before we begin to deal with him I wish to tell about the members of the Aztec tribe who separated and went to live in Tlatelolco, and how they abstained from coming to swear their oath before the new king. Like rebels they remained silent. They paid no attention to the monarch that the Aztecs had elected and they became a separate nation. This was permitted by the original Aztec group but I believe it was done from fear, for no kingdom divided against itself can endure, and all were afraid that both groups might perish if they were not united.

During the reign of King Acamapichtli, the Tecpanecs, people of Azcapotzalco and of Coyoacan, seeing that the Aztecs had elected a king, became offended and felt insecure. King Tezozomoc, holding court at Coyoacan, called together his chieftains, exclaiming:

"O people of Azcapotzalco, you have seen how the Aztecs have not only taken lands that belonged to us but have elected a king and become independent. We have pretended to be indifferent and it is convenient that we continue to do so. But the day we are dead they may not want to obey our sons and successors. They may even want to make them vassals and tributaries and become lords of our own state. Little by little the Aztecs are rising, becoming proud and climbing to our heads. Lest they rise more let us order them to pay double the usual tribute, twice as much as they used to give us in fruits of the earth as a sign of subjection."

Everyone thought well of what King Tezozomoc had decided. Taking the matter into hand they sent their messengers to Mexico to give the news to the new king, Acamapichtli. They stated that King Tezozomoc of Azcapotzalco claimed that the tribute they were paying was too small, and that he wished it to be increased. He needed to repair and to beautify his city and consequently, together with the usual tribute of fish, frogs and fruits of the earth, they must add fully grown willow and evergreen trees since he wished to plant such trees in Azcapotzalco. The Aztecs were to construct a floating garden sown with different plants: corn, chilli, beans, squash and amaranth.

When the Aztecs heard these orders they began to wail and show great sadness. However, on the following night the god Huitzilopochtli spoke to Ococaltzin, one of his priests, saying:

"I have seen the affliction and the tears of the Aztecs. Tell them not to be anguished for I will bring them peace and spare them all this labor. Let them pretend to accept the payment of the tribute and tell my son Acamapichtli to be courageous. Let him take the willows and evergreen trees that are demanded of him! Let them make the raft in the form of a floating garden, let them sow upon it all the plants that are demanded of them. I will make everything simple for them."

When morning had come, Ococaltzin went to King Acamapichtli and told him about the revelation which he had had the night before. The monarch was greatly consoled and ordered the people immediately to accept the payment of the tribute or tax. And thus they obtained the willows and evergreens with great ease and took them to Azcapotzalco. They planted them in the places which had been indicated by the king of this city. Then the raft garden, sown with fully grown maize plants, chilli, tomatoes and amaranth, beans, squash and flowers, was floated to Azcapotzalco.

When Tezozomoc had marvelled at all of this, he said to his people:

"Brethren, this has seemed to me almost a supernatural thing. When I ordered this to be done I thought it was an impossible task. Call the Aztecs now! I want you to realize that they are the chosen people of their god and that some day they will rule over all the nations of the earth."

The Aztecs then came before him and he addressed them: "Friends, it seems to me that everything is easy for you and that you have acquired great strength. My new order is that the next time you bring the tribute you do it in the following way: You must have the floating garden sown with greens, sprouted corn and other seeds and plants already growing and mature. But in the midst of those plants there must be a female duck sitting upon her eggs and a heron hatching her eggs. And at the moment that the raft with the tribute arrives in Azcapotzalco, the chicks of the duck and the heron must come out of their eggs. If this is not done you will all perish."

The Aztecs considered this an awesome thing but gave the message to their king, telling him what the monarch of Azcapotzalco had demanded. The news spread quickly throughout the city and caused sorrow and restlessness. However, King Acamapichtli, with faith in his god, ordered the people not to be troubled nor to feel cowardice. And so all withdrew from his presence in apparent good spirits in spite of their deep apprehensions.

And that night the god Huitzilopochtli spoke to his keeper Ococaltzin:

"My father, do not be afraid!
Let not the threats daunt you!
Tell the king my son that I know what is best.
I know what must be done and let him obey me.
Let him understand that all the demands of the foes
Will be paid with their blood and their lives!
They will perish,
They will become slaves before a few years have passed.
Let my children suffer and weep now
But their time will come!"

Old Ococaltzin told all of this to the king, and he and all in the entire city were reassured by the news. They made the raft and sowed it with all kinds of plants and among them set a duck upon its eggs and a heron in the same manner. They took these things to King Tezozomoc in Azcapotzalco together with some large loaves made of *ezcahuitl*, a type of small red worm from the lagoon.

When King Tezozomoc saw the tribute he was amazed and he realized the truth of what he had said to his nobles the previous year. He repeated now what he had said then.

The Aztecs continued to pay the same tribute for fifty years, pretending to be content and feigning obedience but waiting for their numbers to become larger and stronger. King Acamapichtli had already reigned forty years in the city of Mexico and he had ruled in peace and quiet. He had built the city, he had organized its houses and canals, and had done other things necessary to the good order of the state.

But now this sovereign became ill and ended his days, leaving the city sad and disconsolate over his death as he had been much loved and respected by his vassals. On his deathbed he called his nobles and spoke to them for some time, charging them to care for the things of the state and for the women and children. He did not indicate his successor but asked the state to elect someone to govern, stating that he wished to give them liberty of choice. He also showed great sorrow in not having been able to free the city from the subjection of Azcapotzalco.

The city performed funeral rites and lamented his passing with great ceremony. But the wealth with which the people were later to bury their dead, the slaves, pages and servants who were to be killed at funerals, was displayed in a limited manner because they were still poor, humble and destitute. At that time even the king had barely enough to eat. After the death of their monarch the chieftains and nobles began to prepare for the election of a successor.

Acamapichtli had begun his reign at the age of twenty and had ruled forty years, which means that he died at the age of sixty. He left valorous sons, strong-hearted men. Many of them became mighty kings, captains and counsellors who will be described later. He died in the year 1404. Three years before his death, in 1402, the great lord and king Nezahualcoyotl of Texcoco had been born. Besides being a close relative of the rulers of Mexico the latter was sympathetic to the Aztec nation and a great friend of this people, such as very few others. In the following chapter will be told the manner and way in which he perpetuated the confederation and friendship of the Aztecs, and how he achieved it without letting the other nations know his intentions.

King Acamapichtli, who had ruled the Aztec nation with wisdom and prudence, who had endeavored to give his people greatness, was dead. The Aztecs then determined to elect a king, consulting among themselves and discussing the matter with the nobles and with the common people. One of the elders spoke:

"O Aztecs, behold that our king and lord is dead!
Who is to be our leader now? Who will be king of this city?
Who will shelter and defend us and have pity on the old,
On the widows and the orphans?
Who will be father of this republic?
Let all speak with freedom and proclaim the one that they favor!
He will be in command, he will sit upon the mat,
The royal seat of this kingdom.
He will defend us; he will guard us from our enemies.
According to what our god has revealed, we will soon need courageous hands
    and hearts.
Who, O Aztecs, will have the courage to be the strength of our arms?
Who will thrust out his chest fearlessly
In order to defend our city and our persons?
Who will be the man
Who will not weaken the name of our god Huitzilopochtli?
This man will have to be the image of our god
And will defend and lift up his name! He will make known to the entire world
That the Aztec nation has enough valor and strength
To subject the earth and make all peoples his vassals!
Now elect the man who will be your father and your mother. We will be the
    feathers on his wings,
The lashes on his eyes,
The hairs on his face!
Speak, Aztecs, say, name, point out the one
Who is to hold the staff of justice!
He is the one who shall sit on the left hand of our god!

## chapter VI

Let him come out, let us see him, let us rejoice in his face!
Behold, we the chieftains are old men, without strength.
You have many from whom to choose:
There are grandsons and sons of the dead king,
Born of our daughters."

When he had spoken, the heads of the four wards (that is, Moyotla, Teopantlaza, Atzacualco and Cuepopan) answered, "Aztecs, we are here in our gathering, in our council. Here without offending anyone we speak freely. Our will is that our king and lord be Huitzilihuitl, Humming Bird Feather, the son of Acamapichtli, our last ruler. He is a young man, well bred, of good heart, kind and peaceable, courageous, and of praiseworthy ways. This is the one that we select to govern and rule over us. Let him be our lord and king, the very image of our god Huitzilopochtli!"

The election having been carried out, one of the elders appeared before the common people who were outside awaiting the decision. He spoke to them—men and women, old and young, adults and children—in a strong voice.

"Brethren, you of the Aztec nation who are gathered here will now hear that the chieftains of the four wards, the statesmen and officials, have elected as king the youth, Huitzilihuitl. He will be your father, he will be your protection in your needs! Express your wishes, because without your approval the election will amount to nothing."

The people, having heard this, answered in one voice, children and adults, men and women, old and young, that they confirmed the election and that it pleased them. They let forth great cries and shouted:

"Strength to our King Huitzilihuitl, image of our god Huitzilopochtli!
Our hearts rejoice in him!
We thank the Lord of All Created Things,
Of the Night, and of the Day,
Of the Wind and of the Water."

All the officials, standing in order, went to the place where the elected king was, and taking him from among the other youths and princes, his brothers and relatives, they led him to the royal place where he was seated and the diadem was put upon his head. The officials anointed his body with the same pitch used to anoint the statue of the idol Huitzilopochtli. After having dressed him in the royal garments, one of the men spoke:

40

"O courageous youth, O king and lord! Do not faint or lose spirit because of the authority which has been given you. You will protect the water and the earth of your new kingdom, which is sunk in this wilderness, in the midst of the canes, the reeds, the grasses and the rushes. Your kingdom is here under the shadow of our god Huitzilopochtli, whose image you are. You know the troubles and labors with which we live because we dwell upon land that belongs to someone else. You know that we are tributaries of the people of Azcapotzalco. I say it to you and remind you of it, not because I believe you ignorant of it, but so you may have new spirit and realize that you have not come to the throne to rest but to work. O lord, we have nothing else to offer you! You well know in what wretchedness and poverty your father reigned, supporting us, resisting our enemies, suffering with courage and wisdom."

The speech having ended, one by one they did reverence to Huitzilihuitl, addressing him with elaborate words. Because of the length of these talks I do not record them here.

Huitzilihuitl began to reign in the year 1404 and, as we have seen, he was elected through the vote and by consent of everyone. This was a custom which had existed since the beginning of this nation; no son would inherit through simple succession or primogeniture as is the custom among us, which is that the eldest son inherits his father's place. Among the natives it was not thus. Successors were chosen through agreement on the part of the electors and all the people. Though Huitzilihuitl had elder brothers he was chosen to be king of Mexico.

The officials began to discuss the problems of the state. They now felt that they had acquired strength and they felt some relief.

"We are weary of being subjects and tributary vassals of the lords of Azcapotzalco," they stated. "We not only are subjected to the Tecpanecs but also are vassals of those of Colhuacan and Texcoco. We cannot be subjects to so many people. Where shall we go? What shall we do? We will labor to find relief from this intolerable load that is upon our shoulders. Let us rest a while and consider the situation: our greatest load is Azcapotzalco, since the court and the king are there. We consider that, since our king is young and still unmarried, we should go to Azcapotzalco and ask for the daughter of King Tezozomoc so that she may be the wife of our king and lord. If he grants us this, he may spare us some of the heavy tribute. How does this appear to you, O Aztecs?"

The elders and the nobles responded that the idea seemed wise to them. Having determined this, they sent two of the eldest men to Azcapotzalco to beseech the king to grant them his daughter, so that she might become the wife of the king of Mexico. They entered his presence and, having greeted him, they spoke:

41

"O lord and son, we have come before your greatness; we are prostrated upon the earth with all humility. We beg and beseech of you a favor. Whom, O lord, should we go to but you since we are your vassals and servants? Awaiting your royal commands, we are attentive to the words of your mouth and eager to comply with all that your heart and your will desire. Behold, O lord, the embassy that we have brought from your servants the officials and elders of Mexico! Great lord, accede to our plea. Have pity upon your servant, the king of Mexico; upon the city which is among the reeds and rushes, where Huitzilihuitl rules and protects your vassals. He is single, still to be wed. What we ask of you is that you surrender one of your jewels and precious plumes—that is, one of your noblewomen. She will not go to an alien place but will stay within her own land and country, where she will be in command. Therefore, O lord, we beg you not to refuse that which we ask of you."

The king, who had listened attentively to what the Aztecs had requested, saw that their petition was a just one. He answered them with affection and benevolence. "O Aztecs, your words, your humility have overcome me and I find it difficult to answer. I have daughters and the Lord of All Created Things has destined them for this end. Behold my beloved daughter called Ayauhcihuatl. You are welcome to take her."

They prostrated themselves upon the earth before the king and gave him thanks. Then they took the noble daughter of the king together with many attendants from Azcapotzalco and brought her to Mexico where she was well received by the people. The future bridegroom received her warmly and she was carried to the palace where she was welcomed and where the marriage ceremony took place. The matrimonial rite consisted of tying the mantles of the groom and bride together as a sign of union.

After the king of Mexico and Ayauhcihuatl were married, she bore a son to him and the city rejoiced greatly. It was decided that King Tezozomoc, father-in-law of their king and father of the queen, should know about it immediately. Therefore they sent messengers to Azcapotzalco with the message:

"Lord, the king of Mexico and all the chieftains kiss your hands and notify you that the queen, our lady, your daughter, has given birth to a son, given to us by the Lord of All Created Things."[28]

"Aztecs," answered Tezozomoc, "with great pleasure have I received this news. Rest while I tell my officials and noblemen about it."

The officials of Azcapotzalco, Tacuba and Coyoacan appeared before him and he told them that his daughter had given birth to a son, whereupon they congratulated him and showed great joy. When he asked them for their opinion as to how

42

his grandson should be named, they looked into the matter and considered the signs under which the child had been born and decided that he should be called *Chimalpopoca*, which means "Smoking Shield." The king then sent the messengers back to their city with congratulations for the king and queen and notified them that the child should be called Chimalpopoca.

After the messengers had departed, the monarchs of Azcapotzalco, Tacuba and Coyoacan followed them to Mexico with the best gifts for the king and the new mother. They asked in the name of their king that the child be called by the name that he had given, and thus it was done. The Aztecs gave many thanks to the Tecpanecs and sent their good wishes to Tezozomoc.

Tezozomoc realized now that he had a grandson in Mexico who would be heir to that kingdom. His daughter, bringing the child before him, spoke about the great labors and sufferings of the city in paying such large tribute. The king was moved by the pious plea of his daughter and he gathered together some of his councilors with the intention of giving relief to the Aztecs. He did not propose to waive the entire payment of taxes, but he hoped that at least part of the tribute could be spared them, and proposed this to his councilors.

The officials and noblemen of Azcapotzalco did not show great pleasure when they heard what the monarch asked of them, but in order not to contradict him they agreed that a large part of the tribute would be remitted. Tezozomoc, having heard this agreement on the part of his councilors, decided to remit the heaviest load, and to demand of the tributaries only the things that could most easily be obtained. And so, he sent messengers to Mexico who told the king and the authorities that he had agreed to have pity upon them since his daughter and grandson were in that city. As a token payment, so as not to annoy his own people, the Aztecs would pay a yearly tax of two ducks from the lagoon together with fish, frogs and other animals from the waters. When the Aztecs heard the good news they went with great humility to thank the lord of Azcapotzalco for the great favor granted to them.

The Aztecs were now relieved, but Queen Ayauhcihuatl, who had been their sympathetic protectress, died, leaving Chimalpopoca a child of nine. The Aztecs were saddened and distressed, having lost their good mediator, the queen, and they feared that they might have to resume the old tributes. Nevertheless, the child was a source of hope to them.

Some say that the king married again and this time a daughter of the king of Cuernavaca by whom he had many children. Others, though they agree that he married the daughter of the king of Cuernavaca, state that in the ancient pictorial manuscripts they do not find evidence of his having had other children than Chimalpopoca. I agree with the latter as I have found no notice of other children in the paintings and manuscripts I have seen. I also believe that the king died one year after his wife. He reigned only thirteen years and died young, a little over thirty years of age.

Huitzilihuitl ruled in peace and wisdom and was much loved by noble and peasant. He was the first to make laws for his republic, especially in reference to the cult of the gods. This was what the lords and kings were most interested in since they considered themselves images of the gods and any honor given to the gods was honor given to them; therefore they were eager to enlarge their temple and magnify the cult of their god. But they also realized that though they desired the liberty of their nation, the time of their prosperity had not yet come. Other peoples who surrounded them had much more liberty and wealth than they, and though this distressed them they did not yield to laziness or complaints. On the contrary, they not only traded constantly with other nations, moving from one group to the other, bringing provisions to their city, and fishing, but they began to make boats and canoes and to practice the arts of war upon the water. They knew very well that, in the long run, they must become expert in these arts because, if the truth must be told, all their friendship with neighboring nations was feigned, and founded on malice and treason. This deceit was practised so that the deed they had to accomplish could be done better. This feigned humility with which they reassured their enemies was well carried out. They began to fill their city with people from the neighboring towns and to take them in marriage.

In this way they won over the people of Texcoco and others. They treated travelers and strangers well, they invited merchants to come to the markets of Mexico with their goods for such commerce always enriches a city. (And this same Aztec nation today has this quality; to the towns where a man is well received and flattered and given to eat and drink he will go willingly, especially if he sees inviting faces, which is what most appeals to him.)

The Aztecs were greatly distressed because of the death of their king and at the fact that the neighboring tribes had been urged not to sell them maize, beans and other foodstuffs.

The officials gathered and formed a council to decide who should reign; the new king should have the aims and desires of the previous one—namely, the enlargement and liberty of the city and the acquisiton of land to sow their own maize and beans.

44

In their council they decided to elect as king the son of Huitzilihuitl, grandson of the king of Azcapotzalco. Though at this time he was only ten or eleven years old, they felt that this would propitiate the grandfather, Tezozomoc of Azcapotzalco.[29]

*Stages in the training of Aztec youth for temple service. From the* Codex Mendoza, *painted in early Colonial times by Aztec scribes. Courtesy American Museum of Natural History, New York.*

The entire Aztec community by common consent elected Chimalpopoca, a boy of ten years, son of Huitzilihuitl the second king, and the entire city was well pleased. They placed the child upon the royal seat and, when he had been given the royal insignia, they crowned him with the diadem and anointed him with what they named divine ointment. They put in his left hand a shield and in the other a sword with blades in it. They gave him weapons which were chosen according to the image of the god that they wished to represent through him. All of this was a sign that he had sworn to defend the city and was willing to die for his people.

Chimalpopoca, the favorite of his grandfather, Tezozomoc of Azcapotzalco, reigned for some years. During this time the Aztecs visited Azcapotzalco with more frequency and dealt with those people in a more familiar way. One day the principal men of Mexico went to their king Chimalpopoca, saying:

"Lord, we all have decided that since your grandfather Tezozomoc loves you well and will listen to you, and since we have become friends with the men under that king, we should ask him to give us some of the water of Chapultepec. We will use it for drinking and we will find a way of conveying it to the city. But we must ask for it first. Up to this time we have lived in huts and in wretched hovels and now we are beginning to build houses of stone and adobe. We are also beginning to dam up the lagoon and we possess canoes that go about the canals. But we still drink troubled, dirty water. That is why we beseech you to send your messengers to ask for this favor."

Chimalpopoca listened to these words and they seemed good to him. He agreed to send envoys to Azcapotzalco to ask for water from Chapultepec. The envoys gathered presents of flowers and other things suitable for such a visit and soon arrived before the king of Azcapotzalco. Once they had made their plea he told them to rest and feel at ease while he asked the opinion of his chieftains. These officials were consulted and everyone agreed that the Aztecs were welcome to the water since Azcapotzalco would not suffer in any way from its loss.

The Aztecs rejoiced greatly in this and they began to take out blocks of earth and make rafts of rushes in order to transport the materials for the causeway over which the water was to come. Very soon with the aid of stakes and canes, banks of earth and other materials, the water began to come into Mexico. It was a difficult task because the causeway was built in the lagoon and it constantly crumbled due to the great impact of the water, the pipe being constructed of clay.[30]

At this point the Aztecs decided that matters with Azcapotzalco must come to a head so they could become free, a condition which they greatly desired. They sent messengers to the king of Azcapotzalco advising him in his grandson's name that the water he had given them was useless, since it traveled in earthen ditches and was lost. They also requested him to give them wooden stakes, stone and lime, and to order his vassals to help them construct a pipe of stone and lime so that the water would pass safely without seeping away.

Tezozomoc was not pleased at what he heard, though he did not show his anger plainly. He told the Aztecs that he would speak to his council. The councilmen, when they had heard the demand made by the Aztecs, responded, "Lord, monarch, what is in the mind of your grandson and of his advisors? Do they think that we are to be their slaves? Is it not enough that we sheltered them and admitted them within our territory, that we permitted them to build their city? Have we not given them the water that they asked for? Now they demand, in a shameless manner, without respect for your dignity, that you and all of us build them a pipe for their water? We do not wish it; it is not our will. We would rather lose our lives! Even though King Chimalpopoca of Mexico be your descendant and friend of the Tecpanec nation, we refuse to be commanded in this manner. He is only a child and what he has done has been provoked by his advisors. We would like to know where they have found such daring and insolence."

Among the councilors was the ruler of Coyoacan, known as Maxtla. Also present were Acolnahuacatl of Tacuba and two others, Tzacualcatl and Tlacahuitlahua. They were rulers of the kingdoms that hated the Aztec people. They plotted against the Aztecs and decided that they would not only refuse the demand but that they would take the water away from them. They also agreed to destroy them, doing away with them to a man and leaving no trace of the place called Mexico.

Rousing the common people, they armed them and inflamed them against the Aztecs. The masses of the people were told that Mexico wanted to make vassals, tributaries and slaves of them. In order to show their anger more clearly, and in order to create a war, they gave orders that, in Azcapotzalco from then on, no one trade or deal with the people of Mexico. No more foodstuffs or merchandise should enter the city, under pain of death. In order to achieve this they placed guards along all the roads, cutting off all contacts between Mexico and its neighbors. They prohibited the Aztecs from using the forests which they had been awarded and where they gathered firewood. Furthermore, the Aztecs were prohibited from using the paths which had permitted them access to the Tecpanecs.

48

Though the monarch of Azcapotzalco saw that his chieftains were enraged and that they had determined to destroy the Aztecs in war, he was desirous of preventing this. However, he realized that the situation was difficult and he begged his men to kidnap the king of Mexico, who was his grandson, so that he might be spared. Some agreed with the king but Maxtla and Tlacahuitlahua refused to agree claiming that even though Chimalpopoca came from the lineage of the Tecpanecs, this relationship was through a woman, and that on his father's side he was an Aztec. He would always be inclined toward his father's people and therefore should be the first to die.

The king was so distressed when he heard this response, so saddened to see that he could not pacify his vassals, that he became sick with sorrow, and soon after died of his grief. He died a very old man.[31]

Tezozomoc of Azcapotzalco was dead and the Tecpanecs were even more determined to carry out their intentions of annihilating the Aztecs and their king through trickery. They swore an oath to be firm in this design and at night sent men secretly to Mexico. These murderers entered the palace while the guards were asleep and, finding the monarch unprepared, they slew him and Tehuetlehuac, his son, upon their mats.

The next morning, when the noblemen of Mexico went to greet their king, they found him and the child dead, covered with great wounds. The Aztecs became inflamed and set up a great hue and cry as the news of the disastrous end of the king spread throughout the city, and every man took up his arms. One of the officials, however, tried to calm them, saying, "Aztecs, compose yourselves, let your hearts be calm. Behold, rash deeds never turn out well. Even though our king is dead, the lineage of his people and of his generation has not ended; we still have descendants of the past kings of Mexico. Will we not have a great leader to guide us in our aims? Do not act blindly! First, elect a king to guide you and give you courage. Choose someone who will be a wall against your enemies! Be not deceived by the passion which you feel now. You must feign tranquillity and prepare to celebrate the funeral rites of your lord and king who lies dead here before you. The time for vengeance will come later!"

Thus the Aztecs were pacified and, showing none of their feelings before their enemies, they invited many guests to the funeral ceremonies. Among those who attended were the representatives of numerous great men from Texcoco and Colhuacan.

Once the rites had ended, the Tecpanecs reproached the envoys of other communities for attending the funeral, though these envoys had been displeased and offended by the terrible assassination committed by the Tecpanecs. Other neighboring peoples also promised the Aztecs not to oppose them or to favor Azcapotz-

49

alco. Friendly tribes permitted the women and children of the Aztecs to obtain merchandise in their towns and bring it into Mexico since the Tecpanecs had cut off all other access to supplies. The Aztecs were delighted with this treatment and gave thanks to their friends. And when, with great humility, they begged them to attend the election of a new king, the neighbors promised to be present at the election.

The council of the Aztecs met to choose the new monarch and one of the elders began the speech which was customary on such occasions. In these times there were great orators and speech-makers who on any occasion could talk lengthily and beautifully and most delicately, filling their addresses with profound and remarkable metaphors. Those who speak this Nahuatl language will agree with me on the profundity and excellence that it carries within it. I dare to affirm, after many years of studying it, that I still find new things, new words and most elegant metaphors to learn.

The elder who was to be the first orator stood up in front of everyone and began his talk.

"O Aztecs, you now lack light in your eyes
Though you do not lack it in your hearts.
The one who was your guide and light is gone.
But the fire in your hearts is still burning!
The noble lineage of Mexico does not end here
Nor has the royal blood perished.
Turn your eyes, look about you.
You will see the noblemen of Mexico around you—
Not one or two, but many excellent princes,
Sons of Acamapichtli your true king and lord.
Choose freely: though you have lost your father,
Here you will find a father and mother.
Make believe, O Aztecs, that for a short time
There was an eclipse of the sun,
The earth grew dark and that afterwards the light shone again.
If Mexico grew dark because of the eclipse of its monarch,
Let the sun come out again!
Elect another king
And observe carefully whom you choose, and whom your hearts desire,
Because the one that you decide upon is the chosen one
Of your god Huitzilopochtli!"

When the speaker had finished, Itzcoatl, a natural son of Acamapichtli, was elected king by common accord. He had been born of a slave girl at Azcapotzalco, yet he had turned out to be so courageous, a man of such excellent life, that he outshone all of his brothers. With general applause, Itzcoatl was elected and the lords of Texcoco were especially pleased.[32] The father of Nezahualcoyotl, Ixtlilxochitl, who was at that time reigning in Texcoco, was married to a sister of the new king, Itzcoatl. In later times Nezahualcoyotl was to regain his kingdom through the favor of Itzcoatl, after having fled from the Tecpanecs who wished to assassinate him.

So it was that Itzcoatl, after the death of his nephew, occupied the royal seat. One of the orators cried:

"Son, lord and king, keep up your courageous spirit, be strong and firm! Let not your heart grow faint, do not lose the might necessary for the royal burden that has been placed upon you. If you become weak, who will give you strength for governing and defending your state? Do you think, by any chance, that your mighty ancestors, fathers and grandfathers, will come to life again? O great monarch, they have passed from this life and nothing is left but the shadow of their memory. We barely remember their strong hearts and the might of their arms and chests with which they faced affliction and labor. Your ancestors have been hidden away by the Lord of All Created Things, of the Wind and of the Night and Day. Will you let your fatherland slip from your hands? Will you let the burden that you carry on your shoulders fall from them? Are you going to permit the old man, the old woman, the orphan and the widow to perish? Courage, courage, O valorous prince! Behold that the nations are against us, that they scorn us and have contempt for us. Have pity upon the babies who are just beginning to crawl upon the ground. They will die if our enemies prevail against us. Prepare to open your mantle to shelter your children. They have faith in the shade of your mantle and in your benevolence. Mexico-Tenochtitlan is joyful and proud of this shelter. Mexico-Tenochtitlan was like a widow, but the husband, the spouse, has been reborn. Let him come back and give it the sustenance it needs. My son, do not fear the work nor the burden; do not be troubled. The god whose image you are favors you and he will aid you."

The Tecpanecs of Azcapotzalco, Tacuba and Coyoacan were much angered when they heard of the new election, and again they placed watchmen on all the roads. They felt vulnerable and they guarded the causeway to Tacuba, that of Chapultepec and that of Tlatelolco. The people of Azcapotzalco were not permitted to go to Mexico and those of the latter city could not go to the Tecpanec capital. The Aztecs saw that the moment had come and that there was no hope of any peace with Azcapotzalco. As the only solution was to fight, they began to arm their men and to discuss the coming war. Up to this time the Aztecs had been intimidated and had had little experience in the arts of war. It was the courage of the king, his valor, which led the common people and the nobles to take spirit.

Our Lord decreed that there be at that time a brave man among them by the name of Tlacaelel, a nephew to Itzcoatl, son of his brother. Tlacaelel was to become the greatest warrior, the bravest and mightiest, that the Aztec nation has ever had—the most cunning man ever produced by Mexico. All of these things will be described later in this history.[33]

CHAPTER IX WHICH TREATS OF THE ELECTION OF KING ITZCOATL
AND HOW HE LIBERATED THE CITY OF MEXICO, WITH A DESCRIPTION
OF OTHER THINGS THAT OCCURRED IN HIS TIME

So it was that in 1424 Itzcoatl was elected to the royal seat and the people of the city were comforted by the choice of the council. The king immediately began to prepare for war, knowing that Azcapotzalco was at the point of attacking. All the people of Mexico were on the alert, though many of the common people, seeing the strength of the Tecpanecs, feared that victory would be impossible.

Many of them, filled with timidity and dread, tried to persuade the king and the great leaders to make peace, and the ruler was dismayed to see their fear. They claimed that the new king of Azcapotzalco was a merciful man and that the best course would be to carry their god Huitzilopochtli to Azcapotzalco and deliver him to the new ruler. Perhaps, they thought, in this way they would be pardoned. These weaklings were on the verge of offering themselves as slaves.

Some of the leading men also thought that this was good counsel and wished to take refuge in Azcapotzalco together with their god. They went so far as to take the idol upon their shoulders and prepare to depart for Azcapotzalco.

At this point a valiant youth by the name of Tlacaelel, nephew of Itzcoatl, appeared and exclaimed, "What is this, O Aztecs? What are you doing? You have lost your wits. Wait, sit still! Let us consider this matter more fully. Are you such cowards that you feel you must take shelter in Azcapotzalco?"

He then turned to the king and said, "Great lord, what is this, how can you permit such a thing? Speak to your people. Seek a way to defend our honor."

The king addressed the people, saying, "Are you still desirous of going to Azcapotzalco? This seems to me a slavish act. We must move with pride. Which of you

52

will appear before the king of Azcapotzalco to hear his decision? The messenger will surely be killed. But, if you insist—whoever wishes to do this—let him rise and go."

After hearing these words there was not one among the people who dared to go to Azcapotzalco with any message. Tlacaelel then exclaimed in a brave and loud voice, "Lord and king: let not your heart be timorous, do not let yourself be easily overpowered. Still, if someone must go to Azcapotzalco, I offer myself to carry the message, since I do not fear death. I well know that I must die some day and it matters little whether it be today or tomorrow. How could I die a better death than by defending the honor of my homeland? Therefore, O lord, I will go."

"I am gratified, dear nephew," said the king, "by the bravery and courage of your decision. If you undertake this task I will reward you with great liberality, and if you die in this mission your children will receive my favor. You will be remembered eternally for this brave act."

People were astonished at Tlacaelel's daring since it was obvious that his life was at stake. But the king had singled him out, considering it better that one die rather than many. Sorrowfully, reluctantly, he commanded him to go and Tlacaelel departed from the city.

Boldly he approached the two guards at the gate who said, "This is a strange thing to see! Are you not the nephew of Itzcoatl, the king of Mexico? Are you not called Tlacaelel?"

Tlacaelel answered, "Yes."

"Where are you going?" they asked. "Do you not know that we have been commanded to forbid any Aztec to enter the city and that we have been told to kill any on sight?"

Tlacaelel responded, "I well know what you have been commanded, but it is also well known that messengers are not to be blamed. And I am an envoy to your king from the sovereign of Mexico and his chieftains. And so I beg you to allow me to pass. I assure you that I will return by the same way. If you then wish to slay me I will put myself in your hands."

They relented and permitted him to pass, whereupon he went straight to the king and saluted him. The ruler was amazed at his presence, saying, "How have you managed to enter the city without being put to death by the guards?"

Tlacaelel explained the manner in which he had entered the city and the king asked him what he wished. Tlacaelel, the messenger, declared that he had come to sue for peace and that the king should have mercy upon his people. Tlacaelel besought the king to calm the wrath of his chieftains.

The king was half inclined to listen to the plea but said he must speak to his

53

councilors first. He said that he would try to placate them but that if he failed, the matter was no longer in his hands. Having agreed to return on the following day for the answer, Tlacaelel asked for some security in order to pass the guards, but the ruler answered that his only security would be his own cunning.

On reaching the guards, now a larger number and more fully armed, Tlacaelel uttered these words, "My brothers, I have just spoken to your sovereign and I carry an answer to mine. If you will allow me to pass I will be grateful. I have come here to talk of peace and I deceive no one. I must return to Mexico to settle this matter. Whether you kill me today or the next day matters little, since I give you my word that I will place myself in your hands tomorrow."

The ruler of Mexico was filled with gladness at the return of Tlacaelel, saying, "How did you enter the city without being slain by the guards?" and the king then heard the story that the messenger had to tell.

On the following day Itzcoatl spoke to his nephew, "I am filled with gratitude that you risked your life and now I will tell you what you must say to the ruler of Azcapotzalco. Ask him if his people are determined to leave us in peace and admit us again to their friendship. If he answers that there is no remedy, that he must annihilate us, then take this pitch with which we anoint the dead and smear it upon his body.[34] Feather his head as we do to our dead and give him the shield, sword and gilded arrows, which are the insignia of a sovereign, adding that he must be on his guard since we will do everything in our power to destroy him."

Tlacaelel, carrying the pitch and feathers, proceeded to Azcapotzalco where the guards, respectful of him because he was a man of his word, allowed him to pass. He stood before the king and addressed him in the following way.

"O powerful sir: your subject and vassal, Itzcoatl of Mexico, wishes to know the decision of your advisors. Are you going to carry out that which you have begun, or are you, O lord, going to favor us? Will you abandon us or will we receive your favor?"

"Tlacaelel, my son," said the king, "what can I answer? Even though I am the ruler, the people of my country have decided to wage war on you. What can I do? If I try to oppose them I risk my life and that of all my children. My men are bitter and wrathful against you and ask that you be destroyed."

"Very well, O lord," responded Tlacaelel, "your vassal, the king of Mexico, sends you this message: Take care, be strong, prepare yourself—at this moment he challenges you and your people. He is now your mortal enemy, and either you or we will be slain upon the field or become a slave forever. You will deeply regret having begun a thing which you cannot conclude in victory. My sovereign sent this pitch, which we use as an ointment of the dead, so that it might be rubbed

*Stages in the training of Aztec youth. From the* **Codex Mendoza,** *painted in early Colonial times by Aztec scribes.*
*Courtesy American Museum of Natural History, New York.*

upon you; in this way you can prepare yourself to die! He has also sent you these shields and arrows and has ordered that I anoint you and arm you with my own hands."

The king allowed himself to be anointed and armed by Tlacaelel, and after he had donned the warrior's insignia he requested him to thank King Itzcoatl for his message. He then commanded his servants to make a hole in a wall in the back of the palace.

As Tlacaelel was ready to depart, the ruler of Azcapotzalco addressed these words to him. "Son Tlacaelel, do not go out by the main gate because there they await you to kill you. I have ordered a hole made in the back of the house, through which you may escape. However, I do not wish you to leave without a gift since you are a friend and a brave man. Take these weapons, this shield and sword, and defend yourself with them if you are attacked." The Aztec armed himself, thanked his protector and escaped through the hole in the palace. He moved cautiously along secret paths until he had outstripped the enemy.

When he reached the boundary between the two cities, he showed himself to the sentinels, with these words, "O Tecpanecs of Azcapotzalco! How poorly you carry out your task of defending the city! Prepare yourselves! Soon there will not be a Tecpanec left in the world. Not one stone will be left upon another; none will be spared. Prepare yourselves to perish in fire and in blood. Itzcoatl, king of Mexico, has challenged you!"

When the Tecpanec sentinels heard these words they were bewildered and wondered how he had escaped alive, and they moved toward him with the intention of killing him. But Tlacaelel faced them all and took the lives of several. Then, when he saw that other warriors were approaching, he withdrew rapidly toward the gates of Mexico, his enemies pursuing him the entire way.

War had been declared. The people of Mexico now knew that it could not be avoided but the common man was fearful and requested permission to leave the city. The leaders reassured the people, and the king himself spoke to them. "Do not fear, my children, we will free you and no one will harm you."

But they were doubtful, exclaiming, "And if you do not succeed, our sovereign, what will become of us?" The king and his men replied, "If we do not achieve what we intend, we will place ourselves in your hands, so that our flesh becomes your nourishment. In this way you will have your vengeance. You can eat us in the dirtiest of cracked dishes so that we and our flesh are totally degraded."

"Let it be as you have said," answered the people. "You yourselves have delivered your sentence. We answer: if you are victorious, we will serve you and work your lands for you. We will pay tribute to you, we will build your houses and be your servants. We will give you our daughters and sisters and nieces. And when you go to war we will carry your baggage and food and your weapons upon our shoulders and we will serve you along the way to battle. In short, we will sell and subject our persons and goods to your service forever."

The officials, hearing the answer of the common people, agreed, making the people swear that they would keep their oath. And thus it was done.

The king then told Tlacaelel to recruit warriors and prepare them for combat. The sons of past kings were made commanders and so were the brothers and nephews of Itzcoatl together with other relatives of his. The king spoke before the soldiers, urging them to conquer or die, reminding them of the glorious history of the Aztec nation. He reminded them that this would be their first great battle and that from it they would bring such honor that other nations would tremble before them. He told them not to be timorous, that the large number of Tecpanecs was unimportant, what really mattered were their own courageous hearts. He commanded the men to follow their officers, and thus began the march toward Azcapotzalco.

When they reached a spot known as *Xoconochnopallitlan,* "The Place of the Cactus That Bears Green Prickly Pears," the warriors of Azcapotzalco came out in good order to meet them, carrying shields with insignia richly done in gold, silver, jewels and feathers and with splendid ornaments upon their backs. When the Aztecs saw them coming, Tlacaelel was filled with boldness and he commanded all the officers and common soldiers to assemble upon an elevation and to wait for the sound of the drums which would be the signal for the attack. He also told certain common soldiers who were lacking in spirit to remain in the rear.

Once all of these instructions had been given, King Itzcoatl took a small drum which he carried on his back and began to sound it, upon which the entire army let out terrifying yells, whistles and shrieks which froze the blood of the enemy.[35]

The officers and all the men, in wing formation, met with those of Azcapotzalco. They struck right and left without order or plan and began to shout, "Mexico! Mexico!" The Tecpanecs were so disconcerted that they fell into confusion, and the Aztecs struck and wounded with cunning and swiftness. The soldiers of Azcapotzalco began to retreat and the Aztecs followed them. The spiritless Aztecs who had remained behind, seeing where victory lay, were swept by a desire for glory and attacked the enemy so vigorously that the forces of Azcapotzalco abandoned the field and took refuge in their city.

58

Tlacaelel, commander of the Aztec army, began to cry, "Victory!" and led his men into Azcapotzalco, killing all in their path. King Itzcoatl ordered the soldiers who had remained with him to devastate the city, burn the houses, and spare neither young nor old, men or women. This was done with no pity but with the greatest cruelty in the world. Not a house was left standing, not a man, woman or child was left alive, except a few who had managed to flee to nearby fields and slopes.

The Aztecs, following up their bloody victory, like meat-hungry dogs, filled with fury and rage, followed those who had fled into the hills. There they found them prostrated upon the earth. The vanquished surrendered their weapons, promising the Aztecs lands and service in their homes and fields. They promised stone, lime and wood as tribute, as well as foodstuffs such as maize, beans, *chian* seeds, chilli, and many other things. Tlacaelel was merciful to them and ordered the pursuit to cease and his men to assemble. He made those of Azcapotzalco swear that they would fulfill what they had promised. And so it was done.

The Aztecs returned victorious and exulting to their city, carrying the spoils which had been taken that day. Great wealth had been acquired, for Azcapotzalco was the capital of the Tecpanec empire and in the city was concentrated the wealth of that nation. There too had lived the merchants and rich men, all now dead. The Aztecs had lost few men in the battle.

The Aztec chieftains reminded the common people what they had promised. The natives of the city agreed to fulfill their promise, serving the nobles in everything.[36]

"Lord," said Tlacaelel to the king, "your noble brothers and cousins, who with such bravery, courage and fearlessness have gone to war, should be rewarded. You well know that the survivors in Azcapotzalco promised us land for our crops. Let us not lose this occasion. Let us go and distribute the land among ourselves since we have won it with the strength of our arms!" The king then ordered that a count be made of the nobles who had gone to war and who had distinguished themselves in battle in order to reward them according to their merits. The count included men that I will mention here, men who were the main cause of the victory. The first was Cuauhtlecoatl, the second was Tlacahuepan, the third Tlatolzaca, the fourth Epcoatl, the fifth Tzompantli. All of these were brothers of King Itzcoatl.[37]

Then a count was made of his nephews; the first was Tlacaelel, the second Huehue Moteczoma, the third Huehuezaca, the fourth Citlalcoatl, the fifth Aztacoatl, the sixth Axicoyotzin, the seventh Cuauhtzitzimitl, and the eighth Xiconoc. All of these were descended from Huitzilihuitl. They brought great glory to Mexico; their conquests were splendid though cruel, and always to magnify their country. It is admirable that in all the wars in this land the Aztecs never provoked anybody; they were always provoked and incited to fight. Generally they asked for peace once or twice before attacking and except for a few times they were always the victors.[38]

The largest and best fields were given to the royal government. Other lands were distributed among the nobles and a third group of fields was divided among the wards of Mexico, each ward receiving a certain amount of land to maintain the cult of its gods. These are the lands which we now call *calpolalli*, that is to say "lands of the wards."

The first individual to be given land was Tlacaelel, who was awarded ten pieces of property, all formerly belonging to Azcapotzalco but in different parts of the empire. All the other great warriors received two plots each. The common men who had fought in the war but had been timid and fearful and had sworn to become serfs of the nobility were not given land or anything else, except for some who had shown a certain amount of valor. The soldiers were also given one plot of land to be used in the cult of their gods. With it they could buy what was most commonly used in ritual, that is paper,[39] rubber,[40] incense,[41] red ochre paint together with blue and yellow colors, with which they painted the mantles and headdresses of the idols.

Azcapotzalco was ruined.

At this point the Tecpanecs of Coyoacan, seeing that their allies had been ravaged, showed anger and a desire for revenge. They sent messengers to the surviving lords in Azcapotzalco to tell of their grief and anger and to offer help in a war of vengeance. The people of Azcapotzalco thanked them but despaired of regaining their previous power. The King of Mexico had commanded that never again should there be a king in Azcapotzalco. Itzcoatl would be the sovereign of all.

When the inhabitants of Coyoacan heard this decree they became fearful and thought, "Let it not be that the Aztecs treat us in this way—take our lands away from us and make us tributaries. Let us be alert, lest moved by their good fortune and by their presumptuousness they attack us." In this they were mistaken, for the Aztecs had no such intentions.

CHAPTER X WHICH TREATS OF HOW THE TECPANECS OF COYOACAN WAGED WAR ON THE AZTECS, AND HOW THEY WERE VANQUISHED

The Aztecs rejoiced that they had obtained their freedom and land enough for all. But the lord of Coyoacan, whose name was Maxtla, and his councilor, Cuecuex, spoke to the people with unbecoming levity. "Friends, Coyoacan has always been famous for the liberty in which it has lived. You have seen how Azcapotzalco was destroyed by the Aztecs and how it was stripped of its lands. The Tecpanecs were massacred—no one was spared, old or young, and the few survivors have become vassals of Mexico. Would it not be fitting for us to avenge that deed, lest they conquer us and divide our lands among them? O Tecpanecs of Coyoacan, defend your city, act wisely!

"We will make alliances with other nations," continued Maxtla, "until we destroy the Aztecs. And we will promise the men of Azcapotzalco to restore their wealth and their lands."

The people received his words with delight and appointed a messenger, a nobleman by the name of Zacancatl, to plant the seeds of vengeance and to make alliances with neighboring towns. The first city he visited was Azcapotzalco, where he tried to arouse the spirit of rebellion among the people. The ruler of Azcapotzalco responded, "Behold, Zacancatl, you have made your proposal in front of me and my chieftains and I will now answer you. What folly, that of your king and of your people, to ask us to wage war at this point against people as bellicose, cunning and sly as the Aztecs! Are we to see the streets of our city bathed in blood again, covered with entrails, with arms and heads and severed legs? What ails your sovereign? Why did he not come to our aid—when he saw us sword in hand—if he loves our city so much? Why did he remain still? Why was he inactive? Now that our people have been humiliated and enslaved he is full of wrath! No, we do not wish war. If Maxtla wants to fight let him do so without our aid."

Disappointed by this reply, Maxtla ordered all of his followers to prepare themselves and take up arms. They also prohibited the Aztecs from approaching the town of Coyoacan.

One fine day three Aztec women were on their way to the market at Coyoacan with their merchandise, to buy and sell as usual. They had no suspicion that they would be attacked and violated since they knew nothing of Maxtla's prohibition. When they reached the place of the guards, the latter came out, robbed them of everything they carried, raped and outraged them. The women, tearful and full of anguish, returned to the city of Mexico and told their husbands what had occurred. Everyone was overwhelmed and the king of Mexico gave orders forbidding his people to go to the market of Coyoacan.

But some of them disobeyed since they believed that it had been common thieves who had despoiled the Aztec women. And so the Aztecs continued to be robbed and assaulted by the guards.

Meanwhile, Maxtla persevered in his attempt to form alliances. He sent his messengers to Xalatlauhco and Atlapulco and proposed to form a pact with these rough mountaineers. The messengers urged them in the following way:

"Chichimec brethren, the monarch of Coyoacan sends you greetings! He wishes you to aid him against the Aztecs with men, shields and swords. Let the warriors be young, valiant men, capable of facing the foe with daring."

The mountaineers of these two towns answered, "So you wish to fight the Aztecs! Know then that we are not their enemies and will do nothing to harm them. Give this answer, then, to those who sent you and do not return, for this is our last word."

Maxtla now sent other envoys to Xochimilco, Chalco and Texcoco with the same message and plea, warning them that the Aztecs wished to conquer the entire land and enslave the other nations. He also stated that the Aztecs were newcomers, had invaded a land that was not theirs; that they were troublesome, difficult people.

Xilomatzin, sovereign of Colhuacan, had his own plan when he heard of the warlike intentions of Maxtla. He resolved to gather all the rulers of neighboring provinces into the meeting house at Chalco and there deliberate the matter.[42] Many towns were invited to take part in these discussions: Xochimilco, Cuitlahuac, Mizquic and others.

When Quitztototzin, sovereign of Mizquic, heard about the proposed gathering, he cried out, "I am bewildered, Tecpanecs, by your fury against a people who have not provoked us or harmed anyone. You know that I am of the generation and lineage of the Toltecs who migrated from Tula, and according to our traditions, we are all descended from Aztecs. Therefore, by no means will I accept what you propose. Go with god; do not return for you will not be well received, and tell your king to take care."

The embassy then went to see King Nezahualcoyotl in Texcoco. This monarch had recently been made ruler with the approval of his uncle Itzcoatl of Mexico. The messengers made their proposals, distorting the deeds of the Aztecs in many ways. They called them usurpers of the Tecpanec lands, tyrants, highwaymen, and asked for help in destroying them, since they were a cursed people.

King Nezahualcoyotl, who had listened carefully to all these words, smiled. "Come here, Tecpanecs; are you ignorant of the fact that Huitzilopochtli, god of the Aztecs, fights for them and protects them with all his might? It seems to me folly to try to fight against gods! I do not wish to be present at the meeting in Chalco nor will I fight against those who have not harmed me. Take care; later you will have only yourselves to blame. From me you will get no help!"

Since the people of Xochimilco, Colhuacan and Cuitlahuac had agreed to the meeting in Chalco, Maxtla, having no time to lose, did not heed the warnings of Texcoco and Mizquic.

And so, on a certain day, the gathering took place in the meeting house at

62

Chalco. Toteociteuctli and Cuateotl, rulers of Chalco, were present. One of them resided in the city we call Chalco-Atenco and the other in Amecameca. The representatives of the different nations were received with the great solemnity and honor due their high station. After many polite words the deliberation began.

By this time, of course, rumors of this meeting had spread far and wide over the countryside, and the chieftains of many states began to fear such an alliance. Those who attended the meeting in Chalco also were desirous of acting swiftly since they feared that the Aztecs might obtain help from their neighbors.

During the gathering a number of opinions were given as to the warlike proposal of the representatives of Coyoacan. The ruler of Amecameca was afraid of the power of the Aztecs and of their alliances, saying, "Tell me this—when the Aztecs come to beg mercy of us and offer to be our tributaries, whose vassals will they be—Coyoacan's? No, because Chalco will say that it has won the war. And so will Xochimilco and Colhuacan and Cuitlahuac, and there will be dissension among us. It seems to me that he who has a toothache must take out his own tooth. Therefore, I think that those who wish to fight a war should do so independently, and whoever conquers Mexico may keep it."

The other representatives agreed with the ruler of Amecameca and told the Tecpanecs to wage their own wars. The meeting then broke up, much to the disappointment of the Tecpanecs.

When Maxtla heard of the decision of the council he said, "O Tecpanecs, we cannot turn back now. Must we go into hiding? We have already infuriated the Aztecs and all we can do now is to conquer or die. Therefore, take courage; we can do nothing else.

"Lest they think that we fear them," continued Maxtla, "let us play a trick on them. Let one of the noblemen dress in his warrior clothing and go spy out if the Aztecs have guards on the boundary and whether there are signs of war."

Cuecuex, a great and bold lord, dressed himself in a quilted cotton jacket, which was the armor of the Tecpanecs, and took up his shield and sword. On his head he placed a helmet, also of quilted cotton, in the form of a tiger or lion or eagle such as was customarily worn by warriors in battle. When he reached a place called Temalacatitlan, near Mexico, he saw no signs of war.

When he returned, Maxtla said, "It would be good to invite them to the feast of our god. Let them come to honor us and when they are here they will be so careless that we will be able to play a joke upon them."

"It would be better, O lord," responded Cuecuex, "that while the feast is going on, we kill them all, sparing no one."

But Maxtla said that such treachery was used only against the most vile and dastardly of men. "If this is done, the other nations will look upon us as cowards and will have nothing but contempt for us. If they must die, let them die in the open field."

When the month of Xocotl Huetzi came,[43] the feast of the people of Coyoacan, the Aztecs were invited to be present. They accepted the invitation and a few of the great men of Mexico, among them Tlacaelel, went to the feast without fear. Before leaving, Tlacaelel said to King Itzcoatl, "Sir, we do not want you to go to these festivities, partly because it is not proper that you condescend to a minor chieftain—it would lower the dignity of your majesty and that of the Aztec kingdom—and partly because we do not know why this feast is being celebrated. In fact, we would not go if we were not carrying with us a full defense. They may wish to attack us treacherously."

The Aztecs arrived in Coyoacan, spoke to the monarch and to the noblemen, giving them gifts typical of the city of Mexico: fish, frogs, ducks, and greens of different types. The Tecpanecs were highly pleased and gave them shelter in the palace. A drum was brought out, a dance accompanied by song began, and many excellent dishes were served. When they had eaten, in place of the flowers that were usually distributed after banquets, each guest was given, by order of Maxtla, a blouse and skirt of a woman.

"Our lord Maxtla orders that we dress you in woman's clothing," the Tecpanecs said to them, "because these are the proper garments for men whom we have been trying to provoke and incite to war."

The Aztecs allowed themselves to be dressed in such a manner, and, wearing the shameful womanly clothes, they returned to Mexico and presented themselves before their king. The king consoled them and told them that the insult would in the long run honor them. He charged them not to be sorrowful since he would presently take vengeance, bringing death and destruction to all of the Tecpanecs. Itzcoatl then had all the paths to Coyoacan guarded and decided to play a trick on their enemies.

The king said, "Let the guards take all the ducks, water fowl, fish and other small animals from the lagoon which cannot be obtained in Coyoacan. Let them be taken to the gates of that city and there let them be cooked or toasted in such a way that the goodness of the odor penetrates the city. The women will begin to have miscarriages, the children will become sickly, old men and old women will become feeble and die of longing for the food which they cannot have."

The royal orders were carried out and they prepared a great many loaves of *ezcahuitl*, a type of small red worm which abounds in the waters of the lagoon, a delicacy to the Aztecs. They threw these loaves into the fire together with duck,

*Grades of rank attainable through ability in war. From
the* Codex Mendoza, *painted in early Colonial
times by Aztec scribes.
Courtesy American Museum of
Natural History, New York.*

fish and frogs, and the odor was so great that it penetrated the streets of Coyoacan. It made the women miscarry out of desire for the food of the Aztecs; it made the children sickly, their mouths watering with greed; the old men became lax in their bowels from longing and the women's faces, hands and feet became swollen. Many became ill and died, drooling.[44]

Maxtla saw the ills that were coming to his city and the harm caused by the smoke, and he called his councilman Cuecuex, saying, "What shall we do? The enemy is destroying us by making us long for the foods that they eat! They have come with malice to our boundaries, for the odor of their smoke is so appetizing that pregnant women are perishing and children are dying."

"We must wait," answered Cuecuex, "for the moment in which we will go out and overcome them by force. I will be the first to go." He immediately dressed himself in his armor and took up the sword and shield. Unaccompanied, he went to the place where the guards of Mexico were stationed, a place called Momiztitlan. He challenged the Aztecs, telling them that he had come to destroy them, shouting insults at them, playing with his sword and shield and jumping to and fro.

The Aztecs were afraid of an ambush. They ordered the workmen to build a high scaffold. When this had been constructed, the chief of the Aztecs, Tlacaelel, climbed to the top of it, looked about him and spied to see if there were an ambush or whether men were concealed any place. He saw a little smoke coming out of a field of rushes and suspected that the Tecpanec army was there. He climbed down and ordered the watchmen to ascend and watch with great care to see if anyone left the army of the enemy. He told his own captains not to move until he returned.

Carrying his sword and shield, he entered the rushes in the direction of the place where he had seen the smoke. He emerged from the rushes on a bank which was the boundary of Colhuacan. He spied through the reeds and saw three well-armed soldiers. Knowing them to be from Colhuacan and not Tecpanecs, he approached them, asking, "Who are you?" They answered, "Lord, we are from Colhuacan and we have come to work for you and serve you."

Tlacaelel said, "On the contrary, I believe you to be spies from Colhuacan and that you have come to examine our army in order to attack us from behind. We know that you attended a meeting in Chalco and made a pact with the Tecpanecs of Coyoacan."

They smiled and told him, "Lord, we of Colhuacan are not treacherous people but are plain and frank. Treat us as we are."

The Aztec inquired their names. One of them said that his was Acaxel, the other, Atamal, and the third Quil layos. These names were not real but false as they were trying to disguise themselves, being noblemen desirous of gaining glory and playing a great role in the war.

67

"Well, friends," spoke Tlacaelel, "my name is Tlacaelel. I am the chief of the Aztecs. Since you have come to gain glory I request one thing of you: do not move from this place but wait for me until I come back. Should soldiers from Coyoacan come here, kill them without mercy."

The noblemen agreed to do this and the Aztec chieftain returned to his people where he found King Itzcoatl exhorting the troops. The sovereign was told of the three men from Colhuacan and how they had promised to wait at a certain spot for his return.

At this moment the watchmen climbed down and cried out that the troops from Coyoacan were approaching in battle array. Tlacaelel asked the king to move toward the Tecpanecs and face them. He himself took a company of soldiers, led by two captains, to rejoin the three disguised noblemen whom he had left in the marsh near Colhuacan.

There, among the reeds he gave to the three from Colhuacan the insignia of Aztec warriors, as well as swords and shields. With great caution they began to march toward Coyoacan in order to attack the enemy from the rear. By this time a great battle had begun between the Tecpanecs and the Aztecs under their king. Blood drenched the ground, and the shouting on both sides could be heard far away.

When Tlacaelel and his men broke from cover, shouting "Mexico! Mexico! Tenochtitlan!" the Tecpanecs had no defense.

Tlacaelel and his companions massacred them without pity, performing such cunning feats and valiant deeds that no man dared attack them directly. Everyone fled before them as though they were wildcats.

The Tecpanecs, retreating toward their city, intended to use their temple as a last stronghold, but Tlacaelel reached the temple before them and, taking possession of its entrance, ordered one of his men to set it on fire, having made prisoner all those who were within. The inhabitants of Coyoacan, knowing the end had come, fled up the slopes of the Axochco mountain, the Aztecs pursuing them closely. The survivors begged the pursuers to spare them since they had already surrendered. They also begged them to put away their arms, for their vengeance was complete.

But the Aztecs answered, "We refuse to pardon you, traitors! The name of Coyoacan shall be erased from the face of the earth. Today we shall ravage it and cast it to the ground. The names of the treacherous men who provoked others will be forgotten!"

"What will you gain by destroying us?" the vanquished replied. "You have done enough. We are now your slaves forever; we will furnish you with stone, wood, lime, lands, laborers for your houses, clothes, foodstuffs—everything you may demand."

The Aztecs cried out that there would be no pardon and told them to remember the women's dresses with which they had been put to scorn.

The Aztecs finally permitted them to depart, and many of the Tecpanecs reached Ocuilan, Xalatlauco and Atlapulco. The Aztecs then returned to their city, rich in slaves, gold, gems and precious feathers, shields and insignia, clothing and many other spoils.

Tlacaelel and his companions used a trick in this battle in order to ascertain how many prisoners they took. Whenever they captured a man they cut off a lock of his hair. In the end it was found that they had captured twice as many as all the other soldiers.[45]

CHAPTER XI WHICH TREATS OF HOW THE LORDS OF MEXICO REQUESTED
KING ITZCOATL TO GRANT THEM TITLES AND HOW HE ACCEDED TO THIS
BESIDES GIVING THEM THE LANDS OF COYOACAN

Itzcoatl returned to Mexico in triumph and was received with shouts of acclaim because of what he had accomplished for the honor of his nation. The king thanked his subjects in these words:

"Lords and great princes:
I know of your great deeds!
I am also aware of the dauntless spirit
With which you have resisted our foes.
You have now concluded your task
In enlarging our city, our water and our lands.
This is also the task of our god Huitzilopochtli
And that is why he came to us.
He gathers, he draws to his service
All the nations with the strength of his chest and of his head.
Rest now and let us discuss the division of the lands of Coyoacan.
They belong to you since you won them,
And I rejoice that they are given to you."

"Powerful prince," replied the commander Tlacaelel, "we kiss your regal hands for your great liberality. This will be a source of great encouragement for those who doubt, for those who are timid. It will stimulate the children who are just beginning to grow. They will be eager to serve you and willing to die for their king and for their country, and for the benefit of their persons and their possessions. Let your officials go, take the lands and divide them in the way you indicate.

"However, great lord," he continued, "I am going to request something else in the name of the peers who have risked their lives in conquering Azcapotzalco and Coyoacan. I beseech you now to give them a reward which they greatly deserve, that is to say, titles of distinction according to their merit."

The king was well pleased at this advice and asked all the great nobles to meet in the chambers where the royal seat was kept. He made them sit down and ordered Tlacaelel to say the following to them: "Friends and brothers, your sovereign, King Itzcoatl, my close relative and yours, greets you and wishes to honor you according to your merit. He wishes to give you titles and preëminence over others, as well as lands which will support you and your families."

Filled with gratitude, the warriors humbly said they were not worthy of such gifts. In spite of this meek response, Tlacaelel and the king began to consider which titles the nobles should receive.

I do not wish these great and honorable titles to be forgotten and therefore I will take pains to copy them here. Just as Our lord, the King of Spain gives titles to his great men, such as that of Duke, Count, Marquis, Viscount, Archduke, Master of a Military Order and Governor of a Conquered Province, titles were given to the Aztec braves.[46]

All of them were natives of Mexico, brothers, cousins and nephews of the king. Apart from giving them titles, he had stone statues carved of them in order to perpetuate their memory, and he had the historians and painters inscribe their lives and deeds with fine brushes and bright colors in the books. In this way their fame would grow and magnify like the brightness of the sun throughout all the nations. In the same way I have wished in this my history to preserve the fame and memory of those heroes so that their honor may last as long as my work lasts and may be an example for all those who love virtue. Let their memory be a blessing, since such men are the loved ones of God, similar to the saints in Paradise. This is the only type of fame that is worth perpetuating.

As soon as the honors had been given to the Aztec warriors, the three allies from Colhuacan came forth. They were offended by the fact that they had been ignored and they complained to Tlacaelel: "Lord, you have not kept your word! In this war we showed great courage in serving King Itzcoatl. We should not be defrauded of what our hands have gained for us. We risked our lives in this adventure; do not look on us as people of low rank. Even though we wear a peasant disguise, we are people of high lineage, worthy of receiving titles like all the rest."

Tlacaelel saw that they were right and he took them before the King, together with the two Aztec captains. He said to Itzcoatl, "Great sovereign, these five men aided me when I attacked our enemies from the rear and destroyed them. Therefore, it is just that they be rewarded like the rest, since they served you so well."

Itzcoatl then thought it fitting to give one of the Aztec captains the title of Quauhnochtecutli and to the other the title of Cuauhquiahuacatl. He called the three strangers, honored them and gave them gifts. Their titles were to be Yopicatecuhtli, Huitznahuatl and Itcotecatl.

The inhabitants of Coyoacan who had survived were greatly dejected since there was not an Aztec warrior who had not captured one or two of them. Inflamed with anger these Tecpanec survivors now decided to take vengeance upon Azcapotzalco. Maxtla, especially enraged, decided to deal with that city in a cruel manner. He sent certain captains of his there and ordered them to murder the most important officials in the utmost secrecy.

These treacherous men left Coyoacan in the afternoon and arrived in Azcapotzalco at sunset. First they blackened and smeared their faces with soot so as not to be recognized, and after that they entered the home of the sovereign and did not stop until they reached the room where he and other nobles of the city were to be found. Before they could defend themselves the assassins fell upon them. Having done this they fled from the town for the people began to make a great noise, wept and cried out.

When King Itzcoatl heard of the murders, he tried to discover the guilty parties, but he was unable to find out the truth of the matter. Thus were assassinated the highest in office in Azcapotzalco, and from that time on the city lost all its importance. It had once been the greatest and most populous in all the land, royalty had resided in it, and it had conquered thirty tributary states long before the Aztecs had even dreamed of coming to this land.

After a few days had gone by, King Itzcoatl, mindful of the need to gratify his vassals and all those who had served him, called the great chieftain Tlacaelel—who was as important to him as Joseph had been to the Pharaoh in Egypt—and spoke to him thus:

"My lord, you know that those who work must be rewarded and paid for their labor. My men have worked and sweated and it is proper that we now divide the lands of Coyoacan among them."

The first to be awarded its share was the Royal Crown. The king, his family, the courtesans, foreign visitors, messengers from other lands—all of these would be maintained by the fruits of these new possessions. Tlacaelel was given eleven pieces of land and after him the noblemen received two or three according to their merit.

Before we proceed with the story of how Xochimilco rebelled against the Aztecs, I wish to explain something about the titles which were given to the warriors of Mexico.

First, it must be known that once a ruler was elected in Mexico, four other lords taken from among his brothers or near relatives were also elected. They were given the titles of princes and from them was chosen the next king, no others being eligible. Their titles were: Tlacochcalcatl, which is made up of the words *tlacochtli*, which means "propelled lance or dart," and *calli*, which means "house." It is as if one were to say "Head of the House of the Darts." This title was given to a man and his descendants, as in Spain we call a man the Duke of Alba and those of his lineage are known as the House of Alba.

The second title was Tlacatecal which is made up of the words *tlacatl*, meaning person, and of the verb *tequi*, which is to cut or slash. That is what they called the second nobleman, "Man-cutter" or "Man-slasher."

The third nobleman was called Ezhuahuacatl which is composed of *eztli*, blood, and *huahuaca*, which means to scratch or to tear. Therefore it can be translated as "Shedder of Blood" by scratching or tearing.

The fourth titled nobleman was called Tlilancalqui, a word which is made up of *tlilli*, soot or blackness, and *calli*, which means house. It means something like "Lord of the House of Blackness." It should be known that there was a god of blackness and that the title of this lord originated from this idol and his house.

These four lords, having been elected, were made part of the royal council as presidents or officials of the supreme council. Nothing was done without their opinion and if a king died the new ruler was chosen from among them. No one could be given the titles mentioned above unless he was a son or a brother of a king. Once one of these had been exalted to the royal seat, another was elected to take his former place. It is worth remarking that they did not necessarily elect the son of the king to the throne. The sons did not inherit titles or kingdoms by simple succession but by election. Sometimes it would be a son, sometimes a brother, at other times a cousin who would be elected. It was sufficient that he be of the lineage and a close relative. And thus sons and brothers would succeed one another in irregular succession, but the kingship always remained within the same kin.

Each one of these lords had vassals who paid tribute; they had villages, lands which were worked for them and from which they received all kinds of foodstuffs and clothing.

72

The people of Xochimilco sorrowed greatly over the destruction of Coyoacan and the growing strength of Mexico, fearing that the Aztecs might also dispossess and enslave them. There were two rulers of this kingdom: one in the capital city of Xochimilco and he was called Yacaxapotecuhtli. The other resided in Milpa Alta and was known as Pachimalcatecuhtli. They spoke: "We will never surrender to the Aztecs. We have been rulers and we will not turn into vassals. We will never sweep the houses or water the gardens of the Aztecs. We will never be mistreated, we will never serve them water for washing their hands. We will attempt to keep our dignity."

At this time the Aztec women continued to go to the usual market places and the people of Xochimilco, in order to reassure them, continued to buy merchandise from them—fish and water fowl. It was at this time that the people of Xochimilco celebrated a great feast with food bought from the Aztec merchant women. During this feast they planned to perfect their plot against Mexico. The dishes of food which had been sold by the Aztec women were served at the banquet and then there occurred a prodigious, fearsome thing, which bewildered everyone. As soon as the people had sat down to eat, the delicacies in the dishes turned into human hands, arms, heads, hearts and tripe. In their terror the Xochimilca called their soothsayers and asked them what this meant. The soothsayers answered that it was an ill omen, since it meant the destruction of the city and the death of many. "Ah, lords! We are lost!" cried out the rulers of Xochimilco. "There is no remedy for us. O, people of Xochimilco, prepare to die, because the glory of our city will perish as did that of Azcapotzalco and Coyoacan."

At this time the Aztecs were not aware that anything was wrong; as far as they knew, the friendship between the two cities continued to exist as it always had. When they needed a small amount of stone and white pine wood for the temple of the idol Huitzilopochtli, they felt sure that they would not be refused. Therefore they sent their messengers bearing a gift, to request the stone and wood from the officials of Xochimilco, saying, "O, high-born lords! King Itzcoatl and the four chieftains of Mexico kiss your feet and hands, send you this greeting and offer you this present. They beg a favor of your generosity. They wish to build a place for the god Huitzilopochtli and would like you to permit them to take some heavy stone and some white pine wood from your lands."

Cuauhquechol and Tepanquizqui, two noblemen of Xochimilco, cried out, "What do you say, O Aztecs? What do you seek? Are you drunk? Are you out of your minds that you have come here with such a demand? Are we your vassals or slaves that we must provide you with stone and wood and everything you need? Are those who sent you our lords and masters? Go home, Aztecs, and tell them that it is not our will to grant them what they demand!"

The messengers were much surprised at this rough reply and they were sorrowful because they were sure no good would come of it. Thereupon Itzcoatl gave orders that no one should trespass upon the lands of Xochimilco lest some unfortunate incident take place.

Though some of the noblemen of Xochimilco wished to make peace, their ruler discouraged them. "If we now bend to the Aztecs we would be scorned and looked down upon as lowly peasants. If they are to conquer us let it be in a real war."

Thus matters remained quiescent until one day certain Aztec merchants were returning from the Marquesado with loads of cotton which they planned to sell in Mexico.[47] As they passed through the mountainous lands near Xochimilco, soldiers of that city appeared and asked them where they came from. They answered that they were natives of Mexico. Without another word the soldiers attacked them, took the cotton mantles from them, and having stripped them, robbed them and wounded them, sent them to the city of Mexico. The travelers went straight to the royal abode and stood before their king, wounded, beaten and weeping.

When Itzcoatl had heard their story he showed great wrath in his countenance, crying out, "O Aztec brothers, how you have suffered! Bear your suffering and be calm, for your injuries will be avenged and your property will be returned to you."

In a meeting with all his great princes, Itzcoatl argued the following: "Aztecs, you now see how those of Xochimilco have broken the peace without cause. Let five of our officers and five soldiers go, with concealed weapons, to the biggest cornfield on the other side of the boundary and let them tear out ears and stocks of maize. If any come out to defend the fields let them be punished. Spare their lives, however, but devastate the field entirely before the others come out to attack."

The ten men followed his orders and when their enemies tried to defend the fields, they clubbed them and then devastated the fields. By the time other defenders appeared the Aztecs were already on their way back to their own city.

When Itzcoatl consulted his men regarding this matter, Tlacaelel and the four supreme councilors advised him. "Our opinion is that we should send a peace embassy, inquiring of them whether they are determined to wage war or whether they desire our friendship. Let two of our most important brothers go on this errand."

74

Huehuetl, *a great wooden drum, which shows calendrical*
*motifs and eagles symbolic of war. Museum of Toluca,*
*Mexico. Photo National Institute of Anthropology*
*and History, Mexico City.*

The king then sent two valorous and highly esteemed noblemen known as Tocoltecatl and Axicoyo. When the two messengers had arrived at a place called Tizapan, within the limits of Xochimilco, a great number of men carrying arms and insignia, swords and shields, came out to meet them. The Aztecs were unarmed. The Xochimilca asked them what they wanted and where they were going. They replied that they came from Mexico and that they were going to Xochimilco with a message. The enemy refused to let them pass and said that there was no more to be discussed, that this was the last word and resolution of the entire land of Xochimilco, and that it came from young and old, even from women and children.

King Itzcoatl was amazed when he heard that the messengers had not been allowed to pass, even though unarmed. The Aztec council met and ordered the commanders and captains of the army to gather, together with all the seasoned warriors. They had decided to engage in war and began to make their plans and to arm their men, as the people of Xochimilco were numerous and extremely courageous. When everything was ready, Tlacaelel took a count of his men in a place called Teyacac. Choosing the strongest and most willing soldiers he spoke these words to them:

"O valiant warriors, the entire land of Xochimilco is against us and they outnumber us, but let this not trouble you. Strength and spirit are what matter! Be informed that our enemy is very near us, in a place called Ocolco, and the battle will take place there. Therefore, O Aztecs, make your name ring out as you have always done."

Cheerfully, the soldiers, well ordered in files, each file following its captain, began to move. When they arrived in the presence of the enemy, the Xochimilca let out great shouts and yells, screaming, "Come, come Aztecs! Your end is near!" The Xochimilca were so numerous that they totally covered the plain, and the gold, jewels, precious stones and plumes that they carried on their weapons, insignia and shields were so splendid that they shone in the sun as they reflected its rays. What a spectacle it was! Weapons of many hues: green, blue, red, yellow, black, multicolored!

"Oh, wretched Xochimilca!" cried the Aztecs. "We pity you and your wives and children! Who has deceived you to come to this place where you will lose spirit and gallantry? You will soon forget that vain fantasy which you have brought with you and will become our tributaries and vassals!"

Having said these words, the Aztecs began to shoot great numbers of darts and arrows with such fury that the arrows darkened the sun. So great were the shrieks of exultation that the valleys trembled. Presently the Xochimilca abandoned the field and retreated, little by little, though the captains attempted to stir them into fighting.

The cunning, spirited Aztecs broke through the squadrons of Xochimilca and began to push them toward a hill called Xochitepec. Tlacaelel ascended this hill and, twisting his sword and his shield, he shouted to his men: "Hail, my valiant Aztecs; victory is ours! Do not tire yourselves overmuch. Let them die little by little and let those perish who had unjustly wished to destroy us!"

Tlacaelel then entered the fray again and began to perform marvelous feats, knocking down all who stood in his way. This encouraged the Aztecs greatly, while the Xochimilca became terrified and fled toward a wall which had been built for the defense of their city. Once they were behind this wall they began to wound many Aztecs through certain loopholes that pierced the walls. But the Aztecs approached with swords, sticks and hoes and began to tear down the wall.

The rulers of Xochimilco now realized that their city was to be sacked. The wall had been torn down and there were few other defenses, and these had been abandoned. Therefore the chieftains came out weaponless and with their arms crossed in front of them. They prostrated themselves in front of the entire Aztec army, saying:

"You are now our masters, O Aztecs! Here we are, we who are guilty of having provoked your wrath, of having brought you trouble! Let your ire and rage be vented upon us but let not the old people and the children perish. Do not permit our city to be sacked and destroyed! You have avenged yourselves. Lower your arms and your swords! Cast your shields upon the ground! Tell us what you wish and we will serve you. From now on the hills and valleys, the waters, springs, lands and plains that have made this city rich are yours. Stone, heavy and light, wood and firewood, all is yours. Let your hearts be calm. The more of us you kill the fewer vassals will you have to serve you. Take rest, O Aztecs, let there be no more conflict, for you have overcome us."

The Aztecs, in order to scare them even further, answered that they wanted to hear no more promises and that they did not need their stone and wood. They said that once the Xochimilca were dead and erased from the earth, they would do as they pleased and settle the city with other inhabitants. Setting up another great cry, the Aztecs picked up their arms again, shouting, "Death to the traitors! Let no man be spared!"

The Xochimilca bowed again and begged the attack to cease, considering the greed of the Aztec soldiers and their eagerness to sack the city. "Why do you pretend, O lords, valorous Aztecs? If you seek land for yourselves, we will give it to you in great quantities, and very good land it is. We will serve you in your homes, we will give you water for your hands, we will build your houses. We will be your carriers and servants whenever you travel. And should you go to war, we will provide you with food, arms and soldiers. In a word, we will be your vassals forever!"

Tlacaelel ordered his soldiers to lower their arms, since the enemy had surrendered, and he ordered that everyone turn back toward Mexico without entering Xochimilco.

The Aztec soldiers, disappointed, showed their displeasure, and as they turned back to the city of Mexico, complained that they had not been given permission to loot as had been done heretofore.

Xochimilco was one of the richest cities in the land and they could have obtained great spoils. Tlacaelel, however, promised to recompense the soldiers for what they had lost. He then turned to the Xochimilca and ordered the entire city to build a causeway about five yards wide from their town to Mexico. It was to be of stone and earth and the water was to be dammed where the road would run. Bridges were to be built at intervals so that the water could pass from one side to the other. The Xochimilca lowered their heads and repeated these orders to the entire kingdom. Xochimilco had been a great state with territory covering more than twenty leagues in one direction, as far as a town called Tochimilco, or Ocopetlayocan. The entire nation then began to build the causeway and today one can walk upon it from Mexico to Xochimilco.[48]

CHAPTER **XIII** WHICH TREATS OF HOW, AFTER THE PEOPLE OF XOCHIMILCO
HAD BUILT THE CAUSEWAY, KING ITZCOATL ORDERED THE DIVISION
OF THE LANDS OF XOCHIMILCO

The Xochimilca received the aid of those of Coyoacan in constructing the causeway, at least in part. This is the way in which it was built: it was constructed upon many stakes, stones and blocks of grassy earth taken from the lagoon. Once this wide avenue had been built, innumerable people began to travel upon it.

"The causeway you ordered the Xochimilca to build is finished," said Tlacaelel to the king, "and they constructed it with good will. It is now time to give our warriors their reward in pieces of land. Let us give each one of them a plot 330 yards long, since they were not allowed to sack the conquered city."

When the lands were about to be divided, the Xochimilca, seeing themselves thus dispossessed, were greatly disturbed and were unable to hold back their tears. The Aztecs took pity on them, consoled them and tried to encourage them with kind words, saying that they would be under their protection now and that they would care for their needs.

When Itzcoatl heard about these events in Xochimilco he decided to make the sovereign of that city one of his councilors with the right to attend his meals and to eat in his presence.[49] He also promised that the vanquished ruler would be consulted on all his decisions. This was greatly appreciated by the Xochimilca, and it was a great favor which had been granted to no other foreign monarch up to that time.

The Xochimilca tribe had been the third to take possession of lands here, having come out of the seven caves where they had lived for a long time. They had been a great power, having warred with their neighbors, the people of Colhuacan, about lands and boundaries and states. Colhuacan had been the first to elect kings and lords before the arrival of the Aztecs and had always competed with Xochimilco. Up to this time each of these cities had refused to recognize the superiority of the other.

When the Aztecs had first arrived in the land, they had aided Colhuacan against Xochimilco and achieved some victories. A very remarkable battle had once taken place in which the Aztecs had decided to cut off one ear of every Xochimilca that was captured. Thus every captive they caught hold of was deprived of one ear. I have heard it affirmed, besides having seen it in the painted manuscript, that the people of Colhuacan carried away baskets filled with human ears in their canoes. This victory was so renowned and celebrated by those of Colhuacan that even today they sing about it and remember it in their feasts and dances.

Colhuacan has always possessed great fame and even today it is famous since it was the place of origin of the the kings of Mexico and of many other great princes and governors. Out of it came the women that engendered them. Besides this, the people of Colhuacan were the first to arrive in this land and were the most important of all people at one time. Colhuacan was an independent state then and conquered many provinces, notably the people of the Chinampa who then became their neighbors and allies. Among the Chinampa people were the Xochimilca.

The two women who were mothers of the kings and of the Aztec nation were called Atotoztli and Ilancueitl, the latter having been mentioned in a previous chapter. It is the belief that one of them had been barren and had only feigned to have children. It is also a popular opinion that these children had been born to concubines of the king, her husband. I am suspicious of this theory since I have seen a painted manuscript in which Ilancueitl, who was said to have been barren, appeared as the wife of the lord of Coatlichan. This ruler had been killed by a tyrant who had wanted to conquer his state. He had also wished to kill a child who might inherit the royal power. The widow hid her child and came fleeing with him to the city of Colhuacan, her birthplace. These events had taken place after she had been the wife and become the widow of Acamapichtli.

XIV  WHICH TREATS OF HOW THE PEOPLE OF CUITLAHUAC
REBELLED AGAINST THE AZTECS DURING THE REIGN OF KING ITZCOATL
AND HOW THEY WERE VANQUISHED

The people of the town of Cuitlahuac considered now that it would be shameful to remain at peace and to continue their friendship with the Aztecs. They also felt that being surrounded by water was a wall and a defense to their city. They relied on their skill in moving their boats to and fro in the waters of the lagoon. In this they were not wrong, for the Aztecs dreaded to meet their enemies upon the water.[50]

The sovereign of Cuitlahuac was at that time a valorous man by the name of Xochitlolinqui, of strong heart, spoiling to achieve some great feat. Deliberately he began to lose favor with the Aztecs and to abandon their friendship.

The Aztec authorities became suspicious and they used a cunning trick to make sure once and for all. King Itzcoatl called a meeting of the dignitaries in the city of Mexico. It was held secretly and no one heard about it.

"It seems to me," said Itzcoatl, "that the people of Cuitlahuac wish to lose our friendship. To know with certainty whether this be true, I have decided to send two of you to Xochitlolinqui, to invite him to a solemn feast that I will hold in honor of our god Huitzilopochtli. Tell him that in order to make the feast more splendid I wish him to bring his noblemen and all their maiden daughters and sisters, so that they may sing and dance at these festivities. In this way, if he agrees to do what I ask of him, I will be relieved of my suspicions. If he refuses, I will know the truth."

Two envoys went to Cuitlahuac and gave the ruler this message. They added that the young girls should come accompanied by their duennas. In this way no unseeming act, which might dishonor their god, could occur. Furthermore, they asked that the maidens carry flowers and rushes as was customary.

When the monarch of Cuitlahuac heard this message, he showed the utmost wrath and displeasure.

"Do you realize what you are saying?" he answered harshly. "Are our daughters and sisters toys or buffoons of your god that they must dance and sing before him? Tell Itzcoatl that I respect the virgins of my city too highly, even those of the lowest rank, to send them to be the playthings of his god. He has numerous maidens in his own city; let him make use of them. Neither on this occasion nor on any other will I obey him. Tell him that if he is trying to incite us to war we are ready for it. You may go now." He saw to it that the messengers were not given food or gifts.

The dignitaries in Mexico were indignant and sent a last message to the monarch of Cuitlahuac, asking him to obey or to prepare for war. This ruler answered that he was determined to destroy the Aztecs and that he wished to hear no more from them.

"I am pleased, O valiant lords," cried Itzcoatl when he had heard this, "that you will now have another occasion to show your courage." But the Aztec dignitaries were much afraid of the treachery of the people of Chalco and said so to their king. Therefore, a message was sent to Cuateotl and Teteozitecuhtli, the rulers of Chalco, telling them of the rebellion at Cuitlahuac. The Aztecs begged them humbly to reveal if the enemy had asked their aid, since it was unlikely that the people of Cuitlahuac would rely on their own strength alone.

The lords of Chalco responded that they kissed the hands of King Itzcoatl and that he should be told that they knew nothing about the matter. They had no news of any war and this was because of the diligence with which the people of Cuitlahuac isolated themselves in their island kingdom. They also assured the Aztecs that they need have no fear from them.

When the messengers had returned to Mexico, Itzcoatl ordered Tlacaelel to form an army of boys between sixteen and eighteen years of age, in order to mock and show contempt for Cuitlahuac. The youths were to be given their quilted cotton armor, lances, arrows, swords and shields, and were to be trained by the captains.

Tlacaelel chose certain diligent captains to guide and teach the youths. The preceptors and teachers in the schools which existed in all the wards were called and were told the will of the king. Great numbers of youths were brought in from all the wards. They were given captains and immediately showed their eagerness to conquer or perish. Having prepared themselves they were ordered to meet in a place called Yahualiuhcan.

All the boys, dressed in their armor, began to march in good order toward the town of Cuitlahuac. When they had arrived at a place called Tecuitlatenco they stopped and waited for the arrival of the canoes which were being rowed across the lagoon. A thousand boats were filled with men armed with shields, great num-

82

bers of lances, darts and arrows. With them came warriors who were to defend the archers and who were experts at deflecting the arrows with their shields. Their skill was wondrous; when they saw an arrow coming they would hit with their shields, making it turn back.

When the canoes arrived, the entire army embarked and they passed through a deep part of the lagoon where there was no causeway or road. When they arrived in Cuitlahuac they landed easily on the bank even while the natives, armed, were coming out in great and richly adorned canoes, the rowers covered with fine shields and feather work. The warriors were well armed and their weapons were covered with white, red, yellow, blue, green, black and multicolored plumes. On their heads and backs were elaborate feather adornments. From their necks hung many ornaments of gold inlaid with jewels. On their arms were wristbands of shining gold, on their ankles gold bands. Thus they were attired from head to foot.

As soon as the Aztecs saw the Cuitlahuaca, a great yelling started on both sides. They began to throw the darts, which are dangerous weapons since once they have entered they cannot be pulled out. This is because of their barbs which make them like harpoons. In order to remove a dart it is necessary to make a great opening or to push it out the other side. Great numbers of these darts were being thrown and men in both armies were severely wounded, not only by the darts but by the arrows and stones shot by the Aztecs and returned by the men concealed in the marsh.

The soldiers of Cuitlahuac, hedged in by the tireless youths who seemed everywhere, turned to seek help from the little aquatic beasts. They invoked the water snakes, frogs, and fish, the little shrimp and the leeches, and finally the worms and other creatures that live in the water, praying to them in a servile manner and asking their favor and assistance.

But the god of the water creatures reminded them that the Aztecs were bellicose, vengeful people, experts in matters pertaining to the lagoon, and that if they did not wish to perish and be destroyed totally, they must beg for mercy and surrender.

Hearing the answer of the god of the waters, of the fishes, frogs and water snakes, of the little shrimp and leeches, those who had prayed rejoined their companions. Many canoes were now drifting without their occupants and the lagoon was covered with oars and shields, darts and arrows. Many men were dead, and others, badly wounded, were trying to keep afloat on the water.

83

The officials of Cuitlahuac, led by their sovereign Xochitlolinqui and laden with gifts of fish, turkeys, ducks and other fine things, approached Tlacaelel knowing that he was a merciful man. They begged him to have pity on them and told him that they would not only give him their daughters and sisters but that they would also serve the Aztecs and become their vassals. Tlacaelel accepted their surrender and ordered the drum beaten which was a sign of the end of battle. The soldiers gathered the canoes which had floated away, and the shields, darts and arrows. They stripped the dead and despoiled them of all their finery.

The Aztec lords returned to their city and related to the king the events which had taken place, and how the Cuitlahuaca had promised to furnish maidens for the dance of the gods. From now on they would serve the Aztecs and pay tribute, since they did not have any lands that could be divided.

Itzcoatl, though ill at that time, was much gladdened by the victory and expressed his gratitude to the lords and princes.

Soon after this his illness became worse and he knew that he was about to die. He sent messages to the king of Texcoco, Nezahualcoyotl, who was a close relative of his, and charged him not to war with the Aztecs, his relatives and friends, but that he remain on good terms with them.

As he felt death near, he left orders that, from that time on, the king of Texcoco was to be the second ranking monarch of the land and that the third ruler was to be the ruler of Tacuba. At the same time he gathered all his courtiers and charged them with the cult of the gods. And he requested that the king who would take his place build a sumptuous temple to his god Huitzilopochtli and to the other gods as there was now much wealth in the empire. He also ordered that his image and those of the kings his ancestors be carved in stone for an everlasting memorial. Having thus expressed his last words and will, Itzcoatl died, leaving the city joyless and disconsolate. He had been a dauntless king, of invincible spirit, a man who had made the Republic great and who had lifted high the glory of his nation. According to the relation most worthy of belief he died in 1440, having reigned only fourteen years.

According to another curious history or painted manuscript he is said to have reigned nineteen years and to have died in 1445, but I find the first chronicle more truthful. It is also said that this king conquered Chalco, Cuernavaca, Huexotzinco, and Azcapotzalco and that he suppressed these kingdoms, leaving only three, that is, Mexico, Texcoco, and Tacuba. I have also heard that Coatlichan was an independent kingdom and that he conquered it. From this time on the three aforementioned states ruled over the land, but Mexico over them, its ruler being like an emperor in the New World.

The king was buried with great solemnity and a large number of representatives of the neighboring cities were present, lords as well as peasants. His funeral rites lasted for eighty days of sorrow and weeping. In those times the funeral cere-

*Temalacatl, stone of the gladiatorial sacrifice, carved under the Emperor Tizoc (1481-1487). National Museum, Mexico City. Photo National Institute of Anthropology and History, Mexico City.*

monies had not taken the form that they were to assume later. However, there was no lack of funerary food and the usual gifts of clothing were exchanged.

CHAPTER X V  WHICH TREATS OF THE ELECTION OF
THE FIFTH KING OF MEXICO, CALLED HUEHUE MOTECZOMA,
THE FIRST OF THIS NAME, WITH
A DESCRIPTION OF THE PACT OR COVENANT THAT HE MADE
WITH NEZAHUALCOYOTL, KING OF TEXCOCO

Once the funeral ceremonies of Itzcoatl had ended, the Aztecs, both lords and common people, elected a brother of Tlacaelel to the royal seat. His name was Huehue Moteczoma, first of this name, a cousin to King Itzcoatl and one of the Supreme Council of four, his title being Tlacatecatl which is similar in Spanish to a High Military and Judicial Officer.

And so Moteczoma was elected king with all the usual ceremonies and anointments. Mourning for the dead ruler ceased and the city rejoiced over the new election with dance and song. The neighboring kings came to acknowledge the preëminence of the new sovereign and to acknowledge their subjection to this supreme monarch. They brought him great and valuable gifts of rich cloth, weapons, insignia, shields, fine plumes, and jewels used on such occasions by the lords to show reverence to one another. Nezahualcoyotl, king of Texcoco, a state of many great towns, was especially generous in his gifts.[51]

As soon as Nezahualcoyotl heard of the election of Moteczoma he gathered the dignitaries of his kingdom and spoke to them solemnly. "I beg you, lords, brothers, to treat the Aztecs well! Flee from their enmity and from any conflict with them. Let us keep an eternal peace and inviolable friendship. You know them; I do not have to say more regarding their ways. If you meet them on the roads and they ask for something you carry, share it with them. Treat them well because in doing so we lose nothing. Should we oppose them we would only gain wars, trouble, deaths, robbery, the shedding of our blood, and desolation to our kingdom. Therefore be in peace and quiet and urge the people of the cities in my kingdom, especially travelers and merchants, to do likewise, for these traders are the ones who go about the roads and move from province to province gaining their sustenance.

You and I remain at home and have no reason to cause trouble to anyone, much less to the Aztecs, who never make trouble unless they are provoked. It is not fitting that any ignoble act come from us. It is the common people who cause war with their ignorance and their recklessness."

Having made all necessary preparations, Nezahualcoyotl departed toward Mexico where he was well received by the new king. Among his many rich presents were golden jewelry, stones, ear plugs, lip plugs, the most exquisite feather work, shields, arms, mantles, and beautifully worked loin cloths.

When he had delivered his gifts, Nezahualcoyotl explained the cause of his visit and spoke to the king in private. "Supreme lord and monarch, let not your regal person and your heart be anguished over the new burden which is imposed upon you. Keep up your manly spirit according to your true worth.

"I have come here, O lord, to tell you of the misery, the affliction that reigns in your province of Texcoco. In your greatness deign to lift it and ennoble it and shelter it from other nations. You well know, great prince, that all your vassals, nobles as well as common people are under your shade and you have been planted here like a great cedar under which men wish to rest in order to take pleasure in the freshness of your friendship and love. Those who need you most are the old men and women, orphans and widows, the poor and the destitute. All of them are like feathers on your wings and feathers on your head. Also think of the little ones who are beginning to crawl or are still in their cradles, who do not feel, nor hear, nor know, nor understand. They have no hands to defend themselves or feet to flee from the wrath of the Aztecs. All these, and I in their name, beseech your clemency. Preserve us in peace and concord and do not allow Mexico to attack us. If I, without purpose or aim, waged a war, I would do so knowing that the fury of the Aztecs is measureless, limitless. Therefore I beg of you to receive my people as children and servants. They love you like a father and mother who consoles them and they hold all Aztecs as friends."

Moteczoma, with gladness in his face, answered that he was grateful for the love that was offered him and that he would be happy to preserve peace and to have them as perpetual friends. He also said that he desired to communicate all of these things to the officials and dignitaries and that he would later give an answer.

The king of Texcoco was lodged in a room within the royal household with much honor.

Moteczoma repeated the words of Nezahualcoyotl to his men and told them that the latter feared war and the fury of the Aztec nation. "He fears us since he says that the Aztecs when they make war cut down the forests, tear up the fruit trees and the century plants, destroy the prickly pears, ruin the houses, set the temples

88

on fire. In a word, he says that they burn everything and destroy until their hearts come to rest. Therefore, he asks for perpetual peace and concord."

Tlacaelel spoke in the name of all the councilmen. "O powerful king, we accept the peace and concord you propose and we are pleased that a truce be made. But let it be on one condition: we are not to lose our authority or rights lest the nations of the earth think it is we who have cravenly and timorously begged for peace. Let them not wish to make pacts with us and leave us without gain, without authority. They must understand that we are capable of conquering the entire world.

"It would be fitting that everyone hear that we have overcome the great kingdom of Texcoco. Let the people of Texcoco come out to meet us in the field and we will go out to encounter them on the plain of Chiconauhtla or at Chiquiuhtepec which belong to them. Let the word spread that they challenged us, and there we will pretend to fight with them. In the very first encounter let them turn their backs on us and we will pursue them without wounding or killing anyone. We will feign their capture; we will go after them as far as Tequiciztlan. By then only the captains and lords of our army will be following them. When we reach Totoltzinco the king of Texcoco will set fire to the temple and the battle will come to an end.

"Our fame, our honor will then be extolled and they will not have been harmed nor angered. The common people will be ready to serve us and the other provinces and cities will be fearful of us for having destroyed Texcoco and its provinces."

The king was well pleased with the advice of Tlacaelel and ordered him to journey to Texcoco to propose these thoughts to the king.

Even though it was against his honor, King Nezahualcoyotl agreed to these plans and gave orders to his nobles to prepare the warriors with great ceremony. At the same time they spread rumors of a war upon the Aztecs. They forbade all access to Texcoco, by land or water. The Aztecs did likewise.

On the appointed day the two armies, with great show of arms, insignia, and splendid armor met at Chiquiuhtepec and the feigned war began. Many of those who took part in it were ignorant of the agreement that had been made and at the beginning shouted great insults as if they were enemies. But as soon as the conflict commenced, the Texcocans began to abandon the field, retreating toward their city as had been determined. They reached a place called Tecaxtlan pursued only by a handful of Aztecs. When they entered the small town called Totoltzinco, which is at the entrance to Texcoco, Nezahualcoyotl was ready, and he gave orders that the temple be set on fire.

89

Seeing the flames the Aztecs lowered their weapons, for the burning of the temple was the sign of surrender. The king then appeared before his men, pretending great sadness and sorrow, and he begged the commanders of the Aztec forces to lay down their arms and cease their warlike labors, since the Texcocans were now subject to Mexico.

The Aztecs disbanded the army in order to return, not having harmed or injured anyone, nor stolen anything, as they had been prohibited from doing these things under pain of death. Thus the soldiers, who were not especially pleased with false wars, returned to their city. And the Aztec noblemen were taken into the vanquished city where they were received lavishly and given all kinds of splendid gifts for themselves and their ruler.

Nezahualcoyotl in the presence of all his nobles and men of his city, spoke these words: "O Aztecs, we are now your vassals and we have placed upon our shoulders the yoke of servitude forever. You have won this by the valor of your persons and by the strength of your arms. Therefore I will give my father and my mother, which is Mexico, lands to provide food and drink. He who is the image of the god Huitzilopochtli will be served by us."

"Lord," answered Tlacaelel, "we are thankful for what you have done to preserve peace between us and your king. But perhaps your vassals in the future will be offended and will not want to accept what has happened. They may regret that their strength and valor were not tested, and when we ask favors of you they may say they are not our vassals. I warn you of this."

Nezahualcoyotl assured him there would be neither rebellion nor complaints. He added that what he had done had been done with the approval of everyone and with the agreement of his subjects and of all the provinces. Never would they rebel against the royal crown of Mexico.

And so the Aztecs were given lands in Texcoco, beginning with the king and continuing with Tlacaelel and the other great lords and chieftains.[52]

This was the first war waged by the elder Moteczoma, and even though it was feigned it was carried out with all the conditions of a real war. Few or none of the neighboring cities were aware of its falseness, since it had been accomplished in great secrecy. This subterfuge of Nezahualcoyotl does not prove him to be weakhearted. On the contrary, it simply shows the love that he had for the Aztecs who were his relatives. In all the histories, in all that can be read about him, he is shown to be a valorous and spirited man. He performed great feats in his wars which he often attended in person. He was especially brave in the long wars waged against the Tecpanecs before he was enthroned, even though for some years he had been fleeing from them and had been obliged to go into hiding. In the end he made peace with them and was enthroned with the aid of the Aztecs and of his relative Itzcoatl. In payment of this help, he had agreed to the pretended war in order to live in peace with the Aztecs and to give them glory and to honor their name. In this way the entire country would fear them and be subject to them because of their fame as conquerors of such a great kingdom. He also favored them by giving them lands which would maintain them.

Moteczoma gave orders that stewards and overseers be placed on the lands belonging to the crown. They were to be responsible for cultivating them, bettering them, gathering the fruits, and storing the latter in the royal storehouses. And thus Coyoacan and Xochimilco were ordered to provide stewards. And so it was done: a nobleman from each of these cities was sent to oversee the royal farmlands, having been assigned certain privileges and wages.

Moteczoma now wished the three kingdoms of Mexico, Tacuba and Texcoco, together with their provinces, to increase and to live in well-being and tranquillity. And he begged all his chieftains to avoid a war with any nation, unless it was necessary, for he wished to preserve peace for some time.[53]

CHAPTER XVI ABOUT HOW MOTECZOMA THE FIRST, KNOWN AS THE ELDER, IN TIMES OF PEACE BEGAN TO BUILD THE TEMPLE, AND HOW CHALCO WAGED A WAR ON MEXICO AND LOST

For twelve or thirteen years, during the reign of Huehue Moteczoma, there was peace and tranquillity. As he was served and obeyed by all the neighboring cities, he determined to build the temple of his god Huitzilopochtli, like the great king Solomon who, having made peace with all the land, beloved by all the monarchs of the earth and aided by them, built the temple of Jerusalem.

Moteczoma gathered his council and told them his will in the following words: "Lords and chieftains of my kingdom, my heart tells me that I must construct a most sumptuous house to honor our god Huitzilopochtli. You know that he does not yet have a home, even though all of you have dwelling places. Yet he should be the first."

Having obtained approval from Tlacaelel and the council for the building of the temple, the king proposed that messengers be sent to Azcapotzalco, Coyoacan, Xochimilco, Cuitlahuac, Mizquic, Colhuacan and Texcoco, asking that laborers and materials such as lime, stone and wood be sent immediately.

"Powerful lord," protested Tlacaelel, "it would be more proper for you to use your royal authority to the full and treat your vassals as a master and supreme monarch. Every time messengers are sent they are chosen from among the nobility. Where will we find enough noblemen to act as messengers? Remember also that it is a heavy task for them. It would be more fitting if all the rulers, without exception, were brought before you. Standing in your presence, they would then receive your command to build the temple of our god."

Moteczoma agreed with this advice, saying, "Forgive me, lords; even though I am king I sometimes commit errors. That is why it is good that you aid me, giving me advice on things of importance to our city. Let the authorities be called immediately."

When the lords had arrived in Mexico they were brought into the presence of Moteczoma and he spoke to them in this manner: "O sovereigns of Texcoco, Xochimilco, Colhuacan, Cuitlahuac, Mizquic, Coyoacan, Azcapotzalco and Tacuba: You have been brought here because I wish you to consider that our god Huitzilopochtli, father and mother of all, under whose protection we stand, has no dwelling place where he can be worshipped. We have decided to build a sumptuous temple dedicated to his name and to our other gods. You well know you are obliged to serve him and I command you that as soon as you return to your cities you order your vassals to come to this work bringing the necessary materials of stone, lime and wood. All of this will redound to your honor and happiness. Let there be no negligence; let every man put his shoulder to the task so that it can be finished quickly."

"O masters," they answered, "and you especially, ruler of all the land, you who are obeyed by all, whose city stands in a marsh, in the midst of the reeds and the rushes: care for your health and your life; preserve them. We have heard your command and it will be done as well as possible, since it is our duty to obey in all things. Let this work be done for our lord in whose shade and protection we live and take refuge. Decide what is necessary and it will be brought to you."

The king and his men thanked them, being grateful for the good will they had shown. The king ordered them to bring heavy stone for the foundation and light stone for the building, together with lime and wood. And this was done.

Moteczoma then said to Tlacaelel, "The rulers of all the provinces have done what we ordered them and have obeyed with much willingness. They are beginning to bring the material for the work. Now I would like, with your consent, to send messengers to Chalco to visit Quateotl and Toteocitecuhtli. We will not give them orders but will approach them with great humility. We will tell them that we wish to build a temple for our god Huitzilopochtli and that we lack large stones in order to make the sculptures and images necessary to beautify it. Let them help us with a few stones from their hills, the largest that can be obtained."

92

Envoys were then sent to Chalco to ask for the stones, but they were twice refused by the rulers, Quateotl and Toteocitecuhtli, with harsh words. War broke out between Mexico and Chalco because of this and for several days there were battles and skirmishes with no victory on either side.

One day the Chalca, who were then at a place called Tlapitzahuayan, fearing the outcome of the war, asked for a truce since they wished to say something to the Aztecs.

"O Aztec brothers: know that five days from now we will celebrate the feast of our god Camaxtli and we wish to celebrate it with great solemnity and smear our temple with the blood of Aztecs so that our god will be the more glorified. Therefore, we ask that on that sacred day you join us in battle so that we may honor our god with your flesh. Allow us to pray and offer sacrifice and we will see whether he deigns to grant us this. Go and rest. We are not in a hurry, there will be time for everything."

Thereupon the two armies disbanded and returned to their cities, the Aztecs having left a guard at that place of Tlapitzahuayan.

When Moteczoma heard that the Chalca had promised their deity Camaxtli to celebrate the feast with Aztec blood, he vowed to his own god that he would celebrate his festival with the death of many Chalca. He swore that the Chalca alone would build the temple and that he would make a great and solemn fire sacrifice with the bodies of men from Chalco. Tlacaelel and the rest of the officials made the same oath, speaking lengthily and offensively against the Chalca.

When five days had passed and the truce that Chalco had requested came to an end, the Aztec forces went forth with great eagerness and ferocity. The soldiers were instructed to take prisoners alive so that the vow might be fulfilled.

When the army had left the city, Moteczoma gathered boys upwards of twelve years of age and armed them with bows and arrows, shields and swords. Under their captains, he sent them after the army. This was done with the hope that the Chalca might think that another army had come into the field, and so grow afraid.

The first army arrived at the appointed place and saw the forces of Chalco already on the slope of the hill of Tlapitzahuayan. The Chalca began to shout, "Come, Aztecs, come! Today this matter will be settled! The sacrificial knife is ready and our wives have already put the pots on the fire awaiting pieces of your flesh to be cooked!"

They began to scream even more loudly, and attacked the Aztecs. The Aztecs fought with such fury that the enemy was forced to retreat. At this point the boys, who from far away looked like mighty warriors, arrived. The Chalca were dismayed and began to abandon the field. Very soon they had withdrawn as far as a place called Nexticpac where they tried to regather their forces. However, the

93

Aztecs did not give them time to organize and pursued them as far as Tlapechhua-can. The soldiers of Chalco, climbing the hill of Tlapechhuacan, begged the Aztecs to let them rest and catch their breath.

But the Aztecs answered, "O little girls, do not ask for another truce because we will not grant it to you. We will fight far into the night if necessary! On this spot you will find out who the Aztecs are, and we will see who celebrates the feast, we or you! Let us see how you fulfill the oath that you have sworn to your god!"

With these words they continued to pursue them until they reached Cocotitlan, near Tepopolan. At this point a great number of warriors from Chalco were killed; there was not a man or boy in the Aztec army who did not kill some or take one or two prisoners. The survivors however hid with much cunning.

The Aztecs left soldiers to guard the battlefield in case the Chalca tried to return. The Aztec leaders went back to Tlapitzahuayan where they were received with great fear by the dwellers of that town. There they began to count the prisoners and found that they had caught three hundred seasoned warriors, without counting others of lower rank, which were two hundred. Thus they captured five hundred men of Chalco. These were sent to Mexico and on the day after their arrival, by order of Tlacaelel and the king, they were immediately sacrificed to Huitzilopochtli.

In this way was fulfilled the oath that had been sworn, and the temple was reddened with the blood of five hundred men. A fire sacrifice was ordained—the most terrible and horrendous sacrifice that can be imagined. A great bonfire was made in a large brazier dug in the ground; this was called the divine hearth. Into this great mass of embers men were thrown alive. Before they expired, their hearts were torn out of their bodies and offered to the god.

Thus the steps and the chambers were bathed with the blood of the prisoners.

CHAPTER XVII WHICH TREATS OF THE CRUEL ATTACK MADE BY THE CHALCA UPON THE AZTECS BETWEEN AMECAMECA AND TEPOPOLAN TO AVENGE THE BLOODY SACRIFICE THAT THEY HAD SUFFERED. AND HOW THREE BROTHERS OF THE KING OF MEXICO WERE KILLED AND THE CHALCA FINALLY SUBDUED

Once the sacrifice had ended and the Aztecs were satiated with human flesh and drunk with the victory of which they were so proud, King Moteczoma told Tlacaelel to form the army again. As soon as they were ready they departed in the direction of Chalco, passing through Tepopolan unafraid. Soon they reached a place called Tlacuilocan near Amecameca which was the capital of the kingdom.

The men of Chalco, angered by this boldness, came out of the city of Amecameca in great numbers. Every boy joined them with his shield and sword, together with people from neighboring towns. Having surrounded the Aztecs, the Chalca fell upon them with such fury that the Aztec soldiers found themselves in an extremely difficult position. They were now forced to conquer or die, and they formed a circle. The battle raged with the greatest confusion, both sides slaying men right and left. After some time, weary with fighting the entire day, both sides abandoned the field, taking whatever prisoners they had managed to capture.

The Aztecs withdrew to Itztopatepec, and at a place called Acolco they counted their losses and found that three brothers of the king were missing. They went back to the field and there discovered the bodies of these three warriors covered with deep wounds, surrounded by many dead soldiers. One of the brothers was named Chahuaque, another Tlacahuepan and the third Quetzalcuauh. Their bodies were brought before Moteczoma and Tlacaelel who had remained in Tlapechuacan confident that their valiant countrymen would be victorious.

When the king saw the bodies covered with deep wounds, he and Tlacaelel sorrowed greatly over the death of their courageous brothers. The king began to moan and lament, wailing, "O valorous brothers of mine: happy are you who died proving your great personal courage. Go now in honor, wrapped in the precious stones and rich plumage of your heroic deeds, performed while fighting for your country and the honor of your brother!"

Turning toward Tlacaelel, who was mute, as if turned to stone, he asked, "How does it affect you, Tlacaelel, seeing your brothers lying here dead?"

"O mighty prince," responded Tlacaelel, "I do not marvel at such deaths. That is how wars are fought! Remember Huitzilihuitl the Elder, our lord and king, who died in Colhuacan before we were born; behold how he found eternal fame as a valiant man. The Aztec nation needs bold men such as those who lie before you. There will be more like them in Mexico. How long must we mourn them? If we stay here weeping we will not be able to accomplish more important matters."

At the beginning of the month, Xocotl Huetzi, on the day which was the special feast of the Aztecs, they prepared for the festivities and celebrated them by sacrificing men from Chalco who had been brought as prisoners.

The Chalca also celebrated their feast, but before the sacrifice began they saw among the prisoners a first cousin of King Moteczoma, a spirited youth by the name of Ezhuahuacatl. The Chalca, knowing that the prisoner came from the royal lineage of Mexico, consulted among themselves and decided to free him and make him king of Chalco.

When the young man heard about this he laughed and told the other Aztec prisoners, "Do you know, brethren, that the Chalca want to make me their king and lord? I would be willing if I knew that all of you would be given your freedom. But as this is not so, I will die with you since I did not come here to reign but to fight and perish like a man. I have already sold my life and with it bought the Chalca who are to serve my children and grandchildren and all their descendants. And all of you have done the same!"

When the Chalca came to Ezhuahuacatl and made their proposal, he feigned an agreement. He told them it was well and asked for a favor before he was enthroned. He begged that they bring a tree trunk about twenty yards high and that they place a platform at its top. On this he wished to play and sport with the Aztec prisoners. The Chalca brought him a thick pole and placed on the very top a small platform. When they told him it was ready, he came out surrounded by the other prisoners.[54]

A drum was brought and all began to dance around the pole. Ezhuahuacatl then said farewell to the Aztecs, crying out, "Friends, the time has come! Die like brave men!" Having said these words he began to climb the pole. When he arrived at the wooden platform he began to sing and dance. When the song was finished, he shouted in a loud voice, "O Chalca, know that with my death I will have bought your lives and that you will serve my children and grandchildren! My royal blood will be paid for with yours!" At this he cast himself down and was shattered to bits.

The people of Chalco were astonished at this deed and began to worry over what he had said. In spite of their troubled spirit, they took the prisoners and, having tied them together, sacrificed them by shooting arrows at them. The Chalca always sacrificed in this way: as their god was the deity of hunting they killed their victims with arrows.[55]

Sorrowing over the loss of Ezhuahuacatl and of the flower of the warriors of Mexico, Moteczoma and Tlacaelel ordered that straw houses and huts be made near the same battlefield at Amecameca, and swore that they would not return to their city until they had conquered.

That night the Chalca and Aztec armies were on the alert. They stood watch through the night, fearful of an attack while asleep. In the middle of the night two owls were heard, hooting to one another, and it sounded as if in their hooting one said:

*Ciuacoatl, "Snake Woman," an earth goddess and goddess of childbirth. Page from the post-Conquest* Codex Magliabecchiano. *Courtesy New York Public Library.*

"*Tiacan, tiacan!*—Mighty, mighty!"

And the other answered:

"*Nocne, nocne!*—Alas, alas!"

Both Aztecs and Chalca were terrified by these cries, as they took them to be an ill omen. While they yet trembled with fear the two owls continued their song.

"*Tetec, tetec!*—Cut, cut!"

And the other answered:

"*Yollo, yollo!*—Hearts, hearts!"

For the third time the owls sang their song, hooting:

"*Quetechpol chichil, quetechpol chichil!*—Red throats, red throats!"

And the other answered:

"*Chalca, Chalca!*—O men of Chalco! O men of Chalco!"

On hearing this Tlacaelel arose and went to the king where many of the Aztecs heard his words. "O Aztecs, listen to the owls, hear how they announce our victory! Some divine thing moves those birds to hoot in such a manner. It is not possible that they are doing it by themselves! Someone moves their beaks, announcing our triumph! It is fated, O Aztecs! Courage and strength! Let us not in our weakness lose what has been sent to us from above!"[56]

When morning came, the Chalca, still fearful of the ill omen that the owls had brought the night before, when they had heard their name clearly mentioned, decided to make use of trickery. Cuauhteotl, sovereign of Amecameca, had three sons, adult men already experienced in war. It was decided that these three, feigning fear of death and of the ill omen, should pretend to flee from their city secretly and go over to the Aztec side. There they would declare that they had come to serve them and to show them a certain pass through which the city of Amecameca could be taken easily.

So it was done, and the three sons of Cuauhteotl, "Divine Tree," very secretly—pretending to be fleeing—came to the Aztec army. To Moteczoma they said, "O great lord, we are brothers, sons of Cuauhteotl, king of Chalco, and we have come to serve you through fear of the ruin of our people and our country."

"My brothers and I," said the one whose name was Teoquizqui, "wish to guide your army so that the city can be taken and destroyed."

When Moteczoma consulted Tlacaelel about this, the latter gave the following advice. "I believe that in their despair they have come to seek salvation and not to aid us. They wish to guide us into an ambush or onto rocky cliffs where we may fall. Even if what they promised were true, they would say later that they had won the war and would share none of their glory with us. Let these nobles remain here if they wish, and if they want to go, let them. We will continue with our struggle and we will win. Let us show our manliness through our personal acts of bravery, not through the aid and plans of others!"

On the next day the two armies met on the battlefield and, after a fierce struggle, the Chalca commander was captured and the Aztecs forced the enemy to withdraw. In this way the Chalca began to lead the Aztecs toward a cliff called Cuauhtexcac, Rocky Place of the Eagles, which is on this side of the Iztaccihuatl, Mountain of the White Woman. But the Aztecs, fearing an ambush in that direction, began to force the enemy toward the road which ascends the mountains to a pass between the volcano Popocatepetl, Mountain of Smoke, and the White Woman.[57] They wounded and killed all the people they caught up with, and the old men and women and the children of Amecameca, who had already climbed to those heights to watch the battle, saw that their city was being sacked by the Aztecs and that the latter were pursuing the men of Amecameca without sparing one. The old people, the women and children then fled toward Huexotzinco where Chalca soldiers had been posted.

When Tlacaelel saw the flight of the women and children, he ordered one of his captains to cut off their means of escape but not to harm them. He told the captain to comfort them, calm them and tell them not to take refuge in a strange land, as the war had ended and he did not wish more vengeance.

The captain, known as Tlacatecatl, went with his squadron in all haste and stopped the people who were fleeing toward Huexotzinco and told them Tlacaelel's words. The Chalca returned and having prostrated themselves before Tlacaelel they surrendered their arms and cried out, "O Aztecs, we have done everything in our power to defend ourselves and we can do no more. All we can give you is wood for your buildings, stone, loads of earth, carved canoes, laborers to till your lands and masons for your works, good soldiers for your wars and foodstuffs for your campaigns. These things we can give you."

In another history, not quite so reliable as the one I have been using, it is stated that the war lasted thirteen years and that on the day of their defeat the Chalca also offered to give the Aztecs comely maidens so that they could possess them. It is also said that before the Aztecs broke camp the king ordered that all those who had fulfilled their duty in this war should have their noses pierced as a sign of valor. In this way they would enter Mexico with feathers and golden jewels hanging from their noses like moustaches. These perforations were made in the cartilage of the nose.

It is also said that Tlacaelel ordered all the Chalca who had fought courageously to be adorned in like manner, saying to them, "Friends, until this time we

98

have never fought with a people who could equal you. It is just, then, that since we have fought bravely you should be honored also."

CHAPTER XVIII WHICH TREATS OF HOW THE PEOPLE OF TEPEACA WAGED WAR AGAINST THE AZTECS AND OF HOW THE FORMER WERE DEFEATED, HARSHLY TREATED AND BROUGHT AS PRISONERS TO MEXICO CITY TO BE SACRIFICED. WITH A DESCRIPTION OF THE FUNERAL CEREMONIES IN HONOR OF THOSE AZTECS WHO HAD BEEN KILLED IN THE WAR WITH CHALCO

Shortly after funerals for the war dead had ended, news came to Mexico that the people of Tepeaca had murdered a number of Aztec, Texcocan and Tecpanec merchants who had been trading in that city. All of their merchandise had been stolen from them and their bodies thrown to the wild animals.

Moteczoma informed Tlacaelel and all the important Aztec chieftains of these events, stating that he desired to capture the rulers of Tepeaca, bring them to Mexico and give them a cruel death. Tlacaelel, however, answered that this was not sufficient punishment and that it would be better to prepare for war and to destroy them mercilessly.

Four envoys then journeyed to Tepeaca to challenge Coyolcue, sovereign of that city, with this message: "Most noble sir, Moteczoma and Tlacaelel and the dignitaries of Mexico send you this shield and sword together with these plumes so that you may feather your head. They also bid you wait since they will soon visit you. You have robbed and killed merchants in all the provinces on this side of the Mountain of the White Woman and therefore we do not wish any dealings between our province and yours."

Moteczoma and Tlacaelel then began to prepare their men for war, and sent messengers to the neighboring cities to obtain great quantities of toasted maize cakes, toasted grains of corn, and maize flour. They also obtained great quantities of bean flour, salt and chilli, pumpkin seeds, together with pots, plates, grinding stones and mats in order to make tents and huts in the field.

The brave captains and seasoned warriors of Mexico and its domains arrived at a hill called Coyopetlayo, near the city of Tepeaca. Spies were immediately sent into Tepeaca to see what preparations were being made and to see if a fence or wall had been built. They also wished to find out the number of enemy warriors. But the spies soon returned to the camp saying that they had seen neither wall nor guards nor warlike activities. Moteczoma was annoyed at the slight importance accorded the Aztec army, and spoke the following words to his men:

"O Aztecs, do not make haste! Go slowly, for before the sun rises tomorrow this matter will have been settled. Let the men separate into groups and let us accomplish in one blow what we would have done in a slower manner. Let some go to Tecali, others to Cuauhtinchan, others to Acatzinco, and let us conquer these capitals so that they become our vassals."

By this time the camp had been set up. Each one of the tribes had its own section of tents; the Texcocans on one side, the Chalca on another, the Xochimilca on another and the Tecpanecs on yet another. The soldiers divided into four companies, each with its own captain and banner. At dusk the companies set out in the directions determined, and before dawn the allies had overcome the four cities as Moteczoma had promised.

I am told that the people of Tepeaca did not fight or defend themselves since they felt their resistance would be futile, and in a cowardly way they allowed themselves to be killed like wild animals. Coyolcue, the chieftain, weeping bitterly, crossed his arms and prostrated himself before the Aztecs, begging for mercy. If the men of Tepeaca actually fought or tried to defend themselves this chronicle does not say so, and my only intention in this work is to translate the story from the Aztec language, Nahuatl, into Spanish.

Tepeaca was now a vassal of the Aztecs and promised to be a perpetual tributary, paying in maize, chilli, salt, pumpkin seeds, cloth, sandals, palm leaf mats, and deerskins. The Tepeacans also promised to provide labor, as carriers on the roads and as workmen to build huts and set up tents in war. They later offered slaves for the abominable sacrifice made to the idols.

The Aztecs were taken into the city of Tepeaca and given rich presents of cloth, skins, sandals, stones, jewels, gold, fine plumage, shields, insignia, and weapons. Similar presents were given by the towns of Tecali, Cuauhtinchan and Acatzinco, though they were smaller than Tepeaca. All of these conquered people were given orders to go to Mexico to acknowledge and adore the god Huitzilopochtli as he was now their supreme lord.

The priests and elders from the temples came out to receive the victorious army at a place called Acachinanco at the gates of Mexico. It must be explained here that in the temples there was a regular hierarchy such as exists in our own cathedrals. There were offices similar to those of archbishop, dean, canon, chaplain, acolyte

100

and sexton. The high priest was called by different names; some called him Papa, others called him Topiltzin, "Our Lord." In a word, every province had its own high-sounding name for him. Other priests were called Tecuacuiltin, others Cuauhuehuetque, others Chalmeca, others Tlenamacazque, others Calmecahuehuezteque, others Mozauhque, and others Tlamacazque. There were so many titles and dignities among the priests that I am unable to record them all here.

The priestly hierarchy then came out to greet the conquerors. They were dressed in their tunics of different styles and colors, some down to the floor, others not quite so long, others with fringes, some with the border in the form of circles—all finely worked with different colors and types of thread. On their heads were garlands made of paper or skin and on their foreheads were headbands with which their headdresses were tied. The headbands were in the form of folded shields and painted in various colors. From the backs of the priests called Cuauhuehuetque and Tecuacuiltin hung small gourds strung with leather ribbons. These little gourds were called *yectecomatl*. They all carried in their hands black staffs.

The priests formed a great procession, some walking on one side of the road and some on the other. Those called Tlenamacazque, which means "incense burners," came with their braziers in their hands. When all the prisoners arrived, the priests threw incense into the braziers and incensed the future victims, since they belonged to the gods. Then the priests called Tecuacuiltin (which means "Gods," or "Images of Gods") arrived and broke pieces of maize bread, which were kept in the temples strung on cords, and offered them to the captives. The priests then addressed the prisoners in the following way:

> "We welcome you
> To this city of Mexico Tenochtitlan
> Which is in the great pool of water,
> Where the eagle sang and the snake hissed!
> Where the fishes fly,
> Where the blue waters came out to join the red waters!
> Here among the reeds, here among the rushes,
> Where reigns the god Huitzilopochtli.
> Do not think that you have come here to live;
> You have come here to die,
> To offer your chests and your throats to the knife.
> Only in this way, through your deaths, has it been your fortune
> To know this great city.
> We salute you and comfort you with these words:

## chapter XVII

You have not come here because of weakness,
But because of your manliness.
You will die here but your fame will live forever."

When the prisoners had heard this greeting they were given a sacred wine to drink which is called *teooctli*, meaning literally "Divine Wine." After drinking it, they were taken to the temple where one by one they were forced to pass by the feet of the idol, making signs of great reverence to it. Afterward they were taken to the palace where they were forced to perform the same ceremony in front of the royal seat of King Moteczoma, since the monarchs in this land were adored as gods.

Presently they were given cloaks, loincloths and sandals, and after having eaten they were taken to the market place where a platform stood. They were given a drum and all of the victims danced upon the platform. For this dance they were given shields of splendid feather work, flowers and tobacco to smoke, and the latter comforted them greatly. Tobacco was generally distributed after meals. They say that it was good for the digestion; a feast without tobacco was not a real feast.

At this time the dignitaries from Tepeaca went to acknowledge and adore Huitzilopochtli. Coyolcue, and two other lords, Chichtli and Chiauhcoatl, together with many princes from the domains of Tepeaca, entered the temple and offered the god splendid white fans, rich feathers in different forms, bows and arrows, finely painted bone armbands, the tanned skins of diverse animals, and nose plugs. They then took out some small blades and drew blood from their tongues and ears with them. They also "ate the earth" at the foot of the idol.[58] All of this ceremony was later performed in front of the king and Tlacaelel.

On the next day Tlacaelel spoke to the chieftains of Tepeaca and instructed them on the tribute that must be paid. He also told them, "You are hereby ordered, since your city is situated in a place through which many travel, to take great care of the travelers from all the provinces, natives as well as strangers. Let none of them be mistreated, robbed or offended in any way, and be especially careful of the merchants who trade with Xoconochco and Guatemala since these are the ones who enrich and ennoble the earth. They feed the poor, they maintain villages, and should anyone mistreat them or harm them you will notify us so that they may be punished.

102

"The king also orders," continued Tlacaelel, "that all those who wish to may live in your country. They must be given land where they will dwell and bring honor to your city. The king also wishes that a great market place be built in

Cuauhxicalli, *a great stone in the form of a jaguar.*
*This vessel was used as a container for the hearts of*
*victims of sacrifice. National Museum, Mexico City.*
*Photo National Institute of Anthropology and*
*History, Mexico City.*

Tepeaca so that all the merchants of the land may trade there on an appointed day. In this market there will be sold rich cloth, stones, jewels, feather work of different colors, gold, silver and other metals, the skins of animals such as jaguars and ocelots, cacao, fine loincloths and sandals. A governor, whose name in Coacuech, will be placed over you and you must obey him and consider him to be a representative of the royal person. You may return to your cities now."

Thus it was done. The governor was well received in Tepeaca and he began to collect the tribute for Mexico every eighty days.

CHAPTER XIX WHICH TREATS OF THE GREAT DISCORD
THAT AROSE BETWEEN THE AZTECS AND THE HUAXTECS OF TAMAPACHCO,
TOCHPAN AND TZINCOAC, AND HOW, AFTER HAVING FOUGHT,
THE HUAXTECS WERE VANQUISHED AND KILLED

Huehue Moteczoma, the Elder, had reigned eleven years when an amazing thing took place: it began to snow so heavily and so often that it is said that the snow reached to one's knees. People became so frightened and they were so unprepared in their light clothing, that one could not see a single person on the roads or streets. This snow fell for six days, and the mountains and hills remained covered for many days.

At this time the Aztec nation was at peace, but peace flies from those who long for it. News came that the Huaxtecs had attacked and killed all the merchants and traders who were active in the area. These merchants came from Mexico and its provinces. Having committed this crime, and assumed an aggressive attitude, the Huaxtecs surrounded their towns with five walls, one after the other.

The Huaxtec people were so strong that the entire land trembled with fear of them. Even their young sons played at war and pretended to bring captives home; they were constantly preparing themselves by fasts, thirst and nudity. They would sleep on the ground, they would carry great burdens to harden themselves. It is said that they could gather a hundred thousand men for war.

105

In spite of the strength of the Huaxtecs, Moteczoma and Tlacaelel gathered the armies of their allies and subjects and prepared for war. Soon after this the first armed forces began to depart toward the land of the Huaxtecs.[59]

Many superstitious ceremonies were performed by the wives of the warriors while the war lasted. For example, as a sign of sadness and mourning, they did not wash their faces from the day their husbands left until they returned.

Another custom was to rise at midnight and build a fire. As soon as the firewood was burning the woman would go out into the street and sweep. Once she had swept, she would bathe her body without allowing the water to touch her face or head. Having bathed she would sit down to grind maize and then prepare some very small, square maize cakes together with some small, long breads. Then she would grind a bit of toasted corn and put it into a deep gourd. She would then enter the shrine where the idols were kept; these were small rooms similar to the ones in which they keep the saints today. They were used only for this purpose and the same holds true in our times. Having entered that chamber she would take out the leg bones of the prisoners whom her husband had captured in war and wrap them in paper. Having hung them from the beams she would take a brazier and put fire and incense in it, placing it below these bones. She also burned incense before all the little household idols, which were many, and while the incense was burning, she prayed:

> "O Lord of All Created Things!
> O Lord of the Heavens and of the Earth,
> Of the Wind and of the Sun,
> Of the Water, of the Night and of the Day!
> Have pity upon your servant, upon your creature
> Who now goes about the hills and valleys,
> About the plains and rocky places,
> Offering you his sweat and his panting breath.
> He is your eagle, he is your jaguar!
> He works ceaselessly to serve you
> In this woeful life.
> I beseech you, O Lord, I beg you
> To allow him a few more days in this world.
> Hear me, O Lord!"

Having made this petition, she would lie down again, but before dawn came she would rise and sweep the street once more. All of this was performed again at midday and at sunset, and lasted during all the time that the husband was away at war.

After the Aztec army had passed through Tulancingo, where they had been well received, they set up their camp close to the Huaxtec enemies. An old captain then stood up and addressed the men. "O valorous soldiers, you who come from all the nations and provinces! You who have abandoned your hearths and homes where you lived happily! You have arrived at a place where you may perish, like wild grass when it is set on fire. Contemplate your death and think of nothing else. You have left your fathers and mothers, uncles, aunts, relatives, and you will never see them again. You are now to fight against a cruel and savage people, whose customs and way of life are completely alien to our own. You have come here to conquer or die since this is your mission in life."

After these words had been spoken the army was given a meal and orders were delivered that each squadron carry a high banner with the sign of its ward and to shout the name of this ward during the battle. Then some old men began to marshal the troops and prepare them for battle. These men carried staffs in their hands and wore headbands, long shell ear-plugs and lip ornaments.

The first warriors marshaled into action were those called Cuachic, who were similar to an order of knights. Each one had sworn not to flee even if faced by twenty enemies, nor take a step backward. There was another order called Otomi,[60] whose members were recognized by their hair which was cut short above the ear, and these had made a vow not to retreat even if faced by ten or twelve enemies but rather to die.

All these soldiers were ordered to lie down upon the earth with their shields and swords in their hands, about two thousand men from all the provinces. They were then covered with grass until not a man could be seen. Then the captains and seasoned soldiers were formed into squadrons, and next to each warrior was placed a youth who had never been to war before. Orders had been given to the soldiers that they take care of the younger men and give them protection.

The Huaxtecs soon appeared, yelling, "None of you will return to Mexico to tell about this! We will kill you and cut off your heads! Don't you know that we have herbs with which we can kill you just by touching you with them?" The Huaxtecs then attacked, making a great din with the wooden rattles which hung from their helmets and with the large metal rattles which they wore on their backs and feet, all of these making a weird noise. Their heads were feathered and their bodies and faces painted in different colors, and some wore in their noses large, thick, crystal nose-plugs or plugs of precious stones. The Huaxtec warriors were so hideous that the mere sight of them terrified. They bore shields and carried in their hands darts with sharp flint points.

Once the battle had begun, the Aztecs, hearing the ghastly howling of this ferocious and loathsome enemy, which was enough to make one's hair stand on end, pretended to retreat. They ran to the place where the great warriors waited in ambush. When the enemy had entered the trap, the men concealed by the grass stood up and annihilated them. Not one of the Huaxtecs escaped; all were killed or taken prisoner. Even the youths took many captives.

After this the Aztecs entered the city, sacked and burned the temple and killed old and young. All of this was done with great cruelty and with the determination to remove all trace of the Huaxtec people from the face of the earth. However, many of the rulers promised great tribute—such as cloth, cacao, gold, gems, feathers, brilliantly colored parrots and other fine tropical birds, macaws, as well as chilli, pumpkin seeds and other foodstuffs—and thus were spared.

The Aztecs were taken into the palace and were given barbecued fish, great quantities of shrimp, white honey, turkey, pineapples and other fruits. They were also given great bundles of richly worked and colored cloth.

Some time later the conquering army set out for Mexico, taking the prisoners and captives, all of them with their hands tied behind and collars about their necks. They went along singing sadly, weeping and lamenting their fate, since they knew that they were to be sacrificed.

Whenever the Aztecs arrived in a town they were well received, lodged and given food generously. They were served turkeys, rabbits, deer, chocolate, maize cakes, fruit, and breads of different types. This was done in all the towns through which they passed. If their hosts were careless or indifferent the Aztecs would rob and sack villages, strip people of their clothing, beat them, dishonor them and rob them of all their possessions. The entire land trembled with fear of them. This ill treatment was generally visited upon the natives even when they treated the Aztec army well. The Aztecs were the cruelest and most devilish people that can be imagined because of the way they treated their vassals, worse even than the way the Spaniards treated and treat them. One did not dare to question them at any time.

When the Aztec forces arrived in their capital, Tlacaelel ordered that the captives be distributed among the wards. Each ward was to guard and maintain a certain number of them. Tlacaelel then instructed them in these words:

"Take care that they do not escape
Take care that they do not die!
Behold, they are the Children of the Sun!
Feed them well; let them be fat and desirable for the sacrifice
On the day of the feast of our god.
Let our god rejoice in them since they belong to him!"

The head of each ward, then, took charge of certain prisoners and treated them well, honoring them as if they had been gods. They called them "Children of the Sun," "Children of the Lord of the Earth" and "Gift of the Gods."

When the warriors had returned to their homes to rest, the elders would make ceremonial visits to each of them, beginning with the principal captain. They would arrive at his house and congratulate him on his return. The lord would receive them, give them food and offer them mantles and loincloths. Once the meal had ended, one of the elders spoke:

"Lord, you have returned to Mexico
Which is your birthplace!
You have favored us, you have given us presents,
And we kiss your hands.
Had you died in the war or on the road
We would not be rejoicing in your presence,
O you, who are our jewel and precious feather.
Let us weep for joy!"

The elders then began to weep while the noble warrior consoled them. Every day the elders visited a great captain by order of rank and every day they were given food and splendid clothing, which would last them many years, or until another war broke out. These elders commended the noblemen to the gods and prayed and did penance for them.

CHAPTER **XX** WHICH TREATS OF THE CRUEL SACRIFICE OF
THE HUAXTECS AT THE HANDS OF THE AZTECS. WITH A DESCRIPTION OF
THE SKINNING CEREMONY CALLED TLACAXIPEHUALIZTLI.
AND HOW THE LORDS OF ALL THE NEIGHBORING STATES
AND CITIES WERE INVITED TO WITNESS THIS SPECTACLE
AND GREAT FESTIVITIES

Many days passed after the return of the Aztecs from the war in the land of the Huaxtecs. Tlacaelel then reminded King Moteczoma of the work on the temple, which they had begun to build, and said that it was necessary to carve a wide stone to serve as an altar or table upon which sacrifice would be made. This

Tlacaelel, in addition to being bold and cunning in the trickery of war, also invented devilish, cruel and frightful sacrifices. He then told Moteczoma to order that the stone be carved and that in its carvings appear the war of liberation of their forebears from Azcapotzalco, so that this war might be given perpetual memory.

Tlacaelel gathered the stone cutters and sculptors, saying these words to them: "Master craftsmen, our Lord wishes you to cut a large round stone which we will call *temalacatl*, which means "stone wheel." On it are to be inscribed our wars with the Tecpanecs, since this sculpture must be an eternal reminder of those admirable deeds. I beg you to give yourselves glory in this, since you will be remembered forever if it is well carved. Let it be done as soon as possible."

The craftsmen were happy to carry out his orders, and they sought a large stone about a yard and a half wide. They made smooth its surface and represented in their carving the war with Azcapotzalco. This labor was very finely done and finished so swiftly that some days later they were able to notify the king that the table of sacrifice was ready. The king then ordered a base to be made for it to rest upon. And so a high platform was made, slightly taller than a man, and the carved rock was placed upon it.

Now that the stone had been set up, they called certain youths who lived in seclusion within the temple, and gave them the office of carrying out this sacrifice which the devil had invented and taught them. They were told, "Take care that every day you prepare yourselves to perform this sacrifice, since the lords of all the cities and neighboring provinces will be invited to the feast and you must not put us to shame." The young men thanked them and promised to practice and rehearse according to the instructions that were given to them.

When the beginning of the month called *Tlacaxipehualiztli*,[61] "Skinning of Men,"[62] approached, they invited monarchs from the entire land: they called the kings of Texcoco and of Tacuba, the rulers of Chalco and Xochimilco, kings from the Marquesado, from Cohuixco, Matlatzinco and from the Mazahua tribes.

Once the guests had arrived the king gave them presents—fine mantles and loin cloths, rich clothes of feather work, wide sashes, sandals and lip-plugs of precious stones, golden ear-plugs and nose pendants. A great feast followed, with quantities of fowl, meat from the hunt, different breads, chocolate drinks and pulque. After the guests and eaten and drunk they were assigned booths adorned with flowers and reeds within which they could sit and watch. The strangers sat down in the decorated boxes and awaited the ceremony, which had been unknown till this time.

110

The prisoners were brought out and placed in a line at a place called *Tzompant-itlan*, which means something like "Mount Calvary" or "Place of Skulls."[63] At this place there were long platforms upon which stood a great rack where the skulls of the sacrificial victims were strung and where they remained permanently as relics. The prisoners were arranged in a file and told to dance. All the victims were smeared with plaster, their heads were feathered and on the top of the head each wore some white feathers tied to his hair. Their eyelids were blackened and their lips painted red.

The priests who were to perform the sacrifice stood in a long row, according to their rank. Each one of them was disguised as a god. One of them wore the garb of Huitzilopochtli, Humming Bird on the Left; another was dressed as Quetzalcoatl, Plumed Serpent; another represented Toci, Our Grandmother; another was Yopi, The Yope; still another, Opochtzin, The Left-Handed One; another was Totec, Our Lord; and finally one of them wore the garments of Itzpapalotl, Obsidian Butterfly. One of them was disguised as a jaguar, another as an ocelot and yet another as an eagle. All carried their swords and shields, inlaid with gold and gems, and all these priests were covered with featherwork and rich jewels.

For all of these an arbor, beautifully adorned with flowers and paintings of the gods, had been prepared. This arbor was made of the branches and leaves of a tree called *tzapotl*; that is why it was called *Tzapotl Calli*, "House of Tzapotl." Within it were seats, also made of tzapotl wood, where all of them sat down according to age and rank. This arbor had been erected on the very summit of the pyramid, in a place called Yopico.

When the priests dressed as gods had been seated—and they were the ones who would perform the sacrifice—the elders called *Tecuacuiltin*, and the chanters of the temple, brought forth the drum, and to the rhythm of its beat they began to dance and sing.

The high priest, fully dressed for the rite, then came forth, with tall feathers in his diadem, his arms covered with golden bands, from which hung large, shining, green and blue feathers. Carrying in his hand the great knife of black stone called *ixcuahuac*, he went forward and took his place.

After he was seated, they brought out one of the prisoners from the land of the Huaxtecs and tied his neck with a rope which emerged from a hole in the middle of the great round stone. Once they had tied him they handed him a wooden sword and a shield; the sword was not equipped with blades but was feathered from top to bottom. At this point the high priest, who for this day was called "Drinker of the Night" and "Our Lord," rose from his seat and slowly began to descend the steps until he had reached the place where the prisoner was. He walked around the stone twice, sanctifying it, and having tied the victim again he returned to his seat.

An old man disguised as an ocelot appeared then and gave four wooden balls to the victim, telling him to try to defend himself with them. He wrapped a piece of cloth around the prisoner's body and gave him a little Divine Wine to drink. After this he withdrew, leaving the victim alone.

One of the men disguised as a god then approached the stone dancing, with his shield and sword in his hand; well protected with his helmet he went up to the place where the prisoner stood. The poor wretch upon the stone threw the wooden balls at him. These were evaded by the sacrificer if he was skillful, whereupon the prisoner picked up his feathered sword and defended himself the best he could.

Some of the victims possessed such ability that they wore out two or three attackers before they could be wounded. But as soon as the victim was wounded, four priests, painted black, with long braided hair, dressed in garments similar to chasubles, ascended the stone and laid the wounded man on his back, holding him down by the feet and hands. The high priest then rose from his seat, went to the stone and opened his chest with the knife. He took out his heart and offered the vapor that came out of it to the sun. As soon as the heart was cold he delivered it to certain ministers who placed it in a vessel called the *cuauhxicalli*, "eagle gourd," which was another large stone dedicated to the sun, containing in its center a concavity which was also used for another type of sacrifice.

These ceremonies were performed in the case of all the prisoners, each one in his turn. However, there were some who, on being given the shield and sword, felt the sword with their fingers. When they realized that the sword was not edged with stone but with feathers they cast it away and threw themselves willingly upon their backs on the stone. The priests then took hold of them and the high priest opened their chests and extracted their hearts. Some of the victims, such as those mentioned above, were unwilling to go through so much ceremonial, and they cast themselves upon the stone immediately, seeking a quick death. Whether one defended himself well or whether one fought badly, death was inevitable. That is why all those priests were required; when one was tired of sacrificing another would take his place. At the most it meant another half-hour of life.

After all the victims had died, the corpses were taken back to the place where, as live men, they had stood in a row, and the bodies cast down. Those who had taken part in the sacrifices entered certain rooms of the temple with the high priest, took off their ritual garb and, with great reverence, put it away in a clean place.

The lords from the provinces who had come to observe the sacrifice were

112

shocked and bewildered by what they had seen and they returned to their homes filled with astonishment and fright.[64]

Moteczoma now called those who had performed the sacrifice and ordered them to be dressed in fine mantles, loincloths and sandals, and thanked them for their skillful work. He commanded that they be given maize, chian seed, and cacao in great quantities. This was done to encourage others to imitate these exercises, which, according to the Aztecs, were filled with virtue and honor.

By ancient tradition, the feast was followed, the next day, by another celebration. At this time the king gave his noblemen fine mantles, rich loincloths and sandals, lip-plugs, ear-plugs, shields, beautiful weapons, insignia and gold armbands. These were the rewards for men who were valiant.

Once the rewards had been distributed, those who had been sacrificed were flayed and the *Tototectin,* "Bird Lords," put on those skins and wore them. Carrying their shields in one hand and staffs covered with rattles in the other, they went from house to house. First they visited the houses of the nobility and then the homes of common people, asking for alms, wearing the skins all the time. The rich gave them mantles and loincloths and the common people gave them fistfuls of corn and other edibles.

For twenty days these men begged. At the end of this time they had gathered great quantities of clothing and food. The flayed skins had been worn in honor of the god of the feast.

When the twenty days had passed they took off the reeking skins and buried them in a special room in the temple. In this way ended the feast and the sacrifice of the Huaxtecs, which had been made to solemnize the first use of the carved stone. Here ends also the chapter on this subject which I found written in the Nahuatl tongue.

CHAPTER XXI WHICH TREATS OF WAR WITH ORIZABA.
WITH A DESCRIPTION OF HOW THAT PROVINCE STIRRED UP TROUBLE
AGAINST THE AZTECS AND HOW THEY WERE
KILLED AND DESTROYED

Having sacrificed the Huaxtecs in this terrible way, the Aztecs believed that they had intimidated the whole world. Some days later they decided to send messengers to Cempoala in the province of Cuetlaxtla, asking the rulers there to send them some conch shells, live turtles and scallops and other curious sea products, since these people lived right next to the ocean. The Aztecs had heard about these objects and wished them for the cult of their god.

Laden with gifts, the envoys arrived in the city of Ahuilizapan, now corrupted to Orizaba, and asked to be lodged in that place. Though they were not well received they were given what they requested. While they ate and rested, the authorities sent a message to Cuetlaxtla, capital of that province, saying that the Aztecs had come to ask for large conch shells, turtles and scallops. It so happened that when the messengers arrived in Cuetlaxtla the rulers of Tlaxcala were there celebrating a feast with the monarch of that place. Once the message had been delivered to Ceatonaltecuhtli, ruler of Orizaba, the Tlaxcalans were much surprised, saying to him:

"How is it that the Aztecs dare to ask you for sea snails or any other thing? Are you perhaps their vassals? What contempt, what daring they show you! Kill them, close the roads, do not permit them to enter your domain!" The sovereign, together with another lord Tepetecuhtli, agreed with this advice and ordered the people of Orizaba to assassinate the envoys and all traders who might happen to be in the province.

The royal messengers were then killed and so were the merchants, not only Aztecs but Texcocans, Xochimilca, Chalca and Tecpanecs. None of them were able to proceed to their goal, Cempoala. From this massacre only two men, from Iztapalapa, escaped and managed to return to Mexico.

Tlacaelel, Moteczoma and their allies were greatly offended at the roughness of the coastal peoples and prepared a campaign to punish them. The armies set out for Orizaba. All along the way they were served and worshipped as gods by the natives of those provinces and people did not dare appear in places where the soldiers were to pass. Everyone hid himself, none dared come out on the roads, because they knew well that the warriors would rob them of whatever they carried and if they wished to defend themselves they might be beaten, wounded or even killed. And so the squadrons went their way, stealing from the cornfields, killing turkeys and domesticated dogs. They acted in an evil way, just as our own Spaniards do today unless they are controlled. Such is and was the shamelessness of the soldiery. As soon as they felt themselves under their banner the whole world was theirs. For this reason, the natives of the towns through which the armies were to pass hid themselves and their maize, chilli, turkeys, domestic dogs and all other possessions.

114

Meanwhile the men of Orizaba asked the Tlaxcalans, who had instigated them to fight, for the aid they had promised. Tlaxcala refused. After a great battle during

*A few of the twenty Aztec hieroglyphic day signs.*
*A page from the* **Codex Borgia,** *one of the most elaborate*
*of all pre-Hispanic books, which deals with*
*fortune-telling, lucky and unlucky days. Courtesy New*
*York Public Library. Photo Reg Van Cuylenburg.*

which there were many deaths on both sides, Orizaba was beaten and conquered, together with many neighboring city states such as Chichiquila, Teoixhuacan, Quimichtla, Tzauctla, Macuilxochitla, Tlatictla, Oceleopan, Totonaca and Cuetlaxtla.

The men of Cuetlaxtla, seeing that their cities were sacked and their people massacred, agreed to pay a large amount of tribute to Mexico. Some of this tribute was to be gold, silver, precious stones, richly worked cloth ten yards long, cacao, feathers, certain plants used in the preparation of chocolate, amber, river fish, shrimp and crab, green stones, carnelians, and skins of jaguars and ocelots. The armies returned to Mexico bringing great numbers of captives who would later be sacrificed.

Moteczoma and Tlacaelel now decided that it would be good to place a governor over Cuetlaxtla and the entire province, and a certain prince by the name of Pinotl was chosen. Tlacaelel spoke to him, saying, "O Pinotl; because of your great personal merits the king has decided to send you to govern and hold down the province of Cuetlaxtla. There, every eighty days you will collect the tribute of all that land and you will send it to us with a guard. Go there and perform your duties as is expected of an honest man like you."

The lord Pinotl expressed his gratitude for the favor that had been done to him, and gathering his wife, his children and his household, he set out for that province in order to govern it.

CHAPTER **XXII** WHICH TREATS OF HOW MOTECZOMA WARRED WITH COAIXTLAHUACA BECAUSE CERTAIN MESSENGERS OF HIS HAD BEEN MURDERED. WITH A DESCRIPTION OF HOW THAT CITY WAS DESTROYED

The city of Coaixtlahuaca is located in the lands of the Mixtecs. The Spaniards now call it Cuixtlahuac, but that is a corruption of the word (most of the original names of towns have been corrupted). In ancient times this city was one of the greatest in that land; there was an extremely wealthy market here, attended by merchants from foreign parts such as Mexico, Texcoco, Chalco, Xochimilco, Coyoacan, Tacuba, Azcapotzalco and many other nations. There they traded in gold, feathers, cacao, finely worked gourds, clothing, cochineal,[65] and dyed thread made of rabbit hair.

One day when a great number of foreign merchants had been trading in the market, the authorities of Coaixtlahuaca ordered their people to arm themselves and to rob and kill the Aztec traders as they left the market place. It is generally thought that in this decision they had been influenced by ill-intentioned persons who wished to stir trouble between Aztecs and Mixtecs.[66]

The subjects of the lords of Coaixtlahuaca did what they had been commanded, killing the merchants without sparing any. Only a few men from Tula managed to hide and save their lives. They came to Mexico with great haste and told Moteczoma what had occurred, that one hundred and sixty merchants had been assassinated. The king and Tlacaelel immediately ordered that all the ally and vassal nations prepare for war, and people began to gather from those lands and from Mexicatzinco, Huitzilopochco, Tula and Matlatzinco.

Tlacaelel was now an old man and, being unable to direct a war in such a faraway country, appointed a nobleman known as Cuauhnochtli to take his place, together with a second in command called Tizocyahuacatl.

When the armed forces left the city, it looked so abandoned, so mournful and solitary, that everyone wept. Mothers wept for their sons and wives for their husbands, since this time the war was to be waged in a distant land and no one knew who would return. As that land was immense there was great fear that the cities would confederate against the Aztecs, surround and destroy them.

The Aztecs arrived at the boundary of the domains of Coaixtlahuaca, where they set up an encampment made of tents and huts of straw mats. They fortified themselves as best they could, placed sentinels and spies in strategic places and kept watch with sword and shield in hand. They had reason to look fearfully before and behind, as they were in a strange land, surrounded by enemies. They were especially afraid of the Chochos, a devilish and savage tribe.[67]

Nevertheless, after a great battle the men of Coaixtlahuaca surrendered and offered to pay a vast tribute consisting of mantles ten yards long, loads of chilli and cotton, salt from the ocean and different colored dyes. By the time the army returned to Mexico with their splendid loot, men were so eager to go to war that one seldom saw a soldier in the city. All wished to go to war since they fared so well.

Having gone through the usual ceremonies and having drunk the Divine Liquor, the captives were addressed by Moteczoma:

"Welcome, O prize of the gods,
O gift to him who encircles the earth with his might each day.
To the One who passes over our heads,
To the Lord of the Earth and of All Things."

Through their interpreters the prisoners thanked him and praised him for having considered them worthy of seeing his face and of having been admitted to his revered presence, though they had not deserved it. They were then delivered to the heads of the wards in order to be housed and their wounds cured so that by the day of the feast they might be fat and desirable for sacrifice.[68]

Once the prisoners had been disposed of Tlacaelel said to Moteczoma:

"O Lord, let us have a stone made
Which will be the likeness of the Sun!
Let us place it upon a high place
And let us call it *Cuauhxicalli*, the Eagle Vessel!"

*Xicalli* in the Nahuatl tongue means container or a type of gourd, and *cuauhtli* means eagle, and that is why it was called Cuauhxicalli, "eagle vessel." I used to think, like many others, that it meant "wooden vessel" but I have since been undeceived.

The king immediately gave orders that the stone be carved so that it would be ready for the sacrifice of the prisoners from Coaixtlahuaca.

This stone was recently found and dug up during the building of our cathedral and it now stands by one of the doorways. It is said that the Mexicans now wish to convert it into a holy baptismal font and I think it good that this stone be used in the service of our God so that that which was a container for human blood, sacrificed to the devil, may now be the container of the Holy Spirit. There the souls of Christians will be cleansed and there they will receive the waters of baptism.

CHAPTER **XXIII** WHICH TREATS OF THE SACRIFICIAL CEREMONY
WHICH WAS PERFORMED IN HONOR OF THE STONE CALLED
CUAUHXICALLI, IMAGE OF THE SUN.
WITH A DESCRIPTION OF HOW THE PRISONERS FROM
COAIXTLAHUACA WERE SACRIFICED UPON IT

Once Huehue Moteczoma had determined that the stone in the likeness of the sun be carved for the great feast, the stonecutters were ordered to seek a great stone and to carve upon it an image of the sun, hollowing out a round depression in the center. From the depression, which was to contain the blood of the victims, were to emerge the rays, so that this image of the sun could hold and rejoice in the blood.

All around its sides were to be represented the wars which the Aztecs had waged up to that time and in which they had been victorious through the favor and aid of the sun.

The stone sculptors sought and found a massive, beautiful stone and upon it they carved the image of the sun and the wars of conquest in Tepeaca, Tochpan, the land of the Huaxtecs, in Cuetlaxtla and Coaixtlahuaca, all of the carving being very finely done. Considering that they did not possess iron mallets or chisels, such as those used by our stone workers, and had to carve small fine figures on the Cuauhxicalli, working stone with stone, it was a marvelous feat. The amazing skill of these stone artisans is worth recording in this history, as is their special ability to shape large stones with smaller ones producing the sort of realism which an artist with a delicate brush, or a silversmith with a fine chisel, achieves.

When the stone had been finished and had been seen by the king, he ordered that a platform about as tall as a man be constructed, with four small staircases pointing in the four cardinal directions: north, south, east and west. The whole structure was conceived according to their beliefs, traditions and demonic dreams. The monolith was then put upon the platform with ceremonial reverence.

The sovereigns of the surrounding states were invited to the feast and when they had arrived and seen the stone they admired it greatly. Moteczoma spoke to them:

"Do you see the likeness of the Sun?
Do you see the image of him who warms you
With his heat and with his fire,
Most excellent Lord of Created Things?
You have come here to give honor to this image;
For that purpose have I bid you come."

When the day of the feast arrived, Moteczoma and Tlacaelel blackened their bodies with soot and applied it in such a way that it caught the light. It was so black that they looked like negroes painted black! They placed crowns of fine feathers, adorned with gold and precious stones, upon their heads, and on each arm they wore a sheath of gold reaching from the elbow to the shoulder. On their feet were richly worked jaguar skin sandals, inlaid with gold and gems. They also were robed in splendid royal mantles and loincloths done in the same manner as the mantles. From their backs hung miniature bowls of finely worked jade. These last indicated that they were both kings and priests. Jeweled plugs were attached to holes in their noses, and both these lords carried flint knives in their hands.

The king and Tlacaelel now appeared before the assembly and went to stand upon the stone which was the likeness and image of the sun, one having ascended by one staircase and the other by another. The five priests of sacrifice followed them. They were to hold down the feet, hands and heads of the victims, and they were painted all over with red ochre, even their loincloths and tunics. Upon their heads they wore paper crowns surmounted by little shields which hung to the middle of their foreheads, also painted in ochre. On the top of their heads they wore long stiff feathers which had been tied to their hair and which stood straight up. On their feet were very common, worthless sandals. Each of these ornaments had its special meaning and mystery attached to it.[69]

The five priests entered and claimed the prisoner who stood first in the line at the skull rack. Each prisoner they took to the place where the king stood and, when they had forced him to stand upon the stone which was the figure and likeness of the sun, they threw him upon his back. One took him by the right arm, another by the left, one by his left foot, another by his right, while the fifth priest tied his neck with a cord and held him down so that he could not move.

The king lifted the knife on high and made a gash in his breast. Having opened it he extracted the heart and raised it high with his hand as an offering to the sun. When the heart had cooled he tossed it into the circular depression, taking some of the blood in his hand and sprinkling it in the direction of the sun. In this way the sacrificers killed four, one by one; then Tlacaelel came and killed another four in his turn. And so, four by four, the prisoners were slain, till every last man that had been brought from the Mixteca had perished.

When the sacrifice had ended the priests took from the shrine of Huitzilopochtli a paper serpent coiled about a pole, adorned with feathers. Even today I have seen this in use in certain dances in Mexico and the surrounding towns. A priest carried the snake, twisted about the pole. He then set it on fire and walked about the stone incensing it with the smoke. While it was burning, he climbed to the top of the monolith and threw the still smouldering serpent upon all the blood which bathed the stone. At this moment a great paper mantle was brought and cast upon the stone. It burned together with the serpent until the blood was consumed and dried.

Once the fire had gone out Moteczoma and Tlacaelel descended and, with the kings of Texcoco and Tacuba, withdrew to the royal seats. They anointed the royal guests, dressed them and adorned them with headdresses, mantles, arm-bands, loincloths and nose-plugs, all of these ornaments being of the same type used by the sacrificers. Everyone then took part in a solemn banquet with great festivities to commemorate the first use of the stone which was the image and likeness of the sun.

On the next day a second feast was celebrated by the warriors and knights of the sun, called *Cuacuauhtin*, that is to say, "Eagles." This was the feast of the sun,

121

*Nahui Ollin,* "Four Motion," during which a man painted red was sacrificed in the name of the sun.[70] They handed him a staff and a shield, and they placed on his back a bag filled with pieces of red ochre and soot, together with eagle feathers, paper and many other things. These were messages which he was to carry to the sun reminding the Lord of Created Things that his warriors still served him and thanked him for the great benefits with which he had favored them in their wars.

The victim, carrying the bag of gifts to the sun together with the staff and shield, slowly began to climb the steps of the pyramid. In this ascent he represented the course of the sun from east to west. As soon as he reached the summit and stood in the center of the great Sun Stone, which represented noon, the sacrificers approached the captive and opened his chest. Once the heart had been wrenched out it was offered to the sun and blood sprinkled toward the solar deity. Imitating the descent of the sun in the west the corpse was toppled down the steps of the pyramid. After the sacrifice the warriors celebrated a great feast with much dancing, ceremonial and cannibalism.

The dignitaries of the neighboring cities then returned to their homelands eager to imitate the Aztecs. They began to build pyramids and sacrifice men in a similar way, to elect and form a priesthood to practice these rites. They also organized military orders, practiced with their arms, and created special schools for singing and dancing similar to those of Mexico.

At this time they began to distinguish and draw a line between the great chieftains and the warriors, a difference between the warriors and the squires, between the squires and lower officials and the common people. Each was to be treated in a manner appropriate to his rank, and thus was made clear the distinction between them. These distinctions were so rigidly enforced that in the palaces were special rooms for people of different rank, and when one visited the palace one knew his place and went there directly. The common people had no business entering the royal buildings and never did so unless it was their turn to render personal services such as scrubbing, sweeping and other menial tasks. Only the lords, noblemen and the chief warriors wore sandals on their feet. The rest of the people did not dream of doing so since there were grave penalties involved, and if the chronicle is not mistaken, the pain of death was applicable to any common man who dared to pass the royal doors. In their trials each of these classes had its own place or tribunal for obtaining justice. The decision of the judges passed through several tribunals until it reached the supreme council which gave the final sentence.

The Knights of the Sun had their distinctive insignia which permitted them to be distinguished from other warriors. They were the ones who celebrated the feast of the Sun, who ate human flesh and who were allowed to keep as many women as they could support.

*Sacrifice upon the round gladiatorial stone. To the*
*right are shown Moteczoma I of Mexico and Nezahualpilli of Texcoco.*
*From the* Atlas, *the picture book accompanying Durán's*
*text. Photo Reg Van Cuylenburg.*

The men of Tlaxcala longed to compete with and subject the Aztecs, and their hatred was so great that they began to harass them and demonstrate their enmity. Since Cuetlaxtla is a domain near Tlaxcala, the four lords of the latter state went to visit the principal chieftains of Cuetlaxtla and feasted with them, using this as an occasion for poisoning their minds against the Aztecs. Said the Tlaxcalans:

"How is it that you suffer the Aztecs
To disembowel, to rob your country?
From your land they take gold,
Cacao, clothing, many colored feathers,
Fish, sea snails, shells and turtles.
How can you consent to such a thing?"

The lords began to weep bitterly, but answered that since they had been vanquished they were now vassals and could do nothing about it.

Xicotencatl, one of the chieftains from Tlaxcala, answered:

"Do not fear, do what I tell you.
We will favor you, we will guard your backs.
Cease sending tribute!
Kill the governor that they have placed over you!
And should they ask for tribute kill them all!
If they come I will move my people
And will surround the Aztecs
And not a man will return alive to Mexico."

The wretches, forgetful of Tlaxcala's great defeat in the past war, believed the promise and immediately assassinated the governor. When tribute ceased arriving in Mexico, Tlacaelel sent messengers to Cuetlaxtla. They were well received and told to rest while the governor was notified of their arrival. Then the lords of Cuetlaxtla closed the door of the chamber where the Aztec emissaries rested, and lighted a great pile of chilli which they had placed in an adjoining room. The smoke was so great that the Aztec messengers, trapped, unable to defend themselves, were suffocated.

Once the Aztecs were dead, the lords and their servants entered and ordered

125

that the corpses be opened through the rear and that their intestines be pulled out and bound around their throats. This was done and the bodies were then stuffed with straw, dressed in splendid mantles and placed in seats of honor.

In order to mock them great quantities of food, flowers and tobacco were placed in front of them. Doing great reverence before the bodies, the lords of Cuetlaxtla said:

"Eat, O dead lords, and take pleasure.
Behold: here is food and drink, fruit and flowers!
Why is it that you do not eat?
What more do you wish? Eat!
Are you perchance angry?"

They took the bodies then and threw them to the vultures and beasts and sent messengers to Tlaxcala to tell what they had done.

A traveler from Tepeaca who happened to be passing saw the royal envoys lying with their intestines about their throats, and entrails, lungs and livers scattered upon the ground. He hastened to Mexico and told what he had seen. Moteczoma and Tlacaelel were horrified and immediately began to prepare the army for war. Before the soldiers departed for Cuetlaxtla it was decided to double the tribute paid by these people. Exclaimed Tlacaelel:

"If they used to give cloth ten yards long
Let it be twenty yards long from now on!
If they used to pay us with green stones,
Let them also give us white and red ones.
If they used to offer us spotted skins of jaguar and ocelot,
Let them also give us white skins now! Let them give us live serpents
And a thousand other animals."

When the Aztec forces approached Cuetlaxtla the Tlaxcalans were notified and were reminded of their promise. Again they paid no heed and left Cuetlaxtla to its fate.

When Cuetlaxtla and its allies believed themselves facing defeat, the rulers fled into hiding. It was then that the common people came out, wailing:

"O Aztec lords, why do you kill us?
What fault is it of ours, we who are ignorant, simple people,
Who are free of malice and have nothing to gain?
Why do you take revenge on us?
We have not angered you nor offended you nor troubled you!
And yet you have spared those cursed thieves,
Our chiefs and lords, who have brought nothing but death to us?

Have we not been the ones to pay the tribute?
By any chance do they pay it?
Is it not all the result of our sweat and labor?
When we gave cloth, did they weave it for you?
No, it was woven by ourselves and our wives.
If you received cacao, gold and precious stones,
Rich plumage and fish,
Were we not the ones who offered it to our lord Moteczoma
And to our masters the Aztecs? Spare our lives, O Aztecs."

The common people sought out their rulers in certain caves and, having bound their hands, they brought them before the victorious general. When Moteczoma heard of the events in Cuetlaxtla he consulted Tlacaelel as to whether the rulers of the vanquished city should be executed, since they were great lords and images of the gods. Perhaps the gods would be offended; perhaps it would be a sacrilege. Tlacaelel answered that since they had rebelled against the supreme deity and his likeness, the king of Mexico, they deserved to be punished. It was also true that the common people were asking for justice and this could not be denied them.

And so it was that Moteczoma ordered that the rulers of Cuetlaxtla have their throats slit, not at the front of the neck but at the back. Cuauhnochtli and Tlillancalqui, two great judges of the supreme council, were sent to execute the sentence. The two lords of Cuetlaxtla were then executed by having their throats slit in this way and the people of lower rank were greatly satisfied. New rulers were elected and an Aztec governor was placed over them.

CHAPTER XXV WHICH TREATS OF THE GREAT TRIBUTE AND WEALTH RECEIVED BY MEXICO FROM MANY PROVINCES AND CITIES WHICH HAD BEEN CONQUERED IN WAR

The Aztec *Chronicle* digresses here and enumerates the great tribute and wealth received by Mexico and by those who had won it in war with their labor and sweat and who had shed their blood for their own glory, for the honor of their king and for the defense of the nation. The *Chronicle* remembers in a special way the valorous, bold captains who had been a principal cause in the aggrandizing of the Republic and who had subjected cities and provinces, tribes and peoples. This reminds one of the great feats of the twelve peers of France or of the Cid, or of Bernardo del Carpio or Count Fernán González or Diego García de Paredes in Spain. Our books are filled with the skill and bravery of these men.

In the same way the *Chronicle* tells us of the valiant men who labored and suffered to overcome and subject Azcapotzalco, Coyoacan, Xochimilco, Cuitlahuac, Colhuacan, Chalco, Texcoco, Tepeaca, Ahuizilapan and Cuetlaxtla, Coaixtlahuaca and all the Mixtec province, the province of Poctlan, Oaxaca, Tehuantepec, Xoconochco and Xolotla, Amaxtlaixochtla, Ixhuatlan, Cuextlan, Tziuhcoac, Tozapan, Tochpan, Matlatzinco, Toluca, Mazahuacan, Xocotitlan, Chiapan, Xiquipilco, Cuauhuacan, Cillan. All of these heavily populated towns, provinces and cities were overcome and destroyed by the bold men whom I will name here: the great Tlacaelel, Cuatlehuatl, Tlacahuepan, Tlatolzaca, Epcohuatl, Tzompantli, Huehue Moteczoma, Huehuezaca, Citlalcoatl, Aztacoatl, Axicyo, Cuautzitzimitl, and Xiconoc.

And these were some of the great riches and tribute received by Mexico due to the bravery of those men:[71]

Great quantities of gold, in dust and worked as jewels.

Large amounts of green stones, of crystal, of carnelian, bloodstones, amber, besides many other types of stone which these people loved greatly. The basis of their idolatry was the adoration of these stones together with the feathers which they called, "Shadow of the gods." These feathers were multicolored or green, blue, red, yellow, purple, white and striped.

Vast amounts of cacao.

Cotton in large bundles, both white and yellow.

A bewildering amount of cloth; strips twenty, ten, five, four and two yards long, according to the wealth of each province.

Exceedingly rich mantles for the lords, differently woven and worked, some of them had rich fringes done in colors and feather work; others had insignia on them, others serpent heads, others ocelot heads, others the image of the Sun, and yet others had skulls, or blowguns, figures of the gods—all of them embroidered in many colored threads and enriched with the down of ducks, all beautifully and curiously worked. Even though silk was unknown in this country, the natives were extremely skillful in embroidering and painting cotton cloth.

Also mantles of maguey fiber given as tribute by the Chichimecs—most delicately worked and painted in different colors, some of them showing gilded eagles, weapons and insignia.

Live birds, too, sent by the Chichimecs—green, red, blue; parrots large and small; other splendid and handsomely colored birds such as eagles, buzzards, hawks, sparrow hawks, ravens, herons and wild geese.

128

Wild animals such as ocelots, jaguars, wildcats. All of these fierce animals were brought in cages.

Great and small snakes, some poisonous, others not, some fierce, others harmless.

It was marvelous to see the great variety of snakes and other small beasts that were brought in large pots. Vassals even paid tribute in centipedes, scorpions and spiders! The Aztecs were the Lords of All Creation; everything belonged to them, everything was theirs!

From the coast came everything that could be found in the sea; scallop shells, large and small sea snails, curious fish bones, large turtle shells, great and small turtles, stones from the sea, pearls baroque and smooth, amber stones.

Colors and dyes—red ochre, yellow, green, blue, purple, light green. Cochineal, alum, colors made from *nacazcolotl* and *zacatlaxcatli*, which are herbs, and black earth used for making an ink dye.

Other provinces sent gourds. Some of them were deep, others shallow, some plain, others carved; some were gilded and painted with rich and curious designs. Some of these have lasted until today and are very richly worked. Another type of gourd was wide and flat, and these were used in the same way that we use silver trays or large plates to carry the food to the table or to give water for the hands. They also had curious gourds with handles, similar to chocolate pots. In sum, this tribute consisted of a multitude of large, medium sized, small and miniature gourds of different shapes, types and colors.

Women's clothing: blouses and skirts, as well finished and splendid as it was possible to make, all of them enriched with wide borders embroidered in different colors, and designs and feather work on the front. On the sides of the blouses were designs in colored thread, and on the back, embroidered flowers, imperial eagles or flowers embroidered and enriched with feather work. They were beautiful to see. Splendid skirts of great price were woven richly and with excellent skill. All of these clothes were used by the ladies, wives of the lords and great chieftains. There was another type of female dress which was entirely white and this was used by the old and young women who served in the temples. There was yet another kind of clothing for women, made of maguey fiber, and this was worn by the servant girls in the homes and was divided among them.

From other provinces were brought mats of different weaves and colors, some of palm leaf, others of water reeds, others of thick shining straw, others of cane and some of rushes from the lagoon. Together with these came seats woven in the same way as the mats, and seats with backs, all finely painted and splendidly worked.

Yet other lands sent maize and beans, chian seeds, amaranth seeds, chilli of the many different types that grow in this country and which is used for the different dishes cooked here.

Another tribute consisted of a great quantity of pumpkin seeds.

From other parts came firewood and the bark of certain trees. This is the firewood of the nobility and makes a beautiful flame. There also was charcoal, which was paid as tribute by the towns that had woods.

Other cities paid in stone, lime, boards and beams to build houses and temples.

From other places were brought deer and rabbits and quail, some uncooked and others in barbecue. As tribute also came gophers, weasels, and large rodents, which thrive in the woods.

Toasted locusts, winged ants, large cicadas and little ones, in addition to other small animals. Those who lived near lagoons sent everything that thrives in the water, such as algae, a certain type of insect that walks upon the water, and small worms.

From the towns where fruit was common, such as the hot country, came products such as pineapples, annonas, mameys, numerous types of sweet fruits such as guavas, wild pear-like fruits, yellow, black and white sapotas, avocados and two or three kinds of yams.

These provinces also paid tribute in great loads of flowers of a thousand varieties, all dexterously arranged. Even though sweet-smelling flowers abound in the hot country, some are better than others, since they have a more delicate perfume. The trees upon which these flowers grow were also brought, roots and all, to be planted in the houses of the lords.[72]

And all this tribute shows the magnificence and strength of the Aztec nation and how they came to be called and held to be lords of all created things, upon the waters as well as upon the earth.

All of this has dealt with food and clothing, but there were also provinces that paid in cotton armor. This armor was stuffed and quilted and so thick that an arrow or a dart could not penetrate it. Another tribute consisted of shields made of fire-hardened rods so strong and heavy that a sword could not dent them. The faces of these shields were covered with fine featherwork of many colors, the design being formed by the different shades and colors of the feathers themselves combined with shining gold. These shields were also decorated with designs of weapons, scenes of great deeds in the past, pictures of their gods and of their past monarchs. Even today they use them, or at least keep them put away as a reminder of their ancient history, great deeds and famous men.

Big thick bows were also paid as tribute, together with arrows of different forms and of many types. Finely worked stones in the form of balls for the slings were also sent, and so were numerous slings of maguey fiber.

Other contributions were white and black blades for the swords, flints for the arrows and the darts. Let one try to imagine all the products of this land and he will know what was sent as tribute to Mexico!

Honeycombs were also tribute, some of them with the very bees inside of them, as well as great jars of white honey and yellow honey! Resin from the trees, torches to give light, and sooty materials for painting and blackening came from the vassals.

Provinces that lacked foodstuffs and clothes paid in maidens, girls and boys, who were divided among the lords—all slaves. The girls became mistresses of the lords and had children, and their offspring are now referred to as "sons of slaves." When the natives have disputes, the greatest insult is to call someone "son of a slave girl." These were the children of those young girls who were paid as tribute in ancient times.

CHAPTER XXVI WHICH TREATS OF THE LAWS, ORDINANCES AND STATUTES DECREED BY KING MOTECZOMA I IN THE CITY OF MEXICO

Because Mexico was now at peace, living in order and tranquility, King Moteczoma gathered together all the chieftains of Mexico and the allied states and decreed the following laws for the future.

"1. The king must never appear in public unless the occasion is extremely important.

"2. Only the king may wear a golden diadem in the city, though in war all the great lords and brave captains may wear such. It is considered that those who go to war represent the royal person.

"3. Only the king and the Prime Minister Tlacaelel may wear sandals within the palace. No great chieftain may enter the palace shod, under pain of death. The great noblemen are the only ones to be allowed to wear sandals in the city and no one else, with the exception of men who have performed some great deed in war. But these sandals must be cheap and common; the gilded, painted ones are to be used only by noblemen.

"4. Only the king is to wear the fine mantles of cotton embroidered with designs and threads of different colors and featherwork. He is to decide which type of cloak may be used by the royal person to distinguish him from the rest.

"5. The great lords, who are twelve, may wear certain mantles, and the minor lords wear others.

"6. The common soldier may wear only the simplest type of mantle and is prohibited from using any special designs or fine embroidery that might set him off from the rest.

"7. The common people will not be allowed to wear cotton clothing, under pain of death, but only garments of maguey fiber. The mantle must not be worn below

131

the knee and if anyone allows it to reach the ankle, he will be killed, unless he has wounds of war on his legs."

(And so it was that when one encountered a person who wore his mantle longer than the laws permitted, one immediately looked at his legs. If he had wounds acquired in war he would be left in peace, and if he did not, he would be killed. They would say, "Since that leg did not flee from the sword, it is just that it be rewarded and honored.")

"8. No one but the great noblemen and chieftains is to build a house with a second story, under pain of death. No one is to put peaked or round gables upon his house. This privilege has been granted by the gods only to the great.

"9. Only the great lords are to wear lip-plugs, ear-plugs and nose-plugs of gold and precious stones, except strong men, brave captains and soldiers, but their ornaments must be of bone, wood or other inferior materials.

"10. Only the king and the sovereigns of the provinces and other great lords are to wear gold arm-bands, anklets, and golden rattles on their feet at the dances. They may wear garlands and gold headbands with feathers in them in the style they desire, and no one else. They alone may adorn themselves with chains of gold around their necks, with jewelry of this metal and of precious stones, such as jade. The other valiant warriors may wear common garlands and eagle and macaw feathers on their heads. They may put on bone necklaces and those of small snails, small scallop shells, bones of snakes and small cheap stones."

(Some of the latter, though, were so well polished, painted and carved that they gave a good appearance and looked very fine.)

"11. In the royal palace there are to be diverse rooms where different classes of people are to be received, and under pain of death no one is to enter that of the great lords. Each one is to go to that of his peers. An order of judges is to be set up, but none of them may give the death sentence without notifying the king.

"12. All the wards will possess schools or monasteries for young men where they will learn religion and good manners. They are to do penance, lead hard lives, live with strict morality, practice for warfare, do bodily work, fast, endure disciplinary measures, draw blood from different parts of the body, and watch at night. There are to be teachers and old men to chastise them and to lead them in their exercises and not permit them to be idle or to lose their time. All of these youths must observe chastity in the strictest way, under pain of death.

"13. There is to be a rigorous law regarding adulterers; they are to be stoned and thrown in the rivers or to the buzzards.

"14. Thieves will be sold for the price of their theft, unless the theft be grave, having been committed many times; such thieves will be punished by death."

These laws were accepted as sparks from a divine fire which the great king

Moteczoma had within his breast and they were issued for the health of the entire land. They were like medicine which, given in its time and season, will profit the human body and be the cause of its welfare.

CHAPTER XXVII WHICH TREATS OF HOW KING MOTECZOMA THE FIRST. NOW REIGNING IN GLORY AND MAJESTY, SOUGHT THE PLACE OF ORIGIN OF HIS ANCESTORS, THE SEVEN CAVES. WITH A DESCRIPTION OF THE SPLENDID PRESENTS WHICH HE SENT TO BE OFFERED AND GIVEN TO THOSE WHO MIGHT BE FOUND THERE

At this point our chronicle tells us that Moteczoma, who had now become a great monarch possessing glory and wealth, decided to seek out the place where his ancestors had dwelt.[73] He wished to know about the Seven Caves which his own traditions had so often mentioned. He had heard that the mother of the god Huitzilopochtli was still alive. When he suggested to Tlacaelel that soldiers be sent to explore that ancient land, his prime minister did not agree, saying:

"You must know, O great lord,
That what you have determined to do is not for strong or valiant men,
Nor does it depend upon skill in the use of arms in warfare.
Your envoys will not go as conquerors, but as explorers;
They will seek out the place where our ancestors lived,
They will try to find the place where our god Huitzilopochtli was born.
No, you must look for wizards, sorcerers, magicians;
Because that place is covered thickly with thorny bushes and with great
  brambles.
All of it is in the midst of lagoons which are filled with reeds and rushes
And it will be difficult to find.
When our people lived there it was a delightful land.
There they lived in leisure, they lived long,
They never became old or weary.
But after they departed from their home everything became thorns and thistles.
The stones became sharp in order to wound,
The bushes became prickly, the trees became thorny.
Everything there turned against them
So that they would never be able to turn back."

Moteczoma agreed to accept the advice of Tlacaelel and called the royal historian, an aged man called Cuauhcoatl, "Eagle Serpent," and addressed him:

"O ancient father, I desire to know the true story,
The knowledge that is hidden in your books
About the Seven Caves from which our ancestors came forth,
Our fathers and grandfathers.
I wish to know about the place wherein dwelt
Our god Huitzilopochtli and out of which he led our forefathers."

"O mighty lord," answered Cuauhcoatl, "I, your unworthy servant, can answer you. Our forebears dwelt in that blissful, happy place called Aztlan, which means 'Whiteness.' In that place there is a great hill in the midst of the waters, and it is called Colhuacan because its summit is twisted; this is the Twisted Hill. On its slopes were caves or grottos where our fathers and grandfathers lived for many years. There they lived in leisure, when they were called Mexitin and Azteca. There they had at their disposal great flocks of ducks of different kinds, herons, water fowl, and cranes. Our ancestors loved the song and melody of the little birds with red and yellow heads. They also possessed many kinds of large beautiful fish. They had the freshness of groves of trees along the edge of the waters. They had springs surrounded by willows, evergreens and alders, all of them tall and comely. Our ancestors went about in canoes and made floating gardens upon which they sowed maize, chilli, tomatoes, amaranth, beans and all kinds of seeds which we now eat and which were brought here from there.

"However, after they came to the mainland and abandoned that delightful place, everything turned against them. The weeds began to bite, the stones became sharp, the fields were filled with thistles and spines. They encountered brambles and thorns that were difficult to pass through. There was no place to sit, there was no place to rest; everything became filled with vipers, snakes, poisonous little animals, jaguars and wildcats and other ferocious beasts. And this is what our ancestors forsook. I have found it painted in our ancient books. And this, O powerful king, is the answer I can give you to what you ask of me."

Moteczoma then appointed sixty sorcerers to go seek the land that had given birth to the Aztec people. Laden with rich gifts they departed and some time later reached a hill called Coatepec in the province of Tula. There they traced magic symbols upon the ground, invoked the demons and smeared themselves with the particular ointments which wizards still use nowadays. (Today there are great magicians among them and Indians who are possessed. One might ask, "How is it that they are not exposed?" And I will answer that it is because they conceal one another and hide from us more than any other people on earth. They have no confidence in the Spaniards and thus it is that when by chance some magical practice

134

is discovered there is always some one to cover for the sorcerer and keep him silent.)

So it is that upon that hill they invoked the Evil Spirit and begged him to show them the home of their ancestors. The Devil, conjured by these spells and pleas, turned them into birds or wild beasts such as ocelots, jaguars, jackals, wildcats, and took them, together with their gifts, to the land of their forebears.

On reaching the shores of a great lagoon from the midst of which emerged the hill called Colhuacan, they resumed their human forms. The *Chronicle* tells us that as they stood on the shore of the lake they saw fishermen going about in canoes, whereupon they called to them. The natives, seeing the strangers and hearing them speak the same language, rowed to the shore and asked them what they wanted and where they came from. The Aztec magicians answered, "Sirs, we have come from Mexico and we are the envoys of the authorities there. We have come to seek the homeland of our ancestors."

The people of the place asked them, "What god do you adore?" to which they answered, "The great Huitzilopochtli!" They added that Moteczoma and his prime minister, Tlacaelel, had sent them to find Coatlicue, "She of the Snaky Skirt," mother of Huitzilopochtli, and the Seven Caves, Chicomoztoc. They also wished to deliver a gift to the Lady of the Snaky Skirt if she were still alive or to her servants if she were dead. The fishermen then went to call the custodian of the mother of Huitzilopochtli who ordered that the Aztecs be brought to him.

By canoe the sorcerers were taken across the lake to the hill of Colhuacan where the old priest who took care of the Lady of the Snaky Skirt lived at the foot of the hill. He said to them, "Welcome, my children. Who sent you here?" "Lord," they answered, "Moteczoma and his prime minister, Tlacaelel, also called Cihuacoatl, sent us."

"Who are Moteczoma and Tlacaelel?" asked the old man. "They were not among those who departed from here. Those who went from here were called Tezacatetl, Acacitli, Ocelopan, Ahuatl, Xomimitl, Ahuexotl, Huicton, and Tenoch. These eight men were the leaders of the wards. In addition to these, the four keepers of Huitzilopochtli also departed, two of them being Cuauhtloquetzqui and Axolohua."

"Sir," answered the Aztecs, "we confess to you that we are acquainted with those men but we never met them. The leaders you mention are gone from the earth, all of them are dead. We have heard their histories; that is all."

135

The old man was amazed at this, asking, "Lord of All Created Things, who killed them? Why is it that all of us are still alive here in the place they abandoned? Why is it that none of us have died? Who are your leaders now?" The wizards answered that they were the grandsons of the men he had named. The old man wanted to know who was now the custodian of the god Huitzilopochtli and he was told that it was a great priest called Cuauhcoatl, who could speak to the god and received orders from him. "Did you see the god before coming here?" asked the ancient man. "Did he send a message?"

The Aztec messengers responded that they had not seen him but that they had been sent by the king and his prime minister.

The old man then asked, "Why does he not let us know when he is to return? Before departing he told his mother that he would return and the unfortunate woman is still waiting, sad and tearful, with no one to console her. Do you wish to see her and speak to her?"

They answered, "Lord, we have done what our masters commanded and have brought a gift for the great lady. They ordered us to see her, greet her and make a present to her from the wealth of her son."

The old man said, "Pick up what you have brought and follow me."

They put the gifts on their backs and followed the old man who climbed the hill with ease. They went behind him, their feet sinking into the soft sand, walking with great difficulty and heaviness. The elder turned his head and when he saw that the sand had almost reached their knees he said, "What is the matter? Are you not coming up? Make haste!"

When they tried to do this they sank up to the waist in the sand and could not move. They called to the old man who was walking with such lightness that his feet did not seem to touch the ground. "What is wrong with you, O Aztecs?" said he. "What has made you so heavy? What do you eat in your land?"

"We eat the foods that grow there and we drink chocolate."

The elder responded, "Such food and drink, my children, have made you heavy and they make it difficult for you to reach the place of your ancestors. Those foods will bring death. The wealth you have we know nothing about; we live poorly and simply. Give me your loads and wait here. I will go call the mistress of this land so that you may see her." He picked up one of the bundles and carried it up the hill as if it were a straw. Soon he returned for the others and carried them up with great ease.

Presently an old woman appeared, the ugliest and dirtiest that one could possibly imagine. Her face was so black and covered with filth that she looked like something straight out of Hell. "Welcome, my sons!" she said. "Know that since your god, my son Huitzilopochtli, departed from this place, I have been awaiting his return, weeping and mourning. Since that day I have not washed my face, combed my hair or changed my clothes. My sadness and mourning will last until he returns. Is it true, my children, that you have been sent here by the seven leaders whom my son took away with him?"

The envoys lifted their eyes, and seeing the hideous and abominable woman, they were filled with fear and did reverence. "O great and powerful lady, we did not see or speak to the heads of the tribes. We were sent by your servants Moteczoma and Tlacaelel to visit you and seek out the place where their ancestors lived. They commanded us to kiss your hands in their name. We wish you to know that Moteczoma now rules over the city of Mexico. He is not the first king but the fifth. The previous ones lived with great hunger and poverty until they conquered other provinces. Accept the gifts, part of the wealth of your magnificent son, Huitzilopochtli."

"Tell me, children," said she, "what have you brought me: is it food?"

"Great lady, it is food and drink; chocolate is drunk and sometimes eaten."

"This is what has burdened you!" she told them. "This is why you have not been able to climb the hill. When you return you must tell my son to have pity on me and to observe the loneliness I am in. Look at me; life has become fasting and penance because of him. Let him remember what he said to me when he departed:

'O my mother, I will not tarry!
I am to lead the seven tribes; I am to find them a dwelling place,
I am to settle them in the land that has been promised them.
Once I have rooted them there and have given them happiness
I will return. But this will not be until
The years of my pilgrimage have been completed.
During this time I will wage war against provinces and cities,
Towns and villages. All of these will become my subjects.
But, in the same way that I conquered them they will be torn from me
And I will be expelled from that land.
Then I will return, then I will return here,
Because those I subjected with my sword and shield
Will rise against me. They will pick me up by the feet
And cast me down head first.
My weapons and I will roll upon the floor.[74]
It will be then, O mother, when my time has come, that I will return
For you to shelter me. Until then do not grieve.
But I beg you to give me two pairs of sandals,
One pair to go on this journey and the other for my return.
No! Give me four pairs of sandals,
Two pairs to go on this journey and two for my return!' "

Then the old woman addressed the Aztec messengers, saying:

## chapter XXVI

"It seems to me, my children, that he must be content over there
Since he does not remember his sad mother
Nor does he seek her or care for her.
Therefore I command you to tell him
That as soon as his time comes, he return.
So that he may remember that I wish to see him,
I, his mother, send him this mantle and this loincloth
Of maguey fiber. Let him wear them!"

As the messengers descended the hill they heard the old woman calling after them, "Stop so that you can see how men never become old in this country! Do you see my old servant? Watch him climb down the hill! By the time he reaches you he will be a young man."

The old man descended and as he ran he became younger and younger. When he reached the Aztec wizards, he appeared to be about twenty years old. Said he, "I am a youth now, this is what happens: I begin to climb again and when I am halfway up the hill I will be older." He ascended again and about halfway up he was like a man forty years of age. The farther he went up the older he became.

"Behold, my sons, the virtue of this hill; the old man who seeks youth can climb to the point on the hill that he wishes and there he will acquire the age that he seeks. That is why we live to old age and that is why none of the companions of your ancestors have died since the departure of your people. We become young when we wish. You have become old, you have become tired because of the chocolate you drink and because of the foods you eat. They have harmed and weakened you. You have been spoiled by those mantles, feathers and riches that you wear and that you have brought here. All of that has ruined you."

When they returned to Mexico the magicians told Moteczoma and Tlacaelel all they had seen and heard, and these great men wept and were moved, remembering their ancestors, wistful at not being able to see the land of their origin. The maguey fiber mantle and loincloth were sent to the temple and placed upon Huitzilopochtli since his own mother had sent them as a gift.

CHAPTER XXVIII WHICH TREATS OF HOW THE PEOPLE OF THE CITY OF OAXACA KILLED THE ROYAL ENVOYS WHO WERE RETURNING FROM COATZACUALCO. WITH A DESCRIPTION OF HOW THE AZTECS WARRED UPON THEM, DESTROYED THEM AND SETTLED THE CITY WITH AZTECS, TEXCOCANS AND XOCHIMILCA

The wishes of Moteczoma and Tlacaelel had now been fulfilled; they had learned many things about their place of origin. But they were fearful and uneasy about what the mother of Huitzilopochtli had remembered of the latter's prophecy.

> ". . . I will return. But this will not be until
> The years of my pilgrimage have been completed.
> Until then I will wage war against provinces and cities,
> Towns and villages. All of these will become my subjects.
> But, in the same way that I conquered them, others will take them from me
> And I will be expelled from the land.
> . . . Those I subjected with my sword and shield
> Will rise against me. They will pick me up by the feet
> And cast me down head first.
> My weapons and I will roll upon the floor."

On hearing then that his god and his god's worshippers would be expelled from the land, and that Huitzilopochtli would return to the place from which he had come, Moteczoma tried to discover who would destroy them. He sought to discover this by looking into the ancient traditions, writings and prophecies, and he found that the Children of the Sun would come from the east to cast down their god and to annihilate the Aztec nation.

At this time Moteczoma's messengers were sent to Coatzacualco to obtain a little gold dust and some of the fish bones, shells and sea-snails which abound on the coast, but on their way back, in a town called Mitla, near the city of Oaxaca, they were all killed. Moteczoma was eager to punish the evildoers but Tlacaelel insisted that there was a much more urgent matter: the building of the new temple of Mexico.

The king ordered the ruler of Texcoco to take charge of the construction of the front part of the pyramid. The monarch and people of Tacuba were to build the back. Chalco and Xochimilco were to erect the sides. The Otomi people were to work exclusively in bringing sand for the building, and the nations of the hot country were to contribute lime. The king addressed the conquered peoples:

> "O lords and great sovereigns, life is short!
> If while it lasts we do not glorify our own names
> We will be totally forgotten, for we will not receive fame
> For the deeds of our ancestors. Furthermore,
> If this work is not accomplished we will not take pleasure in it
> While we are alive. Which of us, once he is dead,
> Will return to see and enjoy earthly things?
> Our power, our might, ends with our deaths!"

Master builders were brought to measure the site and to make plans for marking out the foundations of the building. These men stated that it was necessary to build a platform about five hundred and sixty feet wide, of rubble and mortar, and this was constructed upon stakes driven into the ground.[75] The building of the pyramid continued upon this foundation and it grew so quickly that soon it had reached a great height.

One must not wonder at this since our chronicle says that people from all the provinces worked like ants in this feat. Seeing that his temple began to rise, King Moteczoma desired to honor his god even further and gave orders that all the neighboring sovereigns gather precious stones. Every six feet those gems were to be tossed into the mortar. When the building had reached the height of one hundred twenty steps, a large hall was added in which the image of the god was to be kept. It was all beautified with great stone statues and supports in the form of diverse images and carvings which served as frames and corners.

All of these things had great religious meaning. Some of the idols were called *ilhuicatzitquique,* which means "Those who hold up the heavens," and they were placed in such a way that they seemed to support the entire hall. Others were called *petlacontzitzquique,* "Those who hold up the divine vessels and insignia," and on them were hung the rich feather mantles which signified that the temple belonged to Huitzilopochtli.

Soon after this the Aztecs set out to punish the rebellious people of Oaxaca and after having vanquished them they brought back great numbers of victims for sacrifice. The priests of Mexico came out to meet them with incense burners in their hands, intoning hymns to their god. They offered incense to the prisoners, telling them of their fate and giving flowers and tobacco to all. The prisoners set up a frightful wail, shrieking and screaming. It was enough to horrify one.

When Moteczoma proposed that the victims be sacrificed in the new temple, Tlacaelel objected, saying that the building had not been entirely finished, that many statues were incomplete and that the shining mirror which was to represent the sun had not been made.

"Do not sorrow, O lord," said Tlacaelel. "Let it be finished first!
There is time for everything. If you wish it so, let these warriors,
Children of the sun, be sacrificed; but remember
That we will never lack victims for the dedication.
Our god will not be made to wait until new wars arrive.
He will find a way, a market place where he will go
To buy victims, men for him to eat. They will be in his sight
Like maize cakes hot from the griddle ready for him who wishes to eat.

Let our people, let our army go to this market place!
Let us buy with our blood, our heads and hearts and with our lives,
Precious stones, jade and feathers for our wondrous Huitzilopochtli.
This market place will be situated in Tlaxcala,
Huexotzinco, Cholula, Atlixco, Tliliuhquitepec and Tecoac,
Because if we place it in remote lands such as Yopitzinco,
Michoacan, the land of the Huaxtecs, or on either coast, it will be difficult.
Our god does not like the flesh of those barbarous peoples.
They are yellowish, hard, tasteless breads in his mouth.
They are savages and speak strange tongues.
Therefore our market place must be in these six cities.
They will come like warm breads, soft, tasty, straight from the fire."[76]

CHAPTER **XXIX** WHICH TREATS OF HOW THE KING AND
THE NOBILITY DECIDED TO WAGE A PERPETUAL WAR AGAINST
TLAXCALA, HUEXOTZINCO, CHOLULA, ATLIXCO,
TECOAC, AND TLILIUHQUITEPEC. WITH A DESCRIPTION OF HOW
MEN WERE TO BE BROUGHT TO THE SACRIFICES ON
THE GREAT FEASTS AND HOW SOLDIERS AND THE SONS
OF THE LORDS WERE TO PRACTICE WARFARE

Tlacaelel had now become old and could not go to war in person, though he continued to be the principal advisor in war. At this time his interest turned toward matters concerning the honor of the gods. Therefore, he ordered that sacrifices take place more often. Another reason for this increase was that they had acquired a taste for human flesh since they ate it frequently. It is also true that Tlacaelel had been persuaded or blinded by the devil and was now inventing a thousand cruel acts, all of which he made into law before his death. He was obeyed so blindly that all of that which he ordained was done.

The king notified all his great warriors that they were now to fight in a military market place where they would buy honor and glory with their blood and their lives. He asked Tlacaelel to speak to the men, and the latter uttered the following words:

141

"O sons, brothers, nephews who are here
In the presence of the majesty of Moteczoma!

I, Tlacaelel, wish to give more courage to the strong,
And embolden those who are weak. I wish to make a comparison to you:
When you go to the market place and see a precious ear-plug or nose-pendant,
Or when you see splendid and beautiful feathers
Or a rich gilded shield, or weapons done in feather work,
Do you not covet them, do you not pay the price that is asked?
Know now that the king, who is present, has willed that lip-plugs,
Golden garlands, many-colored feathers, ear-plugs, arm-bands,
Shields, weapons, insignia, mantles, and loin cloths
Are not to be bought in the market any longer by brave men.
From now on the sovereign will deliver them as payment
For memorable deeds. Each one of you, when he goes to war to fight,
Must think that he has journeyed to a market place
Where he will find precious stones. He who does not dare go to war,
Even though he be the king's son, from now on will be deprived
Of all these things. He will have to wear the clothing
Of the common man. And in this way his cowardice, his weak heart,
Will be known by all. He will not wear cotton garments,
He will not wear feathers, he will not receive flowers,
Like the great lords. He will not receive tobacco,
He will not drink chocolate, he will not eat fine foods.
He will be held in contempt as a man of low rank.
He will have to do manual work even though he be of royal blood.
He who does not go to war will not consort with, will not converse with,
Will not eat with the brave warriors. He will wait
Until they have eaten and drunk and then receive what is left over."

Tlacaelel also ordered that the king eat alone and that once he had finished the great captains be given of the same dishes that had been prepared for him, considering them remainders from the royal mouth.

"We also order," continued Tlacaelel, "that if sons
Be born of slave girls and maids, even though they be
Bastards, they be considered our blood. If any of these
Be valiant and courageous in war, more than our legitimate
Sons who might be cowards, let them inherit our wealth.
Let them be lords of our legitimate children.
Let the brave command them like the vilest of vassals.
Let them harass them! Let neither father nor mother intercede for them."[77]

142

After the king had confirmed what Tlacaelel had said, and all the allies had gathered to hear the new laws, the Prime Minister spoke again. "Sirs, you are all here together and you know that the city of Oaxaca was destroyed and ravaged. It is not right that this place remain as it is, for it is well situated and its lands are fertile. Therefore it is my opinion that people should gather from all the provinces to settle it once more. Let Nezahualcoyotl bring sixty married men with their wives and children from his province and let King Totoquihuaztli come with sixty families from his province. Let the same be done by those of Xochimilco and Chalco, those from the hot country, the Mazahua tribe, let them all bring people to repopulate Oaxaca. From my city I will bring six hundred families and will make them a land grant which will be distributed among them. My cousin, Atlazol, son of my uncle Ocelopan, who was killed by the Chalca during the war, will be governor. Thus will I reward him for his father's merits and troubles."

The settlers gathered in Mexico and the king told them not to be sad because they were leaving their homeland. He added that they were going to good lands where they would live at ease and be free from paying tribute.

Atlazol, the new governor, arranged the new city of Oaxaca in this way: the Aztecs formed a ward of their own, Texcocans another, and so did the Tecpanec, Xochimilca, and all the other groups. Orders were given that the governor be the father and mother of all those people and that he always be prepared and alert since this place was surrounded by barbarous and evil people.

CHAPTER XXX WHICH TREATS OF THE GREAT FAMINE THAT
DEVASTATED THIS LAND FOR THREE YEARS DURING THE REIGN OF
MOTECZOMA THE FIRST.
WITH A DESCRIPTION OF HOW THIS KING PREVENTED
HIS PEOPLE FROM PERISHING AND ABANDONING THE CITY

143

In the year 1454, which the Indians called *Ce Tochtli*, "One Rabbit," and for the next two years, the drought was so intense in this land that the clouds remained closed as in the time of Elias and it rained not at all, nor was there any sign of rain in the sky. The drought was such that the springs dried up, the streams and rivers ceased to run, the earth burned like fire and, from sheer dryness, cracked in great clefts. The roots of the trees and plants were so burned by the fire which came out of the earth that flowers and leaves fell and branches dried up. The century plants ceased to give juice. The prickly pear cactus no longer gave fruit; its leaves wilted and became limp, baked by the heat. As soon as maize sprouted it turned yellow and withered like all the rest of the crops.

People became faint and walked about shriveled and skinny due to the famine they suffered. Others became ill, having eaten things bad for the health. Others in their despair abandoned their city, homes, wives, and children, and departed toward more fertile lands to seek salvation.

When King Moteczoma saw that the city, together with the neighboring provinces, was being depopulated and that people came from all parts to wail and to tell him their sufferings, he called his authorities from the different cities. He questioned them as to the amount of maize, beans, chilli, chian seed and other foodstuffs kept in the royal storehouses. His stewards answered that there were great quantities of foodstuffs in the granaries that could alleviate the sufferings of the people. Tlacaelel, filled with pity, said to Moteczoma, "Sir, let us not lose time because the city is being depopulated and we can do nothing about it. We are powerless to stop them since we cannot give them what they need. Also, the people become sick because they eat harmful things. My advice is that from the things that are stored enough maize cakes and gruel be made every day, brought to the city in canoes and distributed among the needy. The nobility and the merchants will not starve since they have their own stores."

Moteczoma then, agreeing with Tlacaelel, ordered the stewards to bring into the city of Mexico canoes filled with maize cakes and gruel. The maize dough was to be cooked in the form of *tamales,* each one the size of a man's head. He told them not to bring in corn in grains and ordered, under pain of death, that no maize be carried away to other parts. From this time on twenty canoes of tamales and another ten of gruel, made from the flour of toasted grains and of chian seeds, began to enter the city.

One year went by and the storage began to decrease. The king saw that he could not maintain his people, whereupon he ordered his stewards to gather all the people of the city, old and young, male and female, and give them a last banquet with what was left of the maize and other seeds. After they had eaten he commanded that they all be dressed in mantles and loin cloths and that the women be given blouses and skirts. He then addressed them with sad words, which made them moan and shed bitter tears:

144

"My children, my brethren, be patient in this moment, I beg of you!
We are not fighting against an enemy in the battlefield.
If we were struggling with our foes we would risk our lives to defend ourselves

*Xochipilli, god of flowers and spring, dance and song.*
*In this monumental stone representation the deity*
*is shown dressed in a human skin, symbolic of the*
*renovation of vegetation and the growth of maize.*
*National Museum, Mexico City. Photo National Institute*
*of Anthropology and History, Mexico City.*

And we would die fulfilling our duties. No, he who wages war on us
Is the Lord of All Created Things, the Lord of Night and Day.
Who can fight against him? It is his will
That the clouds do not rain upon us and that the earth burn
And give forth smoke and the air scorch the crops!
This is a thing which was never seen by the living or the dead.
Therefore, O my children, you know that I have done everything in my power
And that the foodstuffs have been used up.
It is the will now of the Lord of the Heavens
That each of you go his way to seek his own salvation!"

Weeping, the people prostrated themselves upon the earth and gave a terrible scream, exclaiming, "O powerful lord, we have seen the succor with which you have favored us and the loving manner in which you have treated us. We know that you can do no more. Therefore, we kiss your royal hands and accept the liberty you give us to seek a remedy for our misery and hunger. We will sell our sons and daughters to those who can feed them so that they do not starve to death."

Weeping bitterly, the people began to leave the city in different directions. Many of them found relief in certain places where the inhabitants were wealthy. There they sold their sons and daughters to merchants and to rulers of towns who could maintain them. They would trade a child for a small basket of maize and the new owner was obliged to maintain the infant while the famine lasted. If the father or mother wished to ransom him later they were obliged to pay for all his maintenance.

During this time the Totonac people had harvested abundant grain and when they heard of the great need of the entire country of Mexico they wrought a vengeance upon the Aztecs. They came to the city of Mexico carrying great loads of maize and they came to buy slaves. They also went to other cities—Texcoco, Chalco, Xochimilco, Tacuba—to buy large numbers of slaves with their corn. They placed yokes around the neck of young and old. The slaves, lined up one behind another, were led out of the cities in a pitiful manner, the husband leaving his wife, the father his son, the grandmother her grandson. They went along weeping and their wails reached the heavens. In this way they bought a great number of slaves from all these nations. Others without having been sold went freely to the land of the Totonacs with their wives and children where they settled permanently and where they remain until this day.

147

Others, in their desire to escape to this province, fell dead along the way, together with the loads that they carried. All of this was something never seen before in the land.

At the end of the three years of famine which God had inflicted upon these people for their abominations, the clouds began to open up and the heaven distilled its dew. It came with such abundance that the people began to revive and to gain strength after their sufferings. Men and women began to come to the market places, all of them so skinny and pale that they looked as if they had gone through grave illness. But the plenty was such that foodstuffs were more than sufficient and parents were able to ransom their sons and daughters. People could return to their cities and recover their houses and wealth, except those who had left for the land of the Totonacs. These never returned to their native towns, and even today in that country there are wards of Aztecs, Chalca, Texcocans, Xochimilca and Tecpanecs. They were unwilling to return to their native state since they feared a repetition of this suffering and they also knew that the country of Mexico was poor in lands for sowing and that foodstuffs would have to be brought from other regions.

CHAPTER  **XXXI**  WHICH TREATS OF HOW KING MOTECZOMA HAD
A ROCK CARVED UPON THE HILL OF CHAPULTEPEC.
WITH A DESCRIPTION OF HIS LAST DAYS AND DEATH

Three years had passed since the famine. The days of abundance had come but King Moteczoma was old and his days were numbered. Desirous of leaving a memorial and image of himself that would last forever, he called Tlacaelel his brother who was no less old than he, saying, "Brother, you have seen the labors and troubles with which we have managed to sustain this republic and how we have made great this Aztec nation. It is only just that a memorial be set up to you and me and I have determined that two statues will be carved within the limits of the gardens of Chapultepec. Let the stone workers choose the part of the living rock that most pleases them and carve our likenesses upon it.[78] It will be a reward for our endeavors, and our sons and grandsons will see our images there, remember us and our great deeds and will struggle to imitate us."

148

Tlacaelel at once ordered the stone cutters to begin the statues at Chapultepec and to carve upon them the year *Ce Tochtli,* "One Rabbit," which is the year when the famine had begun. The sculptors worked rapidly and the statues were soon finished. Tlacaelel said the the king, "Lord, our vassals have done what you commanded them and it would be good for us to go see what statues they have made for us."

One morning, unattended and unseen, they left the city and went to Chapultepec to admire the statues. They found them very lifelike, as much in the features as in the ornamentation. The king said, "Brother Tlacaelel, I am well pleased with these images! They will remain as a perpetual memorial to our greatness in the way that we remember Quetzalcoatl. It is written that before the latter departed he left orders that his figure be carved in wood and in stone, to be adored by the common people. Yet we know that he was a man like us. Let us be glorified in the same way."

When they had returned to the city the king spoke to his brother in private. "I want to come to an agreement with you. Both of us have governed and sustained this Aztec nation and if I die before you, I wish you to become the ruler of the land. From the beginning your deeds have made you worthy of this. I do not want any son of mine, brother or relative to aspire to this post; only you are worthy of it. And if you should die before I do, let one of your sons inherit the throne. You may choose him and he will sit upon the seat and throne of our ancestors, Acamapichtli, Huitzilihuitl, Chimalpopoca, and Itzcoatl, who were kings and sovereigns of this wide world." Tlacaelel then showed his gratitude to the king for the honor he had bestowed upon him.

"Lord," said Tlacaelel, "I wish you to leave another memorial to yourself in this world, and it will not be less worthy of praise than those which you have built heretofore. In the hot country, in provinces like Cuernavaca, Yauhtepec, Huaxtepec, I know that there is an abundance of waters and springs, of fertile and rich lands.[79] I am reminded especially of the famous springs that exist in Huaxtepec; they can serve as a recreation place, as a diversion, for you and your successors. It will be a delightful place and it will be good to make a large pond where the water may gather and rise. With this the entire garden may be watered.

"Let us send to Cuetlaxtla, where Pinotl governs in your name, the order that we wish the following to be brought to us: Cacao trees together with *xochinacaztli*, *yoloxochitl*, *cacahuaxochitl*, *izquixochitl*, *huacalxochitl*, *cacaloxochitl*, and other flowers that grow in the hot country near the coast, and see if they will thrive here. It will cost us little to find out."

The king liked the idea and thought that it would bring him glory and praise after his days were done. He immediately sent messengers to Cuetlaxtla to have many kinds of plants brought, all with great care. He also ordered that gardeners come to plant them with their own hands according to the methods followed in their homeland, while the springs were being dammed in Huaxtepec. They brought to Mexico all these flowers and plants in great quantities, with the earth still about the roots, wrapped up in fine cloth. When the monarch saw them, when he observed that all the plants were fresh and undamaged and that gardeners had come to transplant them, he ordered them taken to Huaxtepec and planted around the springs. This was done with all the ceremonial usual on such occasions. Once the plants were sown, the gardeners fasted for eight days and slashed the upper part of their ears as a sacrifice and smeared the blood upon the leaves. They asked their overseers for large quantities of paper, incense and rubber, and they performed a sacrifice in honor of the god of the flowers. They offered him quail and they scattered the blood upon the plants and upon the earth where they had been set. They did this because they believed that with that rite no plant would be lost and that soon all would burst forth with flower and fruit.

None of the plants was lost. On the contrary, on the third year they gave abundant flowers and the gardeners from Cuetlaxtla were amazed. They said that in their country no tree bloomed as quickly as here and that Huaxtepec was a better land for the plants than their own.

Moteczoma raised his hands to the heavens and thanked the Lord of All Created Things for what he had done. He and Tlacaelel wept with joy because their plan had been successful, and they considered it a special favor of the Lord of the Heights, of the Day and Night, since they could now bequeath to Mexico and all the nations the refreshment and the delights of the flowers that they had lacked until then.

At this time the king became deadly ill; he sickened day by day until he died; he was to be remembered as a most just and merciful king. He died in 1469, having reigned thirty years. It is said that in his last illness he made a war upon the province of Tlatlauhquitepec and conquered it. After his death the usual obsequies were celebrated in his honor and all the kings and chieftains of the land came with their offerings and presents. They killed many slaves to serve him in the after life, and they buried him with a large part of his treasures.

CHAPTER XXXII WHICH TREATS OF THE ELECTION OF KING AXAYACATL AND OF THINGS THAT OCCURRED IN HIS TIME

When the funeral rites of King Moteczoma the First had ended Tlacaelel ordered all the principal people and noblemen of Mexico to meet in the customary place of solemn gatherings. He then spoke.

"The death of my brother is known to you!
He was like one who carries a load on his back for a time.
He carried the burden of being lord of Mexico until the end of his days.
He was like a slave subjected to his master
Sheltering and defending this republic.
What happened to him will happen to me and to all of us.
We enjoy life, its pleasures and happiness.
This is given to us for only a short time.
All of my brothers are dead now and I am alone."

Having said this Tlacaelel began to weep and the noblemen, pitying and consoling him, asked him to be the next ruler.

"O Aztecs," exclaimed Tlacaelel, "I thank you for the honor
You wish to bestow upon me. But how can I be honored more
Than I have already been?
What further sovereignty could I acquire than that which I have now?
None of the past kings have acted
Without my opinion or counsel!
But I am too old to carry the burden that you wish to place upon my back.
Know that I will serve you and aid you until the end of my life
And do not be sorrowful; I will point out the one
Who is to be your king and lord. Go call King Nezahualcoyotl
From the province of Acolhuacan. Go call Totoquihuaztli
Of the Tecpanec nation! I wish to consult them."

When the two sovereigns had arrived Tlacaelel withdrew with them and talked about the election of a new king. Their decision was that a son of the last monarch, Axayacatl, must now rule. And so it was that he was enthroned.

At the beginning of the reign of the new king Axayacatl trouble began between Mexico-Tenochtitlan and Tlatelolco. Some mischievous youths of the nobility of Mexico went to the market place and met there certain maidens, daughters of the lords of Tlatelolco. The young men directed flattering words to them, joking with them. The girls answered in the same tone, thinking that it was only a game. The boys asked to be allowed to go in their company and the girls agreed. But before they had reached Tlatelolco the youths had treated them disgracefully and violated them. These girls returned to complain to their fathers, brothers and relatives, who were highly indignant over the offense.

At this same time—while the Tlatelolca were digging a canal so that canoes could enter the city—another disturbing event took place. One morning the canal was found broken up and filled in. The lords of Tlatelolco were greatly angered over this and they said, "The Aztecs believe that we are of an alien lineage. They do not know that we are Aztecs like them, relatives who originated in the same place as they did. What new thing is this with which they wish to offend us?"

Among the Tlatelolca there was a high priest by the name of Moquihuix. He was promptly made their king to show their indignation over these happenings. Although they had always been subjects of the royal crown of Mexico, they now declared themselves independent and began to seek help beyond the mountains, inciting Huexotzinco, Tlaxcala and Tliliuhquitepec to fight against the Aztecs. In this, though, they were unsuccessful, for these cities refused to aid King Moquihuix.

CHAPTER XXXIII WHICH TREATS OF A FIERCE BATTLE BETWEEN THE AZTECS OF TLATELOLCO AND THOSE OF TENOCHTITLAN

Moquihuix, sovereign of Tlatelolco, began to prepare all his men for war and feigned a contest. A great statue in the image of a man was carved of stone and it was placed upon a platform in the square. The king announced that the youth who aimed best with his slingshot would receive a reward.

A great number of young men, more than two thousand, came out; they were all desirous of receiving the prize which the new king had promised. They were all sons and relative of the nobility. With slings and rounded stones in their hands they attacked the statue and after a little while it fell, broken to pieces. The king was highly pleased with the ability of his men to destroy the statue and, with a smiling face, he thanked all those who had participated in this act. He said that as no individual had outshone another he was going to prepare another test.

On this occasion a great wooden statue was made and put in the same place. This time the youths shot at it with darts and arrows. In a little while the image had been pierced by many arrows and spears, some of them having passed through it though it was about four inches thick. When the king had seen the skill of the boys and their desire to gain glory, he pretended to organize a hunt of water fowl. Many canoes were put in order and a great number of young men entered the lagoon. They were told not to shoot at any duck or heron which might be stand-

152

ing upon the land or swimming in the water but only to aim at those that were in flight. In this way their skill would be known.

Everyone stood ready with his spear in hand and a great quantity of birds which had been in the water were frightened into flight. As soon as they were in the air most of them, ducks, wild geese, heron and other water fowl were killed with these spears and arrows. The young men spent most of the day hunting in this manner.

"O Tlatelolca," said Moquihuix to the young men,
"I have been well pleased to see your ability.
The contest I engaged you in was done on purpose.
If some day you must wage war against the enemy, you will know
That their flesh is not stone, that it is not wood,
And that since your intrepid arms break through wood and stone,
How much easier will it be to destroy flesh!
I also want you to know that our enemies are not birds
Which can fly and can slip between one's hands.
No birds that fly have slipped between your hands today.
Therefore, have courage. Soon you will have need of your hands,
And Mexico-Tlatelolco will be honored and
All the nations will be subjected to us and it will rejoice in
What Mexico-Tenochtitlan has rejoiced in up to now."

The principal noblemen who knew of this affair advised the king not to hurry or be restless but to keep the matter a secret. Their opinion was that Tenochtitlan should be attacked suddenly in the middle of the night. King Axayacatl was still a young man and once his great warriors were dead one need not worry about him. Tlacaelel was old and he was no more to be feared than a little old woman who spends her time sitting.

However, as this kind of secret is difficult to keep, it was made public in the following way: Some women from Mexico-Tenochtitlan went to the market of Tlatelolco and got into a fight with some of the local women in trading. Heated words were exchanged and the Tlatelolca women yelled that soon the others would pay for their insolence and this made the Aztec women suspicious, whereupon they went to King Axayacatl. Since he already knew about the warlike games of the young men his suspicions were confirmed and he summoned his council. It was decided to send certain captains to the market place of Tlatelolco and while they pretended to be idling they would spy on all.

While walking through the market with an air of indifference they heard many spiteful words against them and above all they noted such phrases as "Behold those who are walking so carelessly! Well, let them, soon they will have to pay!" "What merchandise have you brought to sell? Do you want to sell your intestines or hearts?" All these things worried Axayacatl and Tlacaelel greatly.

The ruler of Tlatelolco was married to a daughter or sister of Axayacatl and our chronicle says that while she was asleep she dreamed that her private parts spoke, wailing, "Alas, my lady! Where will I be tomorrow at this time?" She awoke with a great shock and told her husband what she had dreamed, asking him to interpret this dream. He answered by telling her what he had decided to do about Tenochtitlan, and said that her dream might be a prophecy of events. She wept bitterly over her husband's prediction, saying:

"Lord, it is a terrible thing, that which you have begun!
Have pity on the women and children who will perish because of you!
Think of the deaths that will occur on both sides because of you!
Remember that you have small children, and consider
That you and I will be needed by them.
They will become perpetual slaves if we are conquered."

King Moquihuix arose from his mat and sighed, showing that he repented of his warlike intentions. However, he excused himself by saying that his advisor Teconal had been the instigator of the rebellion and that he was not powerful enough to stop it now that it had begun.

The queen answered, "How is it, sir, that being the chief and lord of these people you cannot calm their hearts? Give me permission to speak to them! They may listen to my womanly words. Make peace with Mexico-Tenochtitlan, and our past friendship will be renewed. Do not be a coward; speak to them. Go see Axayacatl; pacify him and embrace him. Do this for me; give me this satisfaction."

The monarch of Tlatelolco left the room to see if there were trouble abroad and, passing through the kitchen, he beheld there an ancient man whom he had never seen before. The man was speaking to a dog and the animal was answering all of his questions. On the fire next to the old man was a pot boiling and within it some birds were dancing. All of these things were considered to be evil omens by the king. It is also said that a mask hanging on the wall began to moan in a sorrowful way and that the king picked it up and dashed it to the floor.

154

Moquihuix then decided to consult the gods and make a celebration in their honor so that these omens could be turned against Tenochtitlan. He invited his neighbors, the people of Azcapotzalco, Cuauhtitlan, and Tenayuca and regaled

*A battle between Mexico-Tenochtitlan and Mexico-Tlatelolco. King Axayacatl and King Moquihuix are shown in the center. From the Atlas, the picture book accompanying Durán's text. Photo Reg Van Cuylenburg.*

them with banquets and dances. The adornments for this feast were all weapons: swords, shields, arrows, darts, slings, bows, and with them they performed a solemn dance. And all the presents brought by the lords of those towns, as well as their offerings to the gods, were of the same nature.

When the meal had ended several chants belittling Tenochtitlan were sung; the chants mourned over this city as if it had been destroyed. However, their tongues became twisted and wanting to say "Tenochtitlan" they said, "Tlatelolco," much as they tried to speak properly.

Teconal, who had instigated this rebellion, fearful that they would weaken on seeing so many signs and omens, said to Moquihuix, "Everything is ready. Whenever you desire we will go kill those wildcats who are our neighbors."

Moquihuix sent his spies to Mexico to see what was brewing and they found King Axayacatl playing ball with his noblemen, apparently ignorant of any trouble. The Aztecs had done this intentionally so as to blind them and convince them that nothing was known about their plans. It was false, though, since the daughter of King Axayacatl had notified her father that the attack would be on that night.

The spies returned to Tlatelolco well pleased, and at midnight the attack took place. Warriors entered Mexico-Tenochtitlan shouting and yelling, but the Aztecs came out to meet them and caught them in different parts of the city. The Aztecs massacred them and the Tlatelolca fled by the way they had entered. Those who escaped leapt into the lagoon and hid themselves under the rushes. The men of Tlatelolco were much humiliated and angered by this, and they decided to meet their enemy on the battlefield. Orders were given that the army gather again, boys and men, and that all rehearse for war.

CHAPTER XXXIV WHICH TREATS OF A SECOND BATTLE BETWEEN THE AZTECS AND TLATELOLCA AND HOW THE LATTER WERE CONQUERED

Tlacaelel was wrathful over all these happenings and he sent an envoy called Cueyatzin to Tlatelolco, carrying the ointments and insignia of the dead.

"O lord," said the envoy to Moquihuix, "the king of Mexico,
Your servant, your brother, sends you these funeral insignia.

I am to anoint you with this pitch of the dead and you must prepare to die."

Moquihuix stood up from his seat, pushed the messenger away and cast him out of the room roughly, saying, "Tell your master that these ointments are for him!" While he yet spoke Teconal appeared, sword in hand, and with one blow cut off the head of Cueyatzin. They carried the body of the messenger and threw it within the boundaries of Tenochtitlan. After this the Tlatelolca set up a great shriek, yelling, "Tlatelolco! Tlatelolco!"

Tlacaelel picked up his sword and shield and ascended to the top of the pyramid where the drums began to beat and the shell horns to sound. At this a great number of soldiers gathered and Tlacaelel shouted to them:

"Sons and brothers, do not be faint, justice is on our side!
They have killed our ambassador without reason.
This time we will not have to go far from our boundaries;
Our enemy lies right behind our houses. You will not have to climb mountains
Or go down cliffs. You will not have to march through valleys.
Imagine that you are just brushing flies from your bodies.
Therefore cover yourselves with your shields, hold your swords tight,
Extend your arms strongly. From here I will watch and I will rejoice
In your bravery."

At this point, and from the summit of the pyramid, Tlacaelel ordered that the drums sound and that the trumpets, shell-horns and other instruments be played for battle. This was done accompanied by much whistling and hideous screams. At the sound of all this, the Aztecs took courage. They forced the Tlatelolca to retreat until they had surrounded them in the market place where the latter tried to make a last stand.

King Axayacatl ordered his men to be still and they all lowered their shields and bows, dropped their slings and spears while he shouted to the Tlatelolca, "O brother Moquihuix, behold how we are about to become masters of this market place and temple! Surrender! Lower your arms! Have pity upon your own selves and upon your children."

"We will do that gladly," answered Teconal, "if you will deliver yourselves to us with your hands tied! With your blood we will redden our temple! We have sworn it, we have promised it to our god Huitzilopochtli!"

When he realized that his words had no effect, Axayacatl ordered his men into the battle again and the attack was so furious that they pushed into the market place while the Tlatelolca withdrew in great confusion. When Moquihuix and Teconal saw themselves and their people lost, they ascended the steps of the pyramid in order to distract them while preparing a feint. A large number of women were gathered, stripped of their clothing and formed into a squadron. They were made to attack the Aztecs who were fighting furiously. The women, naked, with their private parts revealed and their breasts uncovered, came upon them slapping their bellies, showing their breasts and squirting milk at the Aztecs. Next to them appeared a squadron of little boys, naked, with their faces blackened and their heads feathered, making a wailing sound. The Aztecs, dismayed by such crudity, were ordered by King Axayacatl not to harm any of the women but to take them prisoners together with the children.

The Aztecs pressed their victory and, having captured the women, they began to climb the steps of the pyramid, though this was done with great difficulty because of the resistance found there. When Axayacatl arrived at the summit and found Moquihuix and Teconal crouching at the altar of Huitzilopochtli, he walked boldly to the place where the idol stood. He slew the two men, dragged their bodies out and cast them down the steps of the temple.

When the Tlatelolca saw their chieftains dead, they fled from the market place and jumped into the canals among the reeds. Some of them were immersed up to the neck, others to the chest; all hid as best they could in order not to be killed by the Aztecs who were sparing no one. Now a great nobleman from Tlatelolco, an aged uncle of the king of Mexico-Tenochtitlan, called Cuahuauhtzin, appeared and prostrated himself in front of his nephew, beseeching him to give orders that his men cease in the kill. The king agreed and ordered that the statue of Huitzilopochtli be removed and that the temple become a rubbish heap for the Aztecs, just as the Tlatelolca had sworn to do with that of Tenochtitlan.

In order to abase those who had leapt into the water and who were still hidden in the rushes, the Aztecs ordered them to quack like magpies and imitate ducks and wild geese. As soon as they were commanded to do this they began to quack and the Aztecs burst into laughter and mockery. Even today the Tlatelolca are called "quackers" and imitators of water fowl. They are much offended by this name and when they fight the name is always recalled.

In the midst of all the quacking Axayacatl ordered that Tlatelolco be sacked. The houses were robbed of their contents; even the pots, jugs, plates, and bowls were carried away, and what the Aztecs could not carry they smashed to bits, hoping to frighten and humiliate the Tlatelolca forever. Teconal's body was impaled and placed at the entrance to Tlatelolco as an example and warning to the rest.

159

Eighty days later, when their first payment of tribute was due, the Tlatelolca did not bring slaves as they had been commanded. They excused themselves, saying that they had been unable to obtain them. The king and Tlacaelel reprehended them and punished them in the following way: The noblemen of that city were no longer to wear splendid mantles. From now on they must use cloaks of maguey fiber, like people of low rank. And they were not to wear sandals or lip-pendants, ear-plugs or fine feathers. Nor were they to be allowed to appear in the market place or to rest on the crossroads or at the thresholds. Like women they were to stay in their houses until eighty days after their second payment had passed.

The people of Tlatelolco, in order not to be punished further, made great efforts to join in the battles against Tlaxcala, Huexotzinco, Tliliuhquitepec, Cholula, and Zacatlan. They took many prisoners and slaves as tribute and brought them to the Aztecs, and in this way the interdict they had suffered was removed. But whenever they failed in their duties it was placed upon them again. The obstinacy of the Aztecs was such that, until the Spaniards arrived in this country, the Tlatelolca were given no liberty whatsoever. They were not allowed to have their own temple but had to worship at the one in Mexico. Our chronicle tells us that their temple became filled with weeds and garbage, and that the walls and dwelling quarters fell into ruins.

CHAPTER XXXV WHICH TREATS OF HOW THE PEOPLE OF TENANTZINCO BEGGED THE AZTECS FOR AID AGAINST TOLUCA AND MATLATZINCO. WITH A DESCRIPTION OF HOW THIS HELP WAS SENT AND HOW THE LATTER WAS DESTROYED

In the provinces of Toluca and Matlatzinco reigned two powerful sovereigns. The one of Toluca was called *Chimaltecuhtli*, "Lord of Shields," and the other *Chalchiuhquiauh*, "Jade Rain," who governed over the Matlatzinca people. The ruler of Toluca had three valiant sons, daring young men, who were capable of carrying out any great feat, no matter how difficult. In the city of Tenantzinco there ruled a monarch called Tezozomoctli who had three or four young sons, who were also proud of their lineage and gallantry. Among these young men there began to be rivalries and envy and they began to form bands, all based upon childish quarrels. Even though the *Chronicle* tells us about these disputes, it is such an unimportant

160

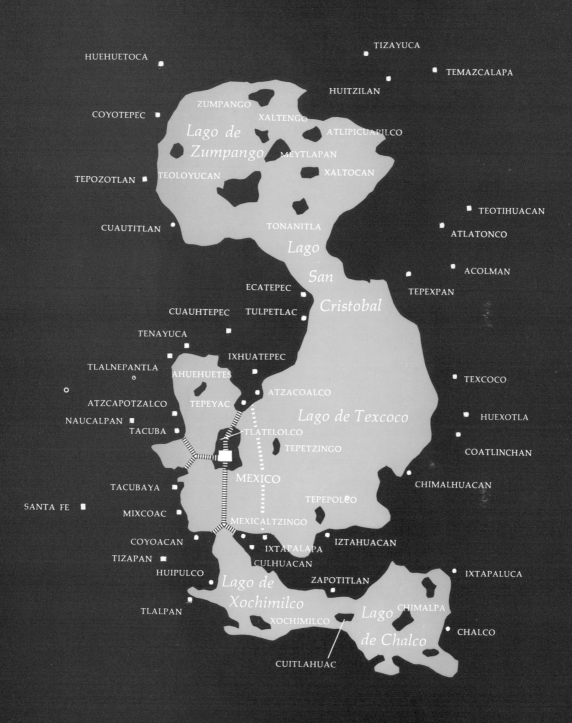

*The lake area of the Valley of Mexico in pre-Hispanic times.*

matter, I will not repeat all the details here. However, it is well known that the young men from Toluca constantly threatened those of Tenantzinco, swearing to wage war upon them and force them to show their strength.

The monarch of Tenantzinco was much troubled by this. He saw that Chimaltecuhtli of Toluca made no effort to control the actions of his sons, but rather encouraged these challenges and feuds. The lord of Tenantzinco decided to try to punish all this trouble-making before any misfortune could happen. He came to Mexico in person and, standing before Axayacatl, he described everything that had happened in the land of Toluca. He told how they had become bad neighbors and how they were trying to take each other's lands and how they challenged each other constantly. King Axayacatl agreed to defend them against the men of Toluca in all that he could.

After Tezozomoctli had departed for Tenantzinco, King Axayacatl became greatly preoccupied in the building of a place for the Stone of the Sun which had been carved, at his orders, by the sculptors. Upon it the master craftsmen had wrought images of the valorous Aztec dignitaries of the past, pictures of the wars in which they had conquered land and of the remote coastal provinces which they had overcome. Men from these conquered regions had already brought offerings and sacrificed upon the stone. In the center were represented the rays of the sun radiating from a round depression where victims were decapitated and from which there ran a channel to carry away the blood.

The king was also occupied in the making of the great and finely worked stone upon which were represented the months, years, days and weeks, all splendidly carved. We were able to see this stone in the great square of Mexico, next to the canal. The most illustrious lord, Don Fray Alonso de Montúfar, Archbishop of Mexico, of happy memory, ordered that it be buried because of the criminal acts that had been committed upon it.

Axayacatl had these two stones carved as tables of sacrifice and he was in the process of constructing places on the top of the temple to set up these stones. He made this the excuse to wage war on Toluca and Matlatzinco. He ordered messengers to these two cities who were to demand cedar and pine wood for certain rooms in the temple. It was not that they lacked wood; rather it was a trick of Tlacaelel to accomplish what he determined. Tlacaelel said that since the time of his brother, Moteczoma, he had been convinced that that province should be conquered, since he feared that its inhabitants might ally themselves to Michoacan.

The Matlatzinca of Toluca refused to send the wood, and the Aztecs prepared for war. At this time the sovereign of Tenantzinco came to Mexico and proposed that the Aztec army meet his men at a place called *Iztapaltetitlan*, "Place Next to the Stone Painted White." Axayacatl asked that the army of Tenantzinco be made ready and, when they saw a great bonfire rising from the top of a hill, attack with cries and shouting. He in his turn would attack the city of Toluca from the road. Thus the enemy would be caught in the middle. He did not wish any Matlatzinca to be killed; he wanted them all taken prisoners in order to redden his temple and the tables of the shrine with their blood in a solemn sacrificial ceremony of the Matlatzinca people.

In this way it was done. The Matlatzinca were caught in an ambush and a great battle occurred near the city of Toluca. King Axayacatl, though a young man, took many captives from among the hardiest warriors and delivered them to his guards. Victorious, this king began to sound the golden drum that he had on his back, and which was played when the enemy retreated. As he went running, without awaiting his guard, an enemy captain who was hidden behind a century plant saw him so careless and in such a hurry. The enemy ran up to Axayacatl and drove a knife in his thigh, almost to the bone. The wounded monarch was on the point of collapse, but he caught his enemy and both fell to the ground where they fought furiously. The king's guard and noblemen, missing him and realizing the danger, searched for him and found him in this struggle. His face was covered with dirt and his arms with blood and, though wounded, he was defending himself bravely like the stout-hearted youth that he was. The soldiers wanted to kill the enemy but the king ordered that his life be spared and that he be taken prisoner. But Tlilcuetzpal, "Black Lizard," a strong and courageous man, managed to defend himself with his shield and sword, even though wounded, and slipped away from their hands.

The Aztecs now entered the city of Toluca, removed the chief god called Coltzin from the temple and burned the sanctuary. The rulers surrendered and the tribal god was carried away, together with all the priests of the temple.

CHAPTER XXXVI WHICH TREATS OF HOW THE TWO STONES WERE SET IN THEIR PLACES AND HOW THE MATLATZINCA WERE SACRIFICED UPON THEM

When the victorious army had returned to Mexico the feast of Tlacaxipehualiztli—Skinning of Men—was approaching, and Tlacaelel spoke to the king:

"My son, you see my white hair, my old age.
I beseech you not to tarry in setting up the tables for the sacrifice.
You know that the feast of the Flaying of Men draws near
And if you postpone this any longer I may be dead tomorrow or
The day after, and I will not be able to take with me the memory
Of this happy event."

All of this was done by that evil old man who never was satiated with human flesh. The king then decided to please him and gave orders that the stones be carried to the top of the pyramid.

Axayacatl also questioned Tlacaelel as to the guests who should be invited to these festivities, and Tlacaelel said that the "Mutes" from Cempoala and Quiahuitztlan should be invited. These were provinces which lie near the coast and which had not yet been conquered.[81] Tlacaelel explained that these people should be invited because if they refused to come it would be an excuse to wage war on them and destroy them.

The Aztec envoys set out for Cempoala and Quiahuitztlan immediately and spoke to Tlehuitzilin and to Quetzalayotl who accepted the invitation and treated the ambassadors well.

When all had gathered for the feast of *Tlatlauhquitezcatl*, "Red Mirror," which is another name for this feast, and when the hour for sacrifice had come, the prisoners were brought out. They were formed in a line at the place of the Skull Rack and were given colored paper loincloths. They were smeared from head to foot with white plaster, their heads anointed with molten rubber and plumed with turkey feathers. Their faces were also smeared with the same rubber pitch. When the Matlatzinca had been lined up, the four sacrificers, two Aztecs dressed as jaguars and two as eagles, appeared. They were called the Elder Jaguar and the Younger, the Elder Eagle and the Younger. Then all the gods appeared, or rather their impersonators, wearing the garb of each divinity.

They ascended to the summit of the pyramid, while the singers brought forth a wooden instrument called *teponaztli* which is commonly played at feasts.[82] They placed the drum in the center of the courtyard and began to beat it and sing special hymns in honor of the new stone, all of which had been composed especially for this occasion. On their backs the singers wore ornaments shaped like millstones, with a hole in the middle made of white featherwork. Cords made of white feathers passed through the holes; and these were called "Singers of the Round Stone." All wore on their heads a decoration made of hair which is called *yopitzontli*, which means hair of the divine Yopi. These wigs are still in use today, as are the different hair ornaments of the various gods, and are brought forth in dances.

When they began to dance a man dressed as an ocelot, moving along to the rhythm of the drum, approached the prisoners and untied one of them; all had been tied at the calves. The victim was brought to the stone, placed upon it and bound with a rope which penetrated the hole in the center. He was given a shield and a feathered sword with four chunks of wood to defend himself. His opponent then emerged and came dancing and singing, encircling the stone two or three times. The unfortunate victim then gave forth great cries and shrieks and began to leap into the air, slapping his thighs loudly with his hand and making gestures toward the heavens. He picked up his wooden sword and shield, raised it to the sun and began to fight. When he was vanquished his heart was torn out.

In this way were all the Matlatzinca sacrificed, and they were so many that in order not to be called a liar or accused of exaggeration, I will not tell the number that died there. It is enough to say that on that occasion the Matlatzinca nation decreased considerably, since many died in that sacrifice.

The bodies were laid out near the skull rack and each warrior went to identify his captive. The body was given to him to eat—the bones to be hung on sticks in his house as a sign of prestige. In this way the Indian nations lost their fear of the dead and ghosts. They are not afraid of sleeping in cemeteries or in churches, either accompanied or alone. They do not claim to have seen ghosts or to have heard moans or other frightful things. In this they are unreasonable people. It is not uncommon to see an old woman or an old man, born before the Conquest, crouching all night next to a corpse without uneasiness or fright, or sitting in a cemetery as a night watchman with only a small light. None of our Spanish people would do these things without great uneasiness no matter how they tried to get up their courage.

The noble guests who had come to the feast and sacrifice were horrified, beside themselves, on seeing the death of so many men. They were so frightened that they hardly dared leave the flower-decorated bowers in which they had been placed. They had handsome fans of rich featherwork to defend them from the sun and all had been sitting upon high seats covered with jaguar skins. All had been given gifts by the king: rich mantles and golden garlands with fine feathers for their heads. They wore bracelets of gold, lip-pendants, ear- and nose-plugs. They carried different types of flowers and had been perfumed.[83]

Once the guests had left old Tlacaelel said to the king:

"My son, you have now rejoiced in the feast which has glorified your name; you have been painted with the colors, with the brush of honor forever. But now you must carry ahead this greatness that you have achieved. You well know that the Stone of the Sun is finished, and that it is necessary that it be set up."

Once this stone had been put in place the great ceremonies connected with its first use were much talked about. It was also at this point that the king and Tlacaelel proposed to their allies that a war be waged against Michoacan.

CHAPTER XXXVII WHICH TREATS OF HOW A WAR AGAINST MICHOACAN WAS DETERMINED. WITH A DESCRIPTION OF HOW THE AZTECS WERE VANQUISHED AND ALMOST ALL OF THEM SLAIN

The next morning Kings Nezahualcoyotl and Totoquihuaztli were called in, together with the sovereigns of other allied nations such as Xochimilco, and Chalco, and the hot country. Axayacatl announced the decision that he and Tlacaelel had come to the previous afternoon, that is to say, to wage war on Michoacan.[84] Although they knew, from what their ancestors had said, that these people were their relatives, the king wished to try out the valor of the Tarascans to see if they could compete with the Aztecs. The main cause, however, for this war was to try to celebrate a great feast in the first use of the Stone of the Sun and to redden the temple with the blood of these people.

The allies sent men in such great numbers that the Aztec army contained twenty-four thousand soldiers. Thinking that these were enough men to conquer Michoacan or even a large province, the army departed from Mexico in the direction of the land of the Matlatzinca. The forces gathered at a point located near the boundaries between Matlatzinco and Tlaximaloyan, next to a lagoon which is not far from Tzipecuaro. The camp was set up with many tents and houses made of mats which were used in war and which today are still in use among the merchants. There a special tent was set up for the king, upholstered in fine cloth with splendid seats for the noblemen who had come with him. Whenever the monarch traveled all his great men went with him, both from the city of Mexico and the other provinces.

Once the camp had been set up, spies were sent to observe the Tarascan army, which was discovered by some Matlatzinca informants. They came back with the news that the enemy had gathered on a plain near the lagoon. The king ordered the spies to find out how many men were there and in what way the army was organized, since he did not know this nation's manner of fighting. He was also desirous of knowing which were their most dangerous weapons. The spies went very secretly and when they arrived near the enemy camp they dug a tunnel which reached the tents of the Tarascans. When they had made a small crack in the earth they were able to hear through it and they listened to everything that was said by the warriors. They found out that the Tarascans were forty thousand strong and that they relied mainly upon their slings and propelled spears, bows and arrows, swords edged with stone blades, clubs, and other offensive arms, together with finely worked shields and gold and feather insignia.

Axayacatl was not much pleased when he heard about this; he called together his great captains, saying, "I have found out that the Tarascans are forty thousand men, all of them robust, tall and brave. They have sixteen thousand more men than we! What shall we do?"

On seeing the indecision of the king, the captains made him take courage, giving him the worst type of advice. They stated that the Aztec nation had never feared multitudes, that it had never turned its face from weapons nor from other warlike devices. If they turned back now, what would the other nations say of them knowing they had come to wage war? They had no alternative but to attack and triumph or die.

The monarch was convinced and he ordered his men to approach the enemy little by little. Along the way went the *Cuauhuehuetl*, "Old Eagles," who were in charge of organizing the men. Then came the old soldiers, lords, captains, and those called *Cuachic*, an order of knighthood that had sworn not to retreat. Soon the Tarascans were seen, in good order, their lords standing in front. They were so covered with gold, gems and feathers, all so shining, glittering with golden bracelets, ankle-bands, ear-pendants, lip-plugs, and golden head-bands, that as the sun rose it blinded the Aztecs to see this.

King Axayacatl was repentant now but he ordered the usual talk of encouragement to be given to the army. Our *Chronicle* tells us that at this point some Tarascans came to the monarch to berate him:

"O great lord, who brought you here? Why have you come?
Were you not happy in your own land? Was it perhaps the Matlatzinca
Whom you overcame a short time ago? Consider carefully, O lord,
What you are to do! You have been deceived!"

The king thanked them and asked them to depart since he wanted to test their strength, as he had come for that reason.

The Tarascan army then attacked with such fury that in a moment the Aztecs had begun to weaken and to turn their backs. When the sovereign saw the situation he began to increase his forces with soldiers whom he had brought from the other provinces, and so it was that the battle lasted the entire day until the sun went down, the Tarascans not retreating but showing great valor and skill.

Once night had come the great lords and warriors appeared before King Axayacatl. Our *Chronicle* tells us that their faces—noses, mouths and eyes—were so covered with sweat and dust because of having fought the entire day, that the king was barely able to recognize them. Those in the most unhappy state were the men who had sworn not to retreat; some of them were badly wounded, some by arrows, others by stones, others by sword thrusts, others pierced with spears. The king sorrowed greatly over them and felt great pity for the multitude, from all the nations, that lay dead upon the field. He had the warriors called and ordered that they be given a beverage which was used to alleviate the pains of war. This was called *yolatl*, "Heart Water," which in Spanish could be translated as "broth of strength."

That night the survivors rested, preparing to defend themselves again. The next morning, with Matlatzinca reinforcements, the Aztecs attacked the Tarascan army. But the assault was so unsuccessful that they were like flies that fall in the water, as our *Chronicle* says. All of them fell into the hands of the Tarascans, and the killing was so great that the Aztecs decided to withdraw those who were still alive in order to save at least a few. In this encounter the Tarascans killed many valiant Aztecs, especially from the military orders called Cuachic and Otomi. Among the fallen was a nobleman who was a close relative of the king and who belonged to the Royal Council of four from which the king's successor was chosen. When the Tarascans realized that this man was of royal blood they carried him into the Aztec camp to show their boldness and to demonstrate their contempt for the Aztecs. Then they returned to their own camp, not wishing to push their victory.

King Axayacatl had his camp dismantled and, with broken spirit because of the few men that had been spared him (most of them wounded and being carried on men's backs), came to a town called Ecatepec. All began to weep there and the survivors were counted. Of the Aztecs, two hundred were left; of the Texcocans, four hundred; the Tecpanecs, Chalca, and Xochimilca, four hundred each; of the Otomi forces from Cuauhtlalpan there were only three hundred; and from the hot country practically none had survived. Twenty thousand men had died in the war, perhaps more!

When Tlacaelel learned of these sad events, he placed guards about the city and ordered drums and conch shells to be played. The gods were invoked and sad hymns were sung from the top of the pyramids. The entire city was filled with sorrow and lamentation, mourning and tears.

When the king and his two hundred men reached Chapultepec, the elders and priests of the temple came out to meet them. They were dressed and adorned as if the king had come victorious. He was offered incense, and great speeches were made to him. This was done, I understand, whenever a king returned from an absence of more than three days, for the kings were held to be divine men, likenesses of the gods, and were therefore honored with godly ceremonies. The king went immediately to offer up his lamentation and to spill some of his own blood in sacrifice, together with the usual offerings of quail.

When he met Tlacaelel he wept, saying, "Lord, it has been my fate to be unfortunate! Things that did not happen to my ancestors happen to me. What a terrible loss! What destruction the Tarascans have inflicted upon us!"

The old man answered, "Son, do not be faint, let not your heart feel dismay! Have courage, your vassals did not die of their hearts, nor spinning like women, but on the battlefield, fighting for the greatness of your crown and for the honor of their country. They won as much honor in their deaths as, in other times, they had gained in their victories! I give thanks to the Lord of All Created Things who has allowed me to see the deaths of so many of my brothers and nephews. But I do not know why I have been spared!" Having said these words he burst into bitter tears. All tried to console the old man, whereupon he ordered that the funeral ceremonies of the dead be prepared.

CHAPTER XXXVIII WHICH TREATS OF THE LONG FUNERAL RITES WITH WHICH THE AZTECS REMEMBERED THOSE WHO HAD DIED IN THE WAR, ESPECIALLY THE BRAVE CAPTAINS

The funeral rites began the following way: the Cuauhuehuetl, who were like field marshals, went to the homes of the deceased and spoke to the widows:

"O my daughter, let not sadness overwhelm you
Or end the days of your life. We have brought you the tears and sighs
Of those who were your father, mother, and strength.
We have brought them to your door. Take courage, show your love
For our sons who did not die plowing or digging in the fields,
Who did not die on the road, trading, but for the honor of our country.

168

*The god Quetzalcoatl shown as Ehecatl, bird-beaked*
*deity of the wind. Museum of Toluca, Mexico. Photo*
*National Institute of Anthropology and History, Mexico City.*

They have departed, holding each other's hands, and with them went
The great lord Huitznahuatl, a close relative of our king and monarch.
All of them are now rejoicing in the shining places of the sun,
Where they walk about in his company, clothed in his light.
They will be remembered forever! Therefore, O illustrious Aztec matrons,
Weep for their memory!"

Those whose profession it was to sing for men who had died in battle came into the square. On their heads were tied black leather bands. They brought out an instrument and began to play a sad and tearful music. The lamentations began with hymns for the dead. When all of this had started the widows of the dead men appeared, carrying the cloaks of their husbands on their shoulders and their loincloths around their necks. The hair of the widows was loose and all of them, standing in a line, clapped their hands to the beating of the drum. They wept bitterly and at times they danced bowing their heads toward the earth; at other times they danced leaning backwards. The children of the dead men were present also, wearing their fathers' mantles, carrying on their backs small boxes containing the lip, ear, and nose-plugs, and other jewelry. They clapped their hands like their mothers, and the other relatives wept with them. The men stood there, dumb, holding the swords and shields of the deceased in their hands, occasionally joining the women in their lamentations. After having wailed for a long time the elders said:

"Rest a while! Let the great resplendent sun, which passes and encircles the world above our heads, console you. To him have you offered your tears and lamentations."

Then certain relatives of the widows, who took charge of the funeral, entered and began to weep, showing great feeling. The instruments were sounded again and the singers renewed their lamentations. A new period of weeping began. The shrieks were so great that they filled one with pity, with fright, as the women clapped their hands to the sound of the instruments. The musicians then ceased to play and there was an interruption in the song. Those in charge of the funeral preparations stood in a line and, one by one, they saluted the widows. They expressed their condolences to them and to the elders who were present. They said, "We give you great thanks, O lord, for the honor that you have given the Sun, Master of the Earth, Creator of All Things! We thank you for the honor you have given those who have died in the war." Many other speeches of gratitude were made on this occasion.

Four days after the ceremony had taken place, images of the dead were made from slivers of firewood, each one with feet, arms and head. Faces were placed upon them—eyes and mouth—and paper loincloths and mantles also. On their shoulders were put wings of hawk feathers, as it was believed that in this way they would fly before the Sun every day. The heads of these bundles were feathered and pendants for the ears, nose and lips were placed upon them. These statues were taken to a room called *tlacochcalco*. The widows then entered and each one placed in front of her statue a dish of a stew called *tlacatlacualli*, which means "food of human flesh," together with some maize cakes called *papalotlaxcalli*, which means "butterfly bread," and a little flour made of toasted maize dissolved in water as a drink. After this food had been offered the drum began to sound again and the singers began their hymns which told of mourning and of tears. The chanters came dressed in filthy stained cloaks and with dirty leather bands tied to their heads. They called this chant *tzocuicatl*, "song of dirt." Their heads were smeared with the ground bark of a tree which is used to kill lice. Each carried a gourd vessel of the white native wine and they placed it in front of each statue. These vessels were *teotecomatl*, the divine gourds.[85] In front of the statues were also placed flowers and tobacco[86] and thick straws for drinking. This type of straw is called "sun drinker." The chanters of the dead then took the gourds of wine in their hands and raised them twice, thrice, in front of the statues. After this they poured the wine in the four directions around the statue.

At dusk the widows offered the singers cheap mantles, loincloths and digging sticks. The elders then gathered the bundles and set them on fire. All the firewood and paper wrapped around it went up in flames, and the widows stood about the fire, weeping with great sorrow.

The old men then addressed the widows.

"O sisters, daughters, be strong, widen your hearts!
We have abandoned our sons, the jaguars, the eagles!
Do not think that we will see them again. Do not imagine that this is
Like the times when your husband left your house sulking and angry
So that he would not return for three or four days;
Nor when he departed for his work, soon to return.
Understand that they have gone forever!
This is what you must do now: you must be occupied in your
Womanly occupations of spinning and weaving, of sweeping and watering,
Of lighting the fire and remaining in the house,
And have recourse to the Lord of All Created Things, or Day and Night,
Of Fire and Water."

172

On hearing this, the women burst forth into tears; it was frightening and made one pity them. From this day on they went into mourning, not washing their clothes or face or head until eighty days had gone by. The dirt that lay on their cheeks was so thick that the elders sent special ministers after the eighty days to scratch the filth from their faces. They would wrap it in paper and take it to the priests, who then ordered that it be cast into a place called *Yaualiuhcan,* which means "round place." Those who went to throw the tears and sadness in this place, which was outside of the city, were given gifts of clothing by the widows. The latter went to the temple, when these rites had been completed, and prayed, offering paper, incense and sacrifice. Their weeping and mourning was over now and they returned to their homes happy and consoled as if nothing had happened. Thus they became free of weeping and sadness.

Soon after this the Aztecs captured seven hundred prisoners in a war with Tliliuhquitepec and a sacrifice took place in Mexico upon the great stone. Once the ceremony had been finished and all the guests had left, King Axayacatl became ill from the exhaustion of the long ceremony and from the smell of the blood which had, according to our chronicle, a bad, sour smell. Feeling very ill, he begged Tlacaelel to have his image carved on the rocks at Chapultepec next to that of Moteczoma.

Tlacaelel gave orders that this be done, and when it was finished, the king, although very sick, was carried to see his likeness. There he said farewell to all his lords since he felt death approaching. The *Chronicle* tells that he did not return to Mexico alive but that he died on the road as he was carried in his litter.

He died young, having reigned thirteen years. Nezahualcoyotl, lord and king of Texcoco, had died earlier and Axayacatl had been present at his solemn funeral. Nezahualpilli was now sovereign of Texcoco. Axayacatl's reign was a period of constant trouble among nearby neighboring nations. There was a great enmity and combat between Ocuilan and Cuernavaca, Ocuilan having vanquished the latter. Huexotla rebelled against Texcoco and waged war. Xiquipilco rebelled and fought against its own brothers and neighbors. In this way ends this chapter.

King Axayacatl died in the year 1481 and once his funeral rites were finished a new ruler was elected: Tizoc. However, before we deal with him, since his life was short and his deeds few, I will tell of the funeral rites of King Axayacatl, since the *Chronicle* describes them in great detail.

Before Tizoc was elected, Tlacaelel sent a message to Nezahualpilli in Texcoco, advising him of the death of the previous king. The rulers of Tacuba and the other provinces were also notified. Once the news was known great mourning and sorrow were prevalent all over the land. The rulers stood in front of the messengers weeping, bemoaning the passing of the youthful and courageous king.

The lord Nezahualpilli rose from his throne and ordered those of his household to prepare all necessary things in order to give condolences to the dead man. He came to Mexico City and having greeted all the authorities he directed himself to the room where the body lay and offered it four slaves, two men and two women, gold lip-plugs, ear-plugs and nose pendants as well as a golden diadem, two gold arm-bands, two anklets of the same metal and a splendid bow with its arrows. He also offered fine green feathers and eagle plumes, a rich mantle, a costly loincloth, beautiful sandals, and an exquisite necklace of stones from which hung a golden jewel. Having placed these presents near the body, he spoke the following words to the dead man,

"O my son, O youthful, courageous and excellent Axayacatl!
This is the last time that I will see your countenance.
You have now gone to the place where you will meet your fathers,
Relatives and noble ancestors. Like the bird that flies
You have·gone there to rejoice in the Lord of All Created Things,
Of the Day and Night, of the Wind and Fire.
I have brought you this small gift for your comfort in that world."

174

When the king of Texcoco had uttered these words the monarch of Tacuba came in and spoke, exclaiming:

"O my son, you have left your city of Mexico, your Republic
Alone and unprotected! It is now in the hands of the Lord of All Created Things;
You have abandoned your labors forever. No one can appeal to you now.
You have reached the land of your lordly kinsmen and ancestors.
There you lie, there you rest in the shades of the somber fields
Of the nine mouths of death with your ancestors;
There you lie in the glittering house of fire of the Sun.
Let your body take rest now, O my son!"

After he had made an offering of slaves, gems and cloth, the lords of Chalco spoke:

"O mighty lord, may you find yourself in bliss!
May your body rest, may your body be calm in death.
The Lord of All Created Things bestowed your presence and strength upon us,
Your Chalca vassals, for a few days."

They offered him five slaves, beautiful mantles and loincloths, many gems, feathers, and a large load of tree bark and torches. This was to be used to burn the corpses of kings and therefore this type of firewood was much revered.

The delegates from Cuernavaca and all the hot country also offered up the same lamentation:

"O powerful lord, unhappy death has cut the thread of your reign
Which had been sustained by the Lord of All Created Things,
Of Night and Day. You have left your noble kinsmen alone and disconsolate.
You have gone to the place where went those who lived before you.
Behold us here in your presence, weeping and filled with sorrow.
The land has lost a great king and lord, one who was the image
Of our god Huitzilopochtli. All of us are orphans now."

The men from Yauhtepec, Huaxtepec, Acapichtlan and Tepoztlan then entered and, having spoken to the dead man, gave him four slaves. These slaves are called *tepantlacaltin* or *teixpanmiquiztenicaltin*, "those who follow the deceased to accompany him." These were the domestic slaves who served the nobility, having been obtained by purchase or through a law suit; prisoners of war were only used for the gods. They also offered paper, bundles of cloth, feathers and many jewels and ornaments. The representatives of Xochimilco spoke:

175

"O mighty sir, our hearts are grieved and burn with pain as we see
That you have lost your speech and can no longer answer us.
You have hidden your face from us and we can rejoice in it no longer.
All we can do is weep and moan over your departure
Since death has taken you away from us forever. Here we have brought you
This small gift against the perils you are about to meet."

The sovereigns of Cuetlaxtlan came in, and having spoken to him they presented five men, five women, cloth, feather work, cacao, precious stones, arm-bands, diadems, lip- and ear-plugs, all of them gold, along with elaborate fans and fine birds of green, blue and red plumage.

After all of these had paid their visits, emissaries from Tlaxcala, Huexotzinco and Cholula came in secretly at night. They conferred with Tlacaelel, consoled him and told him that they sorrowed greatly over the death of King Axayacatl. They had brought with them the tears and sadness of their respective states. They had brought things from their cities for the funeral rites of the king. Thereupon they delivered many bows and arrows, maguey fiber cloaks, and loincloths, animal skins, and other objects made of eagle feathers and also little bells for his feet. After each nation had made its offering, lamented, and spoken to the dead man, the Aztec authorities, including Tlacaelel, thanked them with flowery words, each one speaking in his turn. Food was brought for the guests and it was so well served and so abundant that there was enough left over for their servants—great quantities of breads, fine dishes prepared with fowl, chocolate beverages, flowers, and tobacco. After the meal they brought from the king's treasure mantles and loincloths and gave them to all the guests, except the three enemy sovereigns, who were given weapons, a shield and sword to each.

When these rulers had departed toward their homes on the other side of the snowy mountains, the rest remained in the city. A great bower was prepared; this was called *tlacochcalli*, which means "house of repose." Within the bower was placed a statue which was the image of the dead king. This figure was made of slivers of wood bound together. Its face imitated that of a human being, its head was feathered with plumes called *ichcacaxochitl*, "cotton flowers," and others called *malacaquetzalli*, "spindle-whorl feathers," together with a breastplate of feather work. He was then dressed in the splendid garments worn by the god Huitzilopochtli. Over this garb he was dressed with the garments of the divinity Tlaloc so that he represented that deity. Upon his head was a crown of mixed white and green plumes. In one hand he held a shield of fine quality and in the other a stick carved in the form of lightning, like that of Tlaloc, since he was the god of thunderbolts and rain. He was also attired with a piece of clothing like a surplice.

176

The fourth garment he wore was that of the god Yohualahua which consisted of a diadem of fine feathers, a shield in one hand and in the other a staff with rattles at its top. The fifth attire was that of the deity Quetzalcoatl. On his head they placed a mask in the form of a jaguar with a goose-like beak. Since he was the god of the wind he wore light clothing in the form of wings with rounded edges and a loincloth with rounded borders together with a small mantle called Butterfly Mantle.

After the dead king had been dressed in the manner of the four gods whom he represented, the chanters sang the hymns and songs of the dead. While they chanted, all the deceased's wives, with their hair loose, appeared carrying vessels and dishes of breads and other foods which they had cooked. They placed these in front of the image of Axayacatl together with gourds of chocolate. Then the noblemen entered, each one carrying flowers and tobacco in his hands; these were placed before the statue. Then came the incensers who one by one incensed the statue.

When these rites had ended the unfortunate slaves who were to serve the dead man in the hereafter were dressed. The women were given fine blouses and skirts and on their backs were placed the small boxes and baskets in which the king had kept the finery with which he adorned himself—ear-plugs, lip-plugs, nose-plugs, elaborate cloaks, and loincloths. All of these things were tied to the bodies of the slaves who were to die. Every male or female slave that the king had possessed was brought in, and so were the hunchbacks and dwarfs who served him. All were given jewels, plumes, golden arm-bands, earrings, rattles for their feet, blow-guns with which the king had hunted, his bow, his arrows and string. After this the singers began their funeral chant and everyone wept for some time. Meanwhile priests, carrying gourds of pulque, came and poured the liquid all around the room.

The statue was picked up by the noblemen and carried before the idol Huitzilopochtli together with the body of the deceased. Both were set afire and while they burned, those in charge of the cremation went about poking the fire so that it burned quickly.

Once the statue and the body had been reduced to ashes the priests brought in some green gourds filled with water, and sprinklers made of laurel leaves, and each of the great men, lords, chieftains, and soldiers was sprinkled in the face with the water. So were the widows of the king and the other ladies who were present.

After the sprinkling had ended the noblemen turned to the slaves, saying:

"O brethren, go in peace to serve our master, our lord,
Our dead king Axayacatl! Go along the way consoling him

And giving him courage. See that he lacks nothing in the way of jewelry,
See that you do not drop anything on the way. Serve him with care
And see that he lacks nothing of this food or drink."

The wretches gave thanks to the lords and weeping said farewell. The hunch-backs, dwarfs and other servants were then addressed and told to take great care in preparing the water for the hands of their master, to give him his dress and his sandals, as they had done until now. They were advised to hand him his comb and the mirror they carried, and to furnish him with his blowgun or bow and arrows, should he need them.

All of the ashes were placed in a *teponaztli* drum and the slaves were cast down on their backs next to that instrument and their hearts cut out. The blood was gathered in certain vessels and poured upon the fire where the body of the king had burned.

When all the slaves, hunchbacks, dwarfs and slave girls had been killed (and more than fifty or sixty persons lost their lives on such an occasion), the buriers took the ashes and buried them in a hole at the feet of Huitzilopochtli, along with the hearts of the dead, gems, feathers and mantles.

Four days after these ceremonies in honor of Axayacatl had come to an end, the news spread that Tizoc, also known as *Tlalchitonatiuh*, meaning "Setting Sun," had been raised to the throne. When the rulers of the provinces arrived in Mexico, the king of Texcoco took a golden diadem with green stones and placed it upon the head of the monarch. He pierced the cartilage of his nose and inserted an ornament of green jade of the thickness of a quill for writing. In his ears he placed two jade stones adorned with gold, on his arms two bracelets of shining gold, on his legs were placed two anklets with golden bells hanging from them.

With his own hands Tizoc donned his jaguar-skin shoes handsomely orna-mented with gold. He put on his thin cloak of maguey fiber, all done in gold and embroidered with designs, together with a loincloth of the same kind.

The king of Texcoco led him to a throne called the *Cuauhicpalli* or "eagle seat," also called "the jaguar seat." It was decorated with eagle feathers and jaguar skins. The other chieftains placed him on their shoulders and carried him in his throne to the summit of the pyramid where they set him down next to the image of the god Huitzilopochtli. They placed in his hand a sharp jaguar bone and he pricked himself in the ears, shin bone and calves.

178

When his penance was ended, they carried him out and brought him to the Stone of the Sun, the *cuauhxicalli* or "eagle stone." There he did penance again, and many quail were brought to him and he beheaded them with his own hands upon the stone. Their blood was poured into the round hole. He was given an incense burner and he offered incense to the four parts of the world, that is to say, to the east, west, north, and south. The new king was then carried to the place where the elders slept.

He entered a dark room where the goddess Cihuacoatl was kept. This room was called *tlillan*, which means blackness. There he pricked his body in the same places and killed more quail before the goddess. He then incensed the dark room where all the statues of the gods were kept. After this he visited a place called Yopico where the god Yopi was kept; and there again he bled his ears, arms, and shin, killed quail and offered incense. In this way he visited five gods. After this he was brought back to his dwelling place where he was again placed upon the royal seat.

CHAPTER **XL** WHICH TREATS OF HOW THE AZTECS WAGED WAR ON
METZTITLAN IN ORDER TO BRING VICTIMS FOR THE FESTIVITIES OF
THE CORONATION AND ANOINTING OF THEIR KING

After he was enthroned, King Tizoc ordered a campaign against Metztitlan and Itzmiquilpan. However, the Aztecs lost more men than they captured. Tlacaelel was greatly distressed to see only forty captives brought into Mexico while his armies had lost three hundred men.

After this sad war Tlacaelel called the chieftains, saying, "Let us finish the solemn enthronement of our king since it is our duty. Let us call, let us invite, all the rulers from the neighboring states: Texcoco, Tacuba, Chalco, Xochimilco and that region, Colhuacan, Ixtapalapa, Mexicatzinco, Huitzilopochco, those of the hot country, Cuauhtlalpan, Matlatzinco, Toluca, and Coatlalpan."

All the governors and stewards of these states sent great supplies and food for the feast. Also invited were Cuetlaxtlan, Tochtlan, Tziccoac, Tozapan, Cuernavaca, Yauhtepec, Huaxtepec, Acapichtlan, Cohuixco, Huitzoco, Tepecuacuilco, Tlachmalacac, Yohuallan, Tepetlan, Nochtepec, Teotliztac, Tlachco, Tzacualpan, Ixtapan, Totolapan, Chiauhtla, Piaztlan, Teotlallan, Cuitlatenanco, Cuauhapazco, Xochuehuetlan, Olinallan, Tlalcozauhtitlan, Matlatzinco, Toluca, Tzinacantepec, Tlacotepec, Calimayan, Tepemaxalco, and Teotenanco.

179

Then came all the mountaineers from Malinalco, Ocuilan, Coatepec, Capolhuac, Xalatlauhco and Atlapulco. In sum, all the cities and provinces subject to the royal crown of Mexico. Their emissaries came with wealth and supplies to lodge in the house of the principal steward who was called Petlacalcatl. He was the one in charge of the royal storehouses; he was the keeper of the king's treasure. It was he who brought all the representatives of the provinces before the king, who was sitting upon his throne next to the old man Tlacaelel. Said Petlacalcatl, "O lord, all your stewards and treasurers from the cities and provinces have come and they wish to kiss your royal hands." They prostrated themselves upon the earth before their king, bowing and humiliating themselves. The Indians are people who know well how to feign humility and pretend that they are lower than the earth itself when they are in the presence of their superiors.

After all the emissaries had delivered their gifts, Tizoc's enthronement was completed. On the next day, before dawn, Tlacaelel rose and went to the king's chamber to awaken him and adorn him, and both went out to dance with the noblemen. They said that their days were numbered and that they wished to pass them in contentment and gaiety since in the other world they would not sing or dance nor enjoy the odor of flowers and tobacco. After the dance the nobility came to offer them garlands of flowers delicately arranged and handsomely decorated pipes of tobacco. To make the feast more solemn all ate wild mushrooms which make a man lose his senses. After four days of feasting the guests were given rich gifts by the king, the latter was crowned, the victims from Metztitlan were sacrificed and the visitors departed to their towns.

Our *Chronicle* tells us that this ruler reigned only four or five years and that he spent much of his time in seclusion. He showed no initiative but was pusillanimous and cowardly. During this time Tlacaelel urged him to finish the building of the temple but before the work could begin, members of his court, angered by his weakness and lack of desire to bring glory to the Aztec nation, helped him to die with something they gave him to eat. He died in the year 1486, still a young man. His death was immediately known in the provinces and his funeral rites were the same as those of the last king.

The only remarkable thing about this burial is that after the body had been dressed in the likeness of the four gods and been placed before the statue of Huitzilopochtli to burn, those in charge of the cremation appeared naked. They were painted black and their faces covered with soot, their hair curled, wearing paper loincloths to cover their private parts. They carried pointed sticks made of oak with which they pushed the body to and fro in the fire. These sticks were painted with red ochre.

180

After them appeared the king and lord of the Underworld, dressed up to look like a fierce demon. Instead of eyes he wore shining mirrors; his mouth was huge and fierce; his hair was curled up around two hideous horns, and on each shoulder

*A battle between the Aztecs and the men of Metztitlan.*
*The river Quetzalatl, "Precious Water," is*
*shown in the center, and King Tizoc of Mexico is depicted*
*at the left. From the Atlas, the picture book*
*accompanying Durán's text. Photo Reg Van Cuylenburg.*

he wore a mask with mirror eyes. On each elbow was a mask, on his stomach another and on his knees also other faces with eyes. With the shining of the mirrors which represented eyes on all these parts, it looked as if he could see in every direction. He was so hideous, so abominable, that no one dared to look at him out of fear. This man who represented the Lord of Hell carried in his hand another stick painted with ochre, and he went about the fire giving orders to the others, urging them to hurry in turning the corpse in the flames. The *Chronicle* says that sometimes even he poked at it.

At this funeral there was present a man with a green gourd in his hand and a sprinkler made of laurel leaves. He went about sprinkling all those present. He was dressed to impersonate the goddess of the waters called Chalchiuhtlicue.

CHAPTER XLI WHICH TREATS OF HOW, AFTER THE FUNERAL OF
KING TIZOC, A YOUNGER BROTHER OF HIS WAS ELECTED,
AND HOW THERE WAS SOME CONTROVERSY
IN THIS ELECTION

On the fourth day after the death of King Tizoc there was a gathering in the city of Mexico. All the lords and highborn men, all the officials of the court, and all the chiefs of the wards were present.

The nation had a special official for every activity, small though it were. Everything was so well recorded that no detail was left out of the accounts. There were even officials in charge of sweeping. The good order was such that no one dared to interfere with the job of another or express an opinion since he would be rebuffed immediately; even today they have kept up this order in what they can. As soon as a child is born he is registered with the heads and captains of the wards. One man had in his charge twenty households, another forty, another fifty, others had a hundred, and thus the city and its wards were divided. He who had a hundred houses in his charge would appoint five or six of his subjects and divide them among the hundred homes. If he received fifteen or perhaps twenty households, he was obliged to govern them, collecting tribute and men for public works. And so the officials of the Republic were innumerable.

183

All of these authorities appeared on the day of the new election, which was presided over by Tlacaelel, who had always been the second person of the court. When the discussion of the choice of a new king for Mexico began, there were many opinions among them and even disputes.

Tlacaelel wished to choose the youngest brother of the deceased monarch, because he was his nephew and because he was the son of Moteczoma the Elder. It is said that the succession always passed from brother to brother. Therefore, considering that Axayacatl and Tizoc had reigned, succeeding one another, and that this was the third brother, he had a right to the throne. Tlacaelel said that he had promised King Moteczoma at the time of his death that until his three sons had ruled one after the other he would not permit another to occupy the throne. However, the officials objected, saying that his candidate was yet a child.

After much discussion it was determined to consult the king of Texcoco and to ask his advice. King Nezahualpilli answered that his opinion was that Tlacaelel should be elected since he was the person who most deserved it and that he had rights as brother to King Moteczoma. Ahuitzotl, he said, could live at his side and would master the statesmanship of his uncle. Once the old man was dead Ahuitzotl could be his successor and by then he would be able to govern.

The messengers returned to Mexico with the answer and they entered the presence of Tlacaelel and the other electors shouting, "Long life to King Tlacaelel!" Tlacaelel asked, "I hear you, O Aztecs. I hear you! What shouts are these?" Then they told him of the decision made by the king of Texcoco but Tlacaelel said:

"O my sons, I am grateful to you and the king of Texcoco! But come here: I wish to ask you, what have I been during the eighty or ninety years since the war with Azcapotzalco? What position have I had? Have I been nothing? Why have I not put the diadem upon my head, why have I not worn the royal insignia? Have all the orders I have given been null and void? Have I executed the delinquent or pardoned the innocent unjustly? Have I not been able to appoint chieftains or to remove them? Have I done wrong, have I broken the laws of the Republic in wearing the mantles, loincloths and sandals, golden arm-bands, anklets, and lip-plugs of gold and jade, ear- and nose-pendants? Have I sinned in entering the royal palace and the temple shod, as I have up to now? For no one can do these things but the kings. Have I done wrong in wearing the garments and the costumes of the gods, showing myself as their image, and as a god taking up the knife to sacrifice men? If I could do these things, and I have been doing them for eighty or ninety years, I am then a king and you have held me as such. What more of a king could I have been? And it will continue so until my death. Why are you disturbed, why are you troubled, over the election of my nephew Ahuitzotl? I will always be at his side to punish the evil-doer, no matter how high his position be. I will place him under the mat at my seat, under my seat and throne! I will honor the virtuous man, I will receive guests and strangers and honor rulers and monarchs. I will organize wars and command them. Be calm, my children, obey me, I am king and king I will remain until I die. I want the promise I made to my brother fulfilled. I want all my nephews to rule first and then, should you desire it, you may enthrone my sons. I will accept that in payment for the things I have done for my country and for your own persons."

When everyone had heard Tlacaelel's words and recognized the truth and realized that he would be their protector and shelter as long as he lived, all agreed to accept the election of Ahuitzotl. The principal chiefs and noblemen, followed by the masses of the people, went to the school where the sons of the kings and nobles lived and where they were trained and taught morals, the exercise of war and good manners. When they arrived they took him from among his companions and led him to the royal palace where they seated him upon the throne of the kings of Mexico.

When the boy had been thus enthroned, Tlacaelel sent messages to the different regions to proclaim to all that the sun, which had been darkened, shone again in Mexico and that the city which had been mute could speak again. All were to come and help seat him upon the royal throne, anoint him, crown him, and recognize him as their king and lord. They were advised that his name was Ahuitzotl and that he was the son of Moteczoma the Elder and the brother of the two kings who had recently died.

After all had come to pay homage to the new monarch, Ahuitzotl received the envoys in the temple of Tlillan, the Black Place. The first to kiss his hands was the king of Texcoco, who addressed him:

"O my son, on this day these lords and chieftains of all your kingdom offer you a little closed chest so that you may open it. You are going to find within it a cloth to wrap up the load that has been given you. You will put it upon your back and you will learn how to carry it from one place to another. Do not become weary, do not be careless, do not let the load fall. You will carry the same burden as the god Huitzilopochtli; eyes from the four directions are fixed upon you. They have now given you a sword and a shield so that you may risk your life for your country. They have charged you with responsibility for the mountains, the hills, the plains, caves, cliffs, rivers and seas, pools and springs, rocks and trees. Everything has been commended to you and you must watch out and see that it does not fall apart. You may not have to do this with your own hand but you must give orders that it be done. Until now your work has consisted in sweeping and cleaning in front of the gods; after these tasks you played and enjoyed yourself like a child. But now you must know and care for all existing things under the heavens. For this purpose you have at your side the mighty lord Tlacaelel. Follow his footsteps, observe how he rules and you will not err. He will watch over the way you govern so that you do not let the load that has been given you fall upon the ground. With these words, my son, I end my discourse."

When the guests had departed Tlacaelel gathered the nobles, describing to them the manner in which the king was to be crowned and telling them how victims must be obtained for sacrifice. It was decided to wage war against the province of Chiapan where seven powerful cities were inhabited by mountaineers. The cities were Chiapan, Xilotepec, Xiquipilco, Xocotitlan, Cuauhauacan, Cillan and Mazahuacan. This province was restless, reluctant to serve the Aztecs, and this fact had greatly displeased the Aztecs. They now decided to punish and subject them, and Tlacaelel ordered that war be made on them. In this way prisoners for sacrifice could be obtained for the feast of the new king.

The armies of the various allied nations under the leadership of the Aztecs met in a place called Cilocan. Here Ahuitzotl was taken by his nobles; he had never fought before. They dressed him and gave him his weapons and royal insignia. He was put in a prominent place and, through an interpreter, addressed the army. The soldiers immediately attacked Xiquipilco and soon subdued, destroyed and sacked the town. After this they attacked four other cities which were vanquished. Many were slaughtered and others captured. All the authorities came out to ask for mercy. They carried presents and made promises of service and tribute of all that was asked of them. With this the Aztecs stopped pursuing and killing.

When the five cities had been taken, King Ahuitzotl ordered that under pain of death no one dare flee or absent himself from the army. All were to watch one another and if one were missing, even though he were of high birth, he must be killed as soon as he was found. This was to be done until the war had finished. The two main cities—Chiapan and Xilotepec—had yet to be conquered. No one dared abandon camp because they were watching one another carefully.

That night the army set out for Chiapan and when they drew near they were heard by the guards who carried the alarm to the city. The men of the city defended themselves and a great skirmish took place, but the Aztecs, who had always been crafty and who knew a thousand cunning tricks, managed to get the Texcocans, Tecpanecs, Xochimilca and Chalca in the front lines, while they secretly followed a path which had been revealed to them by some of the inhabitants of that province. They entered the city, captured the pyramid, which was always the main defense of a city, and made it their stronghold. They took all the priests prisoners, together with the other officials, and having tied their hands they set fire to the temple.

When all of this was discovered by the enemy, they abandoned the field and fled. The allies pursued them and captured or killed many who tried to defend

186

themselves in order not to be taken prisoners. Thus the allies were able to enter the city, stealing what they could. The other city Xilotepec, was taken soon after this.

Once these seven cities had been captured they were ordered to pay tribute in maize, beans, and other cultivated seeds, lumber and other things. The vanquished were ordered to bring workers to Mexico for the building of the houses of the nobility, together with slaves for sacrifice.

When Tlacaelel was notified of the victory he ordered horns to be blown and drums to be beaten and the event celebrated in the usual manner. Guards were placed upon the pyramids to watch for the return of the army so that it might be received with due ceremony.

And so Ahuitzotl, accompanied by his chieftains and great nobles, returned to the city of Mexico, where he and the prisoners were received by the elders and priests. Great speeches were made to them, they were welcomed and congratulated for their successful venture. Ahuitzotl was taken to the temple and from there to his home, where, upon his royal throne, he received the old man Tlacaelel who was carried in on the shoulders of a man because of his extreme age. He welcomed his nephew and made a lengthy speech. The same was done by the kings of Texcoco and Tacuba and the other monarchs. If I were to record here these long, curious and elegant talks, I know that they would please the reader but it would lengthen this history too much and be too great an expense of paper and time.

The coronation was set for *Ce Cipactli*, "One Alligator," the first day of the month, and neighboring peoples were invited to attend. All the guests were instructed to bring a contribution for the expenses and to offer turkeys, fowl, deer, rabbits, hares, quail and other types of wild animals, fish from those who lived on the coast, fruit, different types of chilli, cacao for drinking purposes, cloth, jewels, feathers, weapons, shields, firewood, charcoal, seats, mats, and everything that might be necessary.

CHAPTER XLII WHICH TREATS OF THE SOLEMN FESTIVAL THAT WAS MADE ON THE CORONATION OF KING AHUITZOTL, AND HOW MANY MEN WERE SACRIFICED

According to my *Chronicle*, this feast was prepared by the Aztec people with the intention of showing the enemy—Tlaxcala, Huexotzinco, Cholula and other cities in that direction, together with those of Michoacan and Metztitlan—the greatness of Mexico. It was designed to bewilder them, fill them with fear, and make them see the grandeur and abundance of jewels and gifts that were exchanged on such an occasion. All of this was based upon ostentation, vaingloriousness, in order to show that the Aztecs were the masters of all the riches of the earth. This is why they celebrated their feasts so splendidly.

The governors, treasurers and stewards of all the cities were notified to bring the provisions and were warned that if they failed in any way they would be deprived of their positions, exiled from their homeland along with their family and relatives. The jewelers were told to hurry in cutting the precious stones that were necessary for this feast. The same was said to the metal workers, feather workers, potters, those skilled in preparing tobacco, the florists; all of them were threatened with punishment unless they made elaborate preparations. The heads of the wards harassed them, not letting them rest or pause in their work. These officials were so solicitous and untiring that one would think their life depended upon this diligence. This was due to the great fear and reverence in which they held their masters.

Tlacaelel had all the heads of the wards brought to him and he ordered them to obtain mats and baskets for the maize cakes. He had masons and carpenters brought to make the seats and to repair those which had been damaged. He ordered the lime workers to plaster or repair parts that were chipped or badly finished. The wood cutters were told to prepare a great abundance of branches and leaves. On this day the entire city was so busy in adorning, providing and preparing these things that it was admirable.

After this the king and officials decided to invite the lords of Michoacan, Metztitlan, Tlaxcala, Huexotzinco, Cholula, Tliliuhquitepec and Yopitzinco. All these cities and provinces were enemies of Mexico and they had never been subdued, and they were constantly warring and making trouble.

These foreign rulers were invited in order to impress them with the Aztec grandeur. The sovereign of Tlaxcala answered that he was unwilling to attend the feast and that he could make the same celebration in his city whenever he liked. The ruler of Tliliuhquitepec gave the same answer. The king of Huexotzinco promised to go but never appeared. The monarch of Cholula sent emissaries and asked to be pardoned since he was busy and could not attend. The lord of Metztitlan angrily expelled the messengers and told them to take care for the people of his province might kill them if they found out who they were.

When the king of Michoacan received the invitation he laughed, saying:

"What do your masters think? Was it a whim to come and make

War upon us, be defeated and flee having lost so many men?
You must be mad! One day you wish war, another day you wish peace.
If I go there, what security will I have while I eat or drink
Among you after the way I treated you?"

The messengers answered, "O powerful monarch, there are times when one must be an enemy but there are others when one must heed the natural obligations that exist between us, and so my lord the king says that he has forgotten your enmity. Those things have their time and place and it is not our last chance. Ahuitzotl begs you to come together with your chieftains to honor his coronation. He also asks that you enter the palace at night, so that the courageous Aztecs may not think your arrival is a trick between the two of you. There he will receive you with all the honor you deserve." The monarch then answered that he rejoiced in the coronation but that he would not go nor would he allow his court to go, and the messengers returned to King Ahuitzotl with this answer.

Those who had gone to invite the officials of Yopitzinco brought back the noblemen from that city, but failed to bring the ruler himself, who could not be found. The dignitaries of Yopitzinco and those of Cholula were lodged luxuriously and generously supplied with all their needs. They were treated even better than the two allied monarchs who were in the city at that time and who had been given rich gifts.

During the first night torches were lit in the courtyard and so many people held flaming braziers against the walls that it looked as if the house were on fire. Tlacaelel and the king supervised this part of the feast, which lasted four days. Food was brought, stews and chocolate drink. I have noticed one thing in all this history: no mention is made of their drinking wine of any type, or of drunkenness. Only wild mushrooms are spoken of and they were eaten raw. The *Chronicle* says that people became excited, filled with pleasure, and lost their senses to some extent.[57] It never mentions wine except as part of sacrificial or funeral ceremonies. Only the great abundance of chocolate drink is spoken of as part of these festivities.

Many days after this feast, Tlacaelel told the king that the Huaxtecs had rebelled again. The Aztecs and their allies then attacked that country and subdued it, led by King Ahuitzotl in person. When the fighting was over the king was taken into the palace of the local capital and there he and his chieftains were made presents of clothing, for both men and women, cacao, feathers, parrots, macaws, chilli, pumpkin seeds, and their own daughters as concubines. The king accepted all these gifts and divided them among his chieftains. They were given food and drink in great quantities, presents of flowers and abundant tobacco. After such lodgment and entertainment, the Aztecs returned to Mexico immediately. But first they sent messengers to Tlacaelel so that the city could rejoice in their victory. The messengers departed and after them came the army, proud and joyful, with all the captives before them. The Huaxtec prisoners were linked together by cords drawn through the perforations they wore in their noses. Many people had been captured on this occasion and they went along singing in loud voices, moaning over their fate with a pitiful, wailing chant. The maidens, daughters of Huaxtecs, who had been surrendered, and the children and little boys who did not have their ears or their noses perforated, wore wooden yokes on their throats and they were all tied together in this way.

The messengers arrived in Mexico and announced the great victory. The whole city rejoiced, beating drums and sounding horns in the temples, making fires and lighting torches on the top of the pyramids. The feast lasted until the soldiers, the prisoners and the king returned to the city.

CHAPTER **XLIII** WHICH TREATS OF HOW KING AHUITZOTL FINISHED THE TEMPLE AND HOW A SOLEMN FEAST WAS MADE TO HONOR IT AND HOW MANY MEN WERE SACRIFICED

When the war with the Huaxtecs had ended, Ahuitzotl, now in the second year of his reign, which was the year 1487, "Eight Reed" according to the Indian way of counting, decided to finish the building and the decoration of the temple.[88] He wished a great and sumptuous feast to take place on its dedication. He consulted with old Tlacaelel and when the old man heard of his determination, and being eager to see the end of this work, he told the king that he was well pleased with the plans. He added his thanks and, weeping many tears, he showed his joy and his desire to see the temple finished before his days ended. When the king realized that it was pleasing to Tlacaelel, he called his main steward and told him to notify the administrators in all the provinces that they might provide cloth and everything necessary which had been stored in all the subject cities and provinces, as part of the royal tribute. The steward immediately notified everyone to be ready to furnish what had been demanded.

190

Then he called the stoneworkers and told them to finish the temple of the god as quickly as possible. Without hesitation they began to carve the idols which were lacking, some of which I saw in a painted manuscript. One of them was the sharp sacrificial stone and next to it an image of the goddess called Coyolxauh. On the corners were two statues with their cruciform mantles, formed like feathers. The Aztecs also set up some pilasters shaped like the demon Tzitzimitl. And so at last the building was ready; nothing had to be done now, since all had been perfected and finished.

The vassal nations were invited to be present at the dedication, and all were asked to bring victims. Among the kings who attended was Nezahualpilli of Texcoco who came with great pomp, bringing with him a large number of slaves from all the towns and cities for sacrifice. He brought them because he was obliged to acknowledge the superiority of Mexico.

Some have said that the kingdom of Texcoco was free from paying tribute to the Aztec monarch and that it was in no way subjected to him. But I find this told differently in the *Chronicle*. It is true that they did not pay cloth, jewels, feathers or foodstuffs to Mexico as the other provinces did; but I find that the Aztecs used Texcocan lands to sow and reap and that some of them were tenant farmers of the Aztec chieftains. I have discovered that when great feasts took place they paid tribute in slaves and that no one was exempt from this tribute. I also know that when war was waged on a city or province the first one called to form his army was the king of Texcoco. And, as we have seen in this history, the king was called to the city of Mexico as often as was necessary, which means that subjection did exist, considering his preëminence as king and lord of that province Acolhuacan-Texcoco.

Having arrived in Mexico, this ruler went to the royal palace where he was received by King Ahuitzotl with all the courtesy due to a fellow monarch and kinsman. He was lodged in the place called Teccalli, "House of Lords." He delivered his captives to King Ahuitzotl and spoke to him with elegant phrases, offering his services and best deeds. Water was brought for his hands; this was a common custom among the Aztecs, to bring water for the hands of guests and travelers. After having washed he was given the usual royal fare and chocolate. He and his followers were also given flowers and tobacco.

When King Ahuitzotl had received all the royal guests with the applause and courtesy that such high princes deserved, Tlacaelel spoke to him, saying, "You will remember, O mighty prince, how it was that on the feast of your anointment and coronation the Tlaxcalans and their followers, our enemies, refused to accept our invitation, and those of Michoacan and Metztitlan did likewise. It seems to me that it would not be unreasonable to ask them again to this solemn occasion be-cause, even though we are enemies in the wars that we wage, in our festivities we should rejoice together. There is no reason why they should be excluded since we are all one. It is reasonable that there be truces and greetings among the rulers."

The king thought well of this and immediately gave his orders to three cou-rageous captains who were not afraid to pass the guards and sentinels watching day and night on the frontiers. These three messengers were sent to Tlaxcala, Huexotzinco, Cholula, Tecoac, Tliliuhquitepec and Zacatlan to invite the monarchs and noblemen of those cities in the king's name. These emissaries answered that they would do what had been demanded of them. However, they charged the king with their wives and children, which showed the dangers they would encounter. In spite of all of this, forgetting the great peril, they left the city and, having walked all night, they arrived near Huexotzinco shortly before dawn. They entered the city secretly and went to the royal houses where the ruler dwelt. They found the doorkeepers asleep in the outer rooms. Having awakened them they asked that the lord Xayacamachan, which was the name of the king of Huexotzinco, be told of their presence. They were asked from where they came but they replied that they could not talk to anyone but the sovereign himself. The doormen went to their master and told him what had happened, but the king gave orders that unless the strangers told who they were and where they came from they would not be allowed to pass. The envoys begged to be allowed to enter, as they desired to serve him and kiss his hands; they were unarmed and defenseless, being men of peace who wanted only to show themselves to him and deliver their message.

Though the king and lord of Huexotzinco was fearful, he ordered that they be allowed to enter. Once they had come into his presence they bowed, prostrating themselves before him and performing all the ceremonies that were usual when in the presence of a king. They told him they were Aztecs, messengers of King Ahuitzotl of Mexico, and that they had come to invite him to the dedication of the temple of Huitzilopochtli, whose home had now been finished. They assured him that he could make the trip in all safety during this truce since the courageous Aztecs never used treachery or womanly or cowardly tricks. The Aztecs fought with their swords on the battlefield and in war, each one showing the strength of his arm. Therefore, since they had known one another and been related in blood for one generation, they besought the king of Huexotzinco to be present at the feast of the god.

The ruler accepted the invitation and said that he would be pleased to take part in the festivities. He added that he kissed the hands of King Ahuitzotl for the favor that had been granted him in making him a part of such solemn rites. He

dios mayor de las culebras

los q aquy nacen no piden $ aborrecidos de nadie

diez moores

septimo dia
zeno

primero dia
pedernal

segundo dia
llouer

tercero dia
rrosa

quarto dia
uejez

qu

*On the lower part, the list of lucky and unlucky
days of the "month," and on the upper part, the presiding
god. Page from the* **Codex Borbonicus,** *"Book of Days."
Courtesy New York Public Library. Photo Reg Van Cuylenburg.*

ordered that the messengers be given lodging and everything necessary for their comfort, and food and drink, mantles and loincloths, for the journey. After having eaten and drunk they bade farewell to him and continued, well content, to the city of Cholula.

In Cholula the embassy was received in the same way by the sovereign of that city; they were refreshed with food, drink, mantles, flowers and tobacco. The ruler of Cholula accepted the invitation with the same gratitude, and so did the ruler of Tlaxcala.

After leaving Tlaxcala the envoys waited in the forest for the lords and nobles to arrive. This they did that they might all secretly enter the city together. The entire night was spent watching. Before dawn the rulers and chieftains of Cholula arrived. Their customary dress was changed in favor of Aztec garments and, in order to disguise themselves further, they held flowers, branches and leaves in their hands as though they were men who were coming to adorn the temple or royal house. The Aztecs advised the Cholulans not to answer any greeting, not to speak because of the difference in accent that exists among them. The noble visitors were told that the messengers would answer for them. And so it was that all along the way the Aztecs answered all strangers that they met. In this way they entered Mexico secretly.

The visitors from Cholula, Huexotzinco and Tlaxcala were taken to the royal palace where a secret room had been prepared for them. The royal attendant notified the king of their arrival and at that hour of the night King Ahuitzotl called Tlacaelel and told him what had happened. A message was sent to the visitors, asking them to be at ease since the king would visit them in person as soon as the other lords from Michoacan, Tzicoac, Metztitlan, Tliliuhquitepec, Tecoac and Zacatlan arrived. Many gifts were sent to the guests in their private rooms—flowers, tobacco, dishes of fish, frogs, and other amphibia, duck, wild geese, herons, pelicans, sea fowl and other game, and the king sent the message that these were his offerings to them.

At midnight the guests from the other nations arrived together with their allies and all were lodged in the same rooms where the men from Tlaxcala, Huexotzinco and Cholula slept. King Ahuitzotl ordered his steward to provide them with all that was necessary—mantles, loincloths, flowers and tobacco. But all of this was done secretly; only those who had gone to invite them served them, and no other person was allowed to enter the secret places where they were concealed. The reason for all this secrecy was that they did not wish the common people—soldiers and captains—to suspect that kings and rulers made alliances, came to agreements and formed friendships at the cost of the life of the common man, and the shedding of his blood. In order to avoid these suspicions and the possibilities of whispers and trouble-making, they kept these foreign kings and lords hidden. This is the reason given by the *Chronicle.*

After the guests had been lodged, the Aztec messengers, who had just carried out the king's order in the provinces, gathered in the presence of the king. He asked them one by one how they had been received in enemy lands. Every one of them said that he had been received well and that he had seen only smiling faces.

However, the envoys who had gone to Yopitzinco had something additional to tell about their reception. As soon as they had delivered their message they had been housed in a splendidly appointed apartment. When they had been given water for their hands, the king of that province appeared in person with a staff in his hand followed by all his wives and ladies of the court, all very well dressed and adorned. All of these women carried different foods and fruits, and placed them before the emissaries. After them entered certain lords with gourds of chocolate and others with flowers and tobacco. All this time the ruler had stood with his staff in his hand. He had ordered them to eat, to feel at ease and rest. When they had eaten he commanded that the visitors be clothed with fine mantles and loincloths, after which a squadron of armed men entered the courtyard and began to fight one another. They skirmished as if in a tournament, with great cries and shrieks such as the natives use when they fight. When the mock battle had finished, the king of Yopitzinco said to the Aztec messengers, "Do not fear! All of this has been done for your pleasure. Return to your masters; later we will go to serve them." So it was that King Ahuitzotl was surprised at the way in which his emissaries had been received in those parts.

Later the captives that had been brought for the sacrifice were formed in a line. Those who had been captured by the Texcocans were in one line, by Tacuba in another, and those captured by Xochimilca, Chalca, Mazahua and Cuauhtlalpaneca in separate lines. This was done so that a precise count of prisoners could be made. It was found that there were eighty thousand four hundred men to be sacrificed in the dedication of the temple of Mexico. They were men from Huexotzinco, Tlaxcala, Atlixco, Tliliuhquitepec, Cholula, Tecoac, Zacatlan, Zapotlan, Tzicoac, Tuzapan, Tlapan and the land of the Huaxtecs. King Ahuitzotl was greatly satisfied and he sat upon the royal throne, showing his grandeur to all the nations, the magnificence of his empire and the courage of his people. The two allied monarchs from Texcoco and Tacuba sat next to him, and the enemy rulers were seated in a place where they could see without being seen.

194

Ahuitzotl then ordered the royal officials to have the stewards, administrators, and treasurers of all the provinces bring in the royal tribute. One by one they entered his presence. The first tribute bearers were those of the city of Mexico, then those of Xochimilco and its neighbors, Chalco, of Coixtlahuaca in the land of the Mixtecs, of Tochpan, Tochtepec, Tzicoac, Tlatlauhquitepec, Tepeaca, Piaztla, Tlapan, Tlacozauhtitlan, Chiapan, Cohuixco and Tepecuacuilco. Then came the tribute from Huitzoco, Yohualan, Tlaxtlan, Teotitlan, Nochtepec and Tzacualpan. Then entered the tribute bearers from the hot countries: Cuernavaca, Yauhtepec, Huaxtepec, Acapichtla, Matlatzinco, Xoxotlan, Xilotepec, Actopan, and other cities too numerous to mention.

All of these men brought offerings so great in value and quantity that the enemies, guests, and strangers were bewildered, amazed. They saw that the Aztecs were masters of the entire world and they realized that the Aztec people had conquered all the nations and that all were their vassals.

CHAPTER **XLIV** WHICH TREATS OF HOW THE SOLEMN SACRIFICE TOOK PLACE AND HOW AHUITZOTL ORDERED EVERYONE – MEN, WOMEN AND ELDERS – TO BE PRESENT SO THAT THEY WOULD REMEMBER

Once the nobles of the entire land had gathered in the city of Mexico which was the capital of the country in those days, the three allied kings (and among them old Tlacaelel) met, according to what the *Chronicle* tells us. As was usual, the king of Texcoco, Nezahualpilli, was asked to speak first.

"O powerful lord of Mexico," said he, "happy and blessed are you!
The Lord of All Created Things has permitted you to rejoice
In these festivities for your magnificent temple.
These things were not seen by King Acamapichtli, nor by Huitzilihuitl,
Nor by Chimalpopoca or his successor, our close relative Itzcoatl,
Nor were they seen by Moteczoma the Elder, your father, nor your brothers,
Axayacatl or Tizoc, all of whom have departed from this life.
They went away feeling great sorrow for not having seen
What has been granted you today. Therefore, though you be young
You are the emperor of this powerful kingdom, which is the root, the navel

195

And the heart of the world. See that the glory of the Aztec nation increases.
Therefore, call all the lords and officials
Of this city so that I may tell them what they must do!"

All the officials of the city of Mexico and its wards then appeared before Nezahualpilli, monarch of Texcoco, who reminded them that this was a special day,
perhaps a day of triumph, perhaps a day of disaster, and that they should be careful in the preparation of the temples.

On the next day the crowds swarmed through Mexico City. It was an awesome
spectacle: the streets, squares, market places and houses were so bursting with
people that it looked like an ant hill. And all of this was done with the purpose of
lifting up the majesty and greatness of Mexico.

Before dawn the prisoners who were to be sacrificed were brought out and lined
up in four files. One extended from the foot of the steps to the pyramid all along
the causeway that goes to Coyoacan and Xochimilco; it was almost one league in
length. Another extended along the causeway of Guadalupe, and it was as long as
the first. The third went along the causeway of Tacuba and the fourth toward the
east as far as the shore of the lagoon. These four lines moved toward the four
places where sacrifice was to take place. The first and principal altar was before
the statue of Huitzilopochtli, where Ahuitzotl was to kill. The second and third
were for the rulers of Texcoco and Tacuba. And the fourth was the Stone of the
Sun which had been prepared for the sacrifices of aged Tlacaelel.

When all was ready, the three kings put diadems on their heads, donned their
golden ear-plugs, nose-plugs and lip-pendants, their golden arm-bands and
anklets. They dressed themselves in royal mantles, sandals and loincloths. All of
this was done in the presence of old Tlacaelel whom, according to this *Chronicle*,
they considered to be a sovereign. Together with these lords, many priests put on
the garments of the gods and goddesses, and though our *Chronicle* mentions their
names it is not necessary to repeat them here.

All of them ascended to the summit of the pyramid and each lord, accompanied
by priests dressed as gods, went to the place where he was to sacrifice, holding the
knife in his hand. All the lords of the provinces, all the enemies, were watching
from within the bowers which had been built for this occasion. The files of prisoners began to mount the steps, and the four lords, assisted by the priests, who
held the wretches by the feet and hands, began to kill.

196

They opened the chests of their victims, pulled out the hearts and offered them
to the idols and to the sun. When the sovereigns grew weary, their satanic work
was carried on by the priests who represented the gods. The *Chronicle* tells us

CAP.º 44.º

*The sacrifice of 1487 in the great temple of Mexico.*
*The Christianized native who did the drawing showed*
*two devils, of the European type, on the sides of*
*the temples. From the Atlas, the picture book accompanying*
*Durán's text. Photo Reg Van Cuylenburg.*

that this sacrifice lasted four days from dawn to dusk and that, as I have said, eighty thousand four hundred men from different cities, died.[89] All of this seemed incredible to me, but the *Chronicle* has forced me to put it down and I have found confirmation of it in other written and painted manuscripts. Otherwise I would not dare to write these things, since I would be called a liar. He who translates a history is only obliged to reproduce in a new language what he finds written in the foreign tongue, and this is what I have done.

The streams of human blood that ran down the steps of the temple were so great that when they reached the bottom and cooled they formed fat clots, enough to terrify one. Many priests went about gathering this blood in large gourds, taking it to the different temples of the wards and smearing the walls, lintels and thresholds with it. They also smeared the idols and the rooms of the temple both inside and out, and the stench of the blood was so strong that it was unbearable. The *Chronicle* says that it had a sour and abominable smell, to the point that it became unendurable to the people of the city.

The guests thanked the Aztecs for the favor and good treatment that had been given them, and they departed from Mexico bewildered by the majesty of the city and the amazing number of victims who had died. They were also astonished at the wealth that had been given away during those days. The emissaries from Michoacan, Metztitlan and Yopitzinco were pleased at the splendid reception that had been awarded them but they were also awed by what they had seen.

At this time King Ahuitzotl ordered that the old skull rack be destroyed, together with the skulls that had been spitted upon it. All of these were burned and with the eighty thousand four hundred skulls a new rack was set up.

The people of the province of Teloloapan had been invited to these festivities but did not attend, which made King Ahuitzotl suspect that these people were ready to make trouble. He sent his messengers in an attempt to know the cause of their absence at the feast, and when the envoys arrived at the town Teticpac, they were informed that there had been a rebellion and that the roads and paths had been cut off in order to prevent anyone from entering the province. In order to make sure, the Aztecs followed the highway and found that it was obstructed with stones, tree trunks, century plants, cacti, and branches, and that it could not be used for travel. When the Aztecs had seen this they returned to their king and told him that the province was in a state of rebellion and that the roads and paths had been closed.

199

King Ahuitzotl immediately gathered his own people and those of the neighboring provinces of Texcoco, Tacuba, Chalco and Xochimilco. He raised a great army and went in person on this campaign, encouraging the soldiers all along the way.

When he arrived in the province of Teloloapan he attacked it, vanquished and destroyed it, and forced it to continue paying tribute. As a punishment for the rebellion, according to the *Chronicle*, he ordered them to pay the following tribute every eighty days: four hundred loads of cacao, ten loads of cloth, ten loads of women's clothing, together with certain fruits and foodstuffs which are to be found in that land. The men of Teloloapan complained that they had been incited and misled by their neighbors, the people of Alahuiztlan and Oztoman. King Ahuitzotl then ordered that the latter cities be destroyed, and this was done with the help of Teloloapan. The two cities were left desolate; not a man or woman was spared. All were killed except the children who were brought as captives to the city of Mexico. Forty thousand two hundred children, boys and girls, were then distributed among all the provinces and cities of the region of Mexico. The people of Teloloapan then begged King Ahuitzotl to divide up the lands of the conquered territory. He answered that he would do so when he returned to Mexico. He was extremely fond of the cacao, cotton and fruit plantations which existed in that land.

CHAPTER XLV WHICH TREATS OF HOW AZTEC AND OTOMI COLONISTS
WERE SENT TO REPOPULATE ALAHUIZTLAN AND OZTOMAN,
THE TWO CITIES THAT HAD BEEN DESTROYED

About six months after the campaign, King Ahuitzotl and Tlacaelel met with the rulers of Texcoco and Tacuba to discuss the resettlement of the conquered provinces.

"O lords," said Ahuitzotl, "you know that, in the war we waged on Oztoman and Alahuiztlan with the aid of Teloloapan, two of those cities were depopulated. All their fruit, cacao and cotton plantations were left deserted; it would be sad to see those lands lost and made barren forever. Therefore, I have decided to send people to settle that country, to benefit by its riches and make it prosper. I have thought about this and, considering how great and populous those cities were, I wish to send four hundred men together with their families from Mexico. I also desire that each of you send four hundred families so that the total be one thousand two hundred. From the other provinces there will go twenty settlers, which will make a total of eight hundred; the grand total will be two thousand families, one thousand for each city."[90]

King Nezahualpilli of Texcoco replied that the decision seemed wise to him and that the resettlement of abandoned lands was no new thing, since it had been done many times before. However, he considered it unwise to take four hundred heads of families from the city of Mexico since it would weaken the city. His opinion was that only two hundred should be recruited and that they should be taken from the different wards. Each ward must give five men and none was to go against his will. The men were to be told about the fertility and richness of those lands and it was to be explained to them that they were no longer included among the tribute payers. They were to reap the benefits of the cacao, cotton fields and fruit orchards, and to be masters there. They were to go of their own will; if, after the number in each ward had been completed, anyone else wished to go, he must be unmarried.

The allied rulers accepted the advice, and settlers were obtained from many parts of the country. On leaving Mexico they were told that after a time they would forget the love they had felt for their homeland and for all the things they were leaving behind. They were made to believe that it was the will of the gods and of the Lord of All Created Things who rules over all. Eventually those who remained behind would be envious of those who had found such freedom. In time, when the settlers had established their homes in peace and comfort, the relatives whom they had left behind would enter their gates, envious of their success and forced to come by the misery which would eventually visit the city of Mexico. The settlers were also advised to have armed men always ready since they were on the boundary of Michoacan which was their worst enemy. It was wise, they were told, to care for themselves with all diligence since the Tarascans were people who abhorred the Aztecs.

After they had been given this advice on the part of King Ahuitzotl, all the new settlers expressed their thanks and, with many tears, departed from the city of Mexico. Twelve elders from the city went before them. The monarch had ordered these men not to abandon the people until they had settled in their places and were living in peace and calm in their new homes. The elders were advised to conduct the people slowly because of the weakness of the women and children. They were told to send men ahead of them to be sure all things had been made ready in the towns through which they were to pass and that the people of these cities received and welcomed them kindly and made them forget the labors of the journey.

The twelve elders were dressed in long tunics and from their backs hung small gourds filled with incense in powder form. Their hair was tied with red ribbons and adorned with feathers. Each carried a staff in one hand and in the other a fan. They walked in front of the pilgrims as they left the city, and they went their way until they reached the town of Xalatlauhco that same day and were well received by everyone. They were shown kindness and given flowers and tobacco and also new clothing.

This large group finally reached the province of Teloloapan which they were to settle, and there they divided into three parts. The largest group went to Oztoman; another to Alahuiztlan and a third stayed in Teloloapan. The latter were to act as the garrison which guarded the city, for this city had not been totally depopulated as had the others.

Land, houses and foodstuffs, such as maize, chilli, beans, chian and other seeds, were given to them in order that they might survive the first year. This was done at the command of King Ahuitzotl so that they would have enough to eat until the harvest. The elders, who had gone as guards and guides with the people, pacified and consoled them with kind words and then returned to the city of Mexico, where they related to King Ahuitzotl all that had occurred. They told him how all had been led successfully to their new homes, how the cities were now resettled and everyone content. The monarch was very pleased to hear this. In this way these cities were peopled with Aztecs who live there until today and are still subject to the city of Mexico.

CHAPTER XLVI WHICH TREATS OF HOW THE AZTECS WARRED ON TEHUANTEPEC, IXHUATLAN, MIAHUATLAN AND AMAXTLAN. WITH A DESCRIPTION OF HOW THESE FAMOUS PROVINCES WERE CONQUERED

We have mentioned many times that the Aztecs never provoked war against any nation. Conflicts sprang from disobedience or from crimes perpetrated against Aztecs who were sometimes killed along the roads. This is the excuse which the Aztecs gave, and they give it today. In the *Chronicle* I find this justification constantly: "We did not seek trouble; they incited us, they provoked us."

At this time, certain Aztec merchants were killed by the rulers of the province of Tehuantepec. The Aztec army set out with its provisions, such as toasted grains of corn, maize flour, bean flour, crisp toasted tortillas, tamales baked in the sun, great loads of chilli, cakes of ground cacao, all of this in great quantitites. Apart from the supplies provided by the rulers from their great bins and storehouses, each soldier carried on his back his own food, as much as he could. He went along with his sword, shield, and other weapons tied to his load, and with the latter he augmented the ordinary rations that were given to him.

While their husbands were gone the wives prayed for them in the following way:

"O Great Lord of All Things, remember your servant
Who has gone to exalt your honor and the greatness of your name.
He will offer blood in that sacrifice which is war.
Behold, Lord, that he did not go out to work for me
Or for his children! He did not abandon us to obtain things
To support his home, with his tump line on his head,
Or with his digging stick in his hand. He went for your sake,
In your name, to obtain glory for you. Therefore, O Lord,
Let your pious heart have pity on him, who with great labor
And affliction now goes through the mountains and valleys,
Hills and precipices, offering you the moisture from his brow,
His sweat. Give him victory in this war so that he may return
To rest in his home and so that my children and I may see
His countenance again and feel his presence."

This prayer was recited every day at dawn by the women until their sons or husbands, brothers or other relatives, returned.

Ahuitzotl gave orders that in this war all prisoners be slaughtered and that no one bother to take captives since there was much work of conquest to be done and the distance from those provinces to the city of Mexico was great. And so this was a war of slaughter, Tehuantepec was taken and Ahuitzotl returned to Mexico triumphant.

CHAPTER XLVII WHICH TREATS OF HOW KING AHUITZOTL
VISITED ALL THE TEMPLES WHEN HE
RETURNED FROM WAR. WITH A DESCRIPTION OF THE GREAT
OFFERINGS AND SACRIFICES WHICH HE MADE
OUT OF GRATITUDE FOR HIS TRIUMPH

When King Ahuitzotl had rested from the labors of such a difficult war and of the long road, he decided to show his gratitude to the gods for the favor they had done him in granting him this victory. He ordered that oblations be prepared and that the priests in the temples be ready. Messengers were sent to Chalco, Iztapalapa, Mexicatzinco and Huitzilopochco. He had decided to visit these places since his favorite shrines were there.

In this way he first visited the temple of the city of Mexico. The priests and guards were present, all of them dressed in the way which was usual for the return of a king from war. All of them were in their tunics with their little gourds hanging down their backs. The priests were painted black and they carried flaming incense burners in their hands. These priests formed two long lines all the way from the door of the palace to the courtyard of the temple, which was adorned with greenery and festively decorated. Then the king appeared, preceded by all his guards—gallant soldiers, every one of them of noble blood. All these men carried staffs in their hands but no other weapons. On their heads they wore their badges of rank as knights; these consisted of two or three green or blue feathers tied to their hair with red ribbons. Some of the men wore the feathers erect on their heads while others wore them hanging. On their backs were as many round tassels as the great deeds they had performed in battle. These tassels were attached to the feathered head-bands. All the warriors wore splendid jewelry.

Then appeared the king, dressed in his royal mantle, with a magnificent diadem on his head, and with golden arm-bands and anklets, golden ear-, lip- and nose-pendants, wearing great strings of jewels and precious stones around his neck. Behind him came the dwarfs and hunchbacks who served as pages to the king and nobility, together with eunuchs who cared for the wives and concubines. The dwarfs wore ornate mantles, golden arm- and leg-bands, rich feathers and fine jewelry. They had also donned the skins of jaguars and ocelots that had been brought back from the conquest of Tehuantepec and they carried many objects which were part of the spoils of war.

As soon as the king had arrived, the two long rows of priests began to throw incense from their burners, perfuming him as if he were a god. After this he entered the temple courtyard and the drums, conch shells and flutes were sounded. When he reached the top of the pyramid all the music ceased and all prostrated themselves before him. The king received everyone with a smiling face and greeted all the priests of the gods with courtesy and reverence. He thanked them for the honor they had shown him and asked for an incense burner. A richly gilded one was given him and he incensed the wooden and stone gods inside the temple.

204

Many quail were given to him and with his own hands he decapitated them and poured the blood at the foot of the altar and tossed the dead quail at the feet of the gods. This was done with special care before the image of Huitzilopochtli and this

*A few of the twenty Aztec hieroglyphic day signs.*
*A page from the* **Codex Borgia,** *one of the most elaborate*
*of all pre-Hispanic books, which deals with*
*fortune-telling, lucky and unlucky days. Courtesy New*
*York Public Library. Photo Reg Van Cuylenburg.*

peaceful sacrifice was offered to him. The king then asked for a jaguar bone, and a sharp instrument was handed to him. He drew blood from the top parts of his ears, his arms and shins, and this was done in a squatting position, such as the Indians use today, without allowing the buttocks to touch the floor. This position was a reverent one; had he touched the floor he would have been considered disrespectful. This way of sitting was the equivalent of our kneeling. As he squatted there he put his finger to the floor and taking earth with it he put it in his mouth. This ceremony was called, "The eating of holy earth." When the ceremony had ended, he stood up and turned to the people, exclaiming in a loud voice:

"O almighty, powerful Lord of All Created Things,
You who give us life, and whose vassals and slaves we are,
Lord of the Day and of the Night, of the Wind and the Water,
Whose strength keeps us alive! I give you infinite thanks
For having brought me back to your city of Mexico
With the victory which you granted me. I have returned
To the great city of Mexico-Tenochtitlan where our ancestors—
Chichimecs and Aztecs—with great pains found the
Blissful eagle seated upon the prickly pear cactus.
There the eagle ate and rested, next to the springs of
Blue and red water which were filled with flying fish,
White snakes and white frogs. This wondrous thing appeared
Since you wanted to show us the greatness of your power
And your will. You made us masters of the wealth we now
Possess and I give you infinite thanks, O Lord.
Since you did not frown upon my extreme youth
Or my lack of strength or the weakness of my chest,
You have subjected those remote and barbarous nations
To my power. You did all of these things! All is yours!
All was won to give you honor and praise!
Therefore, O powerful and heroic Huitzilopochtli,
You have brought us back to this place which was only water
Before, which was enclosed by our ancestors,
And where they built our city."

207

King Ahuitzotl then visited his other three favorite shrines: Chalco, Iztapalapa and Huitzilopochco.

After these ceremonies, a count was made of the tribute in the royal storehouses and it was found to exceed the imagination. From each province, every eighty days, there arrived a million Indians laden with everything that the land produced. This is not an exaggeration since we read that Moteczoma the Second, with whom we shall deal later, even had lice and fleas brought as tribute. In this the kings showed their tyrannical nature, though they justified these deeds by saying that they were risking their lives for their country.

CHAPTER XLVIII WHICH TREATS OF THE DEATH OF TLACAELEL
AND OF HOW KING AHUITZOTL ASKED THE RULER OF
COYOACAN FOR WATER FROM ACUECUEXCO.
WITH A DESCRIPTION OF THE EXCUSES THAT WERE MADE TO HIM AND HOW
AHUITZOTL THEREFORE HAD THIS RULER KILLED

Shortly after King Ahuitzotl returned from the conquest that has been described, the courageous Tlacaelel became ill. Due to his illness and to his age and lack of strength, he died, having charged King Ahuitzotl with his sons. The monarch ordered that the eldest son be placed in the position which his father had held and be venerated in the same way. Everyone acknowledged him as the principal chieftain of Mexico and he was given his father's title of *Cihuacoatl*. This was a grandiose name which had been bequeathed by the gods. From that day on he was called *Tlilpotonqui Cihuacoatl*, "The Black One Who Feathers, Snake Woman," and this was his divine name.

The body of Tlacaelel was cremated and his ashes were buried next to the sepulchres of the other kings. As has been related, Tlacaelel performed many feats worthy of remembrance, some of which are not told in our *Chronicle*. One story told by other authors is that after his death the Aztecs embalmed him, set him upon a litter with sword and shield in hand and, with his name and presence alone, brought victory to the Aztecs in a battle with Tliliuhquitepec.

At this time, when the valorous Tlacaelel was buried with great honors, King Ahuitzotl realized that the beauty and fertility of Mexico depended upon great quantities of water entering the city. The Aztecs had built floating gardens and orchards where they had sown maize, chian, squash, chilli, amaranth, tomatoes and flowers. With all these plants the city was greatly beautified, but their freshness would be lost if they should lack water. In order to preserve this greenery

King Ahuitzotl tried to bring in water from Acuecuexco. But in the dry season, the water of the canals was so low that it was impossible for canoes to navigate. So it was that the king sent two messengers to ask the ruler of Coyoacan to allow water to be brought in.

The two envoys went to propose this to King Tzotzomatzin, and this ruler gave signs that he was willing to obey. After he had consulted the chieftains in his city, he told the messengers that he was ready to grant the request since he was a vassal and obliged to obey. He said, however, that before the water was drawn he wished to warn them that the spring overflowed once in a while and could be a danger to the entire city. He feared that if the spring were mishandled it would rise and flood the city of Mexico, forcing the inhabitants to abandon their homes. He did not wish to Aztecs to complain that he had not warned them. The water of that spring was plentiful and when it filled the lake it had no outlet for its overflow and could inundate Mexico. The Aztecs, he said, should be content with the water which came from Chapultepec.

When King Ahuitzotl heard this answer he became full of wrath for he did not consider it a courteous response. He began to speak ill of the ruler of Coyoacan, calling him weak, wretched, a man of low rank. He cursed himself for having been too polite to Tzotzomatzin—a mere vassal of the Aztecs. He swore that he would destroy Tzotzomatzin and erase his dynasty from the face of the earth.

When the chieftains saw their king in such a rage they tried to calm him with soft words and excuses, speaking of the good intentions of Tzotzomatzin. However, the monarch was not to be placated, and he ordered two judges from the court to go immediately to strangle the offender in his chambers. "He should not have answered me thus," said Ahuitzotl. "This can be an example for others who might give advice when they had not been asked."

The chieftains saw that the king's command was irrevocable, but knowing that the lord of Coyoacan was a son of the king of Azcapotzalco, who was greatly honored and venerated, they sent him a message saying that he should be on guard since his life was in danger. However, Tzotzomatzin had great faith in sorcery and magical arts. Our *Chronicle* tells us that he was a sorcerer and that he was expert in magical spells. Therefore he remained still and when he was told that the judges from Mexico had arrived, he ordered his attendants to allow them to enter. When the judges entered his chamber they found a great and frightful eagle flying around the royal seat. The Aztecs saw this ferocious eagle and were greatly afraid. They left the room, asking the doormen why they had been deceived. The doormen claimed that they knew nothing about the eagle. The only one in that room, they said, was their master; they had left him there. On entering the room again the messengers found a fierce jaguar at the door, threatening to attack them with its paws and mouth. When the envoys saw this they returned to Mexico with great haste and told King Ahuitzotl what had happened.[91]

The king was much disturbed by this remarkable thing, and he gave orders that twice as many emissaries return to Coyoacan on the next day. Tzotzomatzin ordered that they be allowed to enter and this time they saw in the middle of the chamber a huge serpent, coiled up with its head twisted around. As soon as the serpent saw them it began to uncoil and prepared to attack. Even though they were greatly frightened they tried to kill it as they had been commanded. But in a moment a great fire appeared within the room, and the flames were so terrifying that they were all forced to flee as they had done on the previous day.

They returned to Mexico and explained to King Ahuitzotl that due to magic it was impossible to kill Tzotzomatzin. The king was angered and even more determined. Therefore he sent a message to the royal council of Coyoacan asking that the monarch be delivered to him. "Otherwise," said the Aztec monarch, "I will wage war on them and destroy them like rebels." Tzotzomatzin heard this and, knowing that it was impossible to escape and anxious to avoid the destruction of Coyoacan, he called the Aztecs saying, "Behold me here! I am in your hands! But tell your lord Ahuitzotl that my prophecies will come true. Before many days Mexico will be flooded and greatly harmed. He will be sorry that he did not listen to my advice." The Aztecs then placed a cord around his neck, strangled him and cast his body into the rocks. A spring, they say, promptly gushed forth in that place.

When all this had been done, King Ahuitzotl ordered his allies to bring workmen carrying stone, lime and stakes in order to make a dam and then a pipe in order to bring the water to Mexico. Many men came to his beckoning and built a strong mortar dam around the spring. The best masons to be found in the provinces were present at its construction, as well as those men whose work it was to enter springs in order to clean them and repair cracks and veins through which the water was lost. Then the workmen from Texcoco arrived with stone, heavy and light. Also men from the Tecpanec nation came with heavy stone. Chalco sent poles, stakes, and volcanic stone for the foundation. Xochimilco sent instruments to cut blocks of earth and canoes filled with dirt in order to dam the water. People from the hot country brought great loads of lime, and the same was done by the Otomi of Xilotepec and Cuauhtlalpan. So many people came to aid in the building of this remarkable work that, though two leagues long, it was finished with astonishing rapidity. Each province worked hard to see who would finish first, and in less than eight days everyone was idle. From the spring of Acuecuexco to the gates of Mexico, all the provinces and cities labored at the work assigned them with a great deal of noise and contentment. It is not an exaggeration to say that the men who built the dam and pipe looked like ants on an ant heap.

When this astonishing work had been finished and the structure had dried, King Ahuitzotl ordered that the water be let loose. Children were made ready to be sacrificed at every outlet and the priests prepared the customary offerings to the goddess of the waters. King Ahuitzotl was finally notified that all was ready and, having given thanks to the gods, he commanded a chieftain of his court to dress himself in order to impersonate the goddess of the waters. The day that the water was allowed to flow through the pipe this man was to stand before it and, in his presence, the ceremonies and sacrifices were to take place.

CHAPTER XLIX WHICH TREATS OF HOW THE WATERS ENTERED MEXICO
AND HOW THEY WERE WELCOMED. WITH A DESCRIPTION OF HOW THE CITY
WAS FLOODED AND THE INHABITANTS FLED

The people of Coyoacan were sorrowful over the death of their king because he had loved his city profoundly and had been a brave and kind sovereign to his people. However, they realized it was not the right time to complain of his death. Therefore they dissimulated and feigned as much as they could, waiting for the waters to avenge his death. Those of Texcoco and Tacuba also whispered and murmured among themselves, saying that the execution had been unjust and without reason. It was talked about so much that a rebellion almost occurred. However, since all believed there was no remedy for what had happened, these men were silent and no one dared to speak to King Ahuitzotl regarding the matter. All decided to wait for the right opportunity to take vengeance. Moreover they wished to protect the children and relatives of the dead king from appearing as traitors or disobedient to the royal crown.

King Ahuitzotl was not worried about these things and when the day came he ordered that the water be freed. It began to run toward the city of Mexico and a man disguised as the goddess of waters and springs appeared, dressed in a blue blouse covered by a garment similar to a scapulary. This last was embroidered with costly green and blue stones. He also wore a diadem made of white heron feathers and his face was darkened with liquid rubber. His forehead was colored blue, in his ears were two green stones, another on his lower lip, and on his wrists he wore strings of turquoise and jade beads. In his hands he carried rattles shaped like turtles and a bag filled with flour of blue corn. His legs were painted blue and he was wearing blue sandals, symbolizing the color of water. This man was accompanied by all the priests of the temples with their faces painted black, wearing paper garlands on their heads and on their foreheads large stars which served as knots for the headbands. They were stripped naked, wearing only paper loin cloths to cover their genitals. These priests carried flutes and conch shells and they went along in front of the goddess, blowing their instruments.

Other priests carried cages filled with quail, others bore handfuls of paper, others carried liquid rubber, and some incense. When they reached the spot where the water began to run, one of the priests killed the quail and poured their blood into the gushing water. As the blood was plentiful the water became reddened and carried the blood with it. The priests who had brought the incense and liquid rubber poured these into the water and into the pipe through which the water was to pass. In their burners they offered incense and all of this was done to the sound of flutes and conch shells which were being played loudly. Once in a while the man who was disguised as the goddess took some of the water in his hand and drank of it, and he spilled it on both sides of the pipes, speaking to it with great reverence:

"O precious lady, welcome to your own road! From now on
You will follow this path and I, who represent your image, have come here
To receive you, greet you and congratulate you for your arrival.
Behold, lady, today you must arrive in your own city, Mexico-Tenochtitlan!"

Having uttered these words he took some of the blue maize flour from the bag and tossed it into the water. Having cast the flour upon the surface he picked up his rattles and, as he sounded them, he entered the pipe and began to jump about and dance in the water. After he had done this he followed the flow of the water to each depression where it was allowed to collect.

All along the way were the singers of Tlaloc, god of the Rain and Thunderbolts, and the servants of the goddess, everyone playing musical instruments, dancing and singing songs in honor of the water. At the same time old men came up with tubs filled with live fish and with water snakes in their hands. Others carried containers with frogs, leeches and other amphibia. Occasionally they tossed them into the pipe, telling the pipe to carry them to Mexico in order that they might reproduce there.

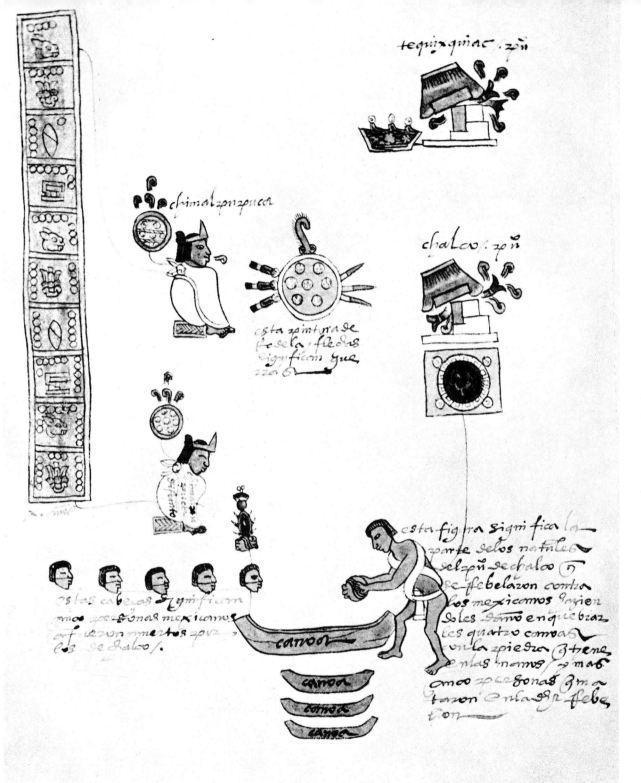

tequixquiac.zpñ

chimalzpuzpuca

chalco.zpñ

esta zpintura de
so se la sfledas
signifisan que
zza

esta figura significa la
parte delos naturales
del zpñ de chalco q̃
se se belazon contra
los mexicanos poyen
do les sano en quebrar
les quatro canvas
en la zpiedra q̃ trene
en las manos y mas
cinco zpersonas q̃ ma
taron en la zzo feberi
tion

canoa

canoa

canoa

canoa

estos cabeças significan
mas zpersonas mexicanos
q̃ fueron muertos por
los ze chalco.

*The reign of King Chimalpopoca, "Smoking Shield," of Mexico. The hieroglyphic dates on the upper left indicate the years of his rule. From the* **Codex Mendoza,** *painted in early Colonial times by Aztec scribes. Courtesy New York Public Library. Photo Reg Van Cuylenburg.*

At the first important culvert, located in a place called Acachinanco, were four six-year-old children waiting. They were painted black with their foreheads blue, wearing paper headbands with stars knotted in front in the manner of the priests. These children were nude except for paper loin cloths and strings of blue beads around their necks. As soon as the waters arrived the first of these boys was laid out upon the pipe, his chest opened and his heart offered to the water with the blood dripping into the pipe. In this way were the other three children sacrificed.

In Mexico City Ahuitzotl welcomed the water with florid words. After he had spoken he cast into the stream many golden jewels in the form of fish and frogs together with great quantities of stones carved in the same manner. All the nobility did the same, throwing in jewels and stones, each one according to his means.

A few days later the water began to increase in such quantities that it flooded some of the floating gardens. When Ahuitzotl saw the harm that was being done he remembered the words of the sovereign of Coyoacan. He asked the advice of those of his council and ordered that a strong dike be erected so that the water which entered the lagoon should not flow into Mexico. And so it was that the nearby cities and towns were asked to come help build the dike.

The dike was constructed a fourth of a league on this side of the Peñol, a knoll on the outskirts of Mexico. However, all their efforts were useless; the more they tried to stop the water the more damage it caused. It began to enter the homes of many inhabitants who abandoned their houses and their city. The situation was such that the heads of the wards came to visit the king and asked him to find a remedy for the harm that was being caused by the flood. The cornfields with their tender cornstalks were lost, and so were the chilli, tomato, amaranth, and flower plantations.

When Ahuitzotl consulted the king of Texcoco the latter said to him, "It is too late to be sorry and alarmed at your own perdition and that of the great city of Mexico. You could have considered and prevented this before. You are not fighting now against your enemies whom you could destroy or force to flee from your cities. You are fighting against water, a fierce element. How can you resist it? The great prince of Coyoacan, Tzotzomatzin, gave you good advice and not only would you not listen to his opinion, which he gave you like a loyal vassal, but you slew him." Having said these words, Nezahualpilli began to weep and show great feeling, exclaiming, "What did Tzotzomatzin do? In what did he sin? In what did he offend? Why did you deprive him of his life so pitilessly? Was he a traitor to the royal crown? Was he an adulterer or a thief? O powerful lord, realize that you have offended, that you have sinned against the gods. It is my opinion that the dam should be removed from the spring and that the water should flow as before. A solemn sacrifice must be made also in honor of the goddess of the waters so that the wrath she feels against you may be placated. She must be offered jewels and feathers, quail, incense, rubber and paper. Let children be brought for sacrifice also. Perhaps with all of this you will calm her and she will control her streams and they will not flow as they do now."

King Ahuitzotl was much moved by this speech and he prepared to placate the great goddess of the waters, who was called Chalchiuhtlicue, "She of the Jade Skirt." Offerings were brought and everyone gathered around the springs. They humiliated themselves, celebrated rites and offered up children, quail, incense, rubber, paper, and other precious things. Then divers leaped into the depths of the water, carrying on their backs many jewels, feathers and precious stones. They offered all these things down at the bottom of the spring and buried them in the mud. Large stone idols were also offered, the most remarkable of which was a likeness of the goddess. In this way the Aztecs calmed the flood to a certain extent. Once this was done the king had the dams removed so that the stream might follow its former course. Ahuitzotl then went to Coyoacan to beg forgiveness for the assassination of the ruler and appointed the son of Tzotzomatzin as legitimate heir to the kingdom. He then ordered his allies to aid him in the rebuilding of the city.

CHAPTER L WHICH TREATS OF HOW NEWS ARRIVED IN MEXICO
THAT THE PROVINCES OF SOCONUSCO, XOLOTLA AND MAZATLAN
HAD MISTREATED THE PEOPLE OF TEHUANTEPEC
BECAUSE THE LATTER HAD BECOME SUBJECT
TO THE AZTECS. WITH A DESCRIPTION OF THE WAR
THAT THE AZTECS WAGED THERE

216

After the city of Mexico had been rebuilt news came that the provinces of Soconusco, Xolotla and Mazatlan had done great harm to Tehuantepec because they had allowed the Aztecs to conquer them. They called Tehuantepec a city of cowards, and used many other offensive womanly epithets. Among the many crimes that the people of Soconusco committed was the killing of merchants from Mexico and its provinces who had gone there to trade. The inhabitants of the rebel provinces had formed gangs and gone about the roads and woods like highway robbers, stripping and robbing travelers and sacking the neighboring villages of the province of Tehuantepec.

King Ahuitzotl called together the rulers of Texcoco and Tacuba and asked them to aid in forming an army to chastise the rebels. Two hundred thousand soldiers gathered; this did not include all the carriers or boys who found it adventurous to go with the army. All of these were gallant men desirous of gaining honor and advancement. When Ahuitzotl saw that the allied monarchs were staying behind and did not wish to go to this war of conquest he played a trick on them. He took from his rooms several shields, swords, and other fine weapons with royal insignia on them and sent them to each sovereign without telling him whether he was to go to war or not. The king of Tacuba realized what Ahuitzotl meant by this and he sent back his excuses. He said that he was too old and that he could not wage war in such a faraway land and on such a long campaign. He begged to be pardoned, as he would have liked to attend. However, in his place would go two courageous sons of his and they would give orders to the men of his army.

According to some authors, King Nezahualpilli of Texcoco took part in this war and showed great bravery; others say that he did not attend. Our *Chronicle* says nothing about this; it states only that the most valiant Texcocans, led by their rulers, went to test their forces in this remarkable enterprise and campaign. However, it is not strange if Nezahualpilli did not go, because the *Chronicle* depicts him as a weak, frail man of little strength, more admired as a prophet than as a warrior. In a certain Texcocan painted manuscript, I saw him portrayed with his weapons, a sword and shield in his hands, holding a man by the hair. In an inscription under the painting were to be found these words: "Here Nezahualpilli captured this captain in the war of Huexotzinco," and the date was shown. However, our Aztec *Chronicle* is not interested in the deeds of other peoples but in its own. It skips the feats which were not achieved by the Aztecs. The only thing the *Chronicle* tells us is that Nezahualpilli was a sorcerer, a magician or witch doctor, together with Tzompantecuhtli of Cuitlahuac, who was honored by his people as a god. He prophesied many things, including the arrival of the Spaniards. This prophecy was couched in a confusing language combined with fables and lies.

Soconusco was conquered, but before King Ahuitzotl returned from that land he was told that other large and wealthy provinces were nearby, such as Guatemala, Atlpopoca, Popocatepetl, and Tlatlatepec.[92] These provinces were rich and densely populated and had continually waged war against Soconusco. The king was told that, if he so desired, the men of Soconusco would aid him in conquering these places. King Ahuitzotl answered that he did not wish to go farther, in part because those people had not offended him in any way and in part because his men were exhausted. He added that he had such faith in the strength of the Aztecs that in time they would conquer the entire world.

When he returned to Mexico he immediately gave thanks to the gods as was his custom, offering them great riches which he had brought from the conquered province. At the end of the ceremonies he bled his ears, arms, shins and tongue, and offered the gods quail which he killed with his own hands.

A few days after his return Ahuitzotl became gravely ill and, as he saw that the end was near, he gave orders that his image be carved next to that of his father on a rock on the Hill of Chapultepec. Thus it was done and visitors can see the carving which is still there today. These images were made in order to perpetuate the memory of the Aztec rulers. A few days after this work was finished he died, leaving many widows, children and concubines, and his own city filled with mourning and sadness.

CHAPTER **LI** WHICH TREATS OF THE DEATH OF KING AHUITZOTL.
WITH A DESCRIPTION OF THE SOLEMN
FUNERAL RITES PERFORMED IN HIS HONOR AND OF THE WEALTH
THAT WAS BURIED WITH HIM

As we have seen, a few days after King Ahuitzotl returned from the war in Soconusco he became ill of a serious disease. It was a strange and terrible illness, and the doctors could not understand it. It was thought that perhaps he had been poisoned in that land. His death was strange since he was a young man, in good health both in body and spirit. With this disease he withered up, began to lose his vigor and when he died he was reduced to skin and bones. No one knew which remedy to administer to him though everything possible was done to restore his health. He was pitied and his death caused immense sorrow. Even children lamented, moved by the frightful weeping and moaning which rose in the city. This was done by the mourners, women who were hired to wail at the deaths of kings and noblemen and for those who died in war. These women had to be of the lineage of the king. The widows and concubines and other old women joined them and, even though they did not shed a tear or feel like crying, it was their task to wail and scream in a terrible way. They also clapped their hands and bowed toward the earth, inclining and raising their bodies from the earth continually.

The neighboring kings came to offer sumptuous presents to the dead man, things that would serve him in the other life, everyone giving as much as he

218

could. (However, this was only done at the funerals of monarchs and great lords, since the common people lacked the means for such splendid obsequies. Poor widows and relatives could offer only food and clay or stone beads of the cheapest kind.)

When the formal speeches made by the princely guests had come to an end, the mantles and loincloths which the king had worn during his life were brought out along with his jewelry. The two hundred slaves who were to die in front of the royal corpse were dressed in all of these garments and jewels. The clothes and gems that remained were placed in small baskets and given to the slaves to carry into the other world. These victims were arranged in lines as if for a procession, all of them garbed in royal vestments. According to the superstition of the Aztecs, these slaves would go to the other world to become great nobles. There they would accompany the king and have the same occupations and privileges which the chieftains had on earth. This was also believed by the wretched slaves and for this reason they offered themselves freely for death.

The divine brazier, filled with the bark of trees which was the firewood of the gods, was lighted, and the wood burned with long-lasting beautiful flames. The nobles cast the corpse, splendidly dressed, into the fire. At this point the priests picked up their sacrificial knives and, one by one, they sacrificed the slaves which the visiting sovereigns and great chieftains had offered. They cast them on their backs upon the wooden drum with which they had been making the death music, and they opened their chests, taking out their hearts. These hearts were thrown upon the burning body and all night the cadaver and the hearts smouldered until they were consumed. The ashes were gathered in a new urn and buried near the Stone of the Sun, the *cuauhxicalli* or "eagle vessel." This is the stone which today stands near the door of the Cathedral in the city of Mexico. Together with this urn was buried all the treasure that had not been burned.

All of the sovereigns and nobility of the country were present at this funeral and when it had ended the king of Texcoco prohibited any one of them from departing from the city until the election of a new king had been carried out, since he wished it to be done with the approval of all.

The day after the ashes of King Ahuitzotl were buried with magnificent ceremonies, King Nezahualpilli of Texcoco, the sovereign of Tacuba, and all the chieftains of the provinces who were subject to the royal crown of Mexico formed a
council to elect the new ruler of the country. Nezahualpilli of Texcoco, as principal
elector, spoke first, saying:

"O valorous monarch of Tacuba and great lords of Mexico! O rulers of the
provinces of Chalco, Xochimilco and the low lands! With your vote and consent
we are to choose the luminary that is to give us light like one of the sun's rays. We
are to choose a mirror in which we will be reflected, a mother who will hold us to
her breast, a father who will carry us on his shoulders and a prince who will rule
over the Aztec nation. He will be the shelter and refuge of the poor, of widows and
orphans, and he will have pity upon those who go about day and night in the wilderness working for their sustenance. This is the one that you must elect, O mighty
lords. Look about you, as there is much to see! You are surrounded by all the Aztec
nobles, who are like rich feathers fallen from the wings and tails of those splendid
turkeys, the past kings. They are the jewels and precious stones which fell from
the throats and wrists of those royal men. Behold the eyebrows and lashes which
have fallen from the courageous sovereigns of Mexico who gave nobility to this
council. Extend your hands to the one who pleases you most.

"The valorous monarch Axayacatl left sons, as did his brother Tizoc. All of them
are highly esteemed princes, remarkable for their boldness and spirit. If these do
not please you, turn your eyes upon other nobles. Among them you will find
grandsons and great grandsons, nephews and cousins of the past kings who
founded this city. It will not be necessary for you to leave this chamber. Extend
your hands, point out your favorite, since anyone you indicate will be a strong wall
against our enemies."

After Cihuacoatl, the son of Tlacaelel, had spoken and some discussion had followed, Moteczoma, son of King Axayacatl, was chosen. There was no opposition
to this choice for he was a mature man, pious, virtuous, generous and of an invincible spirit. He was blessed with all the virtues that can be found in a good ruler
and his decisions had always been correct, especially in matters of war. In the
latter he had performed feats which showed remarkable bravery.

When Moteczoma had been proclaimed king of Mexico by all the electors, everyone looked for him among those who were in the chamber but he was not to be found. (Moteczoma, seeing that all were inclined in his favor, had withdrawn from the meeting.) The king of Texcoco ordered that he be sought and, while this was being done, the brazier that was kept especially for these occasions was lighted. Around it were placed the royal garments, the diadem and an incense burner containing a large quantity of incense. Jaguar bones and the bones of eagles and mountain lions were also placed around the brazier, together with the royal sandals and a splendid loincloth.

Those who had gone to seek Moteczoma went first to a temple, since they knew him to be a religious man. They found him in the Shrine of the Eagles, within a room especially appointed for him. They greeted him and told him the kings and chieftains wished him to return to the council. Moteczoma arose and having greeted them politely, agreed to go with them. When he entered the council chamber all arose and did reverence to him. He did likewise, showing his grave, calm face. Then they seated him next to the brazier, and Cihuacoatl, his uncle, spoke.

"O lord, listen to what I wish to tell you, since it is the decision of all these chieftains, brothers and close relatives of yours. They and I speak to you in the name of the God of All Created Things, the Lord through whom we live and whose creatures we are, the One who with his will moves without being moved! He is the true worker of precious stones and he has chosen you like a gem from among many others. He has polished and engraved you so that you may be a jewel for his arm, a precious stone for his neck. This has also been done by all the chieftains who are present since they too are true lapidaries or goldsmiths who know the value of gems and of gold. They have created thus a precious vessel, a splendid jewel, picked out from among all the others of the earth. All these present have, in one voice, declared and proclaimed that you, because of your virtue, are to reign over Mexico and over its grandeur. They have all confessed your supremacy and so it must be. This is your lot: leave the low seat that you now occupy! Take the throne that has been assigned to you, and rejoice in that which the Lord of All Created Things has granted you!"

After Moteczoma had been enthroned, Nezahualpilli of Texcoco addressed him. "O you most powerful of all the kings of the earth! The clouds have been dispelled and the darkness in which we lived has fled. The sun has appeared and the light of dawn shines upon us after the darkness which had been caused by the death of the king. The torch which is to illuminate Mexico has been lighted and today we have been given a mirror to look into. The high and powerful Lord has delivered his kingdom to you and he has assigned the royal seat to you. Therefore, my son, you will now begin to labor in the fields of the gods like the peasant who works his lands. Cast out weakness from your manly heart, do not be faint, do not be careless in your duties. Remember that all of this has not been given you to sleep away in idleness and pleasure. From now on you must beware of sleep. Because of the cares of the kingdom you must be wakeful. You must rise early and go out to watch the stars in order to observe their movements, signs, influences and omens. You must be ready to receive the morning star and, as soon as it appears, you must take your ritual bath, purifying yourself and anointing yourself with the divine pitch. You will then bleed yourself and, carrying the incense burner, you will offer incense and sacrifice to the gods. Finally, you will contemplate the hidden places and the nine folds of the heavens. You will descend to the place of the abyss, to the center of the earth, where stand the three houses of fire. You will go to the hills and wilderness where the sons of God do penance and live in the solitude of the caves, and you will also contemplate the divine springs and streams.

"You must care for and remember all these things, especially those connected with the divine cult and reverence of the gods and honor of the priesthood. You must see that the latter continue their penance and you must give them courage and aid. With these words I end my discourse."

CHAPTER **LIII** WHICH TREATS OF THE ORDERS GIVEN BY KING MOTECZOMA REGARDING THE SERVICES THAT HE AND HIS HOUSEHOLD WERE TO RECEIVE. WITH A DESCRIPTION OF OTHER THINGS COMMANDED BY THIS GREAT MONARCH

As soon as Moteczoma was enthroned on the royal seat of Mexico, he decided to show the loftiness of his thoughts about the kingship and the esteem due to his exalted person. Even though it is true that, in supernatural and divine matters, these people lacked the light and the knowledge of God, in discipline and good government they surpassed many other nations and were much superior to them. After this great prince had been elected, he called in his main councilor who was his uncle Tlilpotonqui, the second in command in the country. Through the latter's hands passed all things connected with the government.

When Tlilpotonqui appeared, the king spoke to him in the royal chamber and laid down his rules regarding the service and position of his own person. He wished to place new officials in the service of his household and remove those which his uncle Ahuitzotl had appointed because the latter were men of low rank or children of common men. He said that it was undignified and unworthy of a king to be served by lowly people and that he wished to be attended by persons as high ranking as himself. This was to be done in part because he wished to be revered and in part because he wished to teach these sons of chieftains, his cousins and brothers, the virtue of courtly manners and the art of ruling. In this way, when their turn came to govern, it would not seem difficult to them.

Moteczoma then asked his prime minister to go to the places where the sons of the nobility were educated, both to those in Mexico and to those of Texcoco, Tacuba, and other provinces. The king gave orders that no illegitimate boy should be brought before him, even though he be his own brother, son of his father Axayacatl, for he considered that anyone born of a lowly woman or slave might take after his mother and be, therefore, ineligible for his service. All those who served Moteczoma were to be born of lords; all must be legitimate and children of ladies of noble blood.

When the youths had appeared before him he explained to them why they had been brought, how he wished to be served by people of his own blood, and how he would communicate his affairs to them and trust them with his own person and with the royal treasury. These young men were to serve nobles and strangers, who might appear in the palace, with such care that no one ever departed from the court displeased. He also insisted on the respect they must show toward the queens, wives, concubines and other women in the palace. They were to respect the modesty of these women and watch the comportment among the women themselves. The household was to be kept clean and in good order. The new courtiers were also told to be heedful of the commands and messages they were charged with and to beware of any alteration of the words or meaning of the messages. They were told to speak without stuttering, without nervousness or haste. They were to talk in low voices, calmly, slowly and gravely. They were to walk with dignity and were never to tell lies to the king or bear false witness against anyone. If Moteczoma heard any complaints against their comportment, he would have them pierced with arrows or burned alive.

As soon as the monarch had given the young men their instructions he dismissed all the officials that his uncle Ahuitzotl had employed, not sparing one of them. He also changed all the royal officials of the city and substituted them with noblemen. The heads of the wards and the captains of hundreds of men were also changed. It is said that all of these officials were put to death. It would not surprise me if he did this cruel deed because, as king, he showed himself to be the greatest butcher that has ever existed and he did this in order to be feared and held in awe.

If any common man dared to lift his eyes and look upon him, Moteczoma ordered that he be slain. He said that no commoner should gaze upon the one who represented the Deity. Therefore he was given divine honors, and when he passed all prostrated themselves on the ground. I once questioned an Indian on the facial characteristics of Moteczoma and about his height and general appearance, and this is the answer I got: "Father, I will not lie to you or tell you about things which I do not know. I never saw his face!" When I asked him why this was so, he responded that if he had dared to gaze upon the monarch he would have been killed in the same way that others who had looked upon him were slain.

When someone committed a fault within the royal household, the deed was doubly serious because it took place in the house of God. Moteczoma called his home the House of God and the punishment for any negligence or irreverence was death.[93]

This powerful monarch began his reign in the year 1503, the same year in which the Spaniards seized and conquered the island of Cuba. In this same year the great Turkish Emperor Selim was crowned.

CHAPTER **LIV** WHICH TREATS OF THE SOLEMN FESTIVITIES THAT WERE MADE ON THE CORONATION AND PUBLIC ANOINTMENT OF KING MOTECZOMA AND OF THE MANY MEN WHO WERE SACRIFICED

Moteczoma began his reign with a war of conquest and returned triumphant. All victories were attributed to him and the officials determined to celebrate the coronation feast of the king. Emissaries were sent to invite representatives from the enemy states of Tlaxcala, Huexotzinco, Cholula, Tliliuhquitepec, Michoacan, Metztitlan and the land of the Huaxtecs.

When the day appointed for the coronation arrived the foreign kings and nobility began to enter the city. All were well lodged in chambers which had been prepared for them. They were adorned with flowers, reeds and magnificent shields hanging from the walls, together with splendid feathers which these people love greatly. The enemy guests were provided with all necessary things in abundance and they begged the steward who served them to tell his majesty that they desired

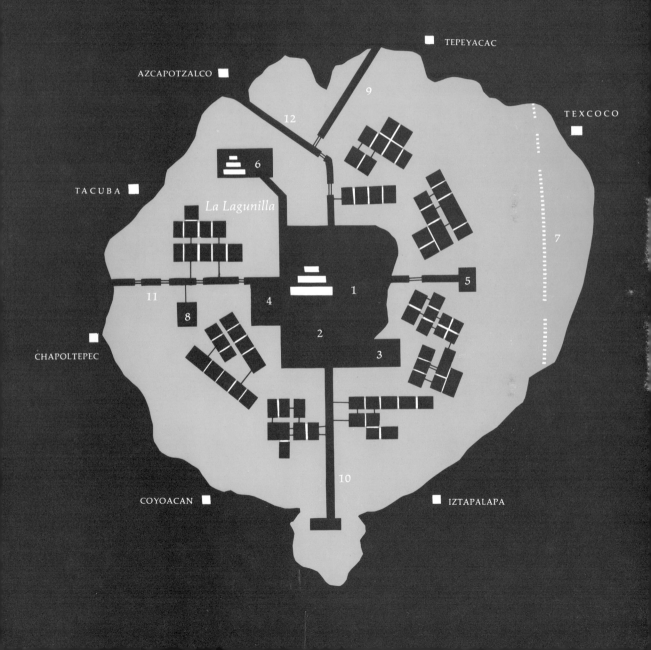

1. ENCLOSURE OF THE GREAT TEMPLE
2. GREAT SQUARE
3. MOTECZOMA'S PALACE
4. PALACE OF AXAYACATL
5. DOCK
6. PYRAMID AND MARKET PLACE TLATELOLCO
7. DIKE
8. ZOOLOGICAL GARDENS
9. TO TEPEYACAC
10. TO IZTAPALAPA
11. TO TACUBA
12. TO AZCAPOTZALCO

TEPEYACAC

AZCAPOTZALCO

TEXCOCO

TACUBA

La Lagunilla

CHAPOLTEPEC

COYOACAN

IZTAPALAPA

Mexico-Tenochtitlan, based on a map attributed to Cortés.
The center of the city is enlarged, and the interpretation
of the size and contours are, to a great extent, a fantasy.

to see him in order to kiss his royal hands. A secret door was opened and all of them were allowed to enter the presence of the king. The monarch of each province made a long oration and offered him fine presents and wealth. They also congratulated him on his election and the beginning of his reign. The powerful sovereign thanked them one by one, showing his peaceful and happy countenance. He received each of the lords with courtesy and seated them next to him by order of their seniority. When they had all been seated, he addressed them in a florid speech for he was an excellent orator. His style was so fine that he could attract and win over others with his reasoning and all were delighted by his pleasant talk.

After they had returned to their chambers, Moteczoma ordered Cihuacoatl to give the guests splendid mantles and loincloths, rich sandals which they called "the royal shoes" and fine jewels, necklaces and precious stones. All of this was done without the knowledge of the kings of Tacuba and Texcoco because, according to the *Chronicle*, they knew nothing about the coming of the enemy to Mexico. King Moteczoma ordered expressly that no one dare disclose their presence or reveal it to the other foreign rulers who had filled the city. In this way the enemies remained unnoticed and they were provided for and served in complete secrecy. When the night of the ceremonial dances came they attended, dressed in the royal vestments, diadems, precious jewels and feathers which the king had given them. When they appeared in the royal courtyard all the torches and lights in the palace were put out, although up to that time there had been so much light that it had seemed like midday. When the enemies had finished dancing they went back into their chambers and the torches were relighted. This was repeated on the four days and nights of the feast.

When the festivities ended, Moteczoma seated himself in the supreme place, the Divine Seat, the Place of the Gods, and the war captives were brought out. All of them were sacrificed to honor his coronation, and it was a pathetic thing to see these wretches as victims of Moteczoma. It had become as common among the Aztecs to sacrifice men on feast days as it for us to kill lambs or cattle in the slaughterhouses. I am not exaggerating; there were days in which two thousand, three thousand or eight thousand men were sacrificed. Their flesh was eaten and a banquet was prepared with it after the hearts had been offered to the devil.

When the sacrifice was finished and the steps and courtyard were bathed with human blood, everyone went to eat raw mushrooms. With this food they went out of their minds and were in a worse state than if they had drunk a great quantity of wine. They became so inebriated and witless that many of them took their lives in their hands. With the strength of these mushrooms they saw visions and had revelations about the future, since the devil spoke to them in their madness.

When the mushroom ceremony had ended and all had recovered, the enemy lords from Tlaxcala, Huexotzinco, and Tliliuhquitepec asked for royal permission to depart. This was granted to them and they were given jewels, sumptuous and rich gifts, weapons and shields with their insignia done in fine feather work. They left the city accompanied by a large number of guards from Mexico so that no one dared molest them in any way. They departed at night and went along hidden paths in order not to be recognized. The guards accompanied them as far as their own boundaries and then returned to their city.

From this day on, says the *Chronicle*, Moteczoma invited the enemy rulers three times a year to great feasts; one of them was known as the Feast of the Lords, another of the Banners, and the third, when they ate mushrooms, was called the Feast of the Revelations. The *Chronicle* does not explain his reasons for these invitations. The Tlaxcalans also invited him to their solemnities and when he attended or sent representatives it was without the knowledge of his own people, nor did the masses of Tlaxcalans know anything about it. However, according to the *Chronicle,* he seldom attended these feasts in person.

CHAPTER **LV** WHICH TREATS OF HOW MOTECZOMA CONQUERED THE PROVINCES OF CUATZONTLAN AND XALTEPEC. WITH A DESCRIPTION OF HOW HE ORDERED THE SLAUGHTER OF ALL THE OLD PEOPLE, THOUGH HE SPARED THE YOUNG

Icpatepec and Xaltepec are towns, or rather populous provinces, whose inhabitants, hearing of the coronation of the new King Moteczoma, thought that he would not become a bellicose, cunning or rigorous man. Therefore they decided to become independent of Mexico. The Indians today will test anyone who has been appointed to a high office and feel his pulse to determine his spirit. In this they are clever and sly, and when they discover a man of good heart and soft entrails they pay little heed to him. Instead of pleasing him they make him drink gall. In this way those provinces wanted to try out the energy of Moteczoma, and they ordered that all the Aztecs and their allies who were within those states be murdered. And so it was done, not a single man being spared. Then, as was the custom, they cut the roads and paths, closed all the gates and placed a roadblock. They encircled their towns with high walls and prepared to defend themselves. These rebels believed that they could sustain themselves as did Michoacan, Tlaxcala, Metztitlan, and the land of the Huaxtecs. They did not remember, however, that

King Moteczoma had explained to all that he did not wish to subject Tlaxcala and the other provinces because they served to give warlike practice to his men and food to his gods.

The Aztecs prepared for war and Moteczoma and his allies, joined by a few soldiers from Tlaxcala and other enemy provinces, set out for Xaltepec. The enemy warriors who joined them did so in order to enjoy the spoils, though others sought practice in war. They mingled with the other soldiers disguised as best they could. Thus it is that the *Chronicle* does not give us the exact number of those who went to war. Our history simply says that they were innumerable men, sometimes comparing them to an ant hill and at other times to the sands of the sea. That is why I am rarely able to give the exact number of combatants in the different wars. The principal reasons for going to war were material gain and glory. Another was to show their contempt for life and the fact that they held those who died in battle as blessed. Therefore war was called *xochiyaoyotl*, which means "Flowery War." The death of those in war was called *xochimiquiztli*, "Flowery Death, Blissful Death, Fortunate Death."

With Moteczoma went Cihuacoatl, son of Tlacaelel, and with them all the great chieftains. At the end of the first day Moteczoma ordered Cihuacoatl to return to Mexico, commanding him to take charge of the government. He was also told to behead all the tutors of his own children and the duennas of his wives and concubines so that they could be replaced by new ones. Cihuacoatl would have been pleased to go to war and so it is that he returned to Mexico in sad spirits. He came back accompanied by the royal councilors, judges and warriors who were no longer obliged to wage war. On his arrival he immediately did what the king had ordered, beheading all the tutors, duennas and other court ladies who lived with the queens and concubines of Moteczoma. Moteczoma sent after him certain spies to see if his orders had been fulfilled. The spies saw that the executions had taken place and returned to tell the monarch. This was characteristic of Moteczoma; all the orders he gave had to be obeyed immediately without any discussion, never admitting pleas or supplications. His reason for slaughtering these tutors and duennas is not explained in the *Chronicle*; it was a secret of the king.

At this time—before King Moteczoma proceeded into battle—he ordered that the rulers of Tlatelolco, now the ward of Santiago in the city of Mexico, appear before him. "You will remember," he said, "that my father waged war on you and subjected you to the royal crown of Mexico. He demanded that you pay a certain tribute because of your rebelliousness. You have complied with this as you should have, especially for this war and for the past one. You know it is your obligation to bring arms and other provisions."

The Tlatelolca answered that he was speaking the truth, but that previous rulers,

Moteczoma's uncles, had relented, as they recognized the people of Tlatelolco to be relatives. Moteczoma responded, "Although my uncles overlooked your failings, I do not wish to do so. I wish to carry out what my father ordered since he won your tribute in a good war. Therefore I command that before I leave this place you bring me what you are obliged to pay. You are fortunate that I am not asking you to pay all the back tribute. I order you to do this and, if you fail, I will bring judgment upon you."

The men then presented themselves, bringing such enormous provisions that when Moteczoma saw the liberality with which they had paid their tribute he was grateful to them. As a special favor he granted that the officers of that company be lodged next to his tent from this time on, and that they be given the same foods that he himself received. He ordered that they be given clothing and he gave them back their titles. He also permitted them to rebuild the temple at Tlatelolco which had lain in ruins and been used as a dung heap since the conquest of that city. In our own Spanish nation it is a custom to destroy the houses of traitors and to sow salt in their fields. A similar custom was this of leaving the temples of traitors in ruins, believing that the advice to rebel had come from these temples.

The men of Tlatelolco were also to be allowed to take their companies to war, as a separate city or province. Moteczoma was very generous with them, showing them affection and friendship, treating them like relatives. However, they were forced to continue to pay tribute, as this was something that he never pardoned.

After this Moteczoma and his armies continued on to the enemy provinces where the king gave orders that no old man or woman over fifty years of age was to be spared. He said that these were the ones who committed treason, caused rebellions and incited the younger people.

So the different cities began to be conquered, the Aztecs killing any man or woman who seemed to be over fifty. They robbed and sacked the houses and villages, leaving them bare. The land was subjected to the city of Mexico and, whenever the king was received in a city, he was recognized as sovereign and offered tribute and presents.

The people of Tehuantepec had been waiting to see the outcome of the war and when they saw that the king had prevailed and that they had not yet acknowledged or congratulated him, the officials came to visit Moteczoma. They saluted him and welcomed his arrival in those parts. They offered him gifts and told him of their great desire to see him. They asked him for a daughter of his to be the wife of the heir to the kingdom of Tehuantepec. He granted them this request and had her taken and married to this lord with much honor, feasting and rejoicing. The people of Tehuantepec considered themselves fortunate in having obtained a lady of such high lineage. This princess some time later was to free her city and her husband by revealing to him an ambush of ten thousand Aztecs who had hidden in the province, sent by Moteczoma to destroy it. The ruler of Tehuantepec, who married the Aztec lady and later had an heir, stopped recognizing his father-in-law. He thought of himself as a fellow ruler and whatever tribute was to be paid he decided to keep for his son, grandchild of Moteczoma. The ambush was revealed by the queen of Tehuantepec to her husband and the latter gave secret orders that each inhabitant kill any stranger who might be in his house that night. This was done, and during the night ten thousand valorous Aztec soldiers were slain.

On his triumphant return to Mexico Moteczoma passed through Chalco where he was received with great rejoicing. From this town he went on to the rocky hill of Tepepulco where beautiful pleasure gardens lay. He said that he wished to rest there a few days, and he pretended to await the arrival of the prisoners who were being brought from war. He sent a message to the governor of Mexico, Cihuacoatl, to receive the great chieftains and treat them royally according to the decrees that had been ordained. The chieftains departed toward Mexico while the dwellers of the lagoon began to arrive in their canoes to bring offerings to the king on the rocky hill.

Once these people had withdrawn, Moteczoma ordered his attendant to prepare a canoe with six rowers and at night, very secretly, he entered the boat and came to the city. He ordered that no one be notified of his arrival since he wished to see how the chieftains were being received. He wished to know if there were deficiencies in the ceremonies when he was not present.

The reception for the officials began with all the usual solemnity and ceremonial, and the king, disguised, was able to watch and notice all that occurred without being seen. Later, when satisfied that all was well, Moteczoma made his presence known.

CHAPTER LVI WHICH TREATS OF WHY MOTECZOMA ATTACKED
AND CONQUERED THE PROVINCES OF QUETZALTEPEC AND TOTOTEPEC.
WITH A DESCRIPTION OF THE STRONG RESISTANCE
HE MET IN CONQUERING THEM

At this time the lapidaries of the city of Mexico, of Tlatelolco, and of other cities heard that in the provinces of Tototepec and Quetzaltepec there existed a type of sand good for working stones, together with emery to polish them until they became bright and shining. The stone workers told King Moteczoma about this and explained the difficulties in obtaining the sand and emery from those provinces, and the high prices that were asked. Moteczoma sent messengers then to Totetepec and Quetzaltepec, asking as a favor that the sand be sent to the master artisans. He stated that he would send them things in return, since he wished this to be an exchange. (In this land the manner of buying and selling was the exchange of one thing for another.)

The people of Tototepec and Quetzaltepec were greatly offended by this request and killed the envoys, throwing their bodies into the river.

Moteczoma prepared an army of four hundred thousand men and set out for those provinces. After great difficulties the guides led the Aztec army to the brink of a river Quetzalatl, which was swollen and raging and poured into the sea with great fury. The soldiers were much frightened by this.[94] Camp was set up on the river bank while the people of Tototepec and Quetzaltepec appeared on the other side, making ferocious gestures and movements with their bodies, faces, hands and feet, meanwhile shouting offensive and obscene words.

When they had arrived there Moteczoma, who was an enemy of lost time, ordered the captains to make balsa rafts and bridges out of the roots of trees and certain reeds. These rafts were called *acatlapechtli*, "bed of reeds." The bridges were made of a root called cuauhmatlatl and were formed like nets. Everything was done carefully and an entire day was employed in these preparations. When night came Moteczoma ordered that the rafts and bridges be set in place and in a moment the entire army had crossed the river. The inhabitants of Tototepec had been free of worry since they trusted the river, swollen and furious as it was, to prevent the Aztecs from crossing.

The Aztecs swiftly entered the city, burned the temple and the royal houses and slaughtered all the people. The looting and killing lasted until daybreak when Moteczoma gave orders that his men gather in one place. However, many of them had gone off to the neighboring villages to steal and at midday they had not returned. It took the whole day to gather the soldiers together.

After much resistance the city of Quetzaltepec was also taken and Moteczoma returned to his capital. He entered the city with his body painted with a yellow pitch called *axin* and pendants in his ears, nose, and lips. Prince Cihuacoatl, who had gone to Iztapalapa to meet the monarch, attired himself in the garb of the goddess Cihuacoatl. These were the female clothes which were called "eagle garments." In this way they entered the city and, coming to the temple, Moteczoma bled his ears, arms and shins as sacrifice, and thanked the god Huitzilopochtli for the victory that he had granted.

230

Many days passed after the two cities of Tototepec and Quetzaltepec had been conquered, and no news of importance reached King Moteczoma. He became weary of so much idleness and of the fact that there was no war in which his soldiers might practice their arts. Therefore, he decided to provoke the people of Huexotzinco, and he brought together the two neighboring kings and their chieftains. He proposed to them what he had in mind. He told them that many days and months had gone by and that there had been no campaigns or military exercises. He was desirous of waging war against Huexotzinco and testing its strength.

When the rulers and lords heard his plan they agreed with him and said that it pleased them very much, since for that very reason the cities of Huexotzinco, Tlaxcala, Cholula and Tliliuhquitepec had been exempt from conquest and tribute. The king immediately sent his messengers to challenge the cities, telling them that he wished to entertain himself for a few days on the battlefield and to give his men some practice in skirmishing. He proposed to them that they appear on the plains of Atlixco and that he would meet them and amuse himself with them.

The men of Huexotzinco were delighted and accepted his challenge with good will. They sent a message saying that they were well pleased and that three days later they would wait for them in the valley and there show the Aztecs why they were so eager for this meeting.

When Moteczoma heard their answer he gave orders that anyone within the three allied kingdoms who wished to gain honor should present himself upon the plains near Atlixco within three days. As supreme commander of the army he appointed a brother of his by the name of Tlacahuepan, presenting him with the device of the god Totec, Our Lord, and splendid weapons with a shield of gold. He urged his brother to be valorous and to gain honor in the battle, as his only risk would be an exercise in warfare and the gaining of honor. Tlacahuepan kissed the king's hands and he and two other brothers went to visit soothsayers to find out what was to happen to them in that war, but they were told that the omens were bad. Tlacahuepan went to say farewell to his royal brother, saying, "O mighty lord, I believe that I shall never see your face again. Care for my wives and children!" In this way he and his brothers left the city and on the third day arrived at the appointed place, a small village called Atzitzihuacan, subject to Papayocan.

One hundred thousand soldiers, the highest and most illustrious men of the three kingdoms, met upon the battlefield, all of them in splendid array. The Huexotzinca then appeared, no less finely attired and in equally good spirits, looking as if they had come to a festival. The Aztec commander ordered two hundred chosen soldiers to begin a skirmish and ordered the rest to remain still until they received new orders. These two hundred warriors went out to the field and began to fight with the Huexotzinca. Both sides struggled in such a way that men began to fall on both sides. The Aztec commander, who was watching carefully, began to send in Texcocans and as more men entered the field, more were killed since the Huexotzinca were showing their great boldness and invincible spirit. When all the Texcocans had entered the fray and had suffered great losses, the general ordered the soldiers from Tacuba to relieve them. The men of Tacuba rushed in and began to perform great feats in the presence of the enemy while the men of Texcoco withdrew to rest. But the Huexotzinca were careful to send in new troops also, and a great slaughter took place, the men behaving like ferocious mountain lions drenched in blood.

At this point Tlacahuepan embraced his two brothers, saying, "Behold, my brothers, the time has come to show the valor of our persons! Let us go to the help of our friends!" After he had given a signal to the Aztecs, they threw themselves into the battle with frightful shrieks, knocking down and killing men. It was a terrible thing to see! The Huexotzinca did not retreat, however, but continued to send all their men to the aid of their brethren, and with these new arrivals a most cruel battle developed. Tlacahuepan, who was eager to gain glory, hurled himself against the enemy with such fury that he seemed like a man who had lost his mind. He behaved with such rashness that when he wished to retreat he was unable to do so surrounded as he was by more than one hundred soldiers. When he realized his situation he began to do marvelous things with his sword; soon he had around him and at his feet over fifty dead. But now he had no strength left after the great deeds he had done, and seeing that he could no longer fight from weariness, though he was unwounded, he dropped the arm that held his sword and also his shield, exclaiming, "Cease, O Huexotzinca! I see that I am yours and that I cannot defend myself. Let the combat end here! You see me here; now do what you will!"

The Huexotzinca seized him, planning to carry him off alive to their city, but Tlacahuepan took hold of the fallen bodies, shouting that he would not go, that he would die there! His sacrifice was to be there, upon those corpses! And so it was

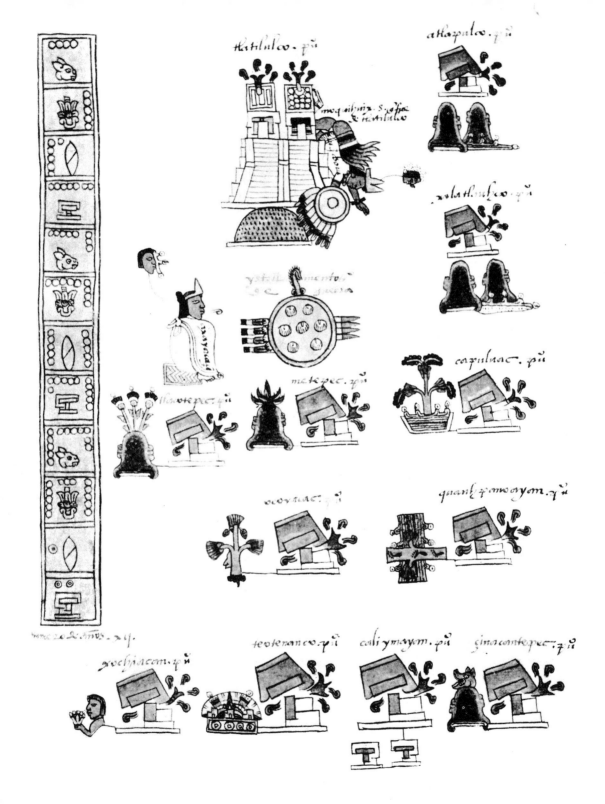

The conquests of King Axayacatl (1469-1481). Most of the conquered city states shown at the right and lower part are in the Valley of Toluca. From the Codex Mendoza, painted in early Colonial times by Aztec scribes. Courtesy New York Public Library. Photo Reg Van Cuylenburg.

that since they could not pull him away they killed him, tore him apart and carried away his body in little pieces, which were saved as relics. Not a bone nor hair of him was left.

The commander was dead and the Aztecs began to withdraw, but in those moments the Huexotzinca slew two other brothers of Moteczoma who had also accomplished great deeds. In addition, they captured many other lords and chieftains from Mexico, Texcoco and Tacuba, and in this way the Huexotzinca returned to their city victorious and boastful.

Moteczoma was notified of the death of his brothers and his nobles. He was also told how his army had been routed. When he heard this mournful news he began to weep bitterly. The tidings spread throughout the city and everyone sobbed in sadness and despair.

When it was known that those who had survived the war were about to return, broken and wounded, Moteczoma commanded that they be received in a manner suiting the occasion. Their reception was a sad thing; the priests who usually wore their hair braided with colored thread appeared with unkempt hair. The old men and officials who generally showed themselves wearing feathers on the top of their heads were seen without their plumes and with the insignia of mourning. The priests who offered incense on other occasions brought no incense this time but instead they brought tears and affliction. The conch shells, trumpets, flutes, and drums were mute.

In this way those who returned from war entered the city, going to the temple where, instead of prayers, were long lamentations and complaints against the gods, to whom no sacrifice was offered. From the temple they went to the king's palace, where they found him sunk in despair. He ordered that the wounded be cured and that those who had returned naked be dressed and that they all be comforted in every possible way. He also ordered that the funeral ceremonies for his brothers be prepared and that three wooden statues of them be carved. These statues were made of the wood used for torches; faces were painted on them and they were covered with paper. The images were dressed in mantles and fine loincloths which carried their insignia as warriors. They wore their arms, feather work, ear-plugs, lip- and nose-pendants, and they carried their swords and shields in their hands.

When the figures had been put in the place chosen for this purpose, people began to come from all the villages, cities, and provinces to give their condolences to Moteczoma. They brought presents and sacrificial victims for the dead and in this way the funeral rites began. I will not stop to describe them since I have already told about these ceremonies in previous chapters and it would be tedious to repeat them here, even though the *Chronicle* narrates them again lengthily.

Once the ceremonies, the weeping of the women and the funeral chants, had ended the officials of the city and of the provinces took the statues on their shoulders and carried them before the idol Huitzilopochtli. There they were set on fire and the slaves which had been offered were killed and burned with them. The ashes were gathered and buried in the Altar of the Eagles that stood next to the Stone of the Sun. With this the foreign chieftains and rulers bade farewell and went home, Moteczoma having thanked them for the honors paid to his brothers.

When the news of these disasters became known in the land of the Mixtecs it was believed that the Aztecs would be unable to take up arms soon, and the sovereigns of Yanhuitlan and Zozola sent a challenge to Moteczoma. In addition, they obstructed the roads and killed many Aztec merchants. However, Moteczoma gathered an army of two hundred thousand men and conquered the state of Yanhuitlan.

Having done this the Aztec lords, led by Cihuacoatl, ordered the soldiers to rest. Three days later they attacked Zozola, but explorers had first been sent to see the state of things. When these men arrived they found the town of Zozola abandoned, without a man, woman or child to be questioned, the houses and huts burned, the latter having been set on fire by the people of Zozola themselves. The explorers returned to Cihuacoatl and told him what they had seen. He ordered that the natives be searched out in the mountains and ravines. For four days the Aztecs sought everywhere but found no trace of them. When the commander saw that the search was fruitless he ordered his men to return and no longer pursue the enemy.

CHAPTER L VIII WHICH TREATS OF HOW MOTECZOMA HAD
THE TEMPLE OF COATLAN BUILT WITHIN THAT OF HUITZILOPOCHTLI;
AND HOW IT WAS CALLED COATEOCALLI,
OR TEMPLE OF THE SERPENT, ALSO MEANING
THE TEMPLE OF THE MANY GODS

At that time King Moteczoma decided that there should be a shrine where all the gods of the country could be adored. Moved by religious zeal, he ordered that one be built and it was constructed within the great temple of Huitzilopochtli, where the house of Acevedo stands now. It was to be called Coateocalli, which means "Temple of the Diverse Gods," and it was called this because in it were housed many gods from the different provinces and lands. They were all placed within one chamber and there were great numbers of them, all of different types, faces and forms. They are to be seen now, some of them lying about streets and homes, others embedded in buildings; and they have done much harm by recalling memories of paganism among the old people and natives of this land.

But, returning to our subject, when this shrine had been finished, Moteczoma began to consider the matter of its dedication. He wondered where victims could be obtained for sacrifice and he remembered that the province of Teuctepec was in a state of rebellion against the royal crown. This was a province close to the sea. Having gathered his allies Moteczoma began a campaign against that province and, having prepared an ambush, attacked the enemy at a river near Teuctepec. Here the *Chronicle* states that some of the conquered warriors who fell into the water were to be seen turning into alligators or fish or other water animals. All of this amazed the Aztec army and filled them with terror.

When the victorious army returned to Mexico Moteczoma dressed himself in the garments of the high priest, anointed his body with the divine bitumen and took a golden incense burner in his hands. He then entered the place where all the idols had been gathered, brought from all the nations and representing all created things. Having incensed them and having performed all the ceremonies that were usual when a temple or house was to be used for the first time, he and Cihuacoatl came to the place of sacrifice which stood outside of the doorway of the shrine. The prisoners who had been brought from Teuctepec were then sacrificed.

CHAPTER LIX WHICH TREATS OF HOW THE CITY OF CHOLULA
DEFIED THE AZTECS ON THE ROAD TO ATLIXCO
WITH A DESCRIPTION OF THE BATTLE THAT TOOK PLACE
THREE DAYS AFTER THE CHALLENGE

After the great King Moteczoma had been elected to the throne the people on the other side of the snowy mountains began to have conflicts with the Aztecs. This happened so frequently that people marveled, for no such conflict had occurred in the times of the previous monarchs. It is to be suspected that Moteczoma himself secretly provoked them in order to give his men practice in war. Or perhaps the inhabitants of those regions were anxious to humble the pride of Moteczoma and his nation. Whatever the reason, the *Chronicle* states that Tlaxcala, Huexotzinco,

Cholula and Tliliuhquitepec, who had never met the Aztecs in the battlefield, wished to test their strength. They sent messengers to the neighboring cities of Cuauhquechollan and Atzitzihuacan, bidding them notify Moteczoma that they wished to fight with him on a certain field. In this way they would please the Lord of the Earth, the Lord of the Battles, and the Sun. They asked him to send his men as, in three days, they would be awaiting him there. The challenge was accepted and the allies gathered.

Three days later the armies met and a great slaughter took place. The enemy nations attacked one another with terrible fury and the battle lasted the entire day. It was fought with such rage that when the Aztecs withdrew that night they found that they had lost eight thousand two hundred soldiers including men from the allied nations. Among the fallen were three most valorous captains, close relatives of King Moteczoma. However, the Aztecs had performed a similar feat against the Cholulans and the fields were covered with dead bodies and many prisoners had been taken. Nevertheless, an envoy was sent to Moteczoma telling him of the happenings of the day and of their significant losses. The Aztecs waited until the next day to see if Cholula wanted to fight again. While the Aztecs were preparing to avenge the deaths of their own lost warriors, the Cholulans sent a message saying they had had enough practice and recreation.

When the Aztec general heard these words, he departed in the direction of Mexico, sad and mournful. No less sad was Moteczoma, who, when he heard the news, wept bitterly and complained about the gods. He cried that he did not know how he had offended them. In this he did not take into consideration that fighting with Tlaxcalans, Cholulans, and Huexotzinca was like Spaniards warring against Spaniards. According to the natives' histories, all these people were of the same origin and the only difference was that they belonged to different parties. However, other nations such as the Mixtecs, Zapotecs, Huaxtecs and the coastal peoples were to them as the Moors, Turks, pagans, or Jews are to us. The name "Chichimec" of which the Aztec nation was so proud, is similar to our use of the word Castilian or Goth and the above-mentioned nations did not use this title. Only those around the Popocatepetl, "Smoking Mountain," bore it, and these people were the inhabitants of Tlaxcala, Huexotzinco, Cholula and Tliliuhquitepec. All of them called themselves Chichimecs before they had come to possess these lands. So it was that Tlaxcala and Mexico fought in order to practice war and not because of enmity.

The Aztec nation was always especially remarkable for the way in which they counted the years, and there existed among them old men who were specialists in the science of the division of time. Their cycle was one of fifty-two years, even though others say that it consisted of eighty years but I think the latter are mistaken. They tell of five ages of the world, including the one that we live in now. Since these people lacked any knowledge of Christ in those times, their count was based on these five ages, as I find shown here in the *Chronicle* where they are called the Five Suns. The *Chronicle* tells us that a cycle ended at this time and that it was called *toxiuhmolpilli*, the "Binding of the Years."

The elders who were in charge of these things advised Moteczoma that it was the year of the end of the cycle. Besides the solemn festivities that took place, the elders pretended that the sun and its light were to be hidden for four days and that everything would be enveloped in darkness. Thus it was ordered that in all the provinces around Mexico the fires should be put out and no one dare burn a fire in secret until, on the hill of Huixachtecatl, a great fire was rekindled from which the inhabitants might ignite their own fires. This hill stands between Iztapalapa and Cuitlahuac. After having been in darkness for four days, not because the sun was eclipsed but because of lack of fire, they performed the rites of the New Fire, similar to our ritual of the Paschal candles, in which one candle is lighted from another. At the end of the ceremony, all took new fire. This feast was celebrated with great solemnity and all the priests were present, led by the high priest dressed in his sacerdotal vestments. There were offerings and incense, together with the sacrifice of many human beings who died as victims of the god of fire. So it is that this god was given the two thousand captives who had been brought from the destruction and conquest of Teuctepec. This sacrifice began at midnight and lasted most of the next day. Triumphant and joyful, the priests were bathed in blood, and the vessels filled with human blood were sent to smear the lintels of the doors, posts and altars of the temples, and to sprinkle the statues of the gods.

Once these rites had been concluded news came that the Tlaxcalans were attacking Huexotzinco and destroying the fields, causing great hunger and privation in that region. The Aztecs decided to aid Huexotzinco, many of whose people had taken refuge in the city of Mexico.

At this point Moteczoma was especially interested in capturing the commander of the Tlaxcalan army, whose name was Tlahuicolli, a most valiant man who had become famous for his outstanding deeds and whose greatness resounded among all the nations. The Aztec forces set out for Tlaxcala and when Tlahuicolli heard of their coming he was much pleased, thinking that he would be able to gain glory in fighting these people. He led his troops into battle and fought with the Aztecs twenty days without interruption. Tlahuicolli was not captured until several days had passed and Moteczoma had sent reinforcements.

This prisoner was brought to the city of Mexico and Moteczoma rejoiced greatly, giving orders that Tlahuicolli be brought to his presence since he wished to see what kind of man this was who had made the entire earth tremble. When the captive entered the presence of the Aztec sovereign, he kissed his hands with humility and reverence and begged pardon for his offenses. Moteczoma received him well, consoled him and said that these were things of war and that all warriors were subject to such conditions. He told him not to be sorrowful and gave orders that he be lodged and all his needs be provided. After many days had passed Tlahuicolli began to remember his wives and children, being moved by the natural desire to see them. Every day he was found weeping, disconsolate, sighing for his family. Moteczoma was told of this because it was considered an ill omen to have a captive become sad. The sovereign was angered and sent a message to the captive saying that he thought that a person like Tlahuicolli, capable of scorning life itself, would not be worried about wives and children. However, since he was so cowardly and fretted in such a way over the absence of his wives, he would be given his liberty. He was to be held in contempt and allowed to go back to his city and retire with his women. It was also ordered that the prisoner not be given food or things from the palace and that the warriors who had accompanied him desert him immediately.

When Tlahuicolli heard the king's message he became mute with sadness. From that day on his food was taken away from him and so was his guard. He went from house to house begging for food and finally in despair he set out for Tlatelolca. There he ascended to the summit of the pyramid and cast himself down the steps. In this way he sacrificed himself to the gods, fulfilling the purpose for which he had been brought to Mexico. He did this because of the offenses that had been committed and he knew that if he returned to his country he and his descendants would be humiliated forever. After his death he was offered to the gods with all the usual ceremonies and solemn rites, and so were the other prisoners that had been brought from Tlaxcala. After this the Tlaxcalans stopped persecuting the Huexotzinca.[95]

WHICH TREATS OF HOW NEZAHUALPILLI, KING OF
TEXCOCO, TOLD MOTECZOMA THAT THE SPANIARDS WERE COMING
AND THAT THE AZTECS WOULD HAVE VERY
FEW VICTORIES OVER HIS ENEMIES

Often have I spoken of how the king of Texcoco, Nezahualpilli, was considered a necromancer or sorcerer and the most common opinion that I find among the natives was that he had a pact with the devil who revealed to him many things regarding the future.

One day when King Moteczoma was at ease it was announced that the ruler of Texcoco had come to see him. Greatly surprised at this sudden visit he came out of his private chambers to receive him. When they had greeted one another with the usual courtesies, they spoke in private in Moteczoma's rooms. When he was asked the reasons for his visit Nezahualpilli answered:

"O powerful and great lord! I do not wish to bring trouble to your peaceful spirit, but the obligation I have to serve you forces me to reveal a strange and bewildering thing which I have been allowed to see by the Lord of the Heavens, of the Night, Day and Wind, something which is to happen in your time. You must be on guard, you must be warned, because I have discovered that in a very few years our cities will be ravaged and destroyed. We and our children will be killed and our vassals belittled. Of all these things you must not doubt. In order to prove to you the truth of what I speak, you will see that whenever you wage war on Huexotzinco, Tlaxcala, or Cholula, you will be defeated. You will always be overcome by losses of your officers and soldiers. I will add this: before many days have passed you will see signs in the sky which will appear as an omen of what I am saying.

"But do not be cast down because of these things, since one cannot turn one's face from that which must be. I will not see these calamities and afflictions because my days are numbered. That is why I wished to warn you before my death, O my most cherished son."

Both of them wept and Moteczoma cried out to the gods asking that his days end so as not to have to see what had been foretold—all those things that were to happen in his time. However, he thanked Nezahualpilli for having warned him and the latter departed, leaving Moteczoma afflicted and fearful, remembering everything.

Since he wished to discover whether that which had been said to him was true, he ordered his soldiers and allies to prepare for war against Tlaxcala. A camp was set up in a place called Ahuayocan where a brave battle took place, the Aztecs being completely vanquished, some killed, some captured. All of the commanders were taken prisoner by the enemy.

When the news of this defeat reached Moteczoma and when he heard that the Aztecs had taken only forty prisoners from Tlaxcala, that Texcoco had taken only twenty, and that Tacuba had only fifteen and Tlatelolco five, Moteczoma rose from his seat in anger, shouting, "What is this you say? Do you know what you are saying? Are not the Aztecs filled with shame? Since when have you lost your vigor, your strength, like weak women? Are you just learning to take up the sword and the shield, the bow and the arrow? What has happened to all the skill acquired since the founding of this renowned city? How has it been lost to the point that I stand in shame before the entire world? Why did so many courageous lords and captains, seasoned in war, go to the battlefield? Is it possible that they have forgotten how to command their squadrons in order to fight with the whole world? I can only believe that they were deliberately heedless in order to mock me!"

The king then called in Cihuacoatl and his councilors, and related to them what had happened. Orders were given that those who were returning from war should not be welcomed. No conch shells or other musical instruments were to be sounded and neither men nor women were to receive them in the city. No sadness or sorrow was to be shown because of their losses and no gladness for those who had come back. Therefore, with the news of the return of the armies a strange silence spread over the entire city; not a man, woman or priest was to be seen anywhere. When, after worshiping in the temple, the warriors went to render homage to the king, the doors were closed in their faces. They were ejected with scorn from the royal household and in shame they returned to their homes and cities.

On another day the great "Angry Lord," for this is what the name "Moteczoma" means, gathered his councilors and, in great anger, he told them that he was ashamed and that he wished to punish the captains, officers, and old warriors. He wished them to be humiliated eternally since they had been lax in the things of war. Everyone approved his decision and the judges and executioners were called together. These justices were sent to the homes of the officers to shear their hair and take their insignia away from them. They were forbidden to wear cotton mantles; from now on these officers were to wear cloaks of maguey fiber like

242

*The conquests of King Tizoc, "Chalk Leg" (1481-1486).
From the* **Codex Mendoza**, *painted in early Colonial times
by Aztec scribes. Courtesy New York Public
Library. Photo Reg Van Cuylenburg.*

those of the common man. They were not to use the sandals of the nobility and they were to refrain from entering the palace for one year. All this was done.

After a year, however, the warriors who had suffered this punishment went of their own accord to another war in Tlaxcala, and many prisoners were taken, whereupon Moteczoma pardoned them.

CHAPTER **LXII** WHICH TREATS OF THE CRUEL SACRIFICE OF
THE TLAXCALAN VICTIMS ON THE FEAST OF THE GODDESS TOCI.
WITH A DESCRIPTION OF HOW
THE HUEXOTZINCA WERE ANGERED BY THIS AND HOW
THEY BURNED HER TEMPLE AT NIGHT

The time for the feast of the goddess Toci, Our Grandmother, now arrived.[96] This feast was celebrated with great solemnity and many ceremonies every year. Toci was considered to be the mother of the gods; she was the daughter of the king of Colhuacan whom the Aztecs, shortly after their arrival in this land, had desired to marry to Huitzilopochtli. She had been killed, skinned and then her image adored as a goddess. From this had come enmity and war between the Aztecs and Colhuacan.

When the day came some of the Tlaxcalan captives were sacrificed in the ordinary way: their chests were opened, their hearts taken out and their bodies rolled down the temple steps. A second group went through the fire sacrifice: they were burned in the divine brazier and half dead they were brought out of the embers where they had been rolling and their hearts were extracted. A third group was taken to the temple of the goddess which was on the outskirts of the city where the first cross now stands as we leave Mexico city. In front of the temple was erected a scaffold of boards and sticks to hold the statue of Toci. It was there that the victims were tied to the sticks and cruelly shot with arrows. This was the special sacrifice in honor of this goddess and it was performed in memory of those who had been wounded with arrows when the Aztecs fled from Coyoacan and had hidden among the rushes and reeds in order not to be slaughtered. Remembering the wounds inflicted by arrows, caused by that goddess, they now offered her men killed in an arrow sacrifice.

245

When the feast had finished Moteczoma was well pleased, and the news of the sacrifice spread throughout the land. But the people of Huexotzinco were angered because of the cruelty with which the prisoners had been treated, though it is true that when Aztecs fell into their hands they were no kinder to them. However, the Huexotzinca were now friends of Tlaxcala and had forgotten their ties with Mexico. So one night they came and burned the temple of the goddess and the four tall poles where the platform and the image of Toci were found. These poles were made of the thickest and tallest trees that could be found in the woods.

Dawn found the structure in cinders, and when the Aztecs realized what had happened the city was thrown into a state of confusion and terror. Moteczoma was filled with wrath as he considered it a personal offense and an ill omen. Therefore he ordered that the priests of the temples be taken prisoners and cast into cages. These cages were paved with small sharp blades or pieces of blades and the prisoners had to sleep upon them until their deaths. They were given food in very small quantities until they starved to death. Every day though, until their death, Moteczoma sent messengers to upbraid them, telling them that it had been their duty to watch the temples of the gods night and day. The unfortunate priests received the rebukes with humility and patience, realizing that they had offended by their carelessness.

Some time later Moteczoma discovered that it had been the Huexotzinca who had burned the temple of Toci and, after rebuilding the temple and the wooden scaffold in a more ornate way, he set out on a campaign against the offending city. The Aztecs were relatively successful, and one hundred and twenty captives were brought back by the Tlatelolca alone. These prisoners were sacrificed in the ways mentioned before.

When the Huexotzinca heard of what had been done to their men, they invited the king of Mexico to a feast which was prepared in honor of their god Camaxtli. Moteczoma refused to go, however, and sent certain chieftains, in whose presence the Huexotzinca skinned a great number of Aztecs. They cut open the breasts of others; some were burned alive and yet others died the death of the arrows. All this was done with the same cruelty that the Huexotzinca themselves had suffered. Among the victims were many important Aztecs and their deaths were ghastly to see.

When Moteczoma was told of these happenings he exclaimed, "Why are you amazed by these things? That is why we were born! That is why we go to battle! That is the blessed death which our ancestors extolled!"

At this point the *Chronicle* tells us that in each temple of the gods there always lived a man who represented the image of the god in that particular sanctuary. He was lodged in a special room where he sat like the idol itself and was revered and served as such. He had his own servants and guards who were changed every year. These were called *Mocexiuhcauhque* which could be interpreted to mean "those who do penance." They abstained from women and did not offend God for one year in the temple of Huitzilopochtli.

One of them was a virtuous young man who represented the god Huitzilopochtli and his name was Tzocoztli. One night around midnight, when he rose to satisfy bodily needs, he happened to look into the sky and in the east he saw a great comet with a large tail that seemed to advance in the direction of Mexico. This youth was frightened and he went to his servants and guards saying, "Awaken, for you will see a marvelous and terrifying comet never seen before in this land." Everyone looked toward the east where they saw it. None of them went to sleep again but all waited in order to discover where the comet would be when dawn came. At the moment of sunrise it hung over the city of Mexico and with the light of the sun it disappeared.[97]

The priest and his servants went to the palace where they told Moteczoma of this strange event. When night came and everyone was asleep the king went to a terrace on the roof. Having watched there until midnight he saw the comet appear with its brilliant tail, whereupon he was astonished. Then he remembered what Nezahualpilli had said, and he was so filled with fear that he thought his death would arrive within the hour.

The next day Moteczoma called in the priests, sorcerers, soothsayers, diviners and astrologers and consulted them, but they claimed that they had not seen any signs in the sky, for which the king had them jailed.

Then Moteczoma asked the king of Texcoco to tell him what it meant. "O lord," responded Nezahualpilli, "your vassals, the astrologers, soothsayers and diviners, have been careless! That sign in the heavens has been there for some time and yet you describe it to me now as if it were a new thing. I thought that you had already discovered it and that your astrologers had explained it to you. Since you now tell me you have seen it I will answer you that that brilliant star appeared in the

247

heavens many days ago. It is an ill omen for our kingdoms; terrible, frightful things will come upon them. In all our lands and provinces there will be great calamities and misfortunes, not a thing will be left standing. Death will dominate the land! All our dominions will be lost and all of this will be done with the permission of the Lord of the Heights, of the Day and the Night and of the Wind. You will be witness to these things since it will all happen in your time. For as soon as I depart from the city of Mexico I go to die. You will never behold me again; this is the last visit in which we will see each other in this life. I long to hide, to flee from the labor and afflictions which await you. Do not be faint, do not feel anguish or despair! Make your heart wide, strengthen your spirit and manly chest against these predestined troubles!"

Moteczoma then wept bitterly, saying, "O Lord of All Created Things! O mighty gods who give life or death! Why have you decreed that many kings shall have reigned proudly but that my fate is to witness the unhappy destruction of Mexico? Why should I be the one to see the death of my wives and children and the loss of my powerful kingdoms and dominions and of all that the Aztecs have conquered with their mighty arms and strength of their chests? What shall I do? Where shall I hide? Where shall I conceal myself? Alas, if only I could turn into stone, wood, or some other earthly matter rather than suffer that which I so dread! But what can I do, O powerful monarch, but await that which you have predicted? For this reason I kiss your hands and thank you. Alas, I cannot at this moment become a bird in order to fly into the woods and hide in their depths." With these words, says the *Chronicle*, the two kings said farewell to each other with great sadness.

CHAPTERS LXIV AND LXV WHICH TREAT OF THE DEATH OF NEZAHUALPILLI, KING OF TEXCOCO, AND THE ELECTION OF A NEW RULER CALLED QUETZALAXOYATL

The *Chronicle* deals little with the king of Tacuba, mentions no great deeds of his or famous happenings in that Tecpanec kingdom. I myself am surprised to see that it glosses over everything that does not concern Moteczoma and the previous Aztec kings. It tells only how they called him for council in war, to obtain soldiers, or to take part in an election. He is never mentioned aside from these affairs. All of this I consider strange since I am sure that if I went to Tacuba to ask about the past, the natives there would tell me that they had been greater than Moteczoma's

Aztecs. This situation has tied my hands and has made it impossible to fulfill my wishes of writing a history of each city and state. There is no village, small as it may be, which does not take credit for all the grandeur of Moteczoma. All of these towns claim that they were exempt from tribute, had royal insignia, and were the victors in war. I speak from experience because in a certain town in the hot country I asked about their ancient power or preëminence and they exaggerated to such an extent that I was forced to insist, and with soft words I managed to get them to admit that they had been vassals and had paid tribute to Nezahualpilli of Texcoco.

I explain all of these things because I do not wish to be called a liar. If there is falsehood in what I write, it is not to be attributed to me. I simply wish to record what the *Chronicle* narrates and, as I stated, it glosses over many things. However, I note that it often tells great things regarding the kingdom of Texcoco and the power of King Nezahualpilli. Sometimes it suggests that Moteczoma in some manner owed recognition and servitude to him, since he did not contradict any statement of the Texcocan monarch.

At this point the *Chronicle* speaks of Nezahualpilli's death and states that he was mourned in Mexico as well as in Texcoco. When news of his death came to Moteczoma, he wept in anguish and donned the garments of tears and sadness, exclaiming, "He has now drained the cup that we must all drink from, he who was my father and true friend! He has gone to rest with his ancestors in the place of repose in the other world, and has forgotten the cares and worries of this one."

Moteczoma of Mexico, the ruler of Tacuba, and many other sovereigns sent representatives carrying rich gifts to the funeral and, at its end, they took part in the election of a new ruler of Texcoco. Quetzalaxoyatl, a son of the last king, was chosen and anointed and enthroned in the midst of florid speeches and elaborate ritual.

According to the *Chronicle* and histories of Texcoco that I have consulted, this new ruler lived only a short time. He accomplished no great deeds, and no remarkable events took place in his days. I have seen a painting showing him dressed in a white mantle without insignia or any other mark such as was worn by the other rulers. After his death his brother Tlahuitoltzin was elected, but he too lived only a short time and was succeeded by another brother named Coanacoch; during his reign the Spaniards came to this land. All these sons of Nezahualpilli who reigned over Texcoco were unfortunate in dying soon without enjoying their power. The *Chronicle* tells that Nezahualpilli died ten years before the arrival of the Spaniards and, during this decade, three sons of his were elected to the Texcocan throne. When Cortés came, a fourth son, called Ixtlilxochitl, succeeded his brothers. He was enthroned because of his great deeds during the conquest of the city of Mexico and because of the aid he gave the Spanish conquerors.

Moteczoma was always anxious to have all his accomplishments well known through the entire land, and all the feats of earlier kings seemed of minor importance to him. He considered that the sacrificial stone that his grandfather had set up was too small and cheap and that it did not conform to the grandeur of Mexico. Therefore he ordered a meeting of the chieftains of his council and he spoke to them of setting up another stone, the widest and largest that could be found in the entire province, for the feast of the Skinning of Men. Having heard their opinions he called the stone sculptors of the city of Mexico and told them his decision to set up a great *temalacatl*, "round stone."

The stone cutters went off to different places, and in the province of Chalco, at a site called Acolco near Tepopolan, next to the river that descends from Amecameca, they found a rock which seemed suitable for what the king desired. When he had been notified of this, Moteczoma ordered that the men of Xochimilco, Cuitlahuac, Iztapalapa, Colhuacan, Mexicatzinco and Huitzilopochco bring ropes and stout poles to carry the stone. They were told where to go and Moteczoma ordered that all the stone cutters be provided with food for the entire time it would take them to convey it.

The stone masons went to the site that had been indicated, scraped the rock clean and prepared to tear it from the place in which it was stuck. When it was ready to be removed Moteczoma sent his men there with ropes, poles, and other instruments. Anxious to add superstition or idolatry to these endeavors, the monarch commanded that the priests of the temple carry their burners, paper, incense, little balls of rubber and many quail. Together with them went chanters of the temples to dance and sing in front of the stone when it began to be moved along the road. Jesters and clowns were also sent to perform buffooneries in front of it, feasting and rejoicing, since it was a sacred thing to be used for divine worship.

Those who were to drag the rock arrived and the priests, having attired themselves in their sacerdotal garments, took the paper they had brought with them and covered the stone with it. Going round and round they incensed it with much ceremony, pouring molten incense and liquid rubber upon it, killing quail and splashing the blood upon the rock. The singers began to chant gay and pleasant songs and the clowns and buffoons started their jesting, all of which provoked

*Some of the towns conquered by the Aztecs toward the middle of the fifteenth century. From the* **Codex Mendoza,** *painted in early Colonial times by Aztec scribes. Courtesy New York Public Library. Photo Reg Van Cuylenburg.*

laughter and gladness. While this was being done, the Xochimilca tied a long, stout rope around the stone and the same was done by the men from the other cities. They began to pull with great shouts and yells in order to wrench it from its bed but the ropes snapped as if they had been made of tender cotton.

Moteczoma was notified of these happenings and he begged the king of Texcoco to give him more men to help him bring in the monolith. This was done and when the same ceremonies had been performed by the priests, new ropes were tied to it by the Texcocans. At last the stone began to budge and the men managed to carry it as far as Tlapechuacan. They rested there and at dawn the next day new ropes were tied, conch shells and horns were blown, the priests performed their ceremonies and the singers chanted while quail were killed. The people, shouting, began to pull the ropes, but for two days they were unable to make it budge from that place. The *Chronicle* says that it seemed to have sprung roots and that it broke all the stoutest ropes.

Moteczoma then called in the Otomi from the province of Cuauhtlalpan and they, with their strong cords and poles, went to help those who were struggling with the rock. These newcomers also tied the stone, and as they began to pull it with many yells and whistles, the stone spoke:

"O wretched people, O unfortunate ones! Why do you persist in your desire to take me to the city of Mexico? Behold your work is in vain since it is not my will to go there. But as you wish it this way, pull me and I will go as far as I wish but it will be to your harm!"

The voice was then silent and everyone was bewildered by this extraordinary event. They began to pull again and the stone moved with such ease that they barely felt its weight. In that way it was carried as far as Tlapitzahuayan. When Moteczoma heard of these things he laughed and had the messengers thrown into jail. However, when he later found out that it was true he released them.

When the men tried to move the stone again it spoke these words, "Poor wretches! Why do you labor in vain? Have I not told you that I will never arrive in Mexico? Go, tell Moteczoma that it is too late. He should have thought of this before. Now he no longer will need me; a terrible event, brought on by fate, is about to happen! Since it comes from a divine will, he cannot fight it. Why does he want to take me? So that tomorrow I be cast down and held in contempt? Let him know that his reign has ended. Soon he will see what is to come upon him, and this will happen because he has wanted to be adored more than God Himself. Therefore leave me; if I go any farther it will be to your harm."

The stone moved quickly after this and was brought with great ease as far as a bridge which Moteczoma had built especially for this occasion. When it reached

253

the middle of the bridge, with a tremendous crash it broke all the beams, falling into the water and carrying with it numerous men who had been attached to it by the ropes. Many of them were drowned and others severely wounded.

Moteczoma commanded divers to seek the stone in the water, but in spite of their efforts they were unable to find it. Eventually the divers told Moteczoma that they wondered if it had not gone back to its original place and the king, considering that this was possible, told certain people to go seek it where it had first been extracted. The messengers found it there, all covered with paper and with signs of the sacrifices that it had been offered. It was still bound by the ropes just as it had been when it had fallen. The bewildered messengers returned in great haste to Mexico and told Moteczoma of the terrible thing they had seen. In terror, the king went in person to see the rock. He made offerings to it, prayed and sacrificed some slaves. Having done these things he returned to Mexico and said the following words to his chieftains:

"Truly, O brethren, I now believe that our labors and afflictions will be great and that our lives are about to end. And I am determined to allow death to come just as my brave ancestors did. Let the will of the Lord of All Created Things be done!" He called his stone cutters and ordered that his statue be carved on the rocks of Chapultepec. When the work was finished he went to see his image and wept. "If our bodies," he moaned, "were as durable in this life as this carved effigy is upon this rock, who would be afraid of death? But I know that I must perish and this is the only memorial that will remain of me!"

Moteczoma returned to Mexico and bemoaned his fate again:

"O brethren! I find no consolation! I am surrounded by worries and anguish. Am I greater than Nezahualpilli who was a prophet and could tell of things to come and who died in spite of all his knowledge? Am I greater than my kinsman Tzompantecuhtli of Cuitlahuac who also was a prophet, knowing six hundred and ten sciences, all of which he could explain with the greatest of ease? He also died. What will become of me, then, who am ignorant, knowing no science? How am I to avoid the calamities and ills which await me?"

# LXVII WHICH TREATS OF HOW MOTECZOMA DECIDED
TO ABANDON THE CITY IN ORDER TO HIDE HIMSELF.
WITH A DESCRIPTION OF HOW HE CARRIED
THIS OUT, AND AN ILL-OMEN THAT APPEARED
BEFORE THESE EVENTS

Greatly disturbed, Moteczoma was preparing to flee from Mexico when a strange event took place, described in our *Chronicle*. A peasant who was a native of Coatepec in the province of Texcoco was plowing his fields calmly when a mighty eagle descended upon him, took him by the hair with its claws and carried him into the heights until he was lost from the sight of those who had been with him. The peasant was carried to a high mountain where he was taken into a dark cave. There he heard the eagle say, "O powerful lord, I have complied with your wishes; here is the peasant that you ordered me to bring." The farmer heard a voice saying, "Bring him here. Welcome!" The man was taken by the hand into a lighted place and there he saw Moteczoma asleep or perhaps unconscious. The peasant was made to sit next to the sleeping king. He was given flowers and tobacco to smoke and he was told, "Take these things, be at ease, and behold that wretch Moteczoma, unconscious, drunk with his pride and haughtiness! He feels nothing but scorn for everyone and if you wish to see how his pride has blinded him, burn him in the thigh with the tobacco you carry and you will see that he does not feel it." The man was afraid to do this but he was told, "Burn him, do not fear." The peasant then touched him with the fiery tobacco and Moteczoma did not stir or feel the burn.

"Do you see," asked the voice, "how he is unaware of everything? Do you see how drunk he is? Know that for this reason you have been brought here. Return to the place from which you were brought and go tell Moteczoma what you have seen. That he may know what you say is the truth tell him to show you his thigh and point out the place where you scorched him. There he will find the sign of fire. Also tell him that the God of All Created Things is angered and that he himself has sought the evils that are to come upon him. His reign is coming to an end. Let him enjoy what remains of it! Let him be patient since he has been the cause of his own ruin!"

The eagle was told to transport the peasant back to his field. The man was then picked up by the hair and deposited in the place where he had been found. The eagle said, "Behold, peasant and common man that you are, do not fear! Go with spirit and a strong heart and do what the Lord has commanded. Do not forget any

255

of the words that you are to say!" With this the eagle disappeared again into the heavens.[98]

The poor peasant seemed to be awakening from a dream, frightened as he was by what he had seen. However, with his digging stick still in his hand he came before Moteczoma and told him of the strange events, and the king remembered that the night before he had dreamed that a common man had wounded him in the thigh with burning tobacco. He then looked at his thigh and felt such pain that he dared not touch the burned flesh. Without asking the peasant any other questions, Moteczoma called his jailers and ordered that the man be thrown into jail and starved to death. The Indian was then cast into prison and forgotten there.

The pain in the monarch's thigh became worse and he had to spend several days in repose while the doctors cured him. After he was well he called his hunchbacks, together with certain conjurers called *tequitque,* and told them to flay ten men and bring their skins to him.

When the skins had been brought to the king he gave them to his hunchbacked pages, telling them that he had finally discovered a place where he would hide. This place was called *Cicalco* which means "The Place of Hares," a place of joy and pleasure where men live forever.[99] According to what Moteczoma had been told it was a land of clear, crystalline waters. There grew all kinds of foods; there was the freshness of many flowers. Though the king had already decided to go there, he wished his servants to precede him to greet the lord of that place, Huemac, and to give him the human skins as a gift. They were to tell him that King Moteczoma wished to be received as a servant of the god and that he wished these things in order to avoid the fate that had been announced to him. He told the dwarfs to keep all of this in the utmost secrecy.

The hunchbacks went out with the tequitques to seek the mouth of the cave of Cicalco, following the instructions of Moteczoma. According to some opinions this cave was situated in a place called Atlixocan between Mexico and Coyoacan, where, say the old men, a ghost used to appear every night, kidnapping the first man it encountered, who was never to be seen again. Therefore, everyone avoided this place at night.

It was to this place, says the *Chronicle,* that Moteczoma sent his messengers. As soon as they entered the cave they met a black man with a staff in his hand. This man was called Totec, Our Lord. He asked them what they wanted and they answered that they had come to speak to the lord of that cave, Huemac. Totec took them by the hand and led them into the depths of the cave until they were in the presence of Huemac, a god of awesome appearance. After greeting him they offered him the ten human skins and repeated the message that Moteczoma had

1. CIHUATLAN
2. TEPECUACUILCO
3. TLACHCO
4. OCUILAN
5. TOLUCA
6. MALINALCO
7. CUAHUACAN
8. XOCOTITLAN
9. ATOTONILCO
10. CUAUHTITLAN
11. XILOTEPEC
12. AXOCOPAN
13. HUEYPOCHTLAN
14. OXITIPAN
15. TZICCOAC
16. TOCHPAN
17. ATLAN

18. TLAPACOYAN
19. ATOTONILCO
20. ACOLHUACAN
21. CHALCO
22. CUAUHNAHUAC
23. HUAXTEPEC
24. TLALCOZAUHTITLAN
25. QUIAUHTEOPAN
26. TLATLAUHQUITEPEC
27. CUAUHTOCHCO
28. CUETLAXTLAN
29. TOCHTEPEC
30. XOCONOCHCO
31. TEPEACA
32. YOALTEPEC
33. TLAPAN
34. TLACHQUIAUHCO
35. COAIXTLAHUACA
36. COYOLAPAN
37. CITLALTEPEC AND
    TLATELOLCO
38. PETLACALCO

san luis potosi

queretaro

guanajuato

michoacan

METZTITLAN

hidalgo

tlaxcala

MEXICO–TENOCHTITLAN

TLAXCALA

puebla

morelos

Golfo de Mexico

veracruz

tabasco

chiapas

TEOTITLAN DEL CAMINO

YOPITZINGO

guerrero

COATLICAMAC

XOCONOCHCO

MIXTECOS

TOTOTEPEC

Oceano Pacifico

*The Aztec empire at its greatest extension, as the Spaniards found it in 1519. Based on the studies of R. H. Barlow.*

sent. But Huemac answered, "Ask Moteczoma why he wants to come here. Does he think that he is going to find jewels, gold, precious stones, feathers and rich mantles like those that he now possesses? Tell him that he has been deceived! Let him rejoice in what he has and let him be calm. That which has been fated cannot be avoided. Tell him that those who bear me company here are also men like him. They too enjoyed life at one time; now they suffer, as you see. Behold them and observe how different they look from the way they did when they were alive. There is no happiness or gaiety here; all is toil and sorrow. We did not come to this place of our own will but were brought here by force and reside here because of the desires of the Supreme One. Therefore, why should he join us here?"

Moteczoma was greatly disappointed with the message brought back by his pages but he persisted and sent others who were told by Huemac that the king must fast eighty days before being admitted to the underworld. Moteczoma complied with these orders and Huemac agreed then to receive him. He told the monarch to be ready. On the fourth day after the fast Huemac was to await him on the hill of Chapultepec. As soon as he saw Huemac appear, the king was to take a canoe and go to a place called Tlachtonco. There Huemac would meet him and carry him off.

When Moteczoma heard this message he again took up his usual affairs and put in order the things of the Republic. He also began to prepare for his flight. All of this was done secretly. Having given gifts to his attendants and relatives he ordered his slaves to prepare a place at Tlachtonco for his arrival. They did this, adorning the place with sapota branches and arranging seats made of the leaves of this tree.

When everything was ready Moteczoma entered his canoe and began his watch. On the hill of Chapultepec he saw a cave so brilliantly illuminated that it gave light to all the things of the city, the hills and trees, as if it were midday. Knowing then that Huemac had come for him he ordered his dwarfs to row quickly and soon he reached Tlachtonco. There his hunchbacks dressed themselves in the royal garments and Moteczoma put on his golden arm- and leg-bands, feathers and necklaces of gold and rich stones. He sat down upon one of the seats surrounded by his attendants and awaited the coming of Huemac. However, it was fated that he was not to escape his destiny.

That night Texiptla, a priest of the temple and image of the god, heard a voice in his sleep saying, "Awake, Texiptla! Behold, your king Moteczoma is in flight and goes to the cave of Huemac." Texiptla awakened and saw light as if it were day. The priest abandoned the temple and entered a canoe that he found at the edge of the water. With great haste he rowed as far as Tlachtonco where he found

Moteczoma and his hunchbacks. Approaching Moteczoma he said, "What is this, O mighty prince? What folly is this in a person of such courage as you? Where are you going? What would Tlaxcala say? What would Huexotzinco, Cholula, Tliliuhquitepec, Michoacan and Metztitlan say? Think of the contempt they will have for Mexico, the city that is the heart of the entire world. Truly it will be a great shame for your city and for all those who remain behind you when the news of your flight becomes known. If you were to die and they had seen you dead and buried, it would be a natural thing. But how can one explain flight? What will we say, what will we answer, to those who ask about our king? We will have to reply that he has abandoned us. Return, O lord, to your throne and forget this folly because you dishonor us." Removing the feathers from the monarch's head, he forced him to rise.

Greatly ashamed, Moteczoma sighed and on looking back toward the hill of Chapultepec, he saw that the light which had burned there had gone out.

CHAPTER LXVIII WHICH TREATS OF HOW MOTECZOMA ORDERED
THE AUTHORITIES TO INVESTIGATE THE DREAMS OF THE OLD
PEOPLE REGARDING THE COMING OF THE SPANIARDS.
WITH A DESCRIPTION OF HOW HE HAD THEM
KILLED BECAUSE THEY REVEALED DREAMS
CONTRARY TO HIS DESIRES

Moteczoma was so disturbed that he was half desirous that the events which had been predicted take place immediately. In the midst of his preoccupation he called the chieftains of the wards, asking them if they had dreamed anything regarding the arrival of the strangers whose coming he so feared. He told them to reveal these dreams even though they might be contrary to his desires, since he wished to know the truth in this much-talked-of matter.

The heads of the wards told him that they had dreamed nothing nor had they seen or heard anything about this affair. He answered, "Then I beg you, my friends, to tell all the old men and women of the wards to inform me of whatever dreams they may have had, be they in my favor or against me. Also, tell the priests to reveal any visions they may see, such as ghosts or other phantoms that appear at night in the woods and dark places. Let them ask these apparitions about things

258

to come. It will also be good to give this advice to those who wander about in the late hours; if they encounter the woman who roams the streets weeping and moaning, let them ask her why she weeps and moans."[100]

Soon Moteczoma was notified that certain old people had dreamed strange things and they were brought before him. Said one old man, "Powerful lord, we do not wish to offend your ears or fill your heart with anxiety to make you ill. However, we are forced to obey you and we will describe our dreams to you. Know then, that these last nights the Lords of Sleep have shown us the temple of Huitzilopochtli burning with frightful flames, the stones falling one by one until it was totally destroyed. We also saw Huitzilopochtli himself fallen, cast down upon the floor! This is what we have dreamed!"

Moteczoma then asked the old women and received the following answer, "My son, do not be troubled in your heart for what we are about to tell you, although it has frightened us much. In our dreams we, your mothers, saw a mighty river enter the doors of your royal palace, smashing the walls in its fury. It ripped up the walls from their foundation, carrying beams and stones with it until nothing was left standing. We saw it reach the temple and this too was demolished. We saw the great chieftains and lords filled with fright, abandoning the city and fleeing toward the hills. This is what we have dreamed!"

Moteczoma listened attentively to what the old men and women had described. When he saw that it was not in his favor but that it confirmed the earlier ill omens he ordered that the dreamers be cast in jail. There they were to be given food in small measures until they starved to death. After this no one wished to tell his dreams to Moteczoma.

Moteczoma also consulted the people of the provinces about their dreams and as they refused to reveal anything they were jailed also. One of the old men who had been incarcerated exclaimed, "Let Moteczoma know in one word what is to become of him. Those who are to avenge the injuries and toils with which he has afflicted us are already on their way. I say no more."

When the sovereign heard this prediction he said to his attendants, "Go there and question him again! Ask him what kind of men are those who are coming, what road they will follow and what their intentions are!" However, when the messengers tried to comply with his command they found that all the prisoners had disappeared from the jail. The jailers, fearful of the wrath of the king, prostrated themselves before the sovereign, telling him of their innocence. They claimed they had not been responsible for the escape but that it had been achieved through the prisoners' own magic. Moteczoma ordered the jailers to rise and go to the towns of all those who had prophesied evil things. "Tear down their houses," he cried out, "kill their wives and children and dig in the places where the houses had been, until you reach water. All their possessions are to be destroyed. And if any one of them is ever seen in a temple he is to be stoned and his body thrown to the wild beasts!"

All of this was done and the wives and children of the offenders, with ropes about their necks, were dragged through the city, though the sorcerers and magicians were never seen again.

From that day on the heart of Moteczoma was filled with such sadness and affliction that he was never seen with a smiling countenance. He fled from all contact with others and locked himself up in his secret chambers with Texiptla to whom he communicated all that the prophets and magicians had told him.

CHAPTER **LXIX** WHICH TREATS OF HOW A SHIP FROM CUBA
ARRIVED IN THIS LAND AND HOW MOTECZOMA, HAVING BEEN
NOTIFIED OF THIS, SENT EMISSARIES TO
INVESTIGATE THE MATTER

A few days after the wizards, soothsayers and enchanters had disappeared from the jail, a man came before the troubled king and, having greeted him with reverence, said that he wished to speak to him. King Moteczoma observed him and saw that he lacked ears, thumbs and big toes. He hardly looked like a human being and when the sovereign asked him where he came from the man responded that he was a native of the Land of the Fiery Mountain. When he was asked who had sent him, he said that he had come of his own will to narrate the things that he had seen. The stranger described how, while he had been walking near the seashore, he saw a round hill moving upon the waters which had approached some rocks on the beach. He had never seen anything like this and he was now filled with fright and wonder.[101]

Moteczoma then called one of his chieftains, Teoctlamacazqui, giving him orders to go to the sea and take along a slave of his by the name of Cuitlalpitoc. He was to find out the truth or falseness of what had been told to him. He was also to reprimand the rulers and governors of the province of Cuetlaxtla and of the coast because of their great carelessness in not being alert. The chieftain and the slave left Mexico and soon arrived before the governor of Cuetlaxtla whose name was Pinotl. Teoctlamacazqui chided Pinotl for his carelessness and ordered him to send

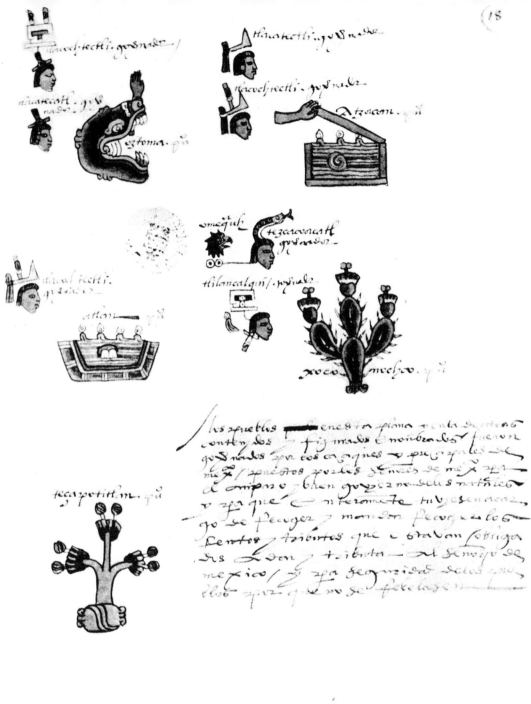

los pueblos — en esta plana y en la de atras
contenidos — figurados e nonbrados fueron
goptados por los caçiques y prinçipales de
mex y puestos por los señores de mex y por
el mismo y bien goptr. de los naturales
y pa que ynteramente tuviesen cargo
yo de recoger y mandar recoger los
çientos tributos que estavan obligados
dar Soan y tributar al señorio de
mexico y pa seguridad delos enç
ellos pa que no se rebelasen

fin dela parte primera de esta ystoria

*Some of the towns conquered by the Aztecs toward the middle of the fifteenth century. From the* **Codex Mendoza,** *painted in early Colonial times by Aztec scribes. Courtesy New York Public Library. Photo Reg Van Cuylenburg.*

men to see if there was a hill in the waters near the rocks of the coast. The lord of Cuetlaxtla sent messengers to the seashore and they soon returned, greatly frightened, saying that they had seen a terrible round thing in the midst of the waters. It moved to and fro and within it there were men who appeared from time to time. Teoctlamacazqui and Cuitlalpitoc said that they wanted to go see for themselves in order to be able to satisfy the desires of their master, Moteczoma. Having arrived at the rocks on the beach they concealed themselves so that the Spaniards could not see them, and they soon realized that everything that had been said was true. In order to observe the strangers better the envoys climbed a large tree and from there they saw a boat being lowered into the water. Men entered it and went fishing near the seashore. Later the boat returned to the ship, carrying the fish that had been caught. When the Aztec emissaries had seen these things, they departed for Mexico with great haste to tell their master what they had observed.

On reaching the presence of Moteczoma, Teoctlamacazqui said, "O powerful lord, you may kill us or have us put in jail to die, but what the man who is your prisoner said to you is the truth. I myself, O lord, with my own eyes, wished to find this out, and with your slave Cuitlalpitoc I ascended a great tree in order to see better. This is what we saw: in the middle of the water a house from which appeared white men, their faces white and their hands likewise. They have long thick beards and their clothing is of all colors: white, yellow, red, green, blue and purple. On their heads they wear round coverings. They put a rather large canoe in the water, some of them jump into it and they fish all day near the rocks. At dusk they return to the home into which they are gathered. This is all we can tell you about that which you wish to know."

Moteczoma lowered his head and, without answering a word, placed his hand upon his mouth. In this way he remained for a long time. He appeared to be dead or mute since he was unable to give any answer. After a long time had passed he gave a mournful sigh, saying to the chieftain who had brought him the news, "To whom shall I give belief, if not to you? Why should I send another messenger if with your own eyes you have beheld the things you have described to me? The best thing to do now is to act."

Moteczoma called an attendant, telling him to liberate the man who was in jail, the one who had come from the coast, saying that he was a native of the Land of the Fiery Mountain. When the assistant reached the jail he found that the cage was empty and the prisoner had left no trace of his means of escape. After the monarch had been told this he stated that he had known that the man was a magician and he was glad that he had escaped, since he had spoken the truth. The king then called one of his officials and told him to bring two goldsmiths, two lapidaries and two feather workers. This was to be done in utmost secrecy, under pain of this official's death, that of his wife, children, and relatives, and under pain of the loss of all his possessions.

When the artisans arrived they were given gold, stones and feathers. They were told to cast golden jewels of different form as swiftly as possible. The lapidaries were told to cut all kinds of precious stones while the feather workers were commanded to make splendid ceremonial ornaments.

Moteczoma then spoke to Teoctlamacazqui. "I have had jewels, precious stones and feather work made and I wish you to carry them as presents to those who have arrived in our land. I want you to find out who their chieftain is, since he is the one to whom you must give all these presents. You must discover with absolute certainty if he is the one that our ancestors called Topiltzin or Quetzalcoatl.[102] Our histories say that he abandoned this land but left word that he or his sons would return to reign over this country, to recover the gold, silver and jewels which they left hidden in the mountains. According to the legends, they are to acquire all the wealth that we now possess. If it is really Quetzalcoatl, greet him on my behalf and give him these gifts. You must also order the governor of Cuetlaxtla to provide him with all kinds of food, cooked birds and game. Let him also be given all the types of bread that are baked, together with fruit and gourds of chocolate. Let all of this be placed at the edge of the sea, and from there you and your companion, Cuitlalpitoc, will take it to the ship or house where they are lodged. Give these things to him so that he, his children and companions may eat of them. Notice very carefully whether he eats or not. If he eats and drinks he is surely Quetzalcoatl as this will show that he is familiar with the foods of this land, that he ate them once and has come back to savor them again.

"Also tell him," continued Moteczoma, "to allow me to die! After my death he will be welcome to come here and take possession of his kingdom, as it is his. We know that he left it to be guarded by my ancestors, and I have always considered that my domain was only lent to me. Let him permit me to end my days here. Then let him return to enjoy what is his!

"Do not go with fear or anxiety and do not fear death at his hands," the king now said to his messenger, "since I swear to you that I will honor your children and give them my wealth and make them members of my council. If, by any chance, he does not like the food that you give him and is desirous of devouring human beings and wishes to eat you, allow yourself to be eaten. I assure you that I will fulfill all my promises regarding your wives, children and relatives."

Teoctlamacazqui said that he would be pleased to go, and he and his companions, laden with the jewels and feather work, left the city secretly. They arrived in

Cuetlaxtla where they ordered the governor and officials to prepare all kinds of stewed fowl and game together with white maize cakes and fruit. Many Indians, carrying these loads, set out for the coast where the Spaniards were still drifting on the sea.

The Aztec emissaries deposited the food close to the seashore without being seen. Teoctlamacazqui bade the carriers depart and he and Cuitlalpitoc remained alone. They climbed the same tree from which they had spied before and they saw that the Spaniards were fishing from their boat. As it was late the two Aztecs did not wish to disclose their presence but decided to wait until morning. One hour before dawn Teoctlamacazqui and his companion took all the dishes to the beach and placed them upon the rocks near the place where the fishermen came in their boat. The two sat down to wait and when the sun rose men from the ship began to appear upon the deck. They saw the two Indians sitting on the beach and swiftly lowered the boat into the water and four Spaniards were soon rowing toward them. However, since Spaniards and Aztecs were unable to understand one another, it was only through signs that Teoctlamacazqui told them to put the food and drink into the boat, as he and Cuitlalpitoc wished to be taken to the ship. The Spaniards understood them and with the help of the two Indians placed the gifts in the boat.

The Spaniards rowed toward their ship and when they arrived delivered the food to it. The Indians boarded the vessel, amazed at such a powerful structure with its many cabins and decks. It seemed like a thing more divine than human, a work of genius, and they asked to be shown the chief or head of those men. Through the Indian lady[103] whom they had brought with them, a speaker of both Spanish and Nahuatl, they were told that the leader was the man she was pointing to. Teoctlamacazqui then prostrated himself in front of the man, presenting him with the jewelry, precious stones and feather work and the *Chronicle* states that when the sacks were opened the Spaniards gazed upon the contents with great joy. They passed the objects from one to another and after they had scrutinized all the wealth, the Indian woman asked who had sent it. The Aztec emissary answered that it came from the great King Moteczoma, his lord, who sent them greetings from his city. The Indian woman then asked where he came from and he responded that he came from the splendid city of Mexico. Then she said, "What is it that you want?"

"Lady," answered the messenger, "I have come to ask this lord why he came here, where he is going, and what he seeks." She responded, "The leader of these men says that he has come to greet your master Moteczoma and that he intends to go to the city of Mexico to salute him and thank him for these presents."

Teoctlamacazqui answered that Moteczoma would be much pleased by this but that the monarch wished to be left in peace until his reign ended and that after his death their leader could journey thither. Then he would recover his kingdom and homeland just as he had left them. He added that the Spanish captain should eat of the presents that his master had sent. The Indian woman answered in the following way, "These gods say that they kiss your. hands and that they will eat. But since they are not accustomed to this kind of food they wish you to taste them first and then all of us will eat them."

The two Aztecs tasted the different foods and when the Spaniards saw them eating they too began to eat turkey, stew, and maize cakes and enjoy the food, with much laughing and sporting. But when the time came to drink the chocolate that had been brought to them, that most highly prized drink of the Indian, they were filled with fear. When the Indians saw that they dared not drink they tasted from all the gourds and the Spaniards then quenched their thirst with chocolate and realized what a refreshing drink it was. Having eaten and drunk, the leader of the Spaniards told the Indian woman to ask the Aztec emissary his name. The answer given was that his real name was Tlillancalqui, Keeper of the House of Ink, that his title was Teoctlamacazqui, and that his companion's name was Cuitlalpitoc.

"This lord says," the interpreter explained, "that he and his men have enjoyed your food and that they desire that you eat some of their own now, even though it is very different from that which you have brought." Biscuits, bacon, jerked beef were brought out and, when they had consumed part of the biscuit and other foods, they saved what was left in order to carry it to Moteczoma. After they had eaten, wine was presented to them and they drank it. Their hearts were gladdened and they said that they kissed his hands since that drink was good and fine. The Aztec envoys slept that night on board because of the wine they had drunk.

The next morning they asked permission of the captain of the ship to return to their master and inform him of the things they had learned. The captain produced a necklace of glass beads together with trinkets and gave them to Tlillancalqui so that they be delivered to Moteczoma. Another string of beads was given to the emissary and yet another to Cuitlalpitoc. By means of the translator a message was sent to the Aztec monarch saying that the Spanish captain kissed his hands and that he would do what he had been commanded. He was to tell the sovereign that they would now go away and leave Moteczoma free to reign peacefully for a long time. The Spaniard added that he had come from a distant country but that in time he would return and that he hoped to find Moteczoma still alive in order to reciprocate his kind actions.

Having said farewell, the Aztec ambassadors left the ship and were brought to the shore in the boat. Once they had been left there they consulted among themselves and decided to climb the tree again to observe. They saw great sheets of cloth being hoisted on the masts of the ship and once this had been done the ship sailed away. They watched it go and remained in the tree observing these strange happenings. They saw the craft move without anyone pulling it upon the waters. They did not leave the tree until the Spaniards were out of sight.

When the two emissaries arrived in the presence of Moteczoma they told him what they had seen and described how they had been given jewels, food and drink. They told of what they had eaten and drunk and said the drink was so good and easy to swallow that they had lost their senses with it. They described how the Spanish captain had promised to go away leaving the monarch to finish his reign, and how he had sailed back to his country which was far away. Even if he did return it would not be soon.

The messengers then presented the food they had brought so Moteczoma might see it. When some bits of biscuit were given to him the king tasted them, saying that they seem like tufa stone. He ordered that a chunk of tufa be brought to him and he compared one with the other, seeing that the rock weighed less than the bread. He called in his dwarfs and ordered them to taste the latter. They found it to be sweet and soft. However, Moteczoma was afraid to eat of it, saying that it belonged to the gods and that to eat it would be a sacrilege. He told the priests to carry it solemnly to the city of Tula and to bury it in the temple of Quetzalcoatl, since those who had arrived here were his sons. The priests took the biscuit, placed it in a gilded gourd, wrapped the latter in rich mantles and made a long procession to Tula. Along the way they incensed it and sang hymns honoring Quetzalcoatl, whose food they carried. Once it had reached Tula it was buried in his temple with great honors.

Moteczoma then asked Teoctlamacazqui if he had seen the Spaniards depart. He answered affirmatively, saying that he had not left the tree until they were out of sight. The messenger then produced the string of beads that had been given to him, saying that it was the only present that the Spanish captain had sent since he had no others. Moteczoma accepted this, considering it a wonderful and divine thing. He said, "I accept the favor and gift which the god has given me." He gave orders that the necklace be buried at the feet of the god Huitzilopochtli, as he was not worthy to wear such a holy thing. And so the beads were buried with much solemnity in the midst of the burning of incense, the sounding of conch shells and other instruments.

When these things had been done Moteczoma thanked Teoctlamacazqui for what he had done, and gave the slave Cuitlalpitoc his liberty. He told both of them to go home to rest but soon he sent gifts of mantles, women's blouses and skirts to them, together with cacao, cotton, maize, beans, and three slaves, one male and two females, to serve them. The two men received these gifts with much gratitude.

Moteczoma was now anxious to find out who the strangers were and where they came from, so he decided to investigate in every possible manner, seeking out old and wise people. All of this was done in the utmost secrecy because what had just taken place was known to no one in the city, not even to the chieftains. The few who had heard of the arrival of strange men at the coast had been threatened with death and the destruction of their families and possessions. Because of fear, everything was kept occult, secret and silent, as if nothing had happened. This secrecy prevailed until Don Hernando Cortés returned to this land with three ships some time later.[104]

CHAPTER LXX WHICH TREATS OF HOW MOTECZOMA ORDERED A PAINTER TO DRAW PICTURES OF THE SPANIARDS ACCORDING TO THE DESCRIPTION OF TLILLANCALQUE TEOTLAMACAZQUI AND HOW THE AZTEC KING WAS DESIROUS OF KNOWING WHAT KIND OF PEOPLE HAD ARRIVED IN HIS LAND

After Teoctlamacazqui had told him all the details described in the last chapter, Moteczoma became even more worried and attempted to discover what kind of people had come to his land, their place of origin, lineage and, above all, whether they planned to return. For this reason he called Teoctlamacazqui and conversed with him in private. He said that he wanted to know more about those who had just departed and that he wished to have a painting made of them. He wished the picture to be drawn in his presence but said that it must be done secretly.

Teoctlamacazqui answered that he was willing to have this picture made, whereupon he ordered that the best artist of Mexico, an old man, be brought. Moteczoma told this man that he should not reveal anything that might happen, under pain of death. The painter was cowed, exclaiming that he was not a man to uncover secrets of such a great and mighty lord. His paints were brought to him and Teoctlamacazqui began to tell him what he should depict. The artist drew a picture of the ship in the way it had been seen, showing the Spaniards with their long beards and white faces. He painted their clothing in different colors, their hats upon their

268

heads and their swords in their belts. When Moteczoma saw this he marveled and gazed upon the painting for a long time. Having looked, he said to Teoctlamacazqui, "Were these things as they have been painted here?" The answer was, "Yes, O lord, they are exactly so; I have not lied or added anything!"

Moteczoma paid the artist for his work, saying, "Brother, I beg you to answer me this question: by any chance do you know anything about what you have painted? Did your ancestors leave you a drawing or description of these men who were to arrive in this land?" The painter answered, "Powerful lord, I will not lie to you or deceive you—you are the image of the god. Therefore I will tell you that I and my ancestors never were occupied with any arts save those of painting pictures and other symbols. My ancestors were merely the artists of past kings and they depicted what they were ordered. Therefore, I know nothing of that which you ask me; if I tried to answer your question my answer would be a lie."

Moteczoma then ordered him to question the other artisans of his profession, asking if they possessed some picture coming down from their ancestors regarding those who might come to this land and possess it. The artist agreed to do so and for several days he inquired. But the painter was unable to find out anything certain and therefore returned to Moteczoma and told him that he had discovered nothing exact regarding these things.

Seeing that his attempts had been ineffectual, Moteczoma called all the oldest painters of books from Malinalco, the hot country to the south, together with those of Chalco. When they arrived he begged them to tell him if they knew anything about strangers who were to arrive in the land, asking them what kind of men might come, from where, and what they looked like. He also wished to know if the ancestors of the painters had left information regarding these things, or painted manuscripts or pictures.

When these things had been asked of them, the Malinalca brought a picture and showed it to him. It portrayed men with a single eye in their foreheads like cyclops. They said that their forebears had told them that these were the ones who were to come to this country and possess it. Other men in this picture were one-legged. The painters of books from the south displayed a drawing in which there appeared men who were fish from the waist down, explaining to Moteczoma that those were the ones who were to come to this land. Others showed the king beings which were half man, half snake. But in the end, none were able to present anything that looked like the painting of the Spaniards.

Having gotten rid of those painters, Moteczoma sent for others from Cuitlahuac and Mizquic, reminding them that they were descendants of the Toltecs, great wise men, and that they should be able to answer his questions. These men informed him, through their ancient paintings, that their ancestors had left a tradition that the sons of Quetzalcoatl were to come to these lands and that they were to possess them and recover that which had been theirs in ancient times. They were also to acquire again that which they had hidden in the hills, in the woods and in the caverns. They showed the monarch what kind of men they were but they did not look like those in his painting and therefore he bade them depart, thanking them for what they had told him and described.

Moteczoma was about to call the painters of books from Xochimilco, but the noble Tlillancalqui Teoctlamacazqui said to him, "Powerful lord, do not tire yourself or waste time in questioning so many men. None of them will be able to tell you what you desire to know as clearly as an ancient man from Xochimilco whom I know well. His name is Quilaztli and he is well informed in all matters which concern ancient history and painted books. If you wish I will bring him to you; I will tell him what you wish to know and he will produce his antique paintings." The king thanked him, commanding him to bring the old man immediately. When the latter appeared he brought with him his painted manuscripts. He appeared before Moteczoma, Angry Lord, who received him well because he was a venerable old man and of fine appearance.

Said Quilaztli to the sovereign, "O mighty lord, if because I tell you the truth I am to die, nevertheless I am here in your presence and you may do what you wish to me!" Before showing him the papers, he narrated that mounted men would come to this land in a great wooden house. This structure was to lodge many men, serving them as a home; within it they would eat and sleep. On the surface of this house they would cook their food, walk and play as if they were on firm land. They were to be white, bearded men, dressed in different colors and on their heads they would wear round coverings. Other human beings were to arrive with them, mounted on beasts similar to deer and others on eagles which would fly like the wind. These men were to possess the country, settle in all its cities, multiply in great numbers and be owners of gold, silver and precious stones.

"So that you may see," continued Quilaztli, "that what I say is the truth, behold it drawn here! This painting was bequeathed to me by my ancestors." He then took out an ancient picture on which were depicted the ship and the men dressed in the same manner as those which the king already knew through his painting. There he also saw other men mounted on horses or on flying eagles, all of them dressed in different colors, wearing their hats and swords.

Moteczoma, seeing the similarity between what the old man described and what appeared upon his painting, almost lost his senses and began to weep and to show anguish. Uncovering his chest to the elder, he cried out, "O brother Quilaztli, I now see that your ancestors were verily wise and well informed. Only a few days ago the men that you have shown me on your painting arrived in this land from the east. They came in the wooden house that you have described, dressed in the same colors and manner that appear in your drawing. I will show you how I ordered that they be painted: behold them here! However, one thing consoles me; I have sent them a present and begged them to go away in peace. They have obeyed me, departed, and I doubt if they will return."

"It is possible, O mighty prince," exclaimed Quilaztli, "that they came and went away again! Listen to the words I will say to you, and if I lie I am willing to have you annihilate me, my children and my descendants! Behold, before two years have passed, or at the most three, the strangers will return to these lands. Their coming was meant only to find a convenient way to return. Even though they said to you that they were returning to their native country, do not believe them! They will not go that far but will turn back when they have gone half way!"

Three years later, when Moteczoma had almost forgotten these things, news came from the sea that a hill was moving to and fro upon the waters again.

CHAPTER LXXI WHICH TREATS OF HOW DON HERNANDO CORTES, OF HAPPY MEMORY, DISEMBARKED AT THE PORT OF CHALCHIUHCUEYECAN, "PLACE OF SHE OF THE JADE SHIRT," AND HOW, WHEN NEWS CAME TO MOTECZOMA REGARDING THESE THINGS, HE ORDERED PROVISIONS BE SENT TO CORTES

Moteczoma was firm in his belief that the Spaniards would not return to this land of New Spain and that they had gone away, never to come back. But after three years they returned, appearing in the port. The governor of Cuetlaxtla, who had maintained spies and lookouts on the coast, heard that the ships were tossing on the waters attempting to reach land. The governor went to see these things in person and immediately sent messengers to Moteczoma, advising him that the ships of the gods had returned. His emissaries arrived swiftly in Mexico, since they did not stop to rest night or day. In four days they were in the city of Mexico where they communicated their news to Moteczoma who, according to the *Chronicle*, almost died of fear. When he had composed himself the king gave orders that his people receive the Spaniards well should they descend from their ship, and sent Tlillancalqui Teoctlamacazqui to the coast for this purpose.

Chief Tlillancalqui departed from Mexico and, walking day and night, arrived in Cuetlaxtla where he was well received and where he gave orders that the governor prepare food for the strangers. The governor stated that everything was ready and departed for the port with numerous men carrying the food and drink. He arrived there and saw that the Spaniards and their horses had already disembarked. Then he approached Don Hernando Cortés whom he recognized to be the leader, greeting him and throwing about his neck a gold necklace set with many jewels and precious stones. Cortés greeted him and ordered that Marina be called, for that was the name of the interpreter.

"O father," said she, "this god wishes to know who you are!"

The chieftain answered, "Lady have you forgotten Tlillancalqui, also called Teoctlamacazqui? I came to see you three years ago on behalf of my lord and king, Moteczoma of Mexico, and now he has sent me on the same errand. I am to serve you food and to provide you with anything else you may need."

The ambassador then ordered that the food be placed in front of the newcomers and their horses, and in their ingenuous manner they gave one turkey to each soldier and another to his horse, a basket of tortillas for the master and another for the animal. This was done until they were told that the beasts ate only corn and grass and soon the Aztec envoys provided the animals with the latter.

All this food was placed before the Spaniards in abundance; all that was necessary for the three hundred men who had arrived, without counting servants and negroes, and all ate with great pleasure. After they had eaten and rested Cortés told Chief Tlillancalqui through the interpreter that he was grateful and that he should carry his gratitude to Lord Moteczoma. The emissary answered that his master had sent a question: "Was it Cortés' will to journey to the city of Mexico where Moteczoma already ruled in his name? If so, the king wished to be notified since it would be necessary to have the throne of the kingdom prepared for him. It belonged to Cortés and Moteczoma was his vassal and the Spaniard would be received as master." The translator spoke to Cortés, who answered through the same interpreter. Marina said, "This god asks you to tell your master Moteczoma that he kisses his hands many times and that it is his will to go to Mexico to see him and enjoy his presence. However, he will not be able to do so immediately as he must organize his men first and unload the ships. As soon as he is able he will journey there, and he begs that chieftains be sent to show him the road that he must travel."

The noble Tlillancalqui bade farewell to Cortés and his men and carried his news to Mexico. Whenever he passed through towns which the Spaniards were to visit he gave commands that everything be prepared for the gods who had arrived.

*CAP.º 71.*

marina        marques

thlaculi

*The arrival of Cortés in Veracruz. To the left of the
Spanish Captain stands Malinche, his interpreter
and mistress; to his right stands the Aztec ambassador,
Tlillancalqui. From the Atlas, the picture book
accompanying Durán's text. Photo Reg Van Cuylenburg.*

Under pain of death no one was to be neglectful of the food of the Spaniards, of their horses, or of good lodgings both for them and the carriers of their supplies.

Tlillancalqui gave his news when he arrived in Mexico, telling how he had given ample provisions to the strangers, how those who had come a few years before had returned in larger numbers, and how the same Indian woman who had spoken to them previously was now the interpreter.

"Welcome," said Moteczoma to the ambassador. "I am grateful for what you have done although it would be more pleasing to hear that the strangers had returned to their own country as they did before. However my fate has been ordained and the Lord of All Created Things is venting his ire against me. Let his will be done since I cannot flee!" Moteczoma then moaned, "I beg a favor of you: after the gods have come and I have received death at their hands, and I know that they will kill me, I beg you to take charge of my children, help them and conceal them from the hands of these gods and from the Aztecs, since you know how evil and perverse the latter are. In the belief that I have surrendered the nation to the strangers, the Aztecs will take vengeance on my wives and children. Therefore I beg you to safeguard them, remembering that I have always considered you as my own son, placed all my trust in you and honored you during my reign.

"This also," continued Moteczoma, "I wish to tell you: all of us will die at the hands of the gods, and those who survive will be made their slaves and vassals. They are to reign now and I will be the last king of this land. Even though some of our descendants and relatives may remain, even though they be made governors and given states, they will not be true lords and kings but subordinates, like tax gatherers or collectors of the tribute which my ancestors and I won. Our descendants' only task will be to comply with the commands and orders of the strangers. And so it was fated that I should be the one to be cast from the throne of my ancestors and leave it in ruins. None of my sons or descendants will restore it or sit upon it again." Having said these words Moteczoma could not control his tears and his bitterness.

Tlillancalqui tried to console the king as best he could, assuring him of the kindness of the gods who had arrived and the affability which they had shown. He spoke of how they had embraced the emissaries and shown them affection, insisting that they would do no harm. Even though Moteczoma might be distrustful, said Tlillancalqui, he should find a way to ingratiate himself with the newcomers in order not to anger or displease them in any way.

Moteczoma thought he would honor the Spaniards in a way that would please them and therefore he ordered that ten slaves be taken to be sacrificed before Cortés, their hearts presented to him as if he had been a god. And so it was done.

Cortés was first offered many jewels, feathers, and other splendid things on behalf of Moteczoma; then certain dances were performed before him. But when it came to the sacrifice of the slaves Cortés and his men prevented it. In another chronicle or painted manuscript it is stated that Cortés ordered the death of the sacrificers who were ready to perform their task. This is not mentioned by our *Chronicle* since it says only that the priests were prevented from sacrificing and I consider the last version the truthful one. Even though the act of sacrificing was the worst of deeds, the intention in this case was to please and honor the newcomers.

At this time the Spaniards were established in the town of Cempoala where they had been well received in the palace by the officials and other natives. Moteczoma meanwhile still persisted in trying to discover in his oracles whether he would be deprived of his power and killed. Since these fears never left him he called his minister Tlillancalqui, saying, "I do not know what measures to take to prevent these gods from reaching the city or seeing my face. Perhaps the best solution will be the following: let there be gathered enchanters, sorcerers, sleep-makers and those who know how to command snakes, scorpions and spiders, and let them be sent to enchant the Spaniards. Let them be put to sleep, let them be shown visions, let the little beasts bite them so that they die. I have decided to send messages to Yauhtepec, Huaxtepec, Malinalco and Tepoztlan to ask that their wizards destroy the strangers with their enchantments."

"O powerful lord," responded Tlillancalqui, "your decision seems good to me, but if they are gods who will be able to harm them? However, nothing will be lost in the attempt. Perhaps these magicians will be able to achieve something and their magic may have some effect."

Moteczoma immediately had all the sorcerers brought to him, telling them to go to Cempoala. They were to pretend that their sole reason for coming was the desire to serve the Spaniards, but they were, instead, to use their tricks and arts to kill the strangers. He ordered the sleep-makers to put them to sleep and the wizards to create frightful visions and images. He commanded those who could control animals to send serpents and scorpions to bite them while they were asleep, together with spiders, centipedes, poisonous lizards, and other mortiferous animals. He also ordered them to enchant the Spaniards, to make them lose their reason and to create infections in their bodies.

The wizards departed for Cempoala where they used all their devilish and fabulous arts to the utmost. But after a few days of trying to assassinate the Spaniards with their magic tricks, they returned to Moteczoma, saying that the Spaniards were gods and that their sorcery had been ineffectual. The strangers had been on guard all night and therefore it had been impossible to send in poisonous animals.

276

Those who knew how to enchant had tried to put a spell on them but it had not worked. The Spaniards had been shown visions but they had paid no attention to them. In fact, if a flea bit them they would get up immediately to look for it and then kill it. These men did not stop talking all night and before day had dawned they were up, had mounted their horses and taken up their arms. These people were of a different manner and disposition than the Aztecs. The flesh of these gods was so tough that no magical device could penetrate it, and their hearts were impossible to locate. Their entrails were so dark that the magicians had been unable to explore their flesh in a way that would cause them harm. No matter how much slumber the wizards had wished to cast upon the Spaniards they had not been able to put them to sleep. They had attempted to catch the Spaniards in order to cast them into the river or into a ravine, but like little birds in trees the strangers had immediately awakened, opening their eyes. While some of them slept at night others moved about. After four nights of failure, the magicians returned to Mexico, saying they were Moteczoma's vassals and perhaps they deserved death, but that they had been unable to accomplish their purpose.

Moteczoma was greatly afflicted to see that his attempts had failed, but he said to the conjurers, "You have done everything in your power; you may rest now. Perhaps when the strangers arrive here your enchantments and power over dreams will be more effective. Let them enter the city, since it is here that we will find a way to destroy them totally. Here my desires will be fulfilled. Not a man will be left alive and no news of them will be carried back to their native land. Therefore, I charge you again to keep up your knowledge and to continue to practice your arts." Having heard his answer, all the wizards went back to their towns awaiting the moment when they should be called.

CHAPTER LXXII WHICH TREATS OF HOW MOTECZOMA SENT
A CHIEFTAIN TO BRING CORTES AND OF HOW HE GUIDED THE SPANIARDS
TO A CLIFF. WITH A DESCRIPTION OF
HOW TWO HORSES FELL, TWO SPANIARDS WERE KILLED AND OF HOW
THE CHIEFTAIN FLED AND WAS LATER EXECUTED BY MOTECZOMA

When Moteczoma saw that the sorcerers had been unable to harm the Spaniards he tried to strengthen his spirit for he was more determined than ever not to allow the Spaniards to enter Mexico. He decided to put obstacles in their way and he could have done this easily had not God blinded his reason, whereupon the Divine Will was fulfilled.

In order to harm the Spaniards Moteczoma sent a chieftain by the name of Motelchiuh, whose title was Huitznahuatl, to Cempoala to receive Cortés. He was instructed to return with him, see that he lacked nothing and to tell him, through the woman who was the interpreter, that he was welcome to come to the city of Mexico where Moteczoma would await him. "Add nothing to my message," said the monarch, "let us see what he answers."

Huitznahuatl Motelchiuh left Mexico with haste, accompanied by other great lords. All were desirous of seeing the famous and fearful gods and soon arrived at a place called Chichiquila where they found Cortés together with his men. When Huitznahuatl arrived he went straight to the Spaniard, with due reverence greeted him and gave him the usual presents of flowers and other things. When the Indians go to visit a person it is not their custom to go empty-handed since this would be considered offensive. This is usual with the hosts as well as with the guests.

After Huitznahuatl had greeted Cortés he said, "O lord and true god! Welcome to this, your country and kingdom!" Cortés answered, asking the emissary where he came from, whereupon Huitznahuatl answered that he had journeyed from the city of Mexico by command of his great master Moteczoma. This great ruler kissed the stranger's hands and welcomed him, advising him to travel slowly and watch his health. Moteczoma was waiting with great eagerness to witness his arrival in that city. Marina interpreted all of these things and then said to the Aztec, "This god asks, O my father, what is your name?" He answered, "O lady, my name is Huitznahuatl Motelchiuh!"

"Well, lord," responded Marina, "this god says that he thanks your master Moteczoma for the interest taken in sending you to visit him and offer gifts. He says that he is on his way to the city of Mexico to enjoy the presence of the king who has treated him so well and put him under obligation."

"Lady," answered the chieftain, "tell this god to rest assured that all his desires will be complied with since King Moteczoma wishes to serve him and has ordered all the towns and provinces, under pain of death, to receive him and his divine companions. He will be greeted with festivities and good feeling since all are Moteczoma's vassals. He will be given provisions for all his needs in a way that he has not known before."

"Huitznahuatl," answered Marina, "this god who is present thanks you and your master for your courtesy and for inviting him to travel to Mexico. He begs you to return to your city and tell your lord of his gratitude. He does not need men

278

to guide him as we have people here who can indicate the way for us." Huitznahuatl returned to Mexico and told all these things to Moteczoma.

After this Cortés journeyed to a town called Nauhtlan where the local prince Coatlpopoca received him well and offered him gifts. Cortés thanked him for the good treatment that he received and presented him with a necklace of blue glass beads which the chieftain appreciated greatly. That night Cortés asked him the straightest way to the city of Mexico. However, the chieftain, disregarding the gift of the necklace and the good treatment and kind words of Cortés, said that he would lead them along a short and quick route to Mexico. All of this was done with malice as he wished to guide the Spaniards to their destruction on a cliff, and in this the chief was guided by the devil. Don Hernando Cortés listened with faith and trust to this prince, and ordered his men to prepare themselves to depart before dawn in order to reach their destination, where they could rest from the sun and the trials of the journey.

The soldiers, having prepared themselves, left the town at dawn, guided by Coatlpopoca. This chieftain led them gradually into a rough country of rocks and cliffs, which were so steep that the horsemen and foot soldiers were panting. As it was not yet light they could not see the way. When Cortés realized the steepness of the path, he asked the guide why he had brought him along such a difficult route. The latter answered that it was simply a shorter way and that it would not last long. But he led them straight toward the cliffs. When they tried to descend, two mounted men who were in front fell from the edge and were killed, together with their horses. When Cortés saw the malice of Coatlpopoca and the harm that he had caused, he ordered him taken prisoner. But when the Indian realized the harm he had caused, and that he would be punished, he fled and concealed himself. Having waited until morning, Cortés returned the same way that he had come, guided by other Indians on the true road to Mexico.

It was there that he sent messengers to Moteczoma, against whom he now felt resentment, as the chieftain's outrageous treason had been at the command of the king. He sent a message that he had had a better opinon of him and that the monarch should take care, since two of his Spaniards had been killed on the cliffs. Cortés added that Moteczoma should order that Coatlpopoca be captured; only in this way he would agree that the treachery had not been due to the king's orders.

When this news was delivered to Moteczoma he became angry and ordered that the chieftain be captured and surrendered to Cortés so that the latter could punish him in the way he desired. The chieftain was found and turned over to the Spaniards. When he confessed his evil intentions and declared that Moteczoma was innocent, the Spanish captain had him put in chains. He gave orders that the traitor be brought to him with great care so that he could deliver him in person to Moteczoma. Later when Cortés arrived in Mexico this was done and Moteczoma had Coatlpopoca torn to pieces. In this way the Aztec king tried to show his innocence in the whole matter.

This same day Cortés arrived at Tecoac, a town near Tlaxcala, belonging to the jurisdiction of the latter town. Before he arrived, however, messengers had come to notify the inhabitants that the gods were to spend the night there, that the people were to come out to receive them and provide them with everything they needed. Tocpacxochiuh, sovereign of Tecoac, was told how he must receive the Spaniards and their horses, and feed them. He was given orders to prepare turkeys, eggs, breads, fruit, and maize, and also grass for the horses. He was also to sweep the rooms of the houses where the strangers were to be lodged. This ruler, however, rose from his seat with great anger, crying out, "Are we vassals of the gods who are coming? Are we vassals of Moteczoma? Are they to command us as if we were their servants? I do not wish it! It is not my will to receive them in my city or to feed them!" He called his officials and all his subjects, saying, "Hear me, O Chichimecs, bold men of Tecoac! Take up your arms, your swords and arrows to defend your nation. Let us destroy and annihilate the gods who have come to create fear among our people. Let us test the strength of these men who have come to our land. Let us discover whether we are really their vassals or tributaries. Let us see if we must provide for all their needs. Prepare yourselves to go out to meet them! Let us destroy them and show ourselves to be valorous men!"

The city of Tecoac was put on guard against the entrance of Cortés. In one moment the fields were covered with Indians, all of them armed for war. Cortés, who was always prepared, ordered his three hundred men to form in squadrons in order not to be surrounded or attacked from the rear. Even when he saw the enormous number of men that faced him he did not fear. In fact he was pleased when he saw that the enemy formed itself in wings and that their squadrons were arranged in their customary way. He saw many gallant men, splendidly arrayed, covered from head to foot with their military ornaments, all the latter incrusted with gold. On their heads and shoulders they wore rich feathers and badges which indicated that they were spirited and courageous people. Filled with contempt, they made scornful signs and faces at the Spaniards. Once these men had been formed in ranks, two valiant Indians came forward. With their shields, gilded and elaborately adorned, and their swords in hand, they defied the Spaniards, ordering them to depart.

The Spaniards were greatly confused and frightened. The native army was

280

large enough to eclipse the sun, and this was the first battle which the strangers had to fight. The Spaniards were few in number, not well equipped, and fearful at finding themselves in this strange and barbarous realm. They were confronted by men as numerous as the sands of the sea, who could have killed them with the greatest of ease. In fact, I heard a conqueror who is now a monk and who was then a layman and was present in that battle, say that many Spaniards shed tears and wished that they had not been born, cursing Cortés for having brought them to this fearful end. But the brave captain, who never lacked spirit in any tribulation of this type, ordered two horsemen to charge wildly and kill the two Indians who had placed themselves in front of the army, since it was obvious that all were depending upon them. Courageously the two cavaliers raised their arms ready to thrust their lances against two who awaited them, but in the moment of the kill one of the native chieftains lifted his right hand with such skill that he slashed at the horse and severed its hoofs, whereupon the horseman fell upon the ground. The Indian leaped to one side and managed to avoid the blow that the Spaniard aimed at him and he hit the horse in the neck in such a way that the severed head hung from the reins and master and beast were left lying on the ground.

Seeing that the Indians were anxious to attack again in order to take them alive, Cortés ordered that a small cannon be shot. All the Indians in the front ranks were killed and the others scattered. This allowed the Spaniards who had fallen to rise from the ground. Taking hold of their swords, they tried to defend themselves from the Indians. With shrieks, while horns, drums and conch shells sounded, the Indians attacked with sling stones, propelled darts and other weapons. The Spaniards shot the small cannon, fired their arquebuses and sent arrows from their crossbows. Little by little land was won from the Indians until the Spaniards had reached a small village on a hill near the city, which was probably a pyramid because they say that a house was there which contained great, spacious chambers. There the Spaniards strengthened themselves and the Indians, having surrounded them, attacked them every day. It is said that this assault lasted ten or twelve days.

During this time Moteczoma kept sending foodstuffs to the Spaniards. Cortés tried desperately to break the siege, asking the enemy for peace many times and telling them to cease their fighting and subject themselves to His Majesty. He told them that he had not come to harm them or kill them. Seeing that they were unwilling to do what he desired, Cortés decided to set up an ambush and finish them off.

Night came and the Indians believed that the Spaniards had gone to sleep. But it was not so, since every one of them was awake. The Spaniards waited until all the fires of their sentries had gone out; when everything was quiet Cortés and his men abandoned their shelter and came forth in groups of ten, some on one side and some on the other, according to the cunning of the good captain. They found the Indians sleeping, notably the captains, in small villages. Cortés gave orders that no one harm or kill any one of them but that the captains be taken prisoners and tied. When they were brought to the camp of the Spaniards none of them was killed but Cortés reproached them through Marina the interpreter. He asked them why they were rebellious, why they made trouble, since he had not come to harm them? He asked them to examine and judge him according to their experiences—though he had been able to massacre all of them, he had not touched them. He also said the fact that he wanted them as friends would be proved by his freeing all the prisoners at dawn.

So it was that when morning came, and the Indian army wished to renew the fight, the men saw that their commanders were not there. Cortés then showed the Aztecs the humiliating situation of their officers. He repeated that, though he could have killed them, his mission was not to kill or to destroy. He besought them to allow him to enter the city to rest, and he freed all the prisoners. When the Indians saw his generosity they lifted the siege, coming in peace to lead Cortés to the city.

All that I have narrated here I heard from a conqueror who was an eye witness to these events. But the *Chronicle* tells us exactly the contrary. It says that the Spaniards entered by force, killing numerous Indians. In a way one thing is not contrary to the other, since it is clear that during the siege a great number of Indians were killed with the cannon and muskets, as a battle took place every day.

And so it became known throughout the land that the gods possessed fiery lightning and with each shot many men perished, whereupon the natives became quiet with fear. Their cowardice was so strong that they fled from the Spaniards, hiding, fleeing into caves, woods and caverns and even threw themselves off cliffs in order not to have to deal with the Spaniards. This situation continues today, for they hide even from the friars as if they were their mortal enemies, although the friars live among them, love and cherish them. In order to illustrate the terror that took hold of the natives, I wish to relate what the Tlaxcalans did when Tecoac surrendered to Cortés and to the Spanish crown.

Tecoac and its cities were now subject to the King and to Cortés who had made them swear that they would never rebel against him. The *Chronicle* says that Cortés took with him the sovereign of that city, Tocpacxochiuh. Soon they reached the limits of Tlaxcala, arriving at a town called Tzopachtzinco. When the Tlaxcalans heard that the gods were approaching, they called together a gathering of all the rulers of the provinces.

Tlaxcala was a great and populous nation, governed by four lords representing four different regions. During the meeting one of the aforesaid nobles spoke lengthily, exclaiming, "O Chichimec lords, natives of the great Tlaxcala! You have heard that certain gods have arrived in our land, from the place where the sun rises. They appeared among the mists and the darkness of the sea, living in wooden hills or houses. All of this was mysterious and it was permitted by the Lord of All Created Things, of the Earth, of the Night and of the Day. Little by little they have been penetrating into our country; therefore decide what we must do! Are we to defend ourselves or not? You have seen how the people of Tecoac were reckless and tried to protect their city. You have also witnessed the deaths of all those who perished from the fire shot by the Spaniards. If you wish to hear my opinion I will give it to you: have pity upon your children, brothers, upon the old men and women and orphans who are to die, all of them innocent, perishing only because we wish to make a defense. All of this will profit us nothing and therefore I believe it will be better to receive them in peace, bring them to our city and furnish them with food and other things for their needs."

All agreed with his opinion, deciding to prostrate themselves before Cortés and offer many presents and themselves as servants of his. And so it was done; gathering many of their chieftains, the Tlaxcalans departed with the best gifts that could be obtained and appeared before Cortés. They did much reverence to him and offered him the gifts, including garlands of flowers to be hung around his neck. Having greeted him, the Tlaxcalan messengers delivered a great speech, which Marina translated for Cortés. In this speech they offered their persons and wealth for the service of the Spanish captain and of His Majesty, whose name Cortés always extolled to these nations. He always begged them to submit themselves to the King and to our Catholic faith.

283

Then Cortés asked the messengers about their country. They responded that they had come from Tlaxcala to serve him, treat him as their master and provide for his necessities. After this they presented him with a number of turkeys, maize breads, fruit, and other edibles for which Cortés thanked them and treated them with much diplomacy. He then asked if they had been subjected to the city of Mexico and forced to pay tribute to Moteczoma or to some other ruler. "Great lord!" they answered, "we are free men! We do not pay tribute nor are we vassals of anyone. That great monarch that you mentioned is the king of Mexico, our mortal enemy, with whom we wage a perpetual war. They come to our lands to die and we go to theirs to perish at the hands of their sacrificers! Our enmity is so great that all our pleasure has been reduced to the seeking out of men for sacrifice and the killing of one another." Cortés had now found that which he desired: discord! He joined the Tlaxcalans against Mexico in case he should need them.

Soon after this the Spanish captain was well received in Tlaxcala with dances and merrymaking. He was given rooms in the best palace, that of Xicotencatl, one of the lords of the city. Xicotencatl was asked by Cortés for men to carry the Spanish possessions. He asked the officials to give him guards to accompany him, together with women to grind corn and to cook.

The Tlaxcalans gave the Spaniards a number of soldiers and carriers and presented them with women to serve them. The latter were accepted by the soldiers with pleasure. The *Chronicle* narrates that from this time on, wherever the Spaniards arrived, they were given young, beautiful maidens, daughters of kings, to serve them well. A notable case of this was in Amecameca on the way to Chalco, where Cortés was regaled with rich presents of gold jewelry, precious stones, feathers, splendid arm-bands, clothing, blouses and ornate skirts, and also with many handsome young girls, all beautiful, well dressed and adorned. On their backs they wore magnificent plumage, their hair was loose and their cheeks were painted in a way that enhanced them greatly. The soldiers received them with thanks, being grateful for this gift. Filled with gratitude, Cortés lingered a few days in the province of Chalco, and during this time all the surrounding towns came to greet him, swore allegiance and gave him gifts. He and his men received them with good will, especially the jewels, gold work and precious stones. All of this whetted their appetite.

When Moteczoma heard that Cortés was approaching Mexico he sent messages to the kings of Texcoco and Tacuba, asking them to come to the capital so that all three might be there to welcome the gods who were now near the city. They acceded to his petition and came to Mexico where they were received in the royal abode of Moteczoma. After they had formally greeted one another, Moteczoma

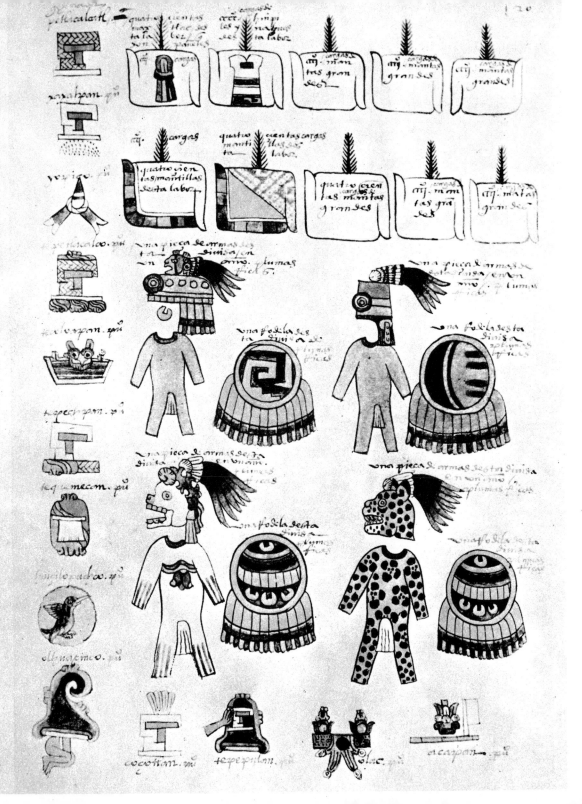

*An Aztec tribute list. On the left and lower parts are shown the towns which paid tribute to Mexico-Tenochtitlan and in the center are depicted cloth, warriors' costumes and shields. From the* Codex Mendoza, *painted in early Colonial times by Aztec scribes. Courtesy New York Public Library. Photo Reg Van Cuylenburg.*

spoke to them, moaning, "O mighty lords! It is fitting that the three of us be here to receive the gods and therefore I wish to find solace with you. I wish to greet you now and also bid farewell to you. How little we have enjoyed our realms which our ancestors bequeathed to us! They—mighty lords and kings—went away in peace and harmony, free of sorrow and sadness! Woe to us! Why do we deserve this? How did we offend the gods? How did this come to pass? Whence came this calamity, this anguish? Who are these who have come? Whence have they come? Who showed them the way? Why did this not happen in the times of our ancestors? There is only one remedy: you must make your hearts strong in order to bear what is about to happen. They are at our gates!"

The other two kings wept in their anguish. And after they had said farewell and embraced each other with feeling, the *Chronicle* tells us that Moteczoma went to visit his oracles again and that in front of the gods he uttered terrible reproaches. He complained bitterly to them for having brought him to this frightful end. He told the gods that he had served them with all possible care and that he had pleased them and promoted their cult. All of these laments to the gods were uttered by Moteczoma in the presence of lords and people. With abundant tears he cried out to the masses that he was terrified over the arrival of the strangers. He begged the gods to have pity on the poor, on the orphans and widows, on the children and aged! Many other prayers did he utter, accompanied by sacrifices, pious offerings and tears. He sacrificed himself, drawing blood from his arms, ears and shins, doing all this in an attempt to show his innocence and to demonstrate his sorrow over the coming of the Spaniards.

When Moteczoma returned to the palace he bade farewell to his wives and children with sorrow and tears, charging all his attendants to care for his family, since he considered himself a man about to die—a man who saw death staring him in the eyes.

It was at this time that Cortés reached Coyoacan where he was well received, in fact, welcomed in a manner such as he had not been shown in any part of the land. The entire Tecpanec nation, led by its rulers, came out to visit and salute Cortés, presenting him with gifts of mantles, jewels, stones, all rich and fine things. They swore their allegiance and promised to serve him in the name of His Majesty. In this way Cortés was gradually taking nations from Moteczoma and the Aztecs. The nations were all turning against the latter and joining Cortés, promising to aid him.

At this time the Tlaxcalans, Tecpanecs and people of Chalco, who had become vassals of His Majesty, warned Cortés not to trust Moteczoma or his people as they were traitors, and also evil, tyrannical and bellicose. The Spaniard was told to beware when the Aztecs acted most amiably and affably to him, for that was the moment to trust them the least. Cortés thanked them for the warning, asking the allies to accompany him in order to guard his own person. The men of Coyoacan gave him guards to serve him.

When Moteczoma and the Aztecs saw that everyone was abandoning them and becoming an enemy, they were much saddened. The people of Coyoacan remained neutral though, not daring to profess their enmity toward the Aztecs nor to show themselves to be true friends of Cortés. However, they served the latter and gave him provisions for his needs, flattered him and treated him with reverence.

When Moteczoma heard that Cortés was in Coyoacan he prepared a solemn reception to welcome him to the city. He ordered that all his nobles, including those of the neighboring cities, be present. But Cortés, who was a sly, cunning man, always stayed a few days in the important towns, resting and coaxing the Indians to join his army. He flattered them, showed them great affection, warned them and persuaded them to become his friends. He said that he had not come to do them harm but to liberate them from the tyranny and oppression of King Moteczoma, promising them freedom from the servitude in which they lived. After he had persuaded them he would depart with his men and go on to the next town.

When Cortés was told that he was now not far from the city of Mexico he sent messages to King Moteczoma telling him that they would soon meet and that he wished to know what the monarch's desires were. The sovereign received the messengers well, answering that Cortés should consider that his home was here and that he, the king, longed to see and welcome him. Only one thing worried him and that was that Cortés was coming in the company of the Tlaxcalans who were his foes and that these mortal enemies had made his people fearful that they might cause trouble in his city. Cortés responded that he was not bringing soldiers but carriers who bore his provisions, the equipment of his soldiers, the presents of cloth and other good things which he had been given in the towns that he had visited.

This clothing was plentiful, well worked in rich designs. There were ornamented mantles for men together with fine women's garments; he had brought a great number of Indians to carry all this wealth which he was planning to distribute among his men in the city of Mexico. And this was to prove fatal to the recipients since later, because of their greed in carrying it during their flight from the city, they lost all these riches. They also lost their lives and perhaps, no, I should not say perhaps—they lost their souls *in aeternum!*

A struggle between Spaniards and Aztecs in Lake Texcoco.
Shown to the left is one of the brigantines built by Cortés
and his men before the siege. A drowning man is being
saved by an Indian ally. Page from the **Codex Azcatitlan,** of the
Colonial period. Photo National Institute of
Anthropology and History, Mexico City.

CHAPTER **LXXIV** WHICH TREATS OF HOW HERNANDO CORTES WAS
RECEIVED IN MEXICO BY MOTECZOMA AND HIS CHIEFTAINS WITH
MUCH SOLEMNITY AND REJOICING.
WITH A DESCRIPTION OF HOW HE WAS LODGED IN A PALACE
IN THE CITY TO BE WELL SERVED THERE.
AND HOW KING MOTECZOMA WAS TAKEN PRISONER

It has never been my intention nor my will, nor is it now, to write a new history of the coming of the Spaniards to this land. It is not my desire to tell of their daring and heroic deeds or to set them up on a pinnacle or give them the praise they deserve. They were worthy of being remembered forever; their chests and hearts were more than human and showed the spirit of Spain which has been lauded, praised and renowned throughout the entire world.

As I have said it is not my intention to deal with their greatness nor their fantastic deeds, nor to reminisce over how Cortés entered the port and scuttled his ships in order to remove any hope that his men might have of fleeing from the land. In this he wished to inspire them to risk their lives like strong men. Nor will I describe how his own men at one time decided to assassinate him, nor the soft and diplomatic words that saved his life. All of this is well known and has been recorded by many authors.

Since I must tell the truth according to the stories and traditions of the Indians, I would have to describe, together with good and heroic actions, Cortés' frightful and cruel atrocities, his completely inhuman acts. In this I may offend those whom I am desirous of serving and who would desire to read these passages with pleasure. Many of these barbarous acts were committed on the way to the city of Mexico but about these I should be silent. One of these took place in the city of Cholula and it was a sorry affair. There, in the courtyard of the temple where Cortés was staying, he slaughtered a great number of men who had come along to serve the Spaniards. These people had carried water, firewood, and grass for the horses, together with other provisions. However, Cortés thought that they were chieftains in disguise, come to harm him, and therefore he had them massacred, sparing no one. I could cite other cases but since that is not my intention I will only describe the events up to the death of Moteczoma, as it is his life I am narrating. I am obliged to describe the end of this powerful monarch who had been feared, served and obeyed in this New World. This sovereign came to such a low, disastrous end that, even at his funeral, there was no one to speak in his favor or to mourn over him. In fact, surrounded by his enemies as he was—he, whose name had made the earth tremble, was not even interred.

Let us continue, as we are nearing the end of our story. It must be noted here how Cortés departed from Coyoacan on his way to the city of Mexico. He was accompanied by many great lords, some of them natives of Coyoacan, others from different areas such as Tlaxcala, Xochimilco, Tacuba and Chalco, all of whom went along to serve and guard him. Aside from the nobles there came many plebeians who wished to observe the spectacle. When Moteczoma was notified of the coming of Cortés from Coyoacan, he surrounded himself with the nobles and kings who had been with him and, seated on a gorgeous litter, covered with splendid cloth, he was carried out of the city on the shoulders of some of his great men. Along the way he showed his grandeur and power. Many of the nobles went ahead while others walked behind, carrying flowers and rich presents which were to be given to the Spaniards, the gods. When the monarch reached a place called Tocititlan he ordered his men to let him descend in order to await Cortés.

When Moteczoma heard that the Spanish captain was approaching, he ascended his litter again and went out to meet him. On seeing Cortés he descended. When the Spaniard saw this, he climbed down from his horse and went to embrace the Aztec sovereign, treating him with much reverence. Moteczoma did likewise, paying homage to the other with humility and words of welcome. From one of his noblemen he took a golden necklace inlaid with precious stones and placed it about Cortés' neck. Then he put in his hands a magnificent piece of feather work, done in the form of a flower. He also placed a garland of flowers about Cortés' neck and another on his head. Holding each other by the hand, they walked to the shrine of the goddess Toci, Our Grandmother, which was near the road, and there the mighty king and Hernando Cortés seated themselves upon thrones that had been prepared for them. Then the rulers of Texcoco and Tacuba came up to kiss the hands of Cortés. They also offered necklaces and flowers befitting their status as rulers. After this all the great lords came and performed the same courtesies which were usual in the service of their god Huitzilopochtli.

When this long and complicated salutation had been completed, Moteczoma spoke to Cortés through the translator, Marina. He welcomed him to his city, telling him that he was overjoyed to receive him. He added that he had been holding the throne for him, governing the kingdom that his father, the divine Quetzalcoatl, had abandoned. Upon this seat Moteczoma had sat, unworthily, reigning over the vassals of Quetzalcoatl. If Cortés had come to rule, he was at his service and the kingdom was now his, because of the written prophecies and traditions of Moteczoma's ancestors. However, if the Spaniard had come only to visit him he considered this a great favor and felt joy in his heart. The Aztec king told Cortés to rest and make known his needs which would be provided in great abundance.

*The goddess Coatlicue, "She-of-the-Snaky-Skirt," Earth Mother. National Museum, Mexico City. Photo National Institute of Anthropology and History, Mexico City.*

Having removed his hat to show reverence, Cortés answered courteously, saying that he had come in the name of a powerful king, whose servant he was. This monarch lived in Spain and was the ruler of a large part of the world. Cortés urged Moteczoma to swear allegiance to him as this would bring him many great favors. He also asked him to receive the Catholic faith of the one true Lord and God, under Whose rule and power heaven and earth are governed. When the sovereign of Mexico had recognizd these two lords, especially the supreme Lord and subjected himself to His Faith and then to the earthly lord, Cortés would become his friend and servant forever. He would never be mistreated nor would his people, as Cortés had come to do no harm. Moteczoma agreed to all these things, placed himself in the Spaniard's hands and offered his subjection to His Majesty at that hour, asking to be instructed in things related to the Holy Catholic Faith.

After having spent some time in that small shrine, both entered the city of Mexico, Cortés on his horse and the powerful Angry Lord in his litter. According to traditions and paintings shown to me by certain elders, it is said that Moteczoma left the sanctuary with his feet in chains. This I saw in a painting that belonged to an ancient chieftain from the province of Texcoco. Moteczoma was depicted in irons, wrapped up in a mantle and carried on the shoulders of his chieftains. This seems difficult to believe, since I have never met a Spaniard who will concede this point to me. But as all of them deny other things which have always been obvious, and remain silent about them in their histories, writings and narrations, I am sure they would also deny and omit this. It was one of the worst and most atrocious deeds committed by them. A conqueror, who is now a friar, told me that, though the imprisonment of Moteczoma might be true, it was done with the idea of protecting the lives of the Spanish captain and his men. The kings of Texcoco and Tacuba, and the sovereign of Xochimilco, who was as great a monarch as the rest and a favorite of Moteczoma, were also taken prisoners.

They entered Mexico preceded by dancers and merrymakers and greeted by the priests who came out to meet them, carrying incense burners and blowing horns and conch shells. They were painted with pitch and decked in their priestly garments. Behind them came the old men and warriors who had retired from war, dressed as eagles and jaguars and carrying their staffs and shields. In the midst of this solemnity and applause Cortés entered Mexico.

The Spanish captain was given rooms in the royal palace that had belonged to Moteczoma's grandfather.[105] These houses were large, divided into numerous chambers, and stood where the Viceroy's palace now stands. There, together with his men, Cortés was lodged and provided for abundantly by the people of the towns that surround Mexico, each in its turn. During this time Moteczoma and the other sovereigns were held prisoners in chains in a room guarded by three soldiers who were changed every other day.

It is said that in the eighty days during which the Aztec king remained there he was instructed in things of the Faith by a cleric whom the Spaniards had brought with them, and that he received the waters of Holy Baptism. My *Chronicle* says no such thing; if I record this event it is only because I have heard certain trustworthy persons speak of it. In order to ascertain the truth I questioned the friar who had been a conqueror and whom I have mentioned before. In a hesitant way he answered that he had not been present at the baptism but he believed that it had taken place at that time. He also stated that the soldiers and Cortés, who were residing in the palace, were more interested in seeking the treasure of Moteczoma (a pious cleric among them) than in converting Moteczoma to the Faith.

My reasons for believing the latter rather than the former are based upon the description given to me by the friar who had been a conqueror. He told me of the frantic search that was made for the secret treasure chambers of Moteczoma. One day the Spaniards' eagerness and hunger led them to a small low door that had been filled in and recently plastered. Having opened it they entered a narrow door and found a spacious chamber in the middle of which stood a pile of gold, jewelry and rich stones, the whole pile as tall as the tallest man. According to the *Chronicle* this treasure did not consist of things acquired by Moteczoma nor were they objects for his own use. This was the treasure that had belonged to all the kings his ancestors, which they had deposited here. When a king died—on that same day—all his wealth and gold, gems, feathers and weapons were placed in that room and guarded as if they were a sacred or divine thing. The king who was about to reign would then begin to acquire wealth so that it could not be said that he used the treasures of his ancestors. So it was that the treasure was guarded as a testimony to the greatness of the city of Mexico.

In this room there were also heaps of fine mantles and clothing for women. Along the walls hung many shields, weapons and insignia of fine workmanship and color. There were piles of golden vessels, of plates and dishes which the kings used to eat from. The most remarkable were four large plates in the form of platters, all beautifully worked in gold, as big as shields and so filled with dust that it was plain that they had not been used for a long time. There were also golden vessels for drinking chocolate, fashioned to look like real gourds, some of them with feet and others without. In the corners of the chamber lay uncut precious stones. In sum, this chamber contained the most amazing wealth ever seen, and the bewildered Spaniards ran to Cortés to show him the golden platters.

The captain entered the room and, after seeing the beauty and richness of the objects, and realizing that they had now gained what they so desired, he ordered that under pain of death no one dare enter the room again. He commanded that the chamber be closed and that guards be placed before it in the name of His Majesty, as here was the best part of the treasure from which the royal fifth was to be taken. And so guards were placed and the door sealed.

But the Spaniards, still possessed of that unsatisfied hunger, did not leave a corner or chamber unsearched or undisturbed. In this way they found a secret apartment where the women of Moteczoma were kept, together with their ladies and duennas. These women had been placed in hidden chambers out of fear of the Spaniards. Others say, however, that these were no other than the cloistered maidens of the temple who lived like nuns, fulfilling their vows under the orders of the duennas who were like abbesses. They had been concealed in that house in order not to be mistreated and violated by the Spaniards who were already giving signs of incontinence.

I have heard it said, though I do not find it in this *Chronicle*, that Moteczoma and the other rulers offered to give an enormous amount of wealth to Cortés if he would return to his own country—enough gold to sink a ship.

But the good Don Hernando Cortés, like a true Christian, was only interested in saving souls! He and his men scorned everything but the extolling of the faith of Christ and the conversion of these blind and idolatrous people! This may be said about the conquerors, that "that which has been won honestly is often lost, and that which has been gained wickedly is also lost, together with its possessor."

And so it is that I have seen the conquerors become wretches, their children dying of hunger and their wealth possessed by others. In order to prove this I wish to refer to a familiar sight in these unfortunate times: the sons of the conquerors as so poor that they are almost driven from door to door begging for food. The secret of all these things is known only to God.

CHAPTER LXXV WHICH TREATS OF HOW CAPTAIN PANFILO
DE NARVAEZ ARRIVED AT THE PORT OF VERACRUZ AND HOW CORTES
CAPTURED HIM AND SENT HIM AWAY.
WITH A DESCRIPTION OF HOW CORTES RETURNED TO MEXICO WITH
HIS MEN AND HOW A REBELLION BROKE OUT AMONG
THE NATIVES AGAINST THE SPANIARDS

We have already seen how the Spaniards discovered the great treasure of Mexico and how they entered the secret, hidden chambers of the maidens who served the gods. Even though the *Chronicle* does not speak of this I do not believe that the virtue of our Spaniards was so great that they insisted that these women persevere in their chastity, modesty and seclusion. If they were the women of Moteczoma, it cannot be believed that they remained faithful to a prince who was now a prisoner in fetters.

The Spaniards at this time were living comfortably, eating and drinking without worry, when Cortés was suddenly notified that Pánfilo de Narváez had landed in Veracruz, and had established his headquarters in the city of Cempoala with his men and artillery. He had entrenched himself there and was preparing to take Cortés prisoner because the latter had left Cuba without permission, not awaiting the commands of his superior officer.

Although Cortés was disturbed at this news, astute and cunning as he was, he left Don Pedro de Alvarado in command of the soldiers in Mexico and departed toward Cempoala with one hundred men. They walked day and night, wearing disguises, since Cortés was so well known to the Indians. No one recognized him and when Pánfilo finally heard of his coming he was not worried; he had faith in his own valor and in the bold men he had brought with him. Narváez had all his artillery ready, at the doors of the buildings in Cempoala, and his men were on the alert. However, Cortés was so determined to succeed in this enterprise that he did not sleep nor was he careless at any time.

And so it was that when Pánfilo de Narváez thought that his enemy was just leaving the city of Mexico, Cortés had already arrived with his men at the doors of the buildings. When Cortés saw their lack of vigilance he waited until the artillery man left the cannon for a moment. In that instant, ten soldiers jumped upon it and took possession. This was done so swiftly that the men of Narváez were unable to make any use of the cannon. At that same moment Cortés, leading his men, sprang with them into the buildings, sword in hand. Others picked up pikes and halberds which they found lying next to the walls. Immediately they began to strike right and left, hurting and wounding, and when Narváez and his men tried to defend themselves, this commander was hit in the eye with a pike and the eye was torn out of its socket. After this he was taken prisoner.

His soldiers also surrendered and begged for mercy. And so we should not be surprised that the local Indians, with their arms crossed, also pleaded to be spared. Cortés received the enemy in a kindly manner and when the soldiers of Narváez saw his friendliness, they gradually joined his army in the name of His Majesty. Narváez' feet were chained, he was placed in a ship and was sent back to Santiago de Cuba.

Once Narváez had been defeated, Cortés gathered his army and returned to

Mexico, leading one thousand more men than he had brought with him. How true it is that when greed and self-interest enter, friendship and justice depart! In this way the men set out for Mexico with Cortés, but soon there came news that his men in the city of Mexico were in trouble and that the Indians had slain some of them. This was false news, sent by Don Pedro de Alvarado so that he could carry out his own plan, which was a cruel, tyrannical atrocity which was to take place as soon as Cortés returned to Mexico.

It must be noted that the Indians were about to celebrate the solemn feast of Toxcatl during which the idol of Huitzilopochtli was transferred from one place to another. Every day the natives came out to dance in preparation for their feast, and Cortés asked Moteczoma to explain to him the meaning of the dance. He was afraid of a rebellion, and he warned the monarch not to stir up trouble since neither he nor his men wished to harm him. Moteczoma reassured Cortés, saying that a rebellion was not their intention. He added that he was a prisoner and that he and his people had no hostile plans. He begged Cortés to be calm as the dances and songs which he heard meant only that the feast of his god was approaching and that certain rites must be performed before the great day. Cortés then asked him as a favor to order that all the sovereigns and lords of the provinces gather to dance in the courtyard of the temple, together with the most courageous men; he wished to gaze upon the grandeur and nobility of Mexico. But all this was a cunning plan to massacre the Indians.

The mistrust which led to this proposal had been communicated to Cortés by Alvarado who had been instigated in turn by the Tlaxcalans who hated the Aztecs. It is also possible that Alvarado was desirous of making himself ruler of the land even though it be at the cost of the lives of many. I have read much about him and his cruelties. Moteczoma, being naive, did not realize that such treachery was being planned and he called together his chieftains and transmitted Cortés' message to them.[106]

When the day arrived the Aztecs, unsuspecting, came out to worship their idol and to show the grandeur of Mexico.[107] Wearing all their finery they formed a circle of some eight or ten thousand illustrious men. While they were dancing Cortés, instigated by Alvarado, ordered ten soldiers to be placed at each of the four gates of the courtyard so that no one could escape. He commanded ten others to approach those who were beating drums where the most important lords had gathered. The soldiers were told to kill the drummer and after him all those who surrounded him. In this way the preachers of the Gospel of Jesus Christ, or rather, disciples of iniquity, without hesitation attacked the unfortunate Indians who were naked except for a cotton mantle, carrying nothing in their hands but flowers and feathers. All of these were killed, and when the other Aztecs saw this and fled to the gates, they were slain by the guards. Others tried to take refuge in the rooms of the temple, fleeing from those ministers of the devil. As they were unable to do so, all were slain and the courtyard was drenched with the blood of those wretched men. Everywhere were intestines, severed heads, hands and feet. Some men walked around with their entrails hanging out due to knife and lance thrusts. Verily it was a terrible thing to behold! The dreadful screams and lamentations in that patio! And no one there to aid them!

The entire city became frenzied, and the frightful shrieks of the women and children resounded in the mountains and should have made the stones weep. Eight or ten thousand men, the entire nobility of Mexico, torn to pieces in the courtyard of the temple! They had done nothing to deserve this fate, unless they were being punished for having given of their possessions to feed and quench the thirst of the Spaniards.

When the priests saw the cruelty with which their own people were being treated and when they realized that the Spaniards were trying to ascend the steps of the pyramid, they knew that they too were to be massacred and that the idol was to be cast down the steps of the pyramid. They prepared to defend themselves and, on watching the ascent of three or four Spaniards whose names I will not record here, the Aztec priests brought out a large heavy beam and sent it rolling down the steps. But it is said that it stuck on the topmost steps and its flight was arrested. This was held to be a miraculous thing, and so it was, since divine mercy did not wish those who had committed that wicked and cruel massacre to go straight to hell but was desirous of giving them an opportunity to do penance. However, not realizing the mercy of God in liberating them from this great peril, they ascended, killed all the priests and cast the idol of Huitzilopochtli down the steps. Many other cruelties were committed by them, always in the belief that they were serving God.

It is also said that when some of the captains heard the clamor of the women and children and the moaning of the entire city they began to sing the ballad:

> From the Tarpeian Rock
> Nero watched Rome on fire.
> Not even the tears of the women
> His pity did inspire . . .

All of the above things I discovered in certain writings which tell that this was the

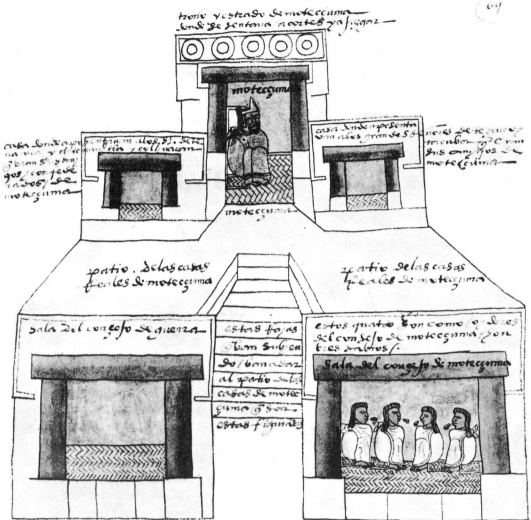

tenio yestrado de moteccuma
onde se sentaua acortes ya su gte ___

moteccuma

casa onde apo senauan los 52 sena
nia vie y el temon tico yel luexom
tecon y y los
gos, con sede
lados se
moteccuma

casa onde apo sentan
con alos grandes sse
nores de te zcuco
tacuba y y eran
dos con dos de
moteccuma

patio. delas casas
peales de moteccuma

patio delas casas
peales de moteccuma

sala del consejo de guerra

estas tojas
tan suben
do / tomadan
al patio dela
casas de mote
cuma q son
estas figuras

estos quatro son como oy dores
del consejo de moteccuma pon
tres alcaldes

sala del consejo de moteccuma

los teontes, en grado de ap clapon
seños alds se presentan p parece
ante los oydores del con
cejo se moteccuma

*The palace of Moteczoma II (1502-1519). From the*
**Codex Mendoza,** *painted in early Colonial times
by Aztec scribes. Courtesy New York Public Library.
Photo Reg Van Cuylenburg.*

most atrocious act ever committed in this land: the end of the flower and nobility of Mexico.

Moteczoma, seeing the treachery and deceit of the Spaniards, wept bitterly and asked the men who guarded him to kill him, as the Aztecs were wicked, vengeful people who might believe that he had advised the Spaniards to commit that deed and who might slay him, his children and wives. The monarch and all those who surrounded him begged to be slain and their wishes were to be granted later.

After this, the Aztecs and the Tlatelolca confederated and raised Cuauhtemoc, "Eagle Which Descends," Lord of Tlatelolco, to the kingship. He was a youth about eighteen years old and a nephew of King Moteczoma. Everyone conspired against the dethroned Moteczoma and killed his children and wives. However, certain people had pity on his relatives, hiding them or removing them from the city in secret. They were taken to towns in the country where they remained concealed until the land was at peace again.

The new king, Cuauhtemoc, had been much grieved over the death of his kinsmen in the massacre, and he gave orders that the city prepare to fight. The palace in which the Spaniards resided was surrounded by many Indians with spears, stones and arrows, and the attack was so fierce that the Spaniards did not dare appear in the doorways or on the roof. The courtyards of the palace were filled with round stones that had been shot by the slings and which destroyed some of the walls. The patios were also filled with spears and arrows, and the bonfires that were lit by the Indians at night were so brilliant that it seemed like day. The Spaniards were not allowed to rest or sleep and they were no longer permitted to obtain food supplies. Their plight was so frightful that they repented their evil deeds.

During all this time Cuauhtemoc placed garrisons around the entire city, as he was determined that the Spaniards must die. He ordered all the neighboring towns, especially those that had not yet seen Cortés and his men, to be ready to be called to arms. Some of these towns were Tenayuca, Cuauhtitlan, Tula, Tulancingo, the province of Xilotepec, Cuauhtlalpan and other Otomi areas. He also called the Matlatzinca nation and people from many towns from the province of Texcoco. Large numbers of men answered the call and if God had not in His mercy seen the tears of those who invoked Him, none of the Spaniards would have escaped with their lives.

Their need for food was so great and their hopes of obtaining any help so slim that they were like men staring into the eyes of death. Among them there were different opinions. Should they go out and die fighting? Escape from the city was impossible! The metropolis was made up of canals with narrow bridges connecting

301

the houses. These ditches were so deep that horses could not traverse them. Risking their lives, the foot soldiers tried several times to leave, but the stones, darts and spears were so furious that they were forced to return rapidly. Any barbed dart that entered the body could not be extracted save by pushing it through the flesh. All those who were wounded were in great danger.

During these days of the affliction of the Spaniards, the new king of Mexico, Cuauhtemoc, realized that he was unable to force them to leave their quarters and that the Aztecs could not enter their hiding place because of the artillery which had been placed at the doors. Therefore he called the old men of the provinces, enchanters and sorcerers, and asked them to frighten the Spaniards by showing them nocturnal visions. In this way the Spaniards were to die of fright.

The wizards came and every night they displayed visions and frightful things. Sometimes the Spaniards would see human heads jumping about in the courtyard. At others they would see a foot still attached to the leg, walking around. Sometimes they beheld corpses rolling on the ground. At other times, they heard screams and moans. At length the tension became unbearable.

Although I have read about these visions in this *Chronicle*, I had already heard of them from the lips of the conqueror who is now a friar, who had been greatly frightened by the mysterious apparitions. So it was that the Spaniards became weary of so much sorrow and affliction, but no one knew what to do since Cortés came to no decisions. He said that he was waiting for the right moment. He encouraged his companions and prayed to Our Lady of the Remedies to alleviate their situation.

Having great faith in the Virgin, Cortés decided to make Moteczoma appear in public and with his own lips command his people to be calm and cease their attacks. One day while the Aztecs were attacking fiercely, almost demolishing the house with stones, Cortés and one of his captains, (one covered with a leather shield and the other with a steel one) took Moteczoma to the flat roof of a housetop. Protecting him, they led the monarch to the edge of the roof, where the king made signs with his hands that the people stop yelling since he wished to speak to them. There was silence and the assault upon the house ceased. The two shields that covered him were removed and in a loud voice he begged the people to stop attacking the Spaniards.

The Aztec captains who stood closest to him began to insult him with ugly words, telling him that he was the mistress of the Spaniards and that since he had planned the massacre of the great chieftains and brave lords, the Aztecs no longer recognized him as king. He, his children and wives, his whole lineage, were to be killed and erased from the face of the earth! With them would die the wicked

Spaniards who had perpetrated such evil upon them! Having said these things, and before Moteczoma could be protected by the shields, one of the Aztecs threw a stone which struck Moteczoma high on the forehead. Although he was wounded it was only a glancing blow which did little harm. Others say that he was injured by an arrow in one foot, but the *Chronicle* does not mention the latter. Moteczoma, wounded, was then carried down into the palace.

The valorous young Cuauhtemoc appeared every day to fight and to encourage his people. Whenever a Tlaxcalan was captured by them he was not spared, and the soldiers of Tlaxcala were in the same difficulties as the Spaniards and were later to suffer greatly, few of them ever returning to Tlaxcala.

# LXXVI WHICH TREATS OF HOW DON HERNANDO CORTES FLED FROM HIS QUARTERS AND HOW THE INDIANS NOTICED HIS DEPARTURE. WITH A DESCRIPTION OF HOW MANY SPANIARDS AND INDIANS WERE KILLED IN THAT FLIGHT

We have already seen the difficulties in which the Aztecs placed Cortés and the other Spaniards. The Captain struggled constantly to find a way of escaping and freeing his companions from the plight they were in. To die and to be eaten by those who, with such fury, surrounded them seemed now their fate. Every day they were told in oaths that their flesh would be devoured and that not one of them would escape. Many soldiers wept bitterly and complained of Don Pedro de Alvarado who was to be blamed for the cruel massacre of the flower of Mexico. The killing in the temple was attributed solely to Alvarado, and a certain conqueror told me that the slaughter took place while Cortés was in Veracruz. However, I do not believe that Cortés was absent during that time, because immediately after the massacre the Indians rebelled against the Spaniards and surrounded them, and not even a bird could have penetrated the city without being seen—much less Cortés leading the men of Narváez.

One night when Our God had been placated by the prayers of Cortés, a great thunderstorm came out of the skies. Then a windstorm and much hail. The Aztecs were forced to lift the siege and the sentinels' fires went out. All the natives, fleeing from the tempest, returned to their homes. When Cortés saw that this phenomenon had been willed by the great and pious Lord and Our Lady of the Remedies, to whom he had prayed, he ordered that everyone be quiet and that all leave the palace in order and silence, since the Tlaxcalans and other natives would be their guides. On seeing that it was still raining in torrents and that the night was dark, the men began to go forth. Cortés ordered them not to carry any of the treasure or to be greedy in taking gold or jewels that might hinder their flight. He told them to leave all treasures, as they would find them when they returned. He did, however, instruct them to carry all the bread they could as a provision until they had escaped across the boundaries of the Aztec lands.

With this advice Cortés, in the utmost silence, led out his soldiers laden with bread and provisions. A number of men did not carry provisions but loaded themselves and their horses with all the gold they could carry. When they departed from the buildings where they had lodged, loaded with treasure, they were unable to move silently. An Indian man and woman happened to appear on one of the roofs and both of them yelled, "Come, Aztecs! The criminals are escaping! Come forth, the traitors are fleeing!"

When these cries were heard, all the Aztec men of war together with those who had come in from the provinces emerged with terrible cries, frightful enough to trouble the strongest heart. The Spaniards most shaken were those who carried no arms but were loaded with gold. Their panic was such that many of them turned back toward the palace from which they had emerged, where they tried to entrench themselves again. Others, having already passed certain bridges, tried to turn back but found the bridges lifted. The Indians fell upon both groups of men, killing every one of them. On this occasion Cortés lost seven hundred men, all of them cut to pieces mercilessly. The canals were filled with corpses, with horses and dead Indians, together with gold and gems, mantles, feathers, and other wealth that the poor wretches had tried to carry with them.

Leading the six hundred survivors, Cortés managed to pass the last of the bridges swiftly and gain safety. There he organized his followers, natives and Spaniards; the Aztecs were still following them, yelling and shooting stones, arrows and darts. Little by little, but in good order, they retreated as far as a place now called Our Lady of the Remedies. The Spaniards arrived there exhausted, wounded and filled with affliction. Many of them had lost their shoes along the way and they wet the earth with the blood of their feet. Others had lost their hats and their heads were exposed to the sun. Many had been severely wounded by stones and spears.

Cortés was filled with sorrow over the many men he had lost. He almost resolved to go back to save those who might still be alive, but he was told that all had died. However, our *Chronicle* narrates that many of them took refuge in the palace where they held out bravely for a few days although finally, lacking wisdom, advice, and above all their courageous leader, they died at the hands of the Indians. I pray to God that these men were not those who had planned the cruel massacre of the Aztec lords and that He did not blind them in their flight in order to punish them for this atrocious deed.

The *Chronicle* tells us that once the Spaniards had fled from Mexico and those who had remained behind been killed, the Aztecs entered the chambers of King Moteczoma in order to treat him more cruelly than they had dealt with the Spaniards. There they found him dead with a chain about his feet and five dagger wounds in his chest. Near him lay many noblemen and great lords who had been held prisoners with him. All of them had been slain shortly before the Spaniards abandoned the building. This *Chronicle* states all of these things, and certain picture writings verify this. Otherwise it would be difficult to believe. However, I am obliged to record what the authors tell, write, or paint for me. I wish to avoid being blamed for having stated something false which the conquerors had not said or written, since it was generally believed that Moteczoma had been stoned to death. I asked my informants again and I insisted that the Indians had killed him with a stone. But they told me that the wound from a stone had been nothing—the head wound was almost healed—and that in truth he had been found knifed.

This was the tragic end of Moteczoma and of the other rulers and lords who had been captives with him in the palace. In this way the omens and prophecies which he himself had revealed were fulfilled—an amazing thing, only permitted by the Most High. It seems that He wished to inflict a rigorous punishment on Moteczoma for his intolerable tyranny, cruelty, unspeakable and filthy vices in which he lived, more than any man in the history of the world.

Some say that the dead king was given a rich and solemn burial and that the funeral lasted many days, attended by many lords and chieftains. However, the *Chronicle* says that the corpse and all the others were burned and turned to dust, without honors or solemnity of any kind. It adds that in order to make the vengeance more complete his enemies sought out his children and wives in order to kill them. This powerful Angry Lord, this unfortunate king, ruled sixteen and a half years. His death took place the year in which the Spaniards reached this land.

When his successor Cuauhtemoc saw that the siege had not been successful and that only half of the Spaniards had been killed, he rebuked the carelessness of the guards who had withdrawn on the night of the storm. However, in order to prevent the further flight of the Spaniards, he sent messengers to all the neighboring towns asking that they send men to join the Aztecs on the plain of Otompan. There they would cut off the retreat of the surviving Spaniards and kill them as they passed on their way back to Tlaxcala. When this message was heard in the towns of Otompan and Teotihuacan, and in the Otomi settlements in that area, so many Indians appeared upon the plain that they eclipsed the sun.

Cortés, his soldiers and allies believed that, with their departure from the province of Mexico, they were safe. But as they approached the plain of Otompan, the multitude of Indians appeared suddenly, screaming, making faces and furious signs at them and leaping about, shaking their swords and throwing spears and stones. When the Spaniards saw this great throng they almost lost their senses, believing that the end had come. But the valorous Don Hernando rebuked their cowardice and showed once more his spirit that was more than human. He reminded them that he had saved them from past trials and promised that he would do so now. He encouraged his followers with spirited words. All of the Spaniards formed a close-knit group and faced the enemy on all sides, more on the defensive than the offensive since they had been surrounded. It was at this moment that Cortés saw a banner flying on a small hill in the plain and next to it an Aztec captain who, judging by his badges and weapons, was a man of great valor and rank. This newcomer spurred on his soldiers from the hill and in him the Indians found their strength, attacking and greatly harming the Spaniards. Cortés then leaped on a colt that one of his soldiers had brought along. This beast had been barely tamed and was strong and spirited. With a lance in his hand, crying out to Our Lord with invincible faith, Cortés all alone attacked the Indians in what seemed to the men a foolhardy way. He passed through their ranks and reached the place where the Aztec stood with the banner. He struck him with his lance whereupon the Aztec fell dead to the ground. When his followers saw this all dispersed and began to abandon the field. But Cortés attacked them again, indicating to his horsemen that they follow him. A skirmish then took place, and many of those who fled were killed. This great number of Indians consisted of people of the Otomi nation together with others from Tula, Otompan, Cuauhtitlan, Tenayuca and Tlalnepantla. Although King Cuauhtemoc had planned to send reinforcements, when news came of the disaster at Otompan, the natives disbanded.

Cuauhtemoc was crowned in Mexico with solemn rites and the inhabitants of the city swore allegiance to him as king. However, this was not done with the rejoicing and solemnity which had been usual in the past, for the city of Mexico was filled with sorrow, the land was troubled and divided against itself. Some wished to make peace with the Spaniards while others wanted war. Some wished to destroy the strangers, and were preparing their warlike equipment and building walls and dikes. But others remained passive, asking only for peace, quiet, and the preservation of their lives and possessions.

For a long time the Spaniards remained in Tlaxcala, healing their wounds,

CAP.º 76.

making plans and seeking a way to return to Mexico as conquerors. This lasted for more than one year, and meanwhile more ships filled with Spaniards arrived in Veracruz. During this time Cuauhtemoc tried to gain the support of the Aztecs who hated the Spaniards. He devoted himself to making the canals deeper, building wide and tall dikes and inciting the natives against the invaders. His activity was so furious that he went to the extreme of asking the rulers of Tlaxcala to forget their friendship with the Spaniards and to rebel against them in order to expel them from the land. He was so insistent that one of the lords of Tlaxcala became persuaded and instigated the others to join in this effort. However, Cortés discovered the plot and denounced them all, whereupon the three other Tlaxcalan rulers delivered the traitor to the Spanish captain. The latter put him in prison and, I believe, finally had him executed.

When Cuauhtemoc realized that he was unable to convince the Tlaxcalans to slaughter the Spaniards, he sent threats telling what he would do to them if he were victorious. He also attempted to attract the people of Chalco, Xochimilco, Tacuba and Texcoco, but Cortés also was busy making allies among the nations. He sent messages to these cities, saying that he had come to liberate them from the tyranny of the city of Mexico and the oppression in which they had lived. When he added that their friendship with the Aztecs had not been of their own choice but had been forced upon them, they decided to become friends and not enemies of the Spaniards. All believed that they would be given their freedom and liberated from the servitude of Mexico.

At this time Cuauhtemoc learned that the Spanish forces were multiplying and that Cortés, preparing to return to Mexico, was looking for help. The news also came that the Texcocans had declared themselves allies of the Spaniards and that Chalco, Xochimilco and Tacuba had done likewise. Therefore the Aztec king filled the city with soldiery, all brave men. He explained to them that Chalco and the other cities were now enemies and that all they could do now was to triumph or die.

Cuauhtemoc sent for help to other cities and began to bring more warriors to Mexico. These men came from the province of Cuauhtlalpan, and from towns in the area af Cuauhtitlan, which alone remained antagonistic to the Spaniards. Other men belonged to the Tlalhuica people of the hot country and they came from the towns of Yacapichtlan, Huaxtepec, Yauhtepec, Tepoztlan, Cuernavaca, Tlayacapan and Totolapan. All of these were inimical to the Spaniards, though Cortés later subjected them one by one. They did not yield to the Spanish forces until Cortés entered their country killing and destroying. Then they abandoned their homes and fled into the hills.

# LXXVII

Cuauhtemoc now saw that the Spaniards were determined to return to Mexico. The vigilant ruler discovered this through his spies and messengers. While he instigated the other nations and asked for their aid, he and his people also offered sacrifice and prayers to the gods. They begged the gods to succor them and give them victory against the Spaniards and their other enemies. But it was too late; even the gods were now silent. It was the general opinion that the gods had become mute or had died since the new divinities had taken away their strength. Although the Aztecs wept bitterly this does not mean that they had given up their intentions of defending their city to the last moment.

This is an example of the Indian way. Once an Indian decides to achieve something and begins to look with scorn upon life, he loses all fear and does not give up until he accomplishes what he desires. It would be easy to prove my assertion, because in our own courts we deal with such cases every day. If a town has a lawsuit against another, or a small town against its capital, or a peasant against his master, each will fight until death or until he has accomplished what he wants. It does not matter if the objective is unjust or unreasonable. The Indian is headstrong and stubborn. When there is trouble he does not respect his father, brother, relative or friend; when he is interested in carrying out his will he is not swayed by reason.

So it was that Cuauhtemoc, anxious to reign and to show his courage, decided to defend his city until death. He was unwilling to listen to the flattering messages of Cortés who asked him to surrender in the name of God and His Majesty, begging him not to be the cause of the destruction and death which would follow his resistance.

When Cortés realized that his pleas went unheeded, he decided to journey to Texcoco to build the ships that were to cover the distance from Texcoco to Mexico. This decision was a wise one, as I believe that it was the principal cause of his subsequent conquest of Mexico which was surrounded by water, canals and great pools, in which horses were of no use. In this way Cortés left Tlaxcala followed by his men and by large numbers of Tlaxcalans, Huexotzinca and Cholulans, all of them enemies of the Aztecs. Along with them came the Texcocans, now friends of the Spaniards, bringing the cargo and wood with which the brigs were to be

310

built. Between the carriers of wood and equipment there were more than ten thousand natives.

Cortés arrived first at a place that is now called Tezmelucan, near the White Mountain and not far from the boundary of Chalco. The Chalca received him again with honor, offering him jewels, mantles, fine feathers and foodstuffs. They also made a pact with him, promising to aid him in the assault on Mexico. The Spanish captain thanked them and told them that they would be recompensed. He stated that he was on his way to Texcoco to build the ships and that he would be grateful if they sent him men to carve the wood. They promised to furnish him with carpenters and this they did. Cortés then departed in the direction of Texcoco where he was well received, where he rested and had time to admire that remarkable and populous city with all its fine and beautifully fashioned buildings, palaces, great pyramids and temples, pleasure gardens with their pools and marvelous groves. All of these had belonged to previous monarchs of Texcoco, to rulers who delighted in them.

In Texcoco Cortés was lodged and served with great reverence, especially by Ixtlilxochitl, son of Nezahualpilli, brother to King Coanacoch. Ixtlilxochitl pleased Cortés to such an extent that the Spaniards took a strong liking to him, kept him near them and honored him in a way befitting a son of the great Nezahualpilli and brother of one of the greatest monarchs of Texcoco. Cortés was aided by Ixtlilxochitl in the conquest of Mexico, during which time the Texcocan sovereign made use of a gilded sword and a shield which the Spanish leader had given him. With these the native monarch performed great deeds, so daring that on hearing the name "Ixtlilxochitl" the Aztecs fled as would the devil on hearing the name of Christ. Later, when Cortés had seen his remarkable feats and the enormous aid he had given in the conquest, he made this prince lord of Texcoco after the death of his brother.

Cortés lingered in Texcoco until the brigs of war were completed. During this time a number of Spaniards arrived in Veracruz and this was a great satisfaction to him because he needed assistance. When the ships had been finished by Martín López, Cortés prepared to attack Mexico. He divided his men into four companies: the first was to be led by himself and it was to attack by way of Coyoacan; the second was to be commanded by Don Pedro de Alvarado and was to proceed by the road that went through Our Lady of the Remedies, which is the causeway to Tacuba; the third was to travel by way of the road of Our Lady of Guadalupe; and the fourth company was to go aboard the brigs. In this order the march toward Mexico began. The allies were also divided into four companies which included men from Tlaxcala, Huexotzinco, Cholula, Texcoco, Chalco, Xochimilco and Tacuba. All of

311

these soldiers were well equipped and they marched in good order. They were to fight against those who had subjected them and whose vassals they had been, and they knew that if the enterprise failed their destiny would be a perpetual misery.

Cuauhtemoc, sovereign of Mexico, on seeing that the entire country was on its way to annihilate him and that the moment had come in which his spirit and his heart would be more useful than his hands to defend himself, spoke to his people.

"O courageous Aztecs, you have seen how all our vassals have rebelled against us! Our enemies used to be Tlaxcala, Cholula, and Huexotzinco, but now we must contend with Texcoco, Chalco, Xochimilco, and Tacuba. All the latter have abandoned us and have gone to join the Spaniards. I charge you now to remember the bold hearts and spirits of the Aztec Chichimecs, our ancestors who, though they were small in number, dared to enter this land. They appeared in the midst of many millions of natives and with their powerful arms conquered this great New World and all its nations. Not a distant coast or province was neglected by them; all fell into their hands! They risked their lives in order to glorify our names! That is why the Aztec name has reached the renown and excellence that it now conveys and is feared throughout the world. Therefore, O valorous Aztecs, do not be dismayed, do not be cowardly. Strengthen your chests and hearts in order to succeed in the most important enterprise that has ever been presented to you. Behold, if you do not succeed, you, your wives, and children, will become slaves forever. And your possessions will be stripped from you! Have pity on the aged, on the children and orphans! If you do not do so they will be left unprotected and in the hands of your enemies, to be torn to pieces or cast into slavery. Do not scorn me because of my extreme youth but consider that what I am telling you is the truth. It is your duty to defend your city and your homeland, and I promise you that I will not yield until I give back its freedom or die."

With great zeal all promised to do likewise, and the valorous youth, in his invincible determination to die rather than be enslaved, filled the city with warriors. However, he forgot to provide foodstuffs in order to maintain the men and, as the Spaniards and his other enemies closed all the entrances, by water or land, food was very soon lacking. So it was that more people died of hunger than by the sword. I have heard it said that a handful of golden jewels, of precious stones, was exchanged for a handful of maize grains. Certain noblemen from nearby provinces managed to enter the city secretly in order to exchange maize for the jewels of Mexico. Men from Cuitlahuac, Colhuacan, Mizquic, and the city of Xochimilco became rich in gold, jewels, stones and feathers during the famine.

In this way the greatest enemy of the Aztecs was hunger. Some of the soldiers were forced to flee from Mexico and return to their lands, leaving King Cuauhtemoc alone with the Aztecs. The latter were few, and feeble from starvation. It is to be noted that these Indian people become thinner than any other people on earth when they lack victuals.

Cortés and his captains were now at the gates of Mexico, each one having come along the path that had been agreed upon. It was then that the Aztecs emerged to defend their city boldly. The dikes were covered with armed men and the canals with warriors in canoes, all awaiting the Spaniards without showing the slightest sign of cowardice. King Cuauhtemoc had divided his people into four parts so that they might meet the Spaniards along the causeways and resist their entrance. The king, in his small canoe, armed with sword and shield, flew from one place to another to watch the activities of his men.

The Spaniards began to attack the city by tearing down the dikes that had been built next to the canals. They gained land by filling in the water with earth, blocks of mud and stones, together with adobe bricks from the houses they demolished. But the diligence and hard work of the Aztecs were marvelous: as soon as a canal was filled in by the Spaniards to be used as a bridge for the horses, they opened it again. Each morning the canals would be found free of rubble, deeper than ever, and all the solid land which the Spaniards had gained the day before would be lost.

Now it is time to tell how the Aztecs, surrounded and harassed by a multitude of men, decided to build a trap for the Spaniards. And the main reason for the building of this trap was to obtain an outlet through which they could seek help and foodstuffs. They realized that the best place to set it would be on the Tacuba causeway, since on that side there were people who would help them. There they placed a false bridge so that when the Spaniards and the other enemies passed the bridge would collapse and all would be slaughtered. This false bridge was constructed in the place where the shrine and hospital of San Hipólito now stand. There was a wide and navigable canal at that place which the Spaniards had filled in. That night the Aztecs opened it again, made it as deep as possible and built over it a false bridge made of wooden beams. It was set up in such a way that the Spaniards would think that it had been unchanged since they had left the day before. The Aztecs prepared an ambush of numerous men, some in canoes and others among the rushes and reeds. All were well equipped with swords, shields and spears, and many of them carried the swords and lances of the Spaniards who had been killed. Near this false pass many warriors gathered, calling to the Spaniards and provoking them to attack. They made faces at them, yelling offensive words and mocking them with gestures and motions of their bodies.

313    Cortés ordered that no one move or attack until the trumpet was sounded. But Don Pedro de Alvarado, whose heart rebelled against the contempt and scorn that

the Indians were showing him, did not wait for the signal. He immediately gave orders that his Spaniards and Tlaxcalans attack the bridge. The Aztecs pretended to flee and the Spaniards followed them, forty foot soldiers, all of them spirited youths, together with a few horsemen and their captain Alvarado and many Indians. When the bridge was laden with men and horses, the Aztecs who lay in ambush pulled the false bridge from their canoes and the entire framework collapsed into the water, together with the Spaniards and Indians who stood upon it. Yelling, "Mexico, Mexico! Fight, valiant Aztecs!" the natives fell upon the invaders, and those who tried to return across the bridge, found that it had fallen into the water. A multitude of Aztecs were attacking and they spared no lives. All were in canoes and none of the Spaniards were able to escape. They had fallen into the canal and therefore were taken prisoners. Don Pedro de Alvarado was able to escape by sinking the point of his lance into the bodies of the dead who lay in the water and leaping to the other side of the ditch. This is what is called the famous "Leap of Alvarado."

The forty Spaniards who were taken were immediately stripped and led up the steps of the great pyramid in front of the entire Spanish army. No one could aid them in any way and they were sacrificed there. Their chests were opened, their hearts torn out and offered to the idols, and finally their bodies were rolled down the steps of the temple. The Spaniards who witnessed this sacrifice wept aloud and screamed to God that He take pity on their companions, but this did not happen.

When Cortés heard the cries and yelling he hurried to the place where the bridge had been, and he did this risking his life. The Indians who moved about in their canoes were killing Spaniards right and left with great fury while Cortés continued in his efforts to aid a wounded soldier who was still defending himself in the water. Two Aztec chieftains came up to Cortés at this point and the latter turned to face them. However, one of them sprang at him from behind and held him by the back, while the other tried to wound him from the front. Both the chieftains struggled with him, trying to drag him into deeper waters. It was at this moment that a Biscayan page of Cortés rushed up with his sword drawn and, striking a blow at the Indian who held the Captain in his arms, cut off his arm at one blow. When the other Aztec saw himself attacked, he let go of Don Hernando and the latter managed to escape. However the page also attacked the native warrior and they tore him to pieces, Cortés not being able to save him.

When the Spanish captain beheld this bloody and dangerous skirmish he gave orders that his men retreat, while the Indians remained triumphant. Cortés felt like hanging or decapitating Don Pedro de Alvarado because of his rash attack without waiting for the signal. Thus ended the battle, and both Spaniards and

314

Indians withdrew. The Indians, however, managed to keep several Spaniards as prisoners. Among them was a young gentlemen who, according to what the conquerors have told me, was a handsome Sevillian who always fought with his crossbow in his hands. The next day the Aztecs brought him out with their warriors, still carrying his crossbow, now shooting arrows at the Spaniards. However, he shot them in such a way that every arrow whistled harmlessly through the air, not one of them touching his countrymen. When the Aztecs realized what he was doing they ripped him to bits then and there. Because of him a shrine was later built on the spot by the conquerors, and it was called "The Martyrs," the walls of which are still standing. Whether the martyrdom of this youth was acceptable to God or not, only His Divine Majesty knows! But my own opinion is that it is an evil thing to try to preach the Faith, sword in hand.

I wish to return to my subject, as my topic is the Aztec nation, its great deeds and its tragic end. And I will not tell of the events that occurred during the eighty days that the Spaniards tried to conquer Mexico. However, I will mention two things. The first is that the *Chronicle* states that when Cortés saw that the Aztecs were holding out so long, he begged the Tlaxcalans to bring more fighting men. When they arrived he ordered them to enter the city in order to expel the Aztecs. But, though they fought an entire day, they were unable to enter Mexico. On the second day he ordered the Texcocans to attack but they failed also. On the third day Cortés called the Chalca to him and Marina spoke the following words: "O valorous men of Chalco, you have now seen how neither Tlaxcalans nor Texcocans have been able to displace the Aztecs. I beseech you to take charge of this enterprise today and to do everything in your power so that we may reach the Great Pyramid of Huitzilopochtli and entrench ourselves there. I charge you with these things because I consider you men of bravery and great spirit."

The Chalca were encouraged by her words and, led by Ixtlilxochitl of Texcoco, who carried his gilded sword in his hand, they attacked the Aztecs furiously. In this they were aided by the Spaniards who used their arquebuses, artillery and crossbows. Having filled many spaces where bridges had been, they made an entrance and managed to take the Great Pyramid. It was there that they established themselves, and they also gained the palace that had been forsaken before.

When the Spaniards had occupied the temple they placed guards in order to avoid being surrounded again. Cuauhtemoc now lacked men and strength to defend himself but, enraged over the death of so many of his people, and because his allies had abandoned him, and because of the great famine, he decided not to show weakness. He pretended that he did not lack warriors to fight for him and therefore had all the women of the city take up shields and swords. Early in the morning the women ascended to the flat roofs of the houses where they made signs of scorn to the Spaniards. Leading the allies from Tlatelolco, brave Cuauhtemoc brought his few remaining men to face the enemy.

When Cortés saw the great number of people covering the flat roofs and filling the streets of the city, he was amazed and became afraid that he would not be able to conquer without bringing much harm to his Spaniards and friends. But he urged the Chalca, Texcocans, Tlaxcalans and Tecpanecs of Tacuba to take courage and finish with the enterprise. All the men returned to the combat and at this time they realized that the warriors who stood on the roofs were women. They sent word to Cortés about this, and the men began to ridicule and insult the enemy. However, the men of Tlatelolco did everything in their power to defend themselves and killed many enemy Indians and some Spaniards, among them a lieutenant from whom they snatched the banner, tearing it to pieces in front of the entire army. In another document I read that they destroyed four Spanish flags and killed a captain by the last name of Guzmán and that the Tlatelolca won glory in this battle.

In the end, though, the Spaniards, greatly aided by their allies, vanquished the Aztecs. King Cuauhtemoc boarded a small canoe, covered himself with a mat and was rowed out of the city by a single man. However, he was taken prisoner by some Spaniards who saw him from their brig, and he was brought before Cortés.

When Cortés faced this youth, a man of refinement and of handsome appearance, he said to Marina, the interpreter, "Ask Cuauhtemoc why he permitted the destruction of the city with such loss of lives of his own people and of ours? Many were the times that I begged him for peace!"

The young king answered:

"Tell the captain
That I have done my duty;
I have defended my city, my kingdom,
Just as he would have defended his
Had I attempted to take it from him.
But I have failed! Now that I am his captive,
Let him take this dagger
And kill me with it!"

Putting forth his hand Cuauhtemoc took a dagger that Cortés carried in his belt and placed it in the latter's hands, begging to be slain. Cortés was greatly troubled by these words and though he did not rise from his seat, he spoke soft and consoling words to Cuauhtemoc and made him sit next to him.

The entire city then surrendered to Cortés, and when he took possession of it,

los qnaçen aqui es el signo
era vahufa hobres mas no
pça em punder a    nadie

mes

| dia | seguodo dia uenado | toravo dia anego | quarto dia agua | quinto dia piro | Sesto dia mono | septimo dio escoba |
|---|---|---|---|---|---|---|

*A page from the* Codex Borbonicus, *the "Book of Days."*
*The Spanish text reads: "Those born under this sign*
*would be brave men but they (were not destined)*
*to take a captive." Courtesy New York Public*
*Library. Photo Reg Van Cuylenburg.*

he went to live in the principal palace of Moteczoma which now belongs to the heir of the Spanish captain. He put guards about the city and gave liberty to Cuauhtemoc to go where he wished, telling him to ask for whatever he might desire. Cuauhtemoc asked him to free the men, women and children whom the Spaniards had captured, many of whom had fled from the famine. Cortés then gave orders that, under pain of death, all the Spaniards liberate those who were being held captives. So it was done and all the refugees, men and women, returned to the city and resettled in it. But the dead on that day were over forty thousand men and women who, rather than fall into the hands of the Spaniards, threw themselves and their children into the canals. The stench of the corpses was so great that even though bodies were carried out of the city continually, many were left and the evil smell was unbearable for a long time.

CHAPTER LXXVIII WHICH TREATS OF HOW DON HERNANDO CORTES, MARQUES DEL VALLE, AFTER HAVING CONQUERED MEXICO, LEFT THAT CITY IN GOOD ORDER. WITH A DESCRIPTION OF THE CONQUEST OF OTHER PROVINCES AND THE DEATH OF CUAUHTEMOC

The valorous Cortés conquered Mexico on the feast of Saint Hippolytus, three days before the Assumption of the Most Blessed Virgin, Our Lady. It is said that the latter appeared during the conquest in order to aid the Spaniards. It is also told that the glorious Patron of Spain, Saint James, appeared just as his image appeared in the church of Tlatelolco. The Indians claim that they saw him in the greatest of the battles when the Spaniards were losing and their banners had been taken from them and torn, to their great shame. At that moment the glorious Saint James appeared, frightening away the Indians and favoring the Spaniards through divine permission.

Once Mexico had been taken in the name of His Majesty, Cortés ordered that the pyramid be demolished, the idols broken, the city razed and the canals filled in. He divided the land into lots, having ordered the people of Chalco, Texcoco, Xochimilco and Tacuba to bring stakes, stone, earth, and other materials to fill in the lagoons and pools that existed. He also built houses and laid out the streets to the best of his knowledge. He considered it safer to found a city where Mexico had been—within the lake instead of outside of it—as the strength of the country was concentrated in the capital and all the inhabitants were ruled from there. He was afraid that if the site of the city were to be changed there might be a rebellion.

While the new city was being planned and Cortés rested, the Spaniards began to seek the treasure that had been found in the secret chamber. The Tlaxcalans, by command of their master, had concealed it in a deep pool which the Aztecs feared due to a certain religious superstition. It was believed that this spring was the place discovered by their ancestors, where the red and the blue waters flowed, where lived the white fish, the white frogs and the white snakes. This pool was never seen by the Spaniards nor has anyone ever discovered its exact location. In order to find it Cortés ordered that many Indians be hunted down by dogs, others hanged and yet others burned alive so that the secret might be revealed. However, it never came to light nor has it been discovered in our times. In fact, it will never be discovered, as those who might have known about it are no longer alive. If this secret is in the possession of anyone it would belong to the rulers of Tlatelolco, to whom it was entrusted. For this treasure the conquerors wept more tears than for the wicked deeds they had committed. They also searched in the canals where many Spaniards laden with gold had lost their lives. But as the Indians had cleaned out and deepened the canals in order to defend their city, all the gold had been removed. It is also true that the Spaniards who had been most heavily burdened with gold had fled back to their palace to entrench themselves. One curious case tells of a horseman who in his flight carried a coffer of jewels and gold on his saddle. He embraced this box with more fervor and desire than he would have embraced the Cross of Christ. In spite of the danger that this man was in, he began to cry when he saw the Indians attack. Everyone yelled to him to drop the coffer and take hold of his sword to defend himself but he refused to let go of the gold. He placed it under his arm while, with the other, he held the sword. With this impediment he could not fight and, still embracing his treasure, he was killed by the Indians. It may be said that greed was the cause of his perdition.

All the gold was picked up by the Indians, concealed and divided among themselves. And it reminds one of the proverb: "In a troubled river the fisherman catches many fish."

After the city had been leveled, after the Spaniards had begun to build their homes in it, the most Christian Don Hernando, Marqués del Valle, saw to it that the natives were instructed in the things of the Faith. He pointed out the site where the church was to be built, he set up crosses and images and ordered that the Indians be taught the doctrines of our Holy Catholic Faith. All of this had been started by a cleric whom Cortés brought with him, though it is my opinion that

320

this man should have been suspended or excommunicated since I have heard that he was more eager to wash his hands in the blood of innocents than Pilate to wash his hands on the death of Christ.

But let us forget my moralizing. In order to convert the natives, a ship was sent to Spain to inform his Catholic Majesty, the Emperor Charles V, then king of Spain, that this land had been conquered in his most serene name. I have heard a trustworthy person say, however, that some advised Cortés not to send any messages to Spain, but to crown himself king of the New World. These persons promised to pay allegiance to him and obey him, but like a true vassal of His Majesty he refused to commit such an act against his oath of obedience.

Cortés also asked that friars be sent to administer the sacraments, and the latter were chosen carefully and dispatched to Mexico. So it was that twelve friars of the order of the glorious Saint Francis arrived in this land three years after the conquest. The twelve gained many converts because of their religious and holy lives, like the original apostles whom they imitated in everything. They preached and baptized in all the provinces with apostolic zeal, filled with spirit and divine fervor. Each barefooted friar went off on foot to a different region and each was such a perfect example of virtue that in this way they attracted the natives. The latter were much moved by the words, labors and abnegation which the friars showed.

Two years after these holy monks had come, men from the order of Our Glorious Father Saint Dominic also arrived, and they were no less holy or zealous in promoting the honor of God and gaining souls. These friars came from the Island of Santo Domingo which is also called Hispaniola. They took charge of the work of conversion and obtained privileges and exemptions in order to protect the natives. They fought the great cruelty and inhumanity of the Spaniards, by whom a great many evil deeds had been done.

Before the Dominicans arrived, Cortés had already gone forth to conquer other provinces, especially those which we now call Marquesado, the hot country. This land defended itself for many days, its ruler being the lord of Yacapichtlan, who was a son or grandson of the great Tlacaelel, of whom I have spoken many times and whose great deeds I have described. The lords of Yacapichtlan are of his lineage. The inhabitants of this land fled to the rocky cliffs of Tlayacapan, Totolapan and Tepoztlan but when the artillery began to be active and the natives fell from the cliffs, the Indians disbanded and fled into the hills. As Cortés conquered these towns he divided them and their people among the conquerors in the name of His Majesty.

Here is a story I was told about a woman who accompanied the army of Cortés

321

and who later was married to Martín Partidor. As Cortés was leaving Huaxtepec after having subdued the entire hot country he passed through Ocuituco where he was received in peace. After this he ascended to a town called Tetela where the Indians were lined up in order to fight, having much confidence in the rugged nature of the place. Other Indians from Hueyapan, which faced the other town across a deep ravine, also appeared in a warlike fashion. When Cortés saw these forces he ordered his men to prepare themselves. But this Spanish woman, advised by certain soldiers, mounted a horse, took a lance and a leather shield and asked the Spanish captain for permission to attack the Indians and demonstrate her personal valor. Cortés granted her this, whereupon she came forth and, spurring on the horse, she attacked the enemy, yelling, "Saint James, and attack them!" The infantry then followed her and when the Indians saw them coming, some fled and others fell into the ravine. The town was taken and all the chieftains with their hands crossed came to surrender to Cortés. When the latter realized the bravery of the woman, he granted her the two towns of Tetela and Hueyapan in the name of His Majesty.

In this way the Spaniards went from conquest to conquest, subjecting the land. After each city was taken a Spaniard asked Cortés to grant it to him, and he received it as an *encomienda*.[108] So it was that *iuste vel iniuste*, justly or unjustly, men, women and children were taken, branded on their faces and sold as slaves for the mines or as servants. In those times they even loaded ships with slaves to be carried away from New Spain. I myself met some of them in the home of my relatives, and they were marked in the face with the name of the man who had sold them. These slaves had not come from nearby towns but were brought from more than ten leagues away from Mexico. Most of them were brought to the city from the province of Guatemala and from the coasts distant to Mexico. And even though I did not actually see slaves branded with hot irons on the face, just like horses in a corral, I did see these men and women liberated through the intercession of the monks in the time of the most Christian Viceroy Don Antonio de Mendoza.[109]

At this time Cortés journeyed to the land that is called Las Hibueras taking with him many chieftains from Mexico, Texcoco, Tacuba, Xochimilco and Chalco, and among the chiefs went the valorous king of Mexico, Cuauhtemoc. He was taken along as it was feared that he might cause trouble if he remained in Mexico, which city had been left unprotected by the Spaniards. It seems that after a few days' journey he was accused of rebelling against the Spaniards and of trying to assassinate them. Several witnesses appeared to denounce him and Cortés had the Aztec ruler hanged. In this way perished the great Cuauhtemoc, who had ruled over

322

Mexico three or four years. That he might not depart this world alone, the other chieftains whom Cortés had brought along were executed also. Some died a natural death, others were hanged or run down by hounds and still others died in different ways. Some Spaniards who attempted to kill Cortés and steal his ship were also hanged.

When Cortés returned from this campaign the Christian religion began to grow and the Indians took to it with love and willingness. After the monks had preached to them they began to abandon their idols. They broke them, mocked them, stepped on them and demolished the pyramids upon which they had worshipped. Turning to God, they accepted the true faith in One Deity. With great fervor they begged to be baptized, and it was an amazing thing to see the millions who came to be baptized and to give up the blindness in which they had lived.

Twelve years after the conquest of New Spain the fathers of the order of Saint Augustine arrived and took up the work of conversion with no less devotion. With their lives and example they began to convert these poor nations. The Augustinians dispersed in all directions and, like the apostles of the two previous orders, they brought forth great fruit in this vineyard of God. In order to present a good example before the Indians, the most Christian Don Hernando Cortés would kneel and kiss the hands of any friar he happened to meet, and when Don Antonio de Mendoza, the viceroy, ruled he treated the monks with the same reverence.

But let us return to our purpose and speak again of the Indians, who have been the subject of my book. After the country had been conquered a plague of smallpox broke out. This had been brought by a Negro who had come with the Spaniards. A multitude of Indians died from this disease since there were no doctors and the illness was new to them. So it was that thousands died, attributing the pestilence to the Spaniards who had brought it.

From the period of the plague to the unhappy present, this most fertile and rich land together with its capital, Mexico, has suffered many calamities and has declined with the loss of its grandeur and excellence and the great men who once inhabited it.

I will conclude this work by honoring and glorifying Our God and Lord and His Blessed Mother, the Sovereign Virgin Mary, subjecting the book to the correction of the Holy Catholic Church, Our Mother, whose son I am, and under whose protection I promise to live and die like a true and faithful Christian.

This work was finished in the year 1581.

NOTES

1. The concepts which Durán expresses on the Hebrew origins of the natives of the Americas are by no means original. The feeling that the American Indian was the result of a long migration from the Near East was a favorite among chroniclers from the time of Columbus. Belief in the ten lost tribes of Israel, based on vague texts in *Genesis*, persisted until the nineteenth century, during which its chief exponent was Lord Kingsborough.

   Other theories, not based on modern scientific discoveries, have also attributed the origin of the Indians to the lost continent of Mu, to transpacific migrations, to Atlantis, etc. Today most anthropologists believe that the natives Columbus found in the New World were the descendants of nomadic tribes that crossed from Siberia via Behring Straits to this continent some thirty or forty thousand years ago.

2. Mexico and Guatemala, areas of high culture in pre-Columbian times, were the lands of written books. No other area in the New World shares this distinction. In Middle America regular books were *written*. Though executed in a type of hieroglyphic writing, totally unknown in the Old World, they fulfilled the needs of the scholar and bookkeeper. Ancient Mexican books, generally written on fine deerskin or bark paper, assumed the form of folded screens. This type of hieroglyphic writing, not yet studied exhaustively, had begun to develop several hundred years before the Christian era, the best-known sites being La Venta, Tabasco, and Monte Albán, Oaxaca. Durán, our chronicler, undoubtedly had at his disposal a number of hieroglyphic writings which are no longer extant. Many Aztec books were destroyed during the conquest by the Spaniards and their native allies. Others were later burned by the Spanish missionaries who feared that the ancient books might keep the native religion alive. Still others disappeared during centuries of neglect and during the revolutions and vandalism of the nineteenth century. Sixteen authentic pre-Columbian codices are now known to survive. All of them are in Europe.

3. Durán's interpretation of a great episode in ancient history is based on the vigorous personality of Quetzalcoatl, a Toltec religious leader. References to this personage, although often confusing, abound in the chronicles which describe the earliest Mexican historical period. Quetzalcoatl's other names are Ce Acatl, "One Reed," the date of his birth; Topiltzin, "Our Lord." As Quetzalcoatl he was the "Feathered Serpent," high priest of the cult of this god, originally a deity of flowing water but later, in Aztec times, regarded as God of the Wind, and called Ehecatl. The worship of the Feathered Serpent had existed since the Teotihuacan period (around the beginning of the Christian era) and later became attached to the divine Quetzalcoatl of the Aztecs hundreds of years later. The name Quetzalcoatl has also been interpreted to mean "Precious Serpent" or "Precious Twin."

   According to an historical reconstruction by Jimenez Moreno, the historical Quetzalcoatl was the son of Mixcoatl, ruler of the nomadic Toltec-Chichimecs, and of Chimalman, "Shield-Hand," a woman of the Valley of Cuernavaca. When Mixcoatl invaded this region, he saw Chimalman and shot at her, but she lifted her hand and turned the arrow aside. Amazed by this feat, Mixcoatl left his weapons and took Chimalman as wife. Soon afterwards the Toltec chieftain was murdered by a usurper to the throne, and Quetzalcoatl's mother died in childbirth. The boy was brought up by his maternal grand-parents in Tepoztlan, near Cuernavaca, where the cult of the Feathered Serpent already existed. When the youth became a man he was made high priest of the cult and therefore adopted the name of the god Quetzalcoatl. One of his first acts was to disinter the re-mains of his father and bury them on a hill near Colhuacan in the Valley of Mexico, deifying Mixcoatl. Next, Quetzalcoatl killed his father's assassin. Soon afterwards the hero founded the city of Tula, north of the Valley of Mexico, and led his people there from Colhuacan. Quetzalcoatl's cult prohibited human sacrifice which was a common practice among the worshippers of Tezcatlipoca, "Smoking Mirror," originally god of the Toltecs. Due to the clash between the followers of Quetzalcoatl and those of Tezcatlipoca, the former was forced to abandon Tula around the year 1000 A.D.

The following text is based in great part upon Garibay's translation of the original Nahuatl of two basic sources, recorded by sixteenth century Aztecs who had learned the Spanish alphabet. The reader will find Dr. Garibay's reconstruction in *Historia de la Literatura Náhuatl*.

"Quetzalcoatl reigned in Tula. Everywhere were abundance and happiness. Pumpkins were so large that a man could hardly embrace them with his arms. The ears of maize were wonderfully long, like the grinder of a *metate*. Corn was to be found everywhere scattered on the ground as if it were worthless. Ears of corn that were not perfect were used to light the fires. Cotton grew in colors: red, yellow, pink, purple, green, light green, reddish yellow, and spotted like a jaguar. All these colors it had by nature; it came out of the earth that way; it grew that way; no one had to dye it.

"Also there were birds of precious feathers: turquoise colored, shining green, yellow, their breasts the color of flame—precious birds of all colors, singing wondrously. And there grew the finest chocolate everywhere. The Toltecs possessed so many precious stones and gold that they did not know what to do with them. All the inhabitants of Tula were rich and happy; they never knew poverty or sorrow; nothing was ever lacking in their homes.

"And there in Tula reigned Quetzalcoatl. There stood his house of jade, his house of fine gold, his house of red sea shells, his house of white sea shells, his house of fine wood, his house of blue turquoise, his house, all covered with precious feathers. This feathered house was his house of fasting, of penance and of prayer. At midnight he would go down to the river to take his ritual bath. At times he would go to the summit of the moun-tain of Xicocotl to prepare his penitential thorns of precious stones. There he would sacri-fice snakes, birds, and butterflies.

"Quetzalcoatl would pray to the heavens; he would invoke the gods. He would cry out to the Omeyocan, 'Place of Duality,' which is above the Nine Heavens. He would pray to the divinities who dwell there.

"During his life Quetzalcoatl never showed himself to the people. He lived inside his

dark and well-guarded chambers. His servants attended him and kept the place well protected. His room was the innermost, and in the others slept his servants on mats of
precious stones, soft feathers, and silver. There dwelt Quetzalcoatl in his abode of fasting.

"Repeatedly the evil spirits tried to induce him to offer human sacrifice, slaying men.
But Quetzalcoatl never wished to do so since he loved his vassals, the Toltecs. His only
sacrifice was that of snakes, birds, and butterflies. It is said that because of this he angered
the demons and they began to persecute him. When he refused to give them what they
wanted they decided to force him to flee from Tula. When Quetzalcoatl refused to pay the
divine debt with human beings, the wizards gathered and plotted against him. Their
names are these: Tezcatlipoca, "Smoking Mirror," Ihuimecatl, "String of Fine Feathers,"
Toltecatl, "The Craftsman." The three sorcerers spoke:

> 'He must abandon his city; *we* will live there.
> Let us make some wine, some *pulque*,
> And let us give it to him to drink.
> Let us corrupt him,
> So that he may no longer live in divine favor!' "

Thus, in a few lines, the Aztec text gives us the setting: a hermit, an ascetic, a holy
man, is about to be tempted by three enemies who are to offer him the world, the devil,
and the flesh.

The first tempter was Tezcatlipoca himself, who went to Tula carrying a mirror concealed in his clothing. After many difficulties the wizard finally stood in the presence of
Quetzalcoatl. Tezcatlipoca spoke:

> " 'My son, Quetzalcoatl, Precious Serpent, I have come to greet you.
> And I have come so that you may see your own body.'
> 'Why have you gone to so much trouble, O little grandfather?'
> Answered Quetzalcoatl. 'Where do you come from?
> What is this you say about my body?'
> 'O my child,' responded Tezcatlipoca,
> 'My priest, I am your servant and I have come
> From the slopes of the mountain of Nonohualco.
> Behold your body! My child, look at yourself,
> Know yourself. You will now appear upon the mirror!'
> 'If my vassals could see my ugliness they would flee,'
> Said Quetzalcoatl when he beheld himself in the mirror.
> His eyelids were swollen, his eyes were sunken in their sockets,
> And his face was bloated! He hardly looked like a man!
> 'My vassals will never see me,' exclaimed Quetzalcoatl,
> 'I will remain here alone!' "

The wizard Tezcatlipoca then departed in triumph. He had made Quetzalcoatl aware
of his ugliness and aroused vanity in him.

The second tempter, the feather worker, Ilhuimecatl, then went to Tula, carrying fine feathers and ornaments. He dressed Quetzalcoatl in fine garments, "a mantle of *quetzal* feathers which fell from his shoulders to his waist. He made a turquoise mask for him. Then he took red paint and reddened Quetzalcoatl's lips with it. Then he took yellow paint and drew two squares on his forehead and decorated his teeth to look like serpent teeth. He made him a wig and a beard of blue feathers and of red macaw feathers. And when all this had been done, Ihuimecatl gave Quetzalcoatl the mirror. When he saw himself reflected in it the priest was delighted with his appearance. It was then that Quetzalcoatl decided to leave his hiding place and his life of austerity."

The second victory had been won. The Toltec holy man had realized the value of artificial beauty and had taken a further step toward worldliness.

The third temptation, in the form of wine, women and song, would now take place. The wizards prepared a great banquet and carried the food to Tula. After Quetzalcoatl had eaten the food he was offered the *pulque*.

> " 'I will not drink it,' he cried out.
> 'I am fasting. Perhaps it will kill me!'
> 'Just taste it with your little finger;
> It is angry *pulque*, it is strong *pulque*.'
> With his little finger Quetzalcoatl tasted it.
> 'Little grandfather,' he said, 'I am going to drink three cups of it!'
> 'You will drink four!' exclaimed the wizards.
> Soon they gave him his fifth cup. And when he had drunk
> They gave each of his vassals five cups.
> Then Ilhuimecatl taught Quetzalcoatl a new song.
> 'This, my house of precious feathers!
> This, my house of red sea shells!
> I will have to abandon it, alas!'
> And in his excitement Quetzalcoatl cried out,
> 'Go, bring my sister,
> Quetzalpetlatl, Precious Mat, the priestess!
> She and I are going to drink together!'
> And so, his messengers went to the mountain of Nonohualco,
> Where she was doing penance.
> 'Quetzalpetlatl, Precious Mat, daughter,' they said,
> 'Noble lady, you who live doing penance,
> We have come to take you away.
> Quetzalcoatl, the priest, awaits you,
> So that he and you may be united.'
> 'It is well, little grandfather, little messenger,'
> She answered, 'Let us depart!'

328

"And when she came she sat down next to Quetzalcoatl. Then they gave her *pulque*; four times she drank, and yet a fifth. 'O my sister,' chanted the wizards to the sister of

Quetzalcoatl, 'O Quetzalpetlatl, Precious Mat, let us drink!' And after their drunkenness the brother and sister no longer said, 'But we are mystics!' They no longer went down to their ritual bath in the river. They no longer pierced themselves with thorns. And at daybreak they were filled with sadness; their hearts were heavy with sorrow.

> " 'O wretch that I am,' moaned Quetzalcoatl.
> 'Let this day not be numbered among those
> I have spent in this my house.
> Ah, that I could remain here, but how can I?
> My body has become of clay! I have only anxiety
> And the desires of a slave!
> Nothing but anguish is left for me now!'

"And when he had finished speaking, all his vassals and servants were also filled with sorrow and they wept.

> 'O little grandfather, O servant,' exclaimed Quetzalcoatl.
> 'I am going to abandon the city.
> Conceal everything, hide all we had possessed—
> Gladness, richness, all our possessions and wealth!' "

Quetzalcoatl then destroyed his palace and his great wealth; he buried his jewels and gold. He turned the cacao trees into cacti and all the precious birds flew away with him. Then he set out for the seacoast. When he reached the Mountain of the White Woman he looked back to Tula for the last time. "He turned his eyes back toward Tula; and then he began to weep. He wept; sobbing, two torrents rolled down his cheeks. His tears dripped down his face; drop by drop his tears fell until they had pierced the rocks." From a distance he beheld Citlaltepetl, Mountain of the Star, and he knew that the coast was not far away.

"Quetzalcoatl finally arrived at the heavenly shores of the divine waters. There he stopped and wept again. He took up his garments and jewels and slowly he put them on, his mantle of precious feathers and his turquoise mask. And thus attired he set fire to himself, and while he was in flames his ashes went up into the air. Then there appeared all the birds of precious feathers that are to be seen in the heavens: the red feathered macaw, the blue birds, the thrush, the shining white birds, and parrots of yellow plumage. When Quetzalcoatl's ashes ceased to burn his heart went up into the heights and the birds watched it as it was taken up into the heavens. Quetzalcoatl was turned into the morning star which appears at the moment of dawn. It appeared then for the first time. That is why he is called Tlahuizcalpantecuhtli, 'Lord of Dawn.' "

Though this version of the disappearance of Quetzalcoatl mentions his death on the Veracruz seacoast, other Aztec texts state that, together with his followers, the Toltec high priest departed on a raft toward the east. His prophetic last words were that he would return some day to the land over which he had ruled. As can be read in the dramatic chapters at the end of Durán's chronicle, Cortés, conqueror of Mexico, was to be taken for Quetzalcoatl by Moteczoma and his people.

4. Undoubtedly Durán is thinking of the Tower of Babel recorded in *Genesis:*

> "Go to, let us go down,
> And there confound their language,
> That they may not understand one another's speech . . .
> Therefore, the name of it is called Babel;
> Because the Lord did there confound
> The language of all the earth,
> And from thence did the Lord scatter them abroad
> Upon the face of all the earth."

5. During early Spanish colonial times, La Florida referred not only to what is now the peninsula of this name in the United States but to the region north of Tampico in Tamaulipas, which would include northeastern Mexico and southeastern Texas.

There are many theories about the location of Aztlan. Jiménez Moreno suggests that it may be the Aztatlan discovered by Nuño de Guzman in 1530, situated on an island in the Mezcaltitlan Lagoon in Nayarit. People of this state today describe a place in a lagoon near the Pacific Ocean, undoubtedly Mezcaltitlan, where the leaves of water plants are so large that children use them as rafts, where shrimps and other seafood are so plentiful that a person need only reach into the water in order to supply the table with food; in short, this is more or less the description of the idealized Aztlan.

There was a confusion as to the place or origin of the Aztecs even before Durán's time, Florida, California, and New Mexico often being mistaken for one another in legend, and all confused with the Seven Cities of Silver, or Cibola, sought by Coronado.

The seven cities of Cibola were located in a legendary region, a paradise of riches, abundance, happiness like El Dorado in South America. News of Cibola was first given by Cabeza de Vaca to a party of Spaniards scouting near the Gulf of California. Cabeza de Vaca had been shipwrecked in 1528 in what is now southeastern United States and for eight years had worked his way westward, accompanied by a few Indians. He stated that to the north were seven cities whose inhabitants lived in silver palaces ornamented with emeralds, turquoise, and sapphires. Among the many people who believed this tale was Francisco Vásquez Coronado (and why shouldn't he . . . having seen the incredible splendor of Moteczoma's court?). Coronado set out with three hundred Spaniards, one thousand Indians and one thousand horses on a great expedition in search of wealth, like Ponce de León's search for the Fountain of Youth in Florida, or Belalcázar's hunt for El Dorado (literally, the man covered with gold, but generally assumed to be a fabulously rich region) in Colombia. But Coronado found nothing but great wilderness and rugged cliffs. He then tried to discover the Gran Quivira, the "land farther on," where dishes were of gold and everyday objects of precious stones—only to find more desert, harsh mountains and failure.

The fact that the Cities of Cibola were seven would lead one to believe that the tradition of the Seven Caves, place of origin of the Aztecs, was confused with a paradise on

330

earth—and the Aztecs certainly described Aztlan, home of the caves, as such. Although no one knows the location of the fabled Cibola, the name signifies "bison" or "buffalo" and this would place it on the plains of the great American Southwest.

At this first mention of agricultural life by Durán, it is appropriate to list some of the plants cultivated in ancient Mesoamerica. The four most important were maize or Indian corn, beans, chilli peppers, and squash. Others were the maguey or century plant, tomato, the tiny *chian* seed, *huauhtli* (the green amaranth vegetable and seed), gourds, *jícama* (turnip-like product), the *texocotl* (which is similar to a crab apple), *nopal* or prickly pear cactus whose fruit and tender leaves were important in the diet, cacao (or chocolate), vanilla, avocado (or alligator pear), manioc, and other plants and berries. All of these were supplemented by a number of wild products. It was not until the arrival of the Spaniards that most cereals such as rice, wheat, and barley, fruits such as apples, pears and oranges, and vegetables like lettuce, carrots, and peas were added to the Indian diet of Mexico, while native American plants found their way to Europe.

6.    Since scientific archaeology had not been born in the time of Durán, it should not be expected that the Dominican missionary would express accurate ideas on the chronology of pre-Columbian Mexico. The dates, controversial even in our own time, may be summed up in the following way:

| | |
|---|---|
| Tepexpan Man | |
|    (nomad, hunter and food gatherer) | 10-5000 B.C. |
| Coxcatlan Cave, Puebla | |
|    (beginnings of agriculture) | 5000-2000 B.C. |
| Preclassic cultures | |
|    (Copilco, Tlatilco, Cuicuilco) | 2000-200 B.C. |
| Classic Period (Teotihuacan) | B.C. 200-750 A.D. |
| Tula and the Toltec Culture | 750-1200 A.D. |
| Chichimec and Aztec invasions | 1200-1428 A.D. |
| Aztec supremacy | 1428-1521 A.D. |
| Spanish Conquest | 1521 A.D. |

7.    It is doubtful that the Aztecs were an agricultural people at this time. They were a semi-barbarian group when they arrived in Tula in 1163 A.D., seventy-three years after the beginning of the Aztec migration from Aztlan; according to the *Anales de Cuauhtitlan* they left the Seven Caves in 1090. This lapse of time would hardly have given them sufficient leisure to sow, wait for the harvest and reap along the route and still cross the entire country from west to east. Furthermore, the Aztecs seem to have acquired their sedentary customs from more advanced peoples whom they contacted or conquered in Tula and in the Valley of Mexico.

8. The Nahuatl language, a branch of the Yuto-Aztecan linguistic family, was spoken all the way from Jalisco to Central America. It was also known as Mexica or Mexicano and was divided into a number of dialects. Several of the Spanish chroniclers comment on the "snobbishness" of the people of Texcoco regarding their particular form of speaking this tongue, apparently considering their accent superior to that of Mexico City. Texcocan Nahuatl stood in a position similar to that of Oxford English in relation to Cockney.

9. The term Chichimec is used here to denote the inhabitants north of the area of Mesoamerica. Mesoamerica, the region of highly civilized native peoples, was found between lines which could be drawn loosely between Tepic in western Mexico and Tampico on the Gulf of Mexico coast. The southern border could be shown as a line drawn between the Gulf of Fonseca, lying between the Republics of Nicaragua and Salvador and the Ulua River in Western Honduras. This culture area was characterized by intensified agriculture, a complex religious and priestly organization, the city-state as the basic political unit, an incredibly complex calendrical and numerical system, and by writing.

10. The legend of the "Giants" is a favorite one in many parts of Mexico, as gigantic bones of Pleistocene-period animals such as the mammoth, *Bison antiquus* and a type of elephant have been found from prehistoric days up to the present and were formerly mistaken for human remains. Sahagún himself mentions that "Giants" of *Quinametin* built Teotihuacan as well as Cholula. So many of these immense bones have been disinterred in the Valley of Teotihuacan that people, before the Conquest, named a site near the pyramids Acolman (*acolli*, "tall" or "broad-shouldered," and *mani*, "where there are"); furthermore, who but men-greater-than-men, giants or gods, could have constructed the pyramids of such extraordinary proportions in Teotihuacan, "Place of Gods"? This legend applies to Cholula not only because remains of the same type have been found there but also because the Teotihuacan civilization was responsible for the beginnings of the city. Mammoth bones were a motive of curiosity to the Spaniards as well as to the Indians. Fossilized bones were sent to Spain during the sixteenth century, the first "Mexican curios," perhaps. Dr. Francisco Hernández, commissioned by the Spanish monarch to investigate many natural phenomena of the New World, judged the "Giants" to be more than five meters tall, based on the size of the mammoth bones. The Museum of Prehistory at Tepexpan in the Teotihuacan Valley has a comprehensive exhibit of gigantic animal bones, together with lithic instruments, discovered here and elsewhere.

11. Huitzilopochtli, who is the god-hero of the whole of Durán's work, is presented by the author in a somewhat confusing manner. At the beginning of the text the reader is led to believe that Huitzilopochtli is a chieftain, an ordinary human being, who leads the barbaric Aztecs during their long migration to find the promised land. Later in the chronicle he appears as a deity represented by an idol in the main temple of the city of Mexico.

12.     It is convenient at this point to define a number of the proper names that appear in Durán's history:

*Aztlan*—"Place of Herons" refers to the legendary place of origin of the people whom Cortés was to find settled in what is today Mexico City.

*Aztec*—means "Man of Aztlan" and refers to the people who formed this great migration which culminated in the founding of Mexico City. The term later was sometimes used to indicate any inhabitant of the Aztec Empire. "Aztec language" refers to Nahuatl.

*Mexico* is a term whose etymology has long been discussed. Two common interpretations of the word are: "In the Navel or Center of the Moon" or "In the Heart of the Century Plant." The name is used by Durán and other early Aztec and Spanish chroniclers to mean the two cities of Mexico-Tenochtitlan and Mexico-Tlatelolco, now both in downtown Mexico City. Beginning with the eighteenth century, the name Mexico has been used to indicate the empire formerly known as New Spain, today the Mexican Republic. Tenochtitlan, "Place by the Prickly Pear Cactus," is now the area of the Zócalo or main square of the city, while Tlatelolco, "Place of Many Mounds," is now the square of Santiago in the northern part of the city.

*Mexica* refers to the Aztec people.

*Tenochca* denotes the inhabitants of Tenochtitlan.

*Tlatelolca*, the inhabitants of Tlatelolco.

*Chicomoztoc*, the Seven Caves, is the mythical place of origin in which Aztlan was thought to have been located.

13.     Actually, these were three different groups. It is doubtful that the Aztecs passed by Patzcuaro on their migration, though it is certain that Toltecs of Nahuatl speech inhabited it in ancient times. The *chacmool*, a half-reclining stone figure that forms an altar, typically Toltec in style, testifies to their presence in the region. The legend of the Tarascans' ire, which made them "change their language" out of spite, is probably due to later rivalry between these people and the Aztecs, both strong political forces in historical times. The Aztecs frequently tried to subdue the Tarascans but never managed to conquer them.

14.     The Aztecs reached Tula toward the end of the twelfth century and their arrival coincided with the collapse of the Toltec empire. It is probable that the Aztecs contributed greatly to this collapse; according to the *Anales de Cuauhtitlan* they were in the area at that time, and Sahagún describes the Toltecs fighting people of the region, who were undoubtedly the Aztecs. The downfall of Tula eliminated the barrier between sedentary cultured groups and nomadic or semi-nomadic barbarians, allowing the latter to invade and occupy the Valleys of Mexico, Puebla and Tlaxcala.

333

15.     The Otomi were an ancient people of the western and northern zones adjoining the Valley of Mexico. The origin and history of this tribe is enigmatic. They had undoubtedly lived in these areas for many centuries before the arrival of the Nahuatl-speaking Aztec

invaders. A timid and rather backward people, they were quickly conquered by the Aztecs and later by the Spaniards. About 350,000 exist today.

16.  The chosen place for the city of Mexico, the "promised land" described by Durán, reminds one of a number of modern legends still circulating among the people of the country, an example of which is this story from Xaltocan, Mexico: "The Aztecs . . . arrived in this town and they found the eagle standing upon a stone, which led them to believe that the city was to be founded here. But a little bird sang to them, 'Let's go! Let's go!' Thereupon the eagle flew away and after it went the Aztecs. The stone is to be seen in the upper part of our village and it is said that when the eagle flew away the water of our lagoon turned salty. Therefore, the city of Mexico was settled where it is today."

Another version refers to Mount Tlaloc, a sacred mountain near Mexico City which is topped by the ruins of a great temple dedicated to the God of the Waters. In nearby towns it is stated that the famous Aztec eagle, omen and symbol of Mexico, had almost decided to indicate that Mount Tlaloc was the promised place. However, certain persons frightened the eagle, causing it to fly down to the lagoon in the Valley of Mexico. This widespread legend, probably in existence since pre-Hispanic times, seems to indicate a certain amount of envy of the rustics toward the urban dwellers of Mexico.

17.  The Valley of Mexico—or rather the completely enclosed basin covered in great part by a lake—had been settled thousands of years before the arrival of the Aztec tribe in the thirteenth century. The cultures of barbaric Chichimec invaders and of the older Toltec civilizations had now merged. Cities such as Colhuacan, Texcoco, and Azcapotzalco were typical of this amalgamation. Therefore it is easy to believe that the Aztecs, on entering territory already occupied by others, were not welcomed in the area. What a spectacle must have greeted the eyes of the newcomers! The great blue-green lake teeming with fish and water fowl, the floating gardens, the island-cities—a scene similar to that which was to enthrall the Spanish conquerors three centuries later.

18.  The traditional date for the founding of the city of Mexico is 1325 A.D. and the locality the present day Zócalo or main plaza of the city. The four wards described by Durán are at the present time four parishes around the Zócalo: San Pablo, San Juan, Santa María la Redonda, and San Sebastián.

19.  Weapons commonly used by the Aztecs and frequently mentioned by Durán are the following:
*Macuauhuitl*—a wooden sword or club edged on both sides with blades of the black volcanic glass called obsidian.
*Atlatl*—a small dart or spear thrower, which propelled these weapons. This warlike arm, used for several thousand years in Mexico, is still employed by the Tarascan Indians in their duck hunts on Lake Patzcuaro.

The bow and arrow, though introduced in very late times by the Chichimec invaders, were also popular among the Aztecs.

*Tepoztopilli*—a lance almost ten feet long tipped by a flint point.

The sling was also an important military arm. It was woven of maguey fiber and the ball cast by the latter was of finely rounded stone or clay.

The blow gun, which shot marble-size clay balls, also played a prominent part in ancient Mexican warfare.

*Chimalli*—a shield of reeds and leather covered with ornate featherwork.

The armor of the Aztec warrior was a tight-fitting and heavily padded quilted cotton suit surmounted by a helmet made of the same material, ornamented with feathers and other devices. A significant aim of these warriors' costumes was to terrify the enemy, and for this reason they were highly decorated with eagles, jaguars, etc.

20.     The *tlacaxipehualiztli* ceremony, "Skinning of Human Beings," was a rite practiced long before the arrival of the Aztecs in the Valley of Mexico. This custom, perhaps of Huaxtec origin, possibly symbolized the ripening of corn within its skin-colored husk.

     Toci, "Our Grandmother" and Tonantzin, "Our Mother" were almost identical in their attributes and revered as powerful fertility goddesses.

21.     This mysterious reference of Durán regarding a "foul" or "obscene" happening in Mexicatzinco has never been clarified but is mentioned by other ancient historians. In the *Codex Aubin* of 1576, in a drawing depicting the Aztecs' stay at Mexicatzinco, is to be seen an almost nude man with a small century plant protruding from his anus.

22.     It is appropriate at this point to discuss the symbols associated with the founding of Mexico-Tenochtitlan. The several dozen ancient texts and paintings show the following: an eagle with open wings posed upon a prickly-pear cactus which stands on a rock located in the middle of burning water. According to some of the sources, Quetzalcoatl himself rested upon this rock in his flight from Tula to the Gulf Coast, leaving signs of his body upon this stone. The snake which now usually appears in the eagle's beak in the modern Mexican coat of arms was possibly introduced in post-Columbian times by the Spaniards. These pictorial elements today form the national emblem of the Republic of Mexico.

23.     The Valley of Mexico, at that time partially covered with water, was farmed by means of a system unique in this part of the world: the *chinampa*. The *chinampa* was a rectangular platform made up of logs, branches and reeds, covered with silt, moss and leaves brought up from the lake bottom. According to some historians, this raft floated upon the surface of the lake and was tied somehow to the mainland, prompting the term "floating garden." Others claim that the platform was built within the shallow waters of the lagoon and adhered to the mud floor of the lake. At any rate, the Aztecs, by means of this ingenious system, were able to create an entire metropolis of islands which eventually joined and reached the mainland.

24. The four wards of Mexico, known as *calpullis* (a form of clan), were the basic sociopolitical unit of the Aztecs. A *calpulli* was as much a division of land as the social group that exploited it. Each member of the *calpulli* was assigned a plot which he might cultivate for a certain period of time. If this "owner" abandoned it for two years, the earth was then assigned to another member of the community. This land could not be sold or leased by the holder, whose title was carefully recorded in hieroglyphs on maps belonging to the community house. Although the plot could not be inherited by the sons of a farmer, certain rights permitted heirs to use it for their own benefit.

    Not all property was individually worked in this manner. Certain lands were worked by all the members of the group for the benefit of the community. Others were exploited for payment of taxes to the central government of Mexico-Tenochtitlan. Yet others existed for the maintenance of the temple and priesthood of the town.

    All of this reminds one strongly of the collectivistic system of the Incas and of certain experiments in collectivism in modern times.

25. Mexico-Tlatelolco, a community only a mile north of Mexico-Tenochtitlan, possesses a history as rich and complex as that of the latter city. Most sources agree that a branch of the original Mexica-Aztec immigrants separated from the tribe in order to found a city of their own around 1370. From this time on a great rivalry existed between Tlatelolco and Tenochtitlan until the latter destroyed the former in 1473.

    Recent excavations at the site of Tlatelolco, the Square of Santiago in modern Mexico City, have revealed that the foundation of this center is much older than the date given by Durán and other chroniclers. The Mexican Instituto Nacional de Antropología e Historia has now created a spectacular showpiece of the ancient city, known as the Historical Center, within the ultramodern Nonoalco-Tlatelolco Housing Development. Enclosed within this enormous urban project stand the ruins of the ancient metropolis of Tlatelolco, the sixteenth century Franciscan monastery now turned museum, and the remains of the *tecpan*, Aztec community house where Cuauhtemoc, last of the native sovereigns, ruled for a brief spell. Within the monastic establishment, Fray Bernardino de Sahagún composed in Nahuatl his monumental work on ancient Mexico based upon the data given by his native informants.

26. At that time Colhuacan was one of the last surviving centers of Toltec culture in the country. Its royal house claimed descent from the dynasty of the kings of Tula. It is obvious that the Aztecs, barbaric newcomers to this land, found it advantageous to intermarry so as to be able to claim kinship with the ancient sovereigns ruled by Quetzalcoatl. Colhuacan is now San Francisco Calhuacán, a suburb of Mexico City.

27. This antagonism on the part of the people of Colhuacan was undoubtedly caused by the skinning of the king's daughter by the Aztecs some time before.

28.  The divinity referred to here is Ometeotl, "Lord Two," male and female, who was thought to have lived in the ninth and topmost heaven. Lord Two was "He-Who-is-Everywhere," "He-Who-is-Near-Us," "The-Ever-Present." The Aztecs attributed to this god the ultimate creation and existence of all things.

29.  The fact that Chimalpopoca, sovereign of the Aztec nation, was only ten years old at the moment of this exaltation to the throne is not surprising. The chronicles that refer to fifteenth century Mexican history frequently mention the election of rulers who were young boys. It is possible that this procedure was based on an ancient custom derived from the Chichimecs, who elected the youngest son to succeed his father.

30.  The building of the first causeway to connect Mexico-Tenochtitlan to the mainland was surely an event of great significance. The city, which had been upon an island, isolated from its neighbors, now began its long cultural and economic expansion. It is not clear how the Aztecs, living in the midst of a salty lake, had previously been able to obtain drinkable water. It was now possible to construct a pipe from Chapultepec to bring in fresh water. As recently as one hundred years ago the water supply of Mexico City came from the same source.

31.  Tezozomoc, king of Azcapotzalco, is not given his proper importance by Durán. This sovereign, a "Prince" in the Machiavellian sense, formed a great empire by means of intrigues, marriage alliances and successful military expeditions. The Tecpanec tribe of Azcapotzalco conquered the entire Valley of Mexico and extended Tezozomoc's domains into the valley of Toluca and Puebla and far south toward the Pacific Coast. His reign was one of the longest in history, lasting from 1343 to 1426, a period of eighty-three years. By 1428, when the Aztecs conquered the Tecpanec empire which had been formed by Tezozomoc they acquired a vast domain including hundreds of tributary towns.

32.  Texcoco, like Azcapotzalco, was another city which had prominence long before the Aztecs founded Mexico-Tenochtitlan. At the beginning of the fifteenth century its ruler was Ixtlilxochitl whose reign covered the period between 1409 and 1418. This sovereign was assassinated by Tezozomoc of Azcapotzalco. His son Nezahualcoyotl (1402-1472) was to be a principal ally of the Aztec kings in their wars of expansion.

There is a wealth of information regarding Ixtlilxochitl, "Black Flower Face," and Nezahualcoyotl, "Fasting Coyote" in the ancient chronicles. In 1418, when the Tecpanec armies invaded Texcoco, the king and his son fled toward the mountainous area to the east of that city. When the enemy approached them, the king gave his young son, Nezahualcoyotl, orders to climb into the branches of a tree, and charged him with vengeance. The sovereign was slain before his son's eyes but the youth managed to escape across the mountains toward the Tlaxcala-Puebla area where he was well received by friends. It was Nezahualcoyotl who later was to aid the Aztecs in destroying Azcapotzalco, and in this way avenged his father's death.

337

Though Durán speaks little of Nezahualcoyotl's cultural achievements, this monarch was the Pericles of ancient Mexico. He was an inspired poet. Several of his compositions, recorded in the European alphabet shortly after the Spanish conquest, still form part of the national literary heritage. He was also the Hammurabi of the New World since he codified the ancient laws of Texcoco. He was perhaps the founder of the first library of the Americas. As an engineer he took an active part in the urbanization of Mexico City and in building its aqueduct. Another of Nezahualcoyotl's inspired creations is his outdoor bath, unique in the world. On the rocky hill called Texcotzingo, near the present day town of Texcoco, is to be found his circular bathtub cut out of the living rock with a view which encompasses hundreds of miles. It was here, at Texcotzingo, that Nezahualcoyotl kept his botanical gardens, his favorite shrines, and his harem.

33. Tlacaelel in many ways is the central character of Durán's *Historia* and is to be considered the driving force in the growth of the Aztec empire. Nevertheless, several modern historians suspect that Durán has actually merged two important political leaders of the fifteenth century into one character and that the name "Tlacaelel" was simply a title similar to our term, "Prime Minister."

34. In Aztec times, on declaring war, it was the custom to send messengers to anoint the enemy chieftain for death with *tizatl* (chalk) and to exchange weapons as a sign of battle.

35. The terrifying shrieks emitted by the native warriors are described with horror by the European eye-witnesses to the conquest. The reader of Bernal Díaz del Castillo's *Conquest of Mexico* will remember his never-to-be-forgotten description of these yells. Another eye-witness, the Conquistador Anónimo, writes, "While the natives fight they dance and sing, giving forth the most bloodcurdling shrieks and whistles, especially when they realize that the battle is to be won by them. Those who are not accustomed to their way of fighting are overwhelmed by their cries and fantastic movements. In war these people are the cruelest in the world since they do not spare a brother, kinsman or friend, nor will they pardon the life of anyone they capture. Even beautiful women are slaughtered and then eaten." These horrifying yells were apparently an excellent psychological weapon which overawed the Spaniards in the early phases of the conquest.

36. This anecdote regarding the bargain made between nobles and plebeians was possibly invented in later times. In the last days of the Aztec Empire it undoubtedly served as an excellent means of reinforcing an order of classes and castes.

37. Little is known regarding the kinship system of the Aztec group and of the other pre-Columbian nations in general. Durán himself does not seem to possess a clear picture of the family or clan relationships of the people he describes. Whenever our chronicler mentions the word "nephew," "brother," or "cousin" it is hard to say what he means. If, for example, a group is addressed as, "My brothers," this may indicate a clan system.

Even the existence of a patrilineal or matrilineal clan organization among the Aztecs is controversial.

38. The reader becomes confused at this stage by Durán's apparent lack of consistency regarding the ethics of the Aztecs. To mention a few examples: at the beginning of the work he claims that these people never provoked another tribe to war. Yet Durán's entire history is an account of a series of provocations on the part of the Aztecs. Though Durán refers to the Mexican natives as a people unparalleled in goodness in the entire world, he writes, "They were the cruelest and most devilish people that can be imagined." While Tlacaelel is sometimes the brave hero and central character of the *Historia*, in one passage he is referred to as "that evil old man who never was satiated with human flesh." Durán was translating a native Aztec text more or less literally, but at the same time was interspersing his own comments in the translation. This indubitably accounts for much of the apparent inconsistency.

39. Paper was made of different materials in pre-Columbian Mexico. While most of the codices or painted manuscripts were written on a fine deerskin covered with a coating of white, two other types of "paper" were widely used for ritual purposes. Bark paper was prepared in the following way: the bark of the *amatl* tree (wild fig) was soaked for several days in water. The pulp was then beaten with sticks and the soggy material placed upon a board to be pounded flat with special stone implements. After this process it was placed in the sun to dry and cut according to specific needs.

Maguey paper, taken from the leaves of the century plant, was made by a similar method. Most of this paper was used for ritual purposes—banners, clothing for the idols, insignia for the priests, etc. Bark paper is still made following the pre-Conquest system in some parts of Mexico.

40. Rubber, native to the New World, grows in the hot lowlands, and in pre-Columbian times was produced in great quantities in the southern part of Veracruz on the Gulf of Mexico. It was called *ollin* which also means "motion." Among the Mexican natives it seems to have been used basically for balls used in the ritual ball game, and for rubber-soled sandals, the first soles of this type in the world. In the Sacred Well at Chichen Itza in Yucatan archaeologists have recently discovered a number of votive offerings in the form of idols made of vulcanized rubber. It is said that the first rubber raincoats were produced in Mexico shortly after the Spanish conquest by coating cotton mantles with fine rubber.

41. The incense referred to by Durán throughout the work is the native *copal*, a resin of a coniferous tree that abounds in the temperate and cool areas of Mesoamerica. As in the Old World, incense was constantly used in religious services in the temples and at the small altars in the homes. In the latter the incense burners seem to have occupied the

position that the candle or vigil light does today. *Copal* is still commonly used all over Mesoamerica—in the graveyards, on domestic altars, and on pilgrimages.

42. The community house or "city hall" of the Aztecs was known as the *tecpan*, literally, "Place of the Lords." It was used as a meeting house and the maps showing different communal lands were guarded there. Policies regarding domestic and external problems were discussed in this place. The *tecpan* could be compared to the modern *palacio municipal* in modern Mexico.

43. The Aztecs, like other Mesoamerican peoples, used two calendars to compute the days of the year. The "civil" or solar calendar consisted of three hundred and sixty-five days. It was divided into eighteen "months" of twenty units each, plus an additional period of five useless or unlucky days at the end of the year. The eighteen months were intimately connected with agricultural rites, and Xocotl Huetzi, "Fall of the Fruits," would today fall within our month of August. This solar year was calculated so accurately by the ancient Mesoamericans, long before the time of the Aztecs, that it excelled the Julian calendar commonly used in Europe at that time.

    The second calendar used by the Aztecs and other Mesoamericans was the *tonalpohualli* or "day count." Durán makes little reference to this in his *Historia* in spite of its great importance. This cycle was made up of two hundred and sixty days, combinations of thirteen numbers and twenty symbols. This system of combining number and symbol could be compared to our own date of the month and day of the week. After a certain period, when the same day coincided in both calendars, the end of the fifty-two year cycle, or Mesoamerican century, had been reached.

44. The incident described by Durán is typical of many passages recorded by Aztec chroniclers who, tongue in cheek, poke fun at their neighbors. It is possible that Durán was unaware that he was repeating jokes rather than historical facts.

45. This description of the warriors identifying their captives after a battle reminds one of an earlier episode in Aztec history not mentioned by Durán. Aztec mercenaries were at one time ordered by the king of Colhuacan to obtain captives in Xochimilco. This they did so zealously that they were unable to bring back their prisoners alive. Instead they filled several bags with the ears of their victims and presented these to the monarch who, in one of the codices, *Tira de la Peregrinación*, is shown turning his head away in disgust at the spectacle of the ear-filled bags.

46. All the titles granted by the Aztec monarch to his captains should not be compared with modern European titles of nobility. There is no doubt that these distinctions carried more weight and power in ancient Mexico than a simple title of nobility today.

47. The Marquesado, so often referred to by Durán, is the state of Morelos in modern Mexico,

south of present-day Mexico City. Lying in the semitropical lowlands it was—and is—a rich territory, at that time remarkable for its production of cotton, chocolate, and tropical fruits and plants. Later, all of Morelos, plus adjoining lands, was granted by the king of Spain to Hernando Cortés when the latter was given the title of "Marqués del Valle de Oaxaca," hence the name "Marquesado."

48. Although Durán, and all the other ancient chroniclers, give the reader the impression that the cities conquered by the Aztecs during this period were remote and foreign kingdoms, they were geographically close, and today most of them are to be found within the city limits of the Mexican capital. It was not until the fifteenth century that the Aztec nation passed the mountains that surround the Valley in order to meet and vanquish distant city-states inhabited by people of other cultures and tongues. The political situation in the Valley of Mexico at the time described by Durán could be compared to that of the early Greek city-states.

49. A much quoted description of Moteczoma's dinner is to be found in Bernal Díaz Castillo's *Conquest of Mexico:*
"He was seated on a low stool, soft and richly worked, and the table, which was also low, was made in the same style as the seat, and on it they placed the tablecloths of white cloth. . . . Four very beautiful cleanly women brought water for his hands in a sort of deep basin which they call *xicallis,* and they held others, like plates, below to catch the water, and they brought him towels . . . As soon as he began to eat they placed before him a sort of wooden screen painted over with gold, so that no one should watch him eating. Then the four women stood aside and four great chieftains who were old men came and stood beside them, and with these Moteczoma now and then conversed, asked them questions, and as a great favor he would give to each of these elders a dish of what to him tasted best."
The table customs of the Aztecs remind one strongly of the way in which the Inca emperors were served. In ancient Peru, the left-overs of the sovereign's meal were burned as divine, since the monarch's hands had touched the food.

50. Cuitlahuac, like several other city-states which are mentioned in Durán's work, was an island. Cuitlahuac is the modern San Pedro Tlahuac, south of Mexico City, near Xochimilco. The name was changed because the prefix *cui,* human offal, was offensive to prudish nineteenth century ears.

51. The constant exchange of gifts to be found throughout the entire chronicle of Durán reminds one strongly of the institutionalized gift exchange systems that occur all over the world among non-European groups. The potlatch of the northwest coast would be an exaggerated form of this custom. Even in our own society, the exchange of presents at Christmas, weddings and other occasions forms an intricate pattern of social behavior.

52. The feigned war between Mexico and Texcoco is probably wishful thinking on the part of the Aztec chroniclers from whom Durán drew his information. According to the Texcocan Ixtlilxochitl's *Historia Chichimeca*, events were totally different from those described here. Ixtlilxochitl writes that in one of the several wars between the two rival cities, "Nezahualcoyotl gathered an army of fifty thousand soldiers and attacked Mexico, entering through Tepeyacac, which is now Our Lady of Guadalupe. . . . Nezahualcoyotl besieged the city of Mexico for seven days, both sides fighting valorously and at the end of these days . . . a Texcocan youth . . . fought against the great captain of the Aztecs who defended the gates of the city. He killed the Aztec and cut his body to pieces. In that way the army entered the city, sacked the houses, burned all the temples and palaces and killed all the soldiers. They spared the personages who were to be found within the city because of the orders Nezahualcoyotl had previously given." The Texcocan text ends in a description of how the Aztecs of Mexico finally recognized the superiority of Texcoco. The interpretation of history often depends upon who writes it.

53. The Triple Alliance formed by Mexico-Tenochtitlan, Texcoco, and Tacuba was to be the major force in controlling a large part of Mesoamerica until the Spanish conquest. These three cities, on conquering the domains of Azcapotzalco, automatically acquired a number of tribute-paying provinces to which they were to add others in later times. The Triple Alliance can be said to have ended on the day Cortés hanged the rulers of Mexico, Texcoco, and Tacuba on his fateful trip to Honduras in 1525.

54. A ceremony practiced in Mesoamerica is suggested by this passage—the famous "Volador" or "Flying Pole" dance. One man, playing the flute and drum, stood upon the top of the pole while four others who were attached to the pole by ropes, threw themselves into the air and as the ropes unwound, made thirteen ever-widening turns until they touched the earth. Several interpretations of this rite are: 1) the four cardinal points; 2) a phallus; 3) the fifty-two year cycle of four groups of thirteen-year periods. This thrilling ceremony is still performed by the Totonacs and other tribes in eastern Mexico, using a pole that is occasionally as high as one hundred feet.

55. This type of sacrifice, known as *tlacacaliztli*, was found not only among the Chalca but also among the Huaxtecs, Nahuas, and other indigenous groups. It possibly originated in Central United States where the Pawnee, a Plains tribe, practiced it until comparatively recent times.

56. Among the many superstitious beliefs of the peoples of ancient Mesoamerica a fear of ill omens is prominent.
    Book Five of Sahagún's *Historia de las cosas de Nueva España* deals entirely with the interpretation of evil signs. The crying of a wild animal at night, the hooting of an owl, ʼnning of a weasel across a road, certain dreams, comets—all of these and many ʼually controlled the daily conduct of the average man in a way so drastic that

some of our modern omens, such as the black cat, the breaking of a mirror, or the number thirteen are insignificant in comparison.

57.   The Popocatepetl, "Smoking Mountain," and Iztaccihuatl, "White Woman," are the two snowy peaks, over seventeen thousand feet high, which separate the Valley of Mexico from the eastern Valley of Puebla Tlaxcala. The Smoking Mountain is a volcano which was active until several hundred years ago and which today still emits fumes. The White Woman, often called Iztactepetl, "White Mountain," looks to the observer in the Valley of Mexico like a reclining woman. Many ancient legends are attached to these peaks and it was between them that Cortés passed on his way from the Gulf coast to the city of Mexico in 1519.

58.   The "eating of the earth" which appears constantly in his *Historia* refers to the native custom of lowering the middle finger to the ground and placing it on the lips as a symbol of courtesy and reverence.

59.   For the first time we see the Aztecs on a campaign outside of their environment. Up to now they had fought with groups of Nahuatl speech, similar in customs, dress, religion, and systems of war, living in a natural environment identical to that of Mexico City. At this point, however, the Aztec army attacked a region several hundred miles away, in the tropics, close to the sea in the northern part of the present-day state of Veracruz and eastern San Luis Potosí. This area was and is known as the Huaxteca, inhabited by a nation known as the Huaxtec, linguistically related to the Maya of Yucatan. The economy of these people, though based on maize, beans, squash, and chilli like that of the Aztecs, was also rich in cotton, vanilla, chocolate, tropical fruits, and seafood, all of which were absent in the Valley of Mexico. Their religion was one of the most ancient in Meso-america, and several of their rites had already found their way into Toltec and Aztec ceremonial. The Aztecs looked upon this region as a sort of Garden of Eden and called it Tonacatlalpan, "Place of Our Flesh," but at the same time considered the Huaxtec natives a sensual, drunken and immoral people. Some of these ideas undoubtedly were based on reality since, according to modern archaeologists, a phallic cult existed in this part of Mesoamerica.

60.   Here Durán contrasts the Otomi warriors with their hair clipped short and the Aztec officers and nobles who were proud of their shoulder length hair, elaborate coiffures similar to our modern "pony-tail" and other hairdos in the form of braids and hanging locks.

343   61.   Based on Dibble and Anderson's translation of Sahagún's *Florentine Codex*, Book Two, the following description will give the reader an idea of the elaborate ritual which composed part of the Tlacaxipehualiztli or "Skinning of Men" ceremony. It should be explained that youths who ventured forth on their first campaign still wore a long tuft of

hair hanging down the left side of their heads. If a young man took a captive the lock was shaved off and another was allowed to grow on the right side.

On his return to the city of Mexico his grandfather addressed the youth in this way: "My beloved grandson: The sun, the Lord of the Earth, hath washed thy face. Thou hast taken on another face, thou hast gone to throw thyself against the foe. Let them take thee if once more thou takest a captive with the aid of others. Take care, lest thou again take a captive with others' help. Cast thyself against our foes." Young men unsuccessful in capturing victims for sacrifice were called "Big tuft of hair on the head." This diminished their prestige in the community and undoubtedly made them reckless in battle. When a warrior finally captured four prisoners ". . . then they placed him on a mat and stool in the warriors' house—there where were gathered the great, brave warriors . . ." which indicates that he had reached the highest rank in military affairs. Undoubtedly all of Durán's great Aztec personages, all the way from Tlacaelel to Cuauhtemoc, had achieved this position.

On the day of the sacrifice the young captor was given a gourd into which the victim's blood would eventually be poured. He was invited to the great ceremony that took place in a courtyard where stood the circular stone upon which the prisoner was to die in a gladiatorial skirmish. According to the same *Florentine Codex* the great procession of captives, captors, priests, and warriors appeared before the stone in splendid array. "When one showed himself strong, not acting like a woman, he went with a man's fortitude; he bore himself like a man; he went speaking in a manly fashion; he went exerting himself; he went strong of heart and shouting with courage, not stumbling, but honoring and praising his city. He went with a firm heart, speaking as he went. 'Here I come! You will speak of me there in my homeland!' "

When the great procession had surrounded the stone there was an uproar, the spectators shouted, trumpets were sounded, sea shells were blown, and men put their fingers to their mouths and whistled. Meanwhile a rope was tied around the waist of the captive and he was made to stand up on the round stone. Four warriors, two dressed as eagles and two as jaguars, began to fight him, trying to wound him in the legs, while the prisoner shouted insults and praised his city.

"Sometimes," continues the *Florentine Codex*, "one went faltering, sinking down on all fours, reeling and overcome in the fray, uselessly and vainly holding the war club, which they snatched from him. And this useless one could do no more; no more could he use his hands; no longer defend himself; no more make himself do anything. No longer did he move; he did not speak. Then, faltering and fainting, he fell upon the surface, tumbling as if dead. He wished that he might stop breathing, that he might perish, that he might cast off his burden of death."

When the priests saw the fallen man's despair they seized him and stretched him over the edge of the gladiatorial stone. The high priest cut a gash in his side, thrust in his hand until he found the heart which he tore out and dropped into the painted gourd. The young captor, who had been standing by all this time, was given part of the captive's blood, whereupon the body was cut up to be eaten later by the family of the youthful warrior.

This ritual cannibalism was based, no doubt, upon the belief that the courage of the deceased would be transmitted to those who partook of his flesh.

Though this description, taken by Fray Bernardino de Sahagún from his Aztec informants, differs slightly from that of Durán, the two texts refer to the same gladiatorial ceremony.

62. The Skinning Rite, Tlacaxipehualiztli, which followed the gladiatorial ceremony, is also described in Book Two of the *Florentine Codex*. It is stated that captors donned the skins of the victims. "Each one of the captors came forth from his house, and appeared in, and went wearing, the captive's skin. They went with paper streamers upon their shoulders and upon the calves of their legs. And so they went jumping, pressing on, arriving together. So foul did they smell that verily the stench wounded the head. It was repellent. All men held their noses when they were met, when they met among people. And the skins, crumpled and crackling, were hardened. And some carried them in baskets—dried up, frayed, stiffened." The *Florentine Codex* then describes how twenty days later the young warriors divested themselves of the skins, cast them into a cave and then bathed in water mixed with corn meal.

This strange ceremony has been interpreted in different ways by modern authors. A prevalent idea is that it was an agricultural rite in which the skin of the victim represented the husk on the ear of corn about to ripen.

63. The skull rack or *tzompantli* was a large wooden affair erected near the great pyramid of Mexico. It stood upon a stone platform adorned with carved skulls and crossbones and was strung with the heads and bones of the victims of the numerous sacrifices performed by the Aztecs.

64. In spite of Durán's emphasis on human sacrifice, it is certain that this custom was by no means an invention of the Aztec nation. Pictorial evidence of the offering up of human lives to the divinity are to be found as early as 600 A.D., and the rite existed among the Maya of the Classic Period in the first centuries of the Christian era. The surrendering of a human life, the most precious possession of man, to the gods, was found not only in Mesoamerica and in northern Mexico but among the Incas to the south. It has existed on all continents in different periods of world history. The early Romans, for example, sacrificed a number of old men in the Tiber as part of a fertility ritual, and the Celts of western Europe and certain Nordic peoples continued the practice well into the Christian era.

65. Cochineal is a dyestuff consisting of the dried bodies of a scale insect known as the *Dactylopius coccus* or *coccus cacti*. This bug was bred in enormous quantities in ancient Mexico, especially among the Mixtec people of Oaxaca. In spite of its diminutive size it was one of the five domestic animals of Mesoamerica, the other four being the dog, turkey, duck, and bee. Cochineal insects reproduced upon the leaves of the *nopal* cactus

and were the source of great wealth to those who kept them. The reddish or purple dye was exported for hundreds of years to Europe, and lost its importance only with the appearance of modern chemical colorings.

66.  The Mixtec confederation of city-states was one of the most ancient and highly developed civilizations of Mesoamerica. Living in the highlands of what is now the state of Oaxaca, the Mixtecs, "People of the Clouds," produced the fabulous gold work now on display in the museum in the city of Oaxaca; they were the authors of seven of the sixteen codices which have survived to the present time; their documented and detailed historical records go back, according to Alfonso Caso, to 692 A.D. There is no doubt that the influence of the elaborate culture of the Mixtec people influenced the city-states of Texcoco, Mexico, Chalco, and many others.

67.  The Chocho and Popoloca peoples were organized as a number of small city-states in northern Oaxaca and what is now the southern part of Puebla. These people, living in a harsh and impoverished area, are often described as a cruel and treacherous tribe, a reputation they maintain to this day.

68.  While congratulatory remarks to those about to die seem paradoxical to us today, they are logical within Aztec theological patterns. While the majority of mankind went to the gloomy underworld after death, both warriors and victims in sacrifice departed toward the Teotlalpan, "Land of the Gods," which was thought to be situated toward the north. There brave soldiers and sacrificed prisoners enjoyed a happy life on a wild plain covered with cacti where the sun rose every day to their warlike shouts of exultation and to the clash of their shields.

   Another special paradise existed for women who had died in giving birth to a child. Another heaven was reserved for infants who had died very young; a "milk tree" kept them alive there. Still another paradise, a sort of Garden of Eden, Tlalocan, "Paradise of the Rain God," was reserved for those who drowned, were killed by lightning, or died of diseases associated with water.

69.  The custom of wearing old and worn sandals was a sign of respect to the deity or person whom one approached.

70.  These religious rites and symbols embody the basic concepts of Aztec cosmogony. These "People of the Sun" believed themselves to be living in a fifth "world" or "creation" which had been preceded by four others. The first world, its people and its sun were devoured by jaguars. The second was destroyed by the wind. A rain of fire then consumed the third world. Finally, a great deluge drowned the people and sun of the fourth creation. The fifth world, the one the Aztecs considered to be their era, was under the sign of movement and was to be destroyed by earthquakes, though the astrologers were not certain of the date of the destruction of this fifth period in the history of humanity.

71.     This chapter of Durán, describing the fabulous wealth delivered to Mexico City every eighty days, is one of the most remarkable in the entire *Historia*. It not only gives us a comprehensive list of objects of ritual or daily use but also shows us what was most prized among the inhabitants of ancient Mexico, including jade, feathers, rich mantles, live birds, jaguars and snakes, winged ants, cacao beans—just to mention a few. While most of the objects enumerated in this list would have relatively little desirability today, and their monetary worth would be almost nil, one must remember that the New World, separated by tens of thousands of years and a vast ocean from the Old, had developed economic systems of its own. Jade, a green stone similar to that of the Far East, was needed to adorn necklaces and other ritual objects which indicated unquestioned rank. Featherwork was esteemed as highly as jade and served very much the purpose of the latter. Live birds, jaguars and snakes were to be the precious occupants of the zoos—each one of these creatures incarnating a sacred concept in Aztec religion. Zoological gardens were unknown in Europe at that time; the Aztec zoos were to amaze the Spaniards on their arrival in Mexico as is attested by Bernal Díaz del Castillo. Winged ants—perhaps repellent to European taste—were one of the greatest delicacies of the Aztec cuisine. And the cacao bean was the money of ancient Mesoamerica, with a purchasing value equal to the coins and bills of today.

72.     These cultivated plants brought from every corner of the empire were to be transplanted in the private gardens of the nobility and in the enormous nurseries maintained by the Aztec government. These botanical gardens were later to be admired and described by the European eye-witnesses of the conquest. Among the many parks of this type should be mentioned Huaxtepec in Morelos, Chapultepec in Mexico City, and the Cypress Gardens of Nezahualcoyotl near Texcoco.

73.     Before considering the fantastic tale that is related in this chapter it is appropriate to remember the fabled origin of the god Huitzilopochtli. According to the ancient sources Huitzilopochtli's mother was a pious woman who lived in the holy city of Tula where she swept the temples and fulfilled other sacred duties. One day a feather came down from heaven. She picked it up and placed it in her bosom. Soon after this Coatlicue discovered that she was pregnant, much to the anger of her daughter, Coyolxauhqui, and her four hundred (*i.e.*, many) sons. When the divine child was about to be born his sister and brothers decided to kill him and his mother. Coatlicue wept in anguish but the voice of the unborn infant reassured her that all would be well. As Coyolxauhqui and her brothers drew their weapons, Huitzilopochtli, fully armed, was born like lightning, and slew his sister and brothers in the first glorious deed of his life.

    Some modern authors have tried to find in this legend a nature myth: Huitzilopochtli is the sun who slays his sister, the moon, and his brothers, the stars, when he is born.

74.     This curious prophecy regarding the fate of the image of Huitzilopochtli, venerated in

347

the great temple in the city of Mexico, was to be fulfilled in 1520 when the Spaniards cast the sacred idol down the steps of the pyramid.

75. The watery subsoil of Mexico City was a problem that the Aztecs had to cope with and which has harassed all architects and engineers, including those of the present day. The solution found by the Aztecs—that of sinking long poles deep under the buildings—reminds one of the methods used by the Dutch some centuries ago in the construction of their cities.

76. These words of Tlacaelel refer to the famous "Flowery War" practiced between the Aztecs and certain enemy states such as Tlaxcala, Cholula and Huexotzinco, a remarkable form of institutionalized warfare whose aim was not the conquest of new territories. Its only object was that of capturing brave warriors to serve as sacrificial victims on the altars of Mexico, or, if the enemy won, on the altars of Tlaxcala, Cholula, or Huexotzinco. Due to the nature of the war, soldiers did their best not to kill the opponent but rather to take him alive.

Tlaxcala, "Place of Maize Cakes," or Texcallan, "Place of Cliffs," as it was originally known, was to become a fierce rival of the Aztecs of Mexico-Tenochtitlan. The tribe that founded Tlaxcala had gone through a migration as harsh as that of the Aztecs. They too were nomadic Chichimecs and had sought the "Promised Land" for centuries. They too had been promised by their god Camaxtli that they would rule the world. The city-state of Tlaxcala was founded in 1328, only three years after the fabled founding of Mexico. The site of both cities had been revealed by birds, the eagle being the symbol of Mexico and the white heron that of Tlaxcala. Both cities were originally formed in four wards representing the four cardinal directions. It is not surprising, therefore, to find that these two vigorous nations should become archenemies and keep up a continual struggle which was still going on when the Spaniards arrived. Tlaxcala, though, had suffered greatly during these years of fighting and was in an inferior position to that of the Aztecs. Hedged in as this nation was by the enemy, the Tlaxcalans were deprived of salt, cotton and many other necessary goods. Therefore the arrival of Cortés (Quetzalcoatl) with his army was a sort of answer to their prayers and it should not surprise one to read that this nation was the principal native ally of the European invaders, receiving many benefits in return after the conquest.

77. These Aztec tenets concerning the treatment of all men as equals were reminiscences of pre-Columbian times which Durán found in the *Chronicle* and which were substantiated by his Aztec informants. However, it must be remembered that in all societies there exist "ideal" conduct and "real" behavior. It is quite possible that Durán's sources idealized the military and political situation of ancient Mexico and expressed a creed more than a reality. Not only Durán's chronicle but several others show inconsistencies and contradict the basic rules which are expressed in these pages.

78. The custom initiated by Moteczoma of leaving a memorial at Chapultepec in the form of a carved image of the royal personage was followed by the other Aztec rulers up to the Spanish conquest. These great carved reliefs were spared by the early conquerors and missionaries who seemed to have realized that they did not represent gods but simply political leaders of pre-Columbian times. In 1580, according to Durán, these memorials were still visible. However, they were dynamited later through fear of a nativistic revival. Parts of one impressive carving, that of Ahuitzotl, brother of Moteczoma II, may still be seen on the rocks at the foot of the hill of Chapultepec.

79. This park, sown with luxuriant plants brought from the Huaxteca and other parts of the empire, exemplifies one of the more refined aspects of the Aztec people. In contrast to some of the barbaric rites described by Durán, it is moving to read of this marvelous pleasure garden bequeathed to later generations. The gardens of Huaxtepec, long neglected, are now a national park near the city of Cuauhtla in the state of Morelos.

80. The Valley of Toluca, to the east of the Valley of Mexico, had been the center of great civilizations since the most ancient times. There the Otomi, Mazahua, Ocuiltec, and Matlatzinca, together with many Nahuatl-speaking groups, had formed important city-states which were now about to be conquered by the Aztec nation. This valley and its people, after the Aztec conquest, were to be exploited, and new towns and cities formed by colonists from the Valley of Mexico were to thrive there. The most spectacular archaeological site in the area is the monolithic temple, hewn out of living rock, in Malinalco, and the circular structure to Quetzalcoatl as a wind god in Calixtlahuaca. Both are near the city of Toluca.

81. The Aztecs, like every other nation, had a number of prejudices regarding the peoples who were their neighbors. Some of the Nahuatl terms used by the Aztecs of Mexico when they referred to other tribes were Nonoalca ("Mutes"), Popoloca ("Barbarians" or "Savages"), Chontal ("Foreigner" or "Speaker of a Strange Tongue"). Therefore, to the average man, the surrounding peoples were "primitive," "backward," "barbarous," and the like. For instance, the Huaxtecs were considered to be drunkards and sodomites, the Otomi were brutish and bestial in their sexual conduct and the Tarascans of the west were wild, nudist people.

82. The *teponaztli* was one of the several musical instruments used by the Aztecs. It was a drum carved out of a log. The *huehuetl* was a large vertical drum whose mouth was covered with stretched skin. Other instruments were the turtle shell drum, the rattle, the whistle, single or multiple flute, rasping bone, copper bells, the conch shell trumpet, and the whistling jar.

83. Perhaps no passage from the *Historia* of Durán shows so clearly the almost incredible

contrast between a barbarous and fierce way of life, exemplified by these brutal cere-monies, and the extreme refinements of the flowers, perfume, fine feather work, elab-orate poetry, and the delicate and refined speech that are to be found throughout the entire work.

84. Michoacan, "Land of Fish," was the home of the Tarascan people, some two hundred miles to the west of the city of Mexico. From ancient times this rich country had been inhabited by the Tarascans or Purepecha, a tribe of unknown origin, speaking a language possibly connected with the Quechua of Peru. This ethnic group possessed a knowledge of metallurgy far superior to that of the Aztecs and this may have contributed to the spectacular defeat of the latter described by Durán. The principal city of this kingdom was Tzintzuntzan on the shores of Lake Patzcuaro.

85. The Aztecs looked upon the universe as a series of superimposed worlds. Above the actual world were the nine heavens, dwelling places of the gods, not to be compared to the "Heaven" of Christianity. Below the earth lay the underworlds, nine in number, the abode of the dead, not to be mistaken for the Christian "Hell." The soul of a dead man was thought to undergo a long and dangerous journey in his efforts to reach the underworld. Along the way he had to pass through a number of trials—ice-cold wind that cut like obsidian blades, mountains that bumped one another and might catch the spirit as it passed, and the River of the World of the Dead where a dog awaited him and could per-haps be talked into helping the soul across the waters. En route a ferocious jaguar stood ready to eat the heart of the individual, but this could be avoided by placing a jade bead in the deceased's mouth at the funeral. This jade, on the terrible journey to the under-world, could be offered to the jaguar in place of the heart. After all these trials the soul eventually reached the ninth underworld where he offered gifts to Mictlantecuhtli, Lord of the Dead and his wife, Mictlancihuatl, Lady of the Dead.

86. Tobacco, a plant native to the Western Hemisphere, was commonly used by the Aztecs for smoking, medicinal purposes, and as an important part of ritual. These three uses were common to practically every native tribe in the New World. The Aztecs smoked tobacco in two ways: in pipes and in elaborate cigarette holders in the form of tubes, scented with liquid amber.

87. The *teonanacatl*, "Divine Mushroom," was a highly important stimulant taken during ritual occasions. In the *Florentine Codex* one reads of the hallucinations produced during a ceremony. On a certain feast day the participants ". . . ate the mushrooms with honey. When the mushrooms took effect on them, then they danced, then they wept. But some, while still in command of their senses, entered and sat there by the house on their seats; they danced no more, but only sat there nodding.

"One saw in a vision that he would die, and the weeping continued. One saw in a vision that he would die in battle; one saw in a vision that he would be eaten by wild beasts; one saw in a vision that he would take captives in war; one saw in a vision that he would be rich, wealthy . . ." Everything, good or bad, that might befall a human being, could be seen under the influence of the mushrooms.

"And when the effect of the mushrooms had left them, they consulted among themselves and told one another what they had seen in visions. And they saw in visions what would befall those who had eaten no mushrooms, and what they went about doing."

These wild mushrooms still play an important role in modern Mexican folk religion, above all in certain Mazatec and Mixtec communities in the state of Oaxaca. In contemporary times they have been studied intensively by modern scientists such as Weitlaner, Wasson, Heim, whose discoveries have found their way into modern psychiatry and whose publications are well known in the medical and anthropological world.

88.  The pyramids of Mexico, unlike those of Egypt, were great earthen mounds covered with cut stone and did not, usually, serve as tombs. They functioned as great platforms upon which temples or shrines were erected and, as Durán's text tells, were often used for defense purposes, a fact the Spaniards were to discover during the conquest. Aside from their military value it is quite probable that in their construction a basic reason for their height was to place the worshipper closer to the Sun and the other gods.

89.  The number of eighty thousand four hundred victims given here by Durán has been one of the most controversial subjects in ancient Mexican history. Those who believe this to be a gross exaggeration point out the problems in disposing of the huge number of corpses, and suggest that the Spanish were always prone to exaggerate the number of sacrificial victims as a justification for the conquest. Those who have defended Durán's statistics have also pointed out that a people as dedicated as the Aztecs were in sacrifice, an act which to them was indispensable in keeping the sun and the universe alive, without doubt possessed a system of disposing of the bodies of the victims.

90.  Little has been written regarding Aztec experiments in the repopulation of devastated zones. However, this does not mean that the Aztecs' experience in these projects was unimportant. The background of the Aztec people, nomadic and wild as it was, possibly had given them an understanding of the importance of mixing with conquered peoples in order to avoid future unrest and trouble. The new settlements founded by the Aztecs remind one of the Inca endeavor to hold together that vast empire by means of new colonies made up of loyal Quechua-speaking Incas. This pattern of resettlement was later to be continued in Mexico by the Spanish conquerors, who sent thousands of Aztecs and other Nahuatl-speaking peoples to the north in an effort to have them merge with nomadic groups there. These Aztec colonists found their way as far north as Zacatecas, Saltillo, and San Antonio, Texas.

351

91.   This passage in the *Historia* reveals one of the principal motifs of ancient Mesoamerican religion: *nahualism,* the belief that human beings are able to change themselves into animals at will. Belief in the *nahual* or werewolf was as widespread in ancient times as it is in rural parts of Mexico today. Folk stories are filled with incidents regarding men and women who are able to transform themselves into jaguars, eagles, hawks, snakes, and even harmless animals such as deer or buzzards. In the village one can hear stories like the following: A certain man was walking along a lonely road when he was attacked by a rattlesnake. The man, however, managed to take out his knife and cut off the head of the serpent. A few hours later, when he arrived back in town he found that his worst enemy had been beheaded in a strange way and had been discovered dead within his home. This means that the decapitated man was a *nahual,* capable of changing himself into a rattlesnake in order to harm others.

92.   This passage in Durán's *Historia,* referring to what are now the Republics of Central America, is curious, yet it is not surprising that the Dominican historian should not dwell on the subject of the rich lands to the south since, as he states several times, his chronicle is to be a history of the Aztecs of Mexico City. Cuauhtemallan, Atlpopoca, Popocatepetl, and Tlatlatepec are regions which undoubtedly lie today within the Republics of Guatemala, El Salvador, and Nicaragua, areas which in those times were inhabited by people who spoke languages of the Maya and Nahuatl families and possessed high cultures.

93.   In disagreement with Durán's description of Moteczoma II, Cortés and Bernal Díaz del Castillo describe the Aztec emperor as the most gentle of men. The character of Moteczoma has been a controversial subject since the moment that the Spanish invaders first set eyes on him. It is possible that Durán's black picture of this sovereign is colored to a certain extent by the traditions that had grown up after the Spanish conquest. In their desire to justify their invasion of the Aztec empire, the Europeans had undoubtedly formed a corps of legends slandering the ancient rulers.

94.   One can believe Durán's description of the panic that gripped the Aztec warriors in their first meeting with the ocean. The Aztecs and many other Nahuatl-speaking people of the highlands, accustomed as they were to their inland mountain peaks and cool climate, generally found the tropical coastal areas unattractive. Acapulco, Veracruz and other seacoast towns conquered by the Aztecs were only to become important in Spanish times.

95.   The Indian, Muñoz Camargo, greatest of all sixteenth century Tlaxcalan historians, tells the story of Tlahuicolli in a different way. He states that the captive warrior from Tlaxcala ingratiated himself with the Aztecs and was made a commander in the army. Moteczoma II placed Tlahuicolli at the head of the great forces which invaded Michoacan. The Tlaxcalan chieftain returned with a record of such glorious deeds that Moteczoma gave him his freedom. However, Tlahuicolli seems to have realized at this moment that his life had come to an end; he could not continue to fight for the Aztecs because they were

the enemies of his own people. He could not return to Tlaxcala as he knew he had betrayed his own nation by fighting on the side of their terrible Aztec enemies. Therefore, Tlahuicolli asked Moteczoma to allow him to die upon the *temalacatl*, the round stone of sacrifice. The victim was given a few days of rest and was finally placed upon the carved gladiatorial rock. So it was that Tlahuicolli, according to the Tlaxcalan chronicler, managed to bash in the heads of eight Aztec Eagle warriors and wound some twenty others before he collapsed upon the surface of the round stone, was sacrificed and his heart torn out by the high priest.

96. Toci, "Our Grandmother," also known as Tonantzin, "Our Mother," possessed many other appellations such as "Earth Mother," "Fertility Goddess," and "Deity of Motherhood." She was a divinity who had been worshipped since preclassic times (2000 B.C.). She was by far the most popular goddess not only among the Aztecs but among the other nations of Mesoamerica. It was inevitable that after the conquest the Virgin Mary should have been confused with this personage. The patroness of Mexico, Our Lady of Guadalupe, is still called Tonantzin, "Our Mother" by Nahuatl-speaking Indians.

97. It is curious to note that the Aztecs looked upon comets as ill omens, just as the contemporary European regarded them as signs of war, famine and pestilence.

98. This curious story is found perpetuated in stone on a Christian monument in front of the church of San Hipólito in Mexico City. It was on this site that hundreds of Spaniards found their death in the confusion of Cortés' midnight flight from the city in 1520. The city of Mexico was finally taken by the Spaniards on the 13th of August, 1521, feast day of Saint Hippolytus, whereupon this Roman martyr was to become the patron saint of Mexico City.

99. Cicalco, "Place of Hares," or Cincalo, "House of Maize," was another name for the underworld, although the place Moteczoma was anxious to journey to sounds more like Tlalocan, the verdant paradise of the Rain God, a sort of Eden which became the home of those who had died by drowning. As can be read in the next passage, Huemac, Lord of Cicalco, undeceives Moteczoma by revealing the true nature of his unearthly domain.

It is strange that Huemac, a true historical personage, last ruler of the Toltecs in the twelfth century, should be described here as sovereign of the underworld. Generally the latter is called Mictlantecuhtli, Lord of the Place of the Dead, and is portrayed as a skeleton.

100. The famous weeping woman to whom Durán refers in this passage is today perhaps the most popular character of any Mexican legend. La Llorona, "She Who Weeps," continues to be in modern times an ill omen who appears to men who wander about in the late hours. She is thought to be dressed in white, with long flowing hair, and her fearful moan, "¡Ay, mis hijos!" "Alas, my children!" is a sign of impending death or other

calamities. She is also looked upon as a seductress of men who are unfaithful to their wives. The theme is a universal one, known not only to many Indian tribes in America but also in Europe and Asia.

101.    There is utter confusion in Durán's chronicle regarding the first Spanish expeditions to Mexico. Francisco Hernández de Córdova led a group of Spaniards to Yucatan and certain points on the Gulf in 1517. Juan de Grijalva captained a second expedition from Cuba, which at that time was the headquarters of the Spaniards in the New World. The voyage of Grijalva was made in 1518, reaching as far as the island of San Juan de Ulúa which today faces the modern port of Veracruz. It was there that the first contact between Aztecs and Spaniards took place. The third expedition was that of Hernando Cortés, who arrived at Ulúa on April 21, 1519.

102.    There is no doubt that Moteczoma was greatly preoccupied with the return of Quetzalcoatl, the Precious Serpent, ruler of Tula in the tenth century A.D., who had abandoned the Veracruz coast and had promised to return. Eventually, Moteczoma and the other dignitaries, as can be seen in chronicles, were to become totally convinced that Cortés and Quetzalcoatl were one. The concept of a messiah, whose coming is anticipated with joy by the masses of the oppressed and is feared by the ruling class, is a universal theme, and in Mexican history Quetzalcoatl filled this prominent role. It is possible that as late as 1864 when the blond, bearded Emperor Maximilian arrived in Veracruz, faint reminiscences lingered in the minds of the Indians which reminded them of the promised return of Quetzalcoatl.

103.    Durán's garbled account and confusion between the Grijalva and Cortés expeditions continues. Malinche, Marina, or Malintzin, as she is referred to in different documents, Indian interpreter and mistress of Cortés, came to Veracruz for the first and only time with Cortés in 1519. Malinche, one of the most remarkable and prominent figures in the entire conquest of Mexico, is not given her proper role by Durán, while other historians, such as Bernal Díaz del Castillo, emphasize her key position in the subjection of the Aztec people. Malinche was born in the tropical area of Tabasco or southern Veracruz and belonged to a Nahuatl-speaking group.

As a child she was sold by her mother and stepfather to certain merchants who carried her south where she apparently learned the Maya language. Young and extremely beautiful, Malinche was given to the Spaniards together with other slave women when the invaders reached a certain point on the Gulf of Mexico. The young woman soon became the mistress of Cortés, leader of the expedition, who quickly realized the shrewdness and inherent diplomacy of the woman. She learned Spanish and her role from this time on was to be vital, not only as a translator but as the one person with the expedition who clearly understood the psychology and ways of the Aztecs in their relation to the Spaniards. Little is known regarding the life of this extraordinary woman after the conquest.

104.    The anxiety and lack of self-confidence shown by the Aztecs throughout all these pages of Durán reveal the true situation of the country at the moment of the arrival of the European invaders. The Aztec empire was formed of a number of subjected and exploited city-states who resented their masters and who could not be trusted to remain loyal. When Cortés set out for Mexico City he had already acquired a large army of Indian allies formed principally of Totonacs, a people of central Veracruz whose resentment was deeply rooted. Later Cortés was to obtain the help of several thousand Tlaxcalans, Huexotzinca and other peoples. Certain modern historians have pointed out that what has been called the "conquest" of Mexico was actually a great native revolution sparked by the arrival of the Spaniards.

105.    The building described by Durán stood on the western side of the Zócalo, main square of modern Mexico City, and occupied the space of what is today the National Pawn Shop. The enormous pyramid and temple enclosure covered some eight blocks to the northeast, on part of which now stands the great Metropolitan Cathedral. On the eastern side of the square was built the "House of Moteczoma" which is today the National Palace. Three causeways led out from this large plaza. The one to the south, used by Cortés on his entry into the city, led toward Iztapalapa and the Floating Gardens of Xochimilco. The road to the north went toward what is now the Shrine of Our Lady of Guadalupe. The causeway to the west led to Tacuba and was to be the scene of the frightful massacre of the Spaniards and their Indian allies when they fled from the city. In these causeways were gaps filled by movable bridges, the purpose of which was to isolate the city in case of attack, and which were to prove fatal to the Spaniards in their attempted escape.

106.    Durán is mistaken in placing Cortés in Mexico City during Alvarado's cruel massacre during the feast of Toxcatl. The Spanish captain was actually in Veracruz during this time, having gone to the coast with the purpose of attacking his enemy Narváez.

107.    Vaillant aptly describes the feast of Toxcatl: "In contrast to the callous brutality of the fire sacrifice, the ceremony in honor of the god Tezcatlipoca was strikingly dramatic, tinged with the pathos with which we view the taking of a life. The handsomest and bravest prisoner of war was selected a year before his execution. Priests taught him the manners of a ruler, and as he walked about, playing divine melodies upon his flute, he received the homage due to Tezcatlipoca himself. A month before the day of sacrifice, four lovely girls, dressed as goddesses, became his companions and attended to his every want. On the day of his death he took leave of his weeping consorts to lead a procession in his honor, marked by jubilation and feasting. Then he bade farewell to the glittering cortege and left for a small temple, accompanied by the eight priests who had attended him throughout the year. The priests preceded him up the steps of the temple, and he followed, breaking at each step a flute which he had played in the happy hours of his incarnation. At the top of the platform the priests turned him over the sacrificial block

and wrenched out his heart. In deference to his former godhood, his body was carried, not ignominiously flung, down the steps, but his head joined the other skulls on the rack beside the temple."

108. The *encomienda* or "trust system" was not a grant of land to be exploited as private property by the Spaniards, but it was a grant of human beings—Indians whom the Spaniards were allowed to use as serfs and whose needs they were supposed to supply. These natives were "entrusted" to the Spaniards who could not sell them or dispose of their lives. The entire system, theoretically sound, led to terrible abuse and unjust exploitation of the conquered peoples under most Spaniards. The *encomienda* was finally abolished in 1710.

109. During the generation that lived after the Spanish conquest of 1521, the Indians of Mexico were often enslaved, bought and sold like chattels, though in Durán's age this was no longer done. Due mainly to the efforts of Las Casas and other Dominicans, the institution had been abolished for the natives, though Negro slaves were brought in from Africa during the three hundred years of Spanish rule. This early abolition of Indian slavery was to change the entire history of Spanish America, for, when the countries became independent at the beginning of the nineteenth century, they did not have to face a wholesale emancipation which could have caused civil wars and social disorganization. Negro slavery, which had always been on a small scale, was eliminated in Mexico as early as 1810.

# TRADITIONAL LIST OF AZTEC SOVEREIGNS

Based on Jimenez Moreno's studies, the following list, though it differs slightly from the chronology given by Durán, gives us these dates for the Aztec emperors:

| | |
|---|---|
| Acamapichtli, "Handful of Reeds" | 1376-1396 |
| Huitzilihuitl, "Hummingbird Feather" | 1396-1417 |
| Chimalpopoca, "Smoking Shield" | 1417-1427 |
| Itzcoatl, "Obsidian Snake" | 1427-1440 |
| Moteczoma Ilhuicamina, "Angry Lord Who Shoots into the Sky" | 1440-1469 |
| Axayacatl, "Water Face" | 1469-1481 |
| Tizoc, "Leg of Chalk" | 1481-1486 |
| Ahuitzotl, "Water Monster" | 1486-1502 |
| Moteczoma Xocoyotzin, "Angry Lord, Youngest Son" | 1502-1520 |
| Cuitlahuac, "Lord of Cuitlahuac, Keeper of the Kingdom" | 1520 |
| Cuauhtemoc, "Eagle That Descends" | 1521 |

The above names undoubtedly evolved from the religious and mythological world of the Aztecs. All these rulers also possessed calendrical names taken from the day of their birth which apparently were kept secret for fear that public knowledge of these names could be used to cause harm to their owners by magical means.

# GUIDE TO THE PRONUNCIATION OF NAHUATL NAMES

The *a* is pronounced like the *a* in *father*.

The *e* as in the word *get*.

The *i* as in *seen*.

The *o* is a sound intermediate between the *o* in *smoke* and the same vowel in *come*.

*C* when followed by *a* or *o* is pronounced like the *k* in *king*. When followed by *i* or *e* it has the sound of *s* in *mess*.

*Qu* when followed by a vowel is pronounced like a *k*.

*Z* is always pronounced like an *s*.

*Hu* when followed by a vowel acquires the sound of the English *w*.

The *tl* is considered an independent sound in Nahuatl, similar to the *tl* in *rattler* but with a harsher, clicking sound.

All Nahuatl words are stressed on the next to last syllable.

Observe the following examples: *Nezahualpilli* (Ness-ah-wahl-*pee*-lee), *Axayacatl* (Ah-shah-*yah*-cahtl), *Xochimilco* (Show-chee-*meel*-coe), *Huitzilopochtli* (Weets-eel-oh-*poach*-tlee), *Azcapotzalco* (Ah-scah-poe-*tsahl*-coe), *Tenochtitlan* (Teh-noach-*tee*-tlan).

# BIBLIOGRAPHY

Acosta, José de. *Historia natural y moral de las Indias.* ("Biblioteca Americana, 38") Mexico: Fondo de Cultura Económica, 1962.

This is perhaps the clearest and most "modern" approach to ancient Mexican history written during the XVIth century. Father Acosta used the same source which was the basis of Durán's *Historia:* the *Crónica X.*

Alva Ixtlilxochitl, Fernando de. *Obras históricas.* 2 vols. Mexico: Editora Nacional, 1952.

The works of Ixtlilxochitl should be read by the student of ancient Mexican history as a contrast to Durán's *Chronicle,* as Texcoco is given credit for most of the great Aztec deeds described by Durán.

Alvarado Tezozomoc, Hernando. *Crónica Mexicana.* Mexico: Editorial Leyenda, 1944.

Again based on the *Crónica X,* this work is a parallel of the *Historia* of Durán.

———*Crónica Mexicayotl.* Mexico: Universidad Nacional Autónoma, 1949.

Tezozomoc's brilliant and poetic work on pre-Hispanic Aztec history.

Anonymous. *Anales de Tlatelolco y Códice de Tlatelolco.* Mexico: Robredo y Porrúa, 1948.

This edition was taken from the original German translation from the Nahuatl, published by Ernst Menghin, in *Baessler Archiv,* Vol. XXII. This Aztec document, written in 1528, is one of the oldest and most thrilling descriptions of the Spanish conquest written by a native eye-witness.

———*Codex Aubin, histoire de la nation méxicaine.* Paris: E. Leroux, 1893.

———*Codex Borbonicus, le manuscrit mexicain de la Bibliothèque du Palais Bourbon.* Paris: E. T. Famy, 1899.

A ritual and calendrical book, painted by an Aztec scribe shortly after the Spanish conquest.

———*Codex Borgia. Il Manoscritto Messicano Borgiano del Museo Etnografico della Santa Congregazione di Propaganda Fide.* Rome: Loubat, 1898.

The most beautiful of all the ancient books; a series of brightly colored paintings dealing with a maze of astronomical and calendrical subjects. Another edition of the codex is that of Eduard Seler, Berlin, 1906.

———*Codex Magliabecchiano XIII, 3, Manuscrit Mexicain post-colombien de la Bibliothèque Nationale de Florence.* Rome: Loubat, 1904.

This is a beautifully illustrated post-conquest book dealing with religious affairs.

———*Codex Mendoza.* Mexico: Museo Nacional de Arqueología, 1925.

A superb English edition of this elaborate pictorial history of the Aztecs and tribute list is that of Cooper Clark (3 vols.), Oxford, 1938.

————*Códice Chimalpopoca—Anales de Cuauhtitlan y Leyenda de los Soles.* Mexico: Universidad Nacional Autónoma, 1945.

These two ancient documents, published in one volume, are of first-rate importance in their description of ancient Aztec history and mythology.

————*Códice Ramírez: Relación del origen de los indios que habitan esta Neuva España, según sus historias.* Mexico: Editorial Leyenda, 1944.

This ancient document is derived from the *Crónica X*, basis of Durán's work. An English version of this text is to be found in Radin's *Sources and Authenticity.*

————*Lienzo de Tlaxcala.* ("Antigüedades mexicanas publicadas en homenaje a Cristóbal Colón") Mexico: Junta Colombina, 1892.

————*Tira de la peregrinación mexica.* Mexico: Librería Anticuaria, 1944.

Bancroft, Hubert Howe. *History of Mexico.* 6 vols. San Francisco: A. L. Bancroft & Co., 1883.

Although outdated, Bancroft's chronicle is well-planned and contains much information which is not found in later works.

Barlow, Robert. *El códice Azcatitlan.* ("*Journal de la Société des Américanistes*, Nouvelle Série t. XXXVIII.") Paris: Musée de L'Homme, 1949.

————*La Crónica "X."* ("Revista Mexicana de Estudios Antropológicos" Vol. VII, 1, 2 and 3) Mexico: Sociedad Mexicana de Antropología, 1945.

The best study of the ancient chronicle upon which Durán relied for his *Historia.*

————*The Extent of the Empire of the Culhua Mexica.* ("Ibero-Americana, 28") Berkeley: University of California Press, 1949.

The geography of the Aztec empire.

Benavente, Toribio de (Motolinía). *Historia de los Indios de la Nueva España.* Mexico: Editorial Chávez Hayhoe, 1941.

Two English versions of this early Franciscan chronicle on the Aztecs have appeared: *Motolinia's History of the Indians of New Spain,* Washington, Academy of American Franciscan History, 1951; and *Motolinia's History of the Indians of New Spain,* Albuquerque, University of New Mexico, 1950.

Bernal, Ignacio. *Bibliografía de arqueología y etnografía. Mesoamérica y Norte de México, 1514-1960.* Mexico: Instituto Nacional de Antropología e Historia, 1962.

————*Tenochtitlan en una isla.* ("Serie Historia II") Mexico: Instituto Nacional de Antropología e Historia, 1960.

This account of life in the Valley of Mexico in pre-conquest times has been translated into English and bears the title of *Mexico Before Cortez,* New York, Doubleday, 1963.

Burland, C. A. *Art and Life in Ancient Mexico.* Oxford: Bruno Cassirer, n.d.

Caso, Alfonso. *El pueblo del Sol.* Mexico: Fondo de Cultura Económica, 1953.
>An English translation of this valuable work is *The People of the Sun*, Norman, University of Oklahoma Press, 1958.

Clavijero, Francisco Javier. *Storia antica del Messico.* Bologna, 1780.
>The best Spanish translation of this remarkable work on the history of the Aztecs is *Historia antigua de México*, Mexico, Editorial Delfín, 1944. The first English edition was printed in London in 1787.

Conquistador Anonimo. *Relatione di alcune cose della Nueva Spagna.* ("Navigationi et viaggi, da Gio Gattista Ramusio.") Venice: 1606.
>A recent English translation of this famous eye-witness account of the conquest can be found in *The Conquistadors*. New York, Orion Press, 1963.
>Another well-known one is entitled *Narrative of Some Things of New Spain*. New York: The Cortés Society, 1917.

Cortés, Hernando. *Cartas de Relación de la conquista de Méjico.* Bilbao: Espasa Calpe, 1932.
>The English edition of the conqueror's letters to the king of Spain are to be found in *Five Letters 1519-1526*. London: Routledge and Sons, 1928.

Covarrubias, Miguel. *Indian Art of Mexico and Central America.* New York: Alfred A. Knopf, 1957.

Díaz del Castillo, Bernal. *Historia verdadera de la conquista de la Nueva España.* Madrid: Espasa Calpe, 2 vols., 1928.
>A popular English translation is entitled *The Discovery and Conquest of Mexico 1517-1521*, Mexico, The Mexico Press, n.d.

García Granados, Rafael. *Diccionario biográfico de historia antigua de Méjico.* ("Publicaciones del Instituto de Historia," No. 23, 3 vols.) Mexico: Universidad Nacional Autónoma de México, 1952-1953.
>This monumental work is a series of biographies of pre-Hispanic personages, the data taken from all the printed sources.

Garibay K., Angel María. *Historia de la literatura náhuatl.* ("Biblioteca Porrúa" I, 2 vols.) Mexico: Editorial Porrúa, 1953.
>In this work Father Garibay has brought to life the songs, hymns, and epic poems of the Aztecs.

Gillmor, Frances. *Flute of Smoking Mirror. A Portrait of Nezahualcoyotl.* Albuquerque, 1949.

Jiménez Moreno, Wigberto. *Notas sobre historia antigua de México.* Mexico: Ediciones S.A.E.N.A.H., 1956.

363

Kingsborough, Lord. *Antiquities of Mexico.* 9 vols. London, 1831-1848.
   Edward King, Lord Kingsborough, was a pioneer in Mesoamerican studies. The fruit of his life's work may be found in these nine enormous volumes.

León-Portilla, Miguel. *La filosofía náhuatl.* Mexico: Universidad Nacional Autónoma de México, 1959.
   Dr. León-Portilla's synthesis of the Aztec world-view is indispensable for any student of ancient Mexico. It has been published in English as *The Mind of Ancient Mexico.* Norman: The University of Oklahoma Press, 1963.

————*Los antiguos mexicanos a través de sus crónicas y cantares.* Mexico: Fondo de Cultura Económica, 1961.

————*Visión de los vencidos.* ("Biblioteca del Estudiante Universitario," Vol. 81) Mexico: Universidad Nacional Autónoma de México, 1961.
   An English translation of these stirring accounts of the Spanish conquest by Aztec eye-witnesses has appeared under the title *The Broken Spears,* Boston, Beacon Press, 1962.

Leonard, Carmen [Ed.] *Esplendor del México Antiguo.* 2 vols. Mexico: Centro de Investigaciones Antropológicas de México, 1959.
   This impressive collection of articles describing every phase of ancient Mesoamerican life was written by prominent experts in the field.

Mendieta, Jerónimo de. *Historia eclesiástica indiana.* 4 vols. Mexico: Chávez Hayhoe, 1945.

Muñoz Camargo, Diego. *Historia de Tlaxcala.* Mexico: Xicohtencatl, Asociación de Tlaxcaltecas, 1947.

Nicholson, Irene. *Firefly in the Night. A Study of Ancient Mexican Poetry and Symbolism.* London: 1959.

Orozco y Berra, Manuel. *Historia antigua y de la conquista de México.* 4 vols. Mexico: 1880.
   Though this history of the Aztecs was written almost a century ago it has not been surpassed by any general work describing the events which took place between the birth and death of this nation.

Peñafiel, Antonio. *Nombres geográficos de Mexico. Catálogo alfabético de los nombres de lugar pertenecientes al idioma náhuatl.* 2 vols. Mexico, 1885.

Peterson, Frederick A. *Ancient Mexico. An Introduction to the Pre-Hispanic Cultures.* London: George Allen & Unwin Ltd., 1959.
   This is one of the most comprehensive modern works on Mesoamerica.

Prescott, William H. *History of the Conquest of Mexico.* New York: The Modern Library, n.d.

Radin, Paul. *The Sources and Authenticity of the History of the Ancient Mexicans.* ("University of California Publications in American Archaeology and Ethnology" Vol. XVII, No. 1) Berkeley: 1920.

Sahagún, Bernardino de. *Historia General de las cosas de Nueva España*. 4 vols. Mexico: Editorial Porrúa, 1956.
   This, the most important work written on the Aztec civilization, serves as an excellent complement to Durán's *Historia*. Father Sahagún, a Franciscan monk, produced another version of his *Historia*, the *Florentine Codex*, in the original Nahuatl, which has been published in a bilingual edition (Nahuatl-English) by the School of American Research, Santa Fe, New Mexico, 1950-1963. A masterly translation into German of the Nahuatl version of the *Florentine* text is to be found in Eduard Seler's *Gesammelte Abhandlungen*, Berlin, 1902-1923.

Sejourné, Laurette. *Burning Water. Thought and Religion in Ancient Mexico*. (Evergreen Edition) New York: Grove Press, 1960.

Soustelle, Jacques. *La pensée cosmologique des anciens mexicains*. Paris: 1940.

———*La vie quotidienne des Aztèques a la veille de la conquête espagnole*. Paris: Librairie Hachette, 1955.

Spence, Lewis. *The Civilization of Ancient Mexico*. London, 1912.

———*The Gods of Mexico*. London, 1923.

Spinden, Herbert J. *Ancient Civilizations of Mexico and Central America*. New York: American Museum of Natural History Handbook No. 3, 1928.

Tapia, Andrés de. *Relación de algunas cosas de las que acaecieron al muy ilustre señor Don Hernando Cortés*. ("Crónicas del Conquista, Biblioteca del Estudiante Universitario, 2") Mexico: Universidad Nacional Autónoma, 1950.
   The English edition of this interesting account of the conquest by an eye-witness is to be found in *The Conquistadors*, New York, Orion Press, 1963.

Tlalocan. *Revista de Fuentes para el Conocimiento de las Culturas Indigenas de México*. Mexico: La Casa de Tlaloc, 1943-1963.
   This journal publishes documents, ancient and modern, on the native cultures of Mesoamerica.

Torquemada, Juan de. *Los Veinte i un libros rituales i Monarchia Indiana*. Madrid. 1723, facsimile edition, Mexico, 1944.

Vaillant, George C. *The Aztecs of Mexico. Origin, Rise and Fall of the Aztec Nation*. ("Penguin Books") Harmondsworth, Middlesex, 1950.

Veytia, Mariano. *Historia antigua de México*. 2 vols. Mexico: Editorial Leyenda, 1944.

# CHRONOLOGICAL TABLE C

## MESOAMERICAN CULTURE

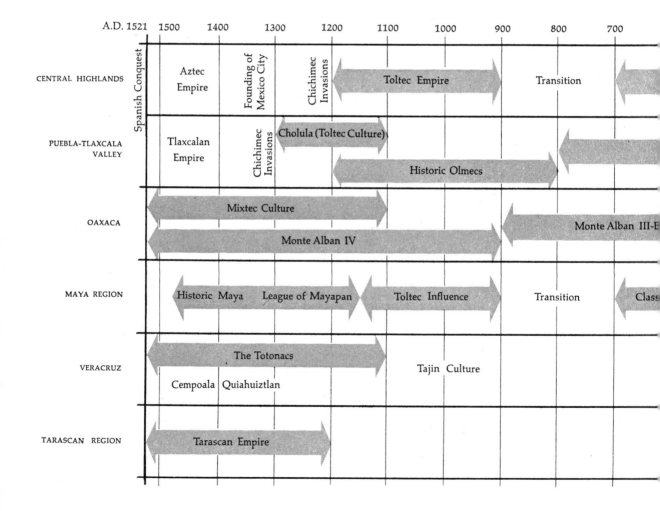

| | A.D. 1521 | 1500 | 1400 | 1300 | 1200 | 1100 | 1000 | 900 | 800 | 700 |
|---|---|---|---|---|---|---|---|---|---|---|
| CENTRAL HIGHLANDS | Spanish Conquest | Aztec Empire | Founding of Mexico City | Chichimec Invasions | Toltec Empire | | | Transition | | |
| PUEBLA-TLAXCALA VALLEY | | Tlaxcalan Empire | Chichimec Invasions | Cholula (Toltec Culture) | Historic Olmecs | | | | | |
| OAXACA | | Mixtec Culture | | | Monte Alban IV | | | Monte Alban III-E | | |
| MAYA REGION | | Historic Maya | League of Mayapan | Toltec Influence | | Transition | | Class | | |
| VERACRUZ | | The Totonacs | | Tajin Culture | | | | | | |
| | | Cempoala Quiahuiztlan | | | | | | | | |
| TARASCAN REGION | | Tarascan Empire | | | | | | | | |

# HE AZTECS AND OTHER

*fter Piña Chan)*

0
500
400
300
200
100
0
B.C. 100
200
2000
5000
10000
Teotihuacan
Preclassic Cultures Copilco, Cuicuilco, Tlatilco
Tepexpan Man
Teotihuacan Occupation
Preclassic Cultures
900
Coxcatlan Cave
Monte Alban III-A
Transition Monte Alban II-III-A
Monte Alban II
Monte Alban I
Maya
Palenque Tikal Kaminaljuyu Copan
Preclassic Cultures Mamom-Chicanel
Olmecs (La Venta Culture)
1500

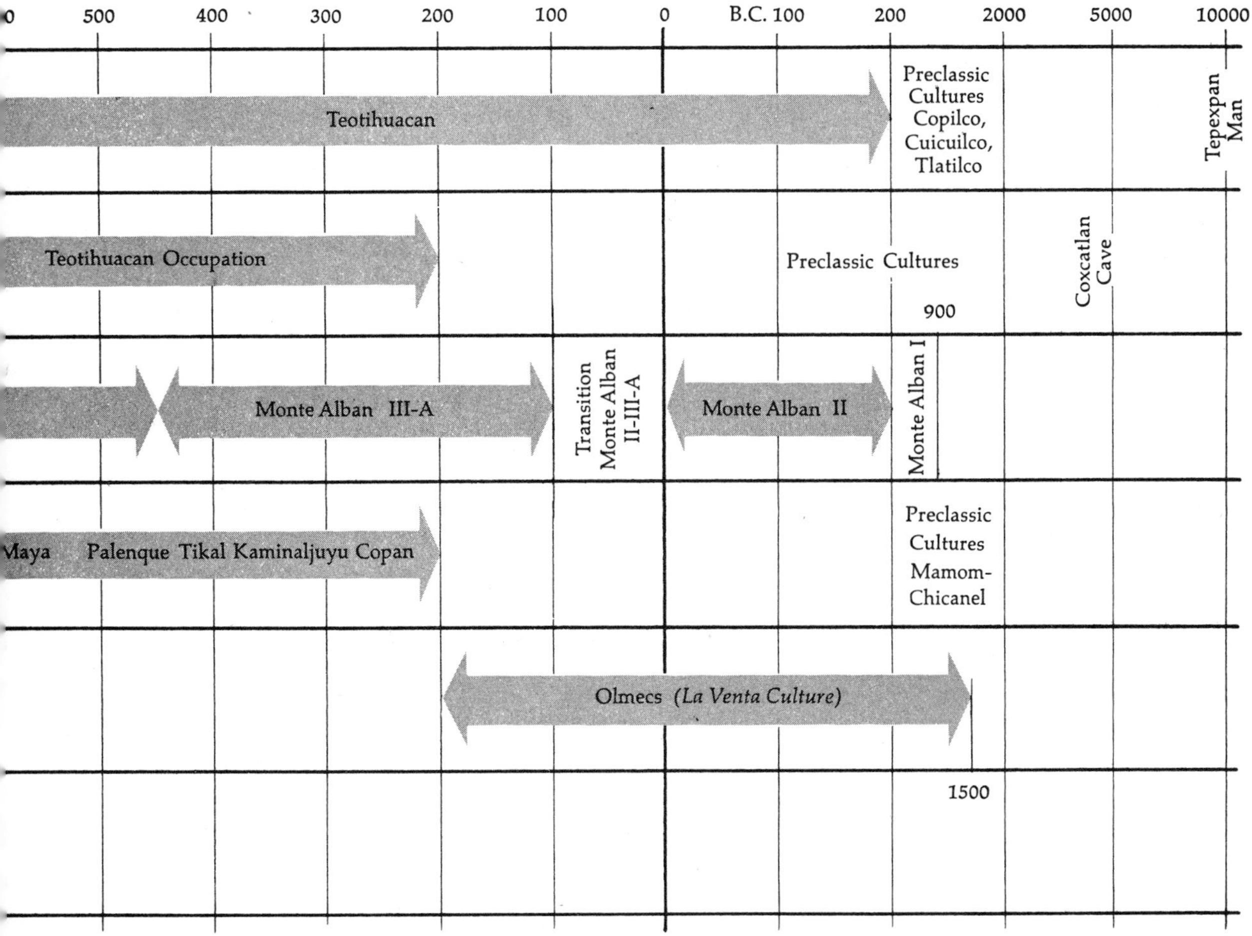

# GENEALOGICAL CHART

# OF AZTEC KINGS

*(According to Durán)*

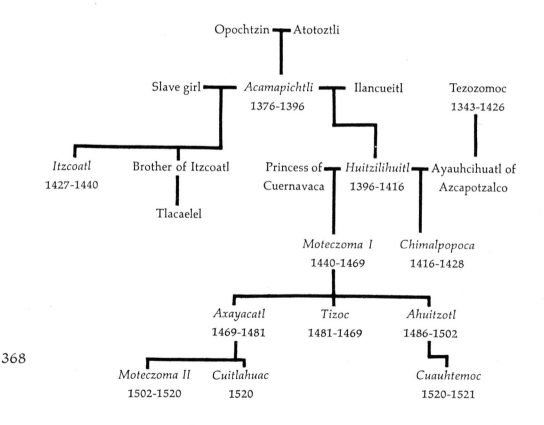

Opochtzin — Atotoztli

Slave girl — *Acamapichtli* — Ilancueitl     Tezozomoc
           1376-1396                         1343-1426

*Itzcoatl*    Brother of Itzcoatl    Princess of — *Huitzilihuitl* — Ayauhcihuatl of
1427-1440                        Cuernavaca    1396-1416     Azcapotzalco

Tlacaelel

*Moteczoma I*     *Chimalpopoca*
1440-1469       1416-1428

*Axayacatl*     *Tizoc*     *Ahuitzotl*
1469-1481    1481-1469    1486-1502

368

*Moteczoma II*   *Cuitlahuac*        *Cuauhtemoc*
1502-1520      1520             1520-1521

# INDEX

371

378

380

to Aztecs, 102; paid by Tlatelolca to Aztecs, 160; promised to Aztecs by Azcapotzalco, 59

Tuchimilco, town of, 10

Tula region, 17, 21, 62, 118 *passim*, 134, 267, 333

Tulancingo region, 106

Tzacualcatl, King, 48 *passim*

Tzauctla, city of, 117 *passim*

Tzicoac region, 193

Tzocoztli, representative of Huitzilopochtli, 247

Tzompanco, *see* Skull rack

Tzompanco region, 21

Tzompantecuhtli, King of Cuitlahuac, 254

Tzopachtzinco, town of, 283 *passim*

Tzotzomatzin, King of Coyoacan, 209, 210, 215; prophecy of, 210; sorcery of, 210

Veracruz, 296, 311

Vision of Cuauhtloquetzqui: *see* Cuauhtloquetzqui, vision of

Wars of Aztecs: against Azcapotzolco, 51-4, 57-60; against Chalca, 23-4; against Chiapan, 186-87; against Cholula, 238; against Coaixtlahuaca, 118-19; against Colhuacans, 27-8; against Coyoacan, 60-4, 67-9; against Cuetlaxtla, 113-14, 117, 125-27; against Cuitlahuaca, 81-4; against Huaxtecs, 105, 106-108, 189-90; against Huexotzinco, 231, 233, 235, 238; against Matlatzinco, 161-62; against Metztitlan, 179; against Michoacan, 165-68; to obtain victims for sacrifice, 348; against Tarascans, 165-68; against Tehuantepec, 203; against Teloloapan, 200; against Tepeaca, 99-100; against Tlatelolco, 151-54, 157-59;

against Tlaxcala, 237-38, 245; against Toluca and Matlatzinco, 161-62; against Xochimilca, 72 *passim*, 73-9

War: methods of fighting, 83, 93, 107, 338; preparations for, 99, 107, 152-53; provisions and supplies, 202; training for, 82; women in, 159, 315-16

Wards: of Mexico City, 32, 33, 60, 201, 334, 335; of Oaxaca, 143

Water ceremony, 211-12, 215, 216

Waterpipe from Coyoacan to Mexico, 210-12, 215

Weapons, 24, 58, 82, 83, 281, 334-35; as gifts, 87, 100, 113, 187, 226; and insignia, 58, 69, 77, 217; paid in tribute, description of, 130; as rewards for valor, 142

Wine, 189; given to Aztecs by Spaniards, 266; used in religious ceremony, 102, 172

"Woman of Discord," *see* Toci

Women: in army, 159; in Battle of Mexico, 315-16

Xalatlauhco, town of, 61

Xaltelolco, *see* Tlatelolco

Xaltocan, town of, 22

Xaltepec, province of, 226; rebellion of, 227, 228

Xayacamachan, King of Huexotzinco, 192

Xicotencatl, Lord of Tlaxcala, 125, 284

Xilomatzin, King of Colhuacan, 62

Xochimilca tribe, 9, 10, 73, 80, 100, 114, 165, 167; and building of pyramid, 139; causeway built by, 79; and colonization of Oaxaca, 143; division of lands of, 79; King of, 92, 110; revolt against Aztecs, 72 *passim*, 73-9; trade, 117; vassalage of, 91

Xochimilco, town of, 10, 62, 63, 73, 91

Xochitepec hill, 78